Lecture Notes in Computer Science 14058

Founding Editors

Gerhard Goos
Juris Hartmanis

The series Lecture Notes in Computer Science (LNCS), including its subseries Lecture Notes in Artificial Intelligence (LNAI) and Lecture Notes in Bioinformatics (LNBI), has established itself as a medium for the publication of new developments in computer science and information technology research, teaching, and education.

LNCS enjoys close cooperation with the computer science R & D community, the series counts many renowned academics among its volume editors and paper authors, and collaborates with prestigious societies. Its mission is to serve this international community by providing an invaluable service, mainly focused on the publication of conference and workshop proceedings and postproceedings. LNCS commenced publication in 1973.

Jessie Y. C. Chen · Gino Fragomeni ·
Xiaowen Fang

Editors

HCI International 2023 – Late Breaking Papers

25th International Conference on Human-Computer Interaction
HCII 2023, Copenhagen, Denmark, July 23–28, 2023
Proceedings, Part V

 Springer

Editors
Jessie Y. C. Chen
U.S. Army Research Laboratory
Adlephi, MD, USA

Gino Fragomeni
U.S. Army Combat Capabilities
Development Command Soldier Center
Orlando, FL, USA

Xiaowen Fang
DePaul University
Chicago, IL, USA

ISSN 0302-9743   ISSN 1611-3349 (electronic)
Lecture Notes in Computer Science
ISBN 978-3-031-48049-2   ISBN 978-3-031-48050-8 (eBook)
https://doi.org/10.1007/978-3-031-48050-8

This Springer imprint is published by the registered company Springer Nature Switzerland AG
The registered company address is: Gewerbestrasse 11, 6330 Cham, Switzerland

Paper in this product is recyclable.

Foreword

Human-computer interaction (HCI) is acquiring an ever-increasing scientific and industrial importance, as well as having more impact on people's everyday lives, as an ever-growing number of human activities are progressively moving from the physical to the digital world. This process, which has been ongoing for some time now, was further accelerated during the acute period of the COVID-19 pandemic. The HCI International (HCII) conference series, held annually, aims to respond to the compelling need to advance the exchange of knowledge and research and development efforts on the human aspects of design and use of computing systems.

The 25th International Conference on Human-Computer Interaction, HCI International 2023 (HCII 2023), was held in the emerging post-pandemic era as a 'hybrid' event at the AC Bella Sky Hotel and Bella Center, Copenhagen, Denmark, during July 23–28, 2023. It incorporated the 21 thematic areas and affiliated conferences listed below.

A total of 7472 individuals from academia, research institutes, industry, and government agencies from 85 countries submitted contributions, and 1578 papers and 396 posters were included in the volumes of the proceedings that were published just before the start of the conference. Additionally, 267 papers and 133 posters were included in the volumes of the proceedings published after the conference, as "Late Breaking Work". The contributions thoroughly cover the entire field of human-computer interaction, addressing major advances in knowledge and effective use of computers in a variety of application areas. These papers provide academics, researchers, engineers, scientists, practitioners and students with state-of-the-art information on the most recent advances in HCI. The volumes constituting the full set of the HCII 2023 conference proceedings are listed on the following pages.

I would like to thank the Program Board Chairs and the members of the Program Boards of all thematic areas and affiliated conferences for their contribution towards the high scientific quality and overall success of the HCI International 2023 conference. Their manifold support in terms of paper reviewing (single-blind review process, with a minimum of two reviews per submission), session organization and their willingness to act as goodwill ambassadors for the conference is most highly appreciated.

This conference would not have been possible without the continuous and unwavering support and advice of Gavriel Salvendy, founder, General Chair Emeritus, and Scientific Advisor. For his outstanding efforts, I would like to express my sincere appreciation to Abbas Moallem, Communications Chair and Editor of HCI International News.

July 2023

Constantine Stephanidis

HCI International 2023 Thematic Areas and Affiliated Conferences

Thematic Areas

- HCI: Human-Computer Interaction
- HIMI: Human Interface and the Management of Information

Affiliated Conferences

- EPCE: 20th International Conference on Engineering Psychology and Cognitive Ergonomics
- AC: 17th International Conference on Augmented Cognition
- UAHCI: 17th International Conference on Universal Access in Human-Computer Interaction
- CCD: 15th International Conference on Cross-Cultural Design
- SCSM: 15th International Conference on Social Computing and Social Media
- VAMR: 15th International Conference on Virtual, Augmented and Mixed Reality
- DHM: 14th International Conference on Digital Human Modeling and Applications in Health, Safety, Ergonomics and Risk Management
- DUXU: 12th International Conference on Design, User Experience and Usability
- C&C: 11th International Conference on Culture and Computing
- DAPI: 11th International Conference on Distributed, Ambient and Pervasive Interactions
- HCIBGO: 10th International Conference on HCI in Business, Government and Organizations
- LCT: 10th International Conference on Learning and Collaboration Technologies
- ITAP: 9th International Conference on Human Aspects of IT for the Aged Population
- AIS: 5th International Conference on Adaptive Instructional Systems
- HCI-CPT: 5th International Conference on HCI for Cybersecurity, Privacy and Trust
- HCI-Games: 5th International Conference on HCI in Games
- MobiTAS: 5th International Conference on HCI in Mobility, Transport and Automotive Systems
- AI-HCI: 4th International Conference on Artificial Intelligence in HCI
- MOBILE: 4th International Conference on Design, Operation and Evaluation of Mobile Communications

Conference Proceedings – Full List of Volumes

https://2023.hci.international/proceedings

25th International Conference on Human-Computer Interaction (HCII 2023)

The full list with the Program Board Chairs and the members of the Program Boards of all thematic areas and affiliated conferences of HCII2023 is available online at:

http://www.hci.international/board-members-2023.php

HCI International 2024 Conference

The 26th International Conference on Human-Computer Interaction, HCI International 2024, will be held jointly with the affiliated conferences at the Washington Hilton Hotel, Washington, DC, USA, June 29 – July 4, 2024. It will cover a broad spectrum of themes related to Human-Computer Interaction, including theoretical issues, methods, tools, processes, and case studies in HCI design, as well as novel interaction techniques, interfaces, and applications. The proceedings will be published by Springer. More information will be made available on the conference website: http://2024.hci.international/.

General Chair
Prof. Constantine Stephanidis
University of Crete and ICS-FORTH
Heraklion, Crete, Greece
Email: general_chair@2024.hci.international

https://2024.hci.international/

Contents – Part V

Gaming and Gamification Experiences

eXtended Reality Interactions

Interaction Techniques to Control Information Clutter in a Pervasive Augmented Reality Scenario

Maxime Cauz(✉) , Thibaut Septon , and Bruno Dumas

Namur Digital Institute, University of Namur, Namur, Belgium
{maxime.cauz,thibaut.septon,bruno.dumas}@unamur.be

Abstract. The recent concept of Pervasive Augmented Reality (PAR) predicts the use of Augmented Reality (AR) in every aspect of our daily life to help access, produce and present information and services from various different sources around users. However, as far as the authors know, no study explored how design interaction techniques can be implemented in a complex and overwhelming PAR environment where information clutter is generated from multiple sources with very different political, social and economic interests. The contributions of this paper are 1) an evaluation of a PAR street-like environment with multiple producers of information, 2) a proposition of four different strategies, and their related interaction techniques, to help users tackle information clutter around them and 3) guidelines on expected interactions for managing such flow of information, based on participants' feedback.

Keywords: Pervasive Augmented Reality · Interaction techniques · Information clutter

1 Introduction

The growing complexity of systems in industries, the will to offer a better health-care, or the need of a better immersion in arts, are examples that lead computer science research to find new solutions. One of them, emerging this last decade due to the improvement in computer hardware, is Augmented Reality (AR). According to Azuma [1], AR can be defined as the integration of virtual data within the real world in real-time and registered in 3D. Such technology can be experienced with a smartphone, or through the use of a Head-Mounted Display (HMD) for instance. It allows immediate access to information in relation with the users' context by placing information directly in the real world. If mobile computing brought the "everywhere, every time" paradigm, AR breaks the frontier between the virtual and the real. Although this is less the case with hand-held smartphones, HMDs will allow, with time, the user to forget that he is going through a screen to consult virtual information. The community named

---

M. Cauz and Thibaut Septon—These authors Contributed equally to this publication.

J. Y. C. Chen et al. (Eds.): HCII 2023, LNCS 14058, pp. 3–21, 2023.
https://doi.org/10.1007/978-3-031-48050-8_1

this approach immersive AR where the real world and the virtual environment tend to be indistinguishable.

Today, AR is proving its effectiveness in numerous domains, as demonstrated by Dey et al. [3]. By giving the right information at the right time and in the right place, this technology is spreading from laboratories, to economic and governmental actors. Industries are deploying AR systems in training and step-by-step guiding systems for maintenance. Some armies have equipped soldiers and/or their vehicles to augment their speed of reaction and their efficiency in the field. It is also used by surgeons to optimize the success rate of surgeries, allowing them to see organs, blood vessels, penetration of their tools, etc. superimposed on the patient's body. Although still limited to smartphones at the consumer level due to high costs, limitations and social constraints, it is plausible to consider that AR will continue to spread within society the same way personal computers, the internet and smartphones did.

Sci-fi works from the media industry have already tried to illustrate dystopian or utopian futures. One of the most thought-provoking is the "Hyper-Reality" video of Matsuda [10]. It presents our world where AR is overused in every aspect of the user life; publicity, entertainment, tourism, etc. (See Fig. 1). Matsuda's work raises many questions. One of them comes from a new possibility offered by such technology; situated information. As stated by Prouzeau et al. [20], situated information is data visualizations which are located close to their physical referent. Considering a world similar to what is depicted by Matsuda, anyone would be allowed to create situated information to be displayed and perceived by other users; professionals, artists, public and private actors. With continuously added information coming from various sources, displayed visualizations might occlude important real world elements and as such, become obtrusive and overwhelming as explained by Lu [13].

In this paper, we focus on how interactions can help users to better appropriate a full Pervasive Augmented Reality (PAR) environment. Following the same approach as Lu et al. [14], we conducted two studies. A pilot study which consisted of semi-structured interviews to assess the feelings of participants in the vision proposed by Matsuda [10]. In response to these results, we elaborate three active interaction strategies and one passive: 1) situated information on-demand with gaze interactions, 2) transparency management for non-readable content depending on the distance to the user, 3) reducing or increasing the number of virtual elements in the user's environment through preferences and 4) situated applications in a virtual smartphone. The experimental study implements and tests these strategies in a real AR environment of a building floor, following the design illustrated in Fig. 1. The goals were, on the one hand, to evaluate the impact of the strategies on the cognitive load and feelings of the participants and, on the other hand, evaluate how well the strategies current implementations perform.

Fig. 1. Illustration of an augmented street by Matsuda in his "Hyper Reality" video.

Our contributions are 1) an evaluation of a Pervasive Augmented Reality street-like environment with multiple producers of information, 2) a proposition of four different strategies, and their related interaction techniques, to help users tackle information clutter around them and 3) guidelines on expected interactions for managing such flow of information, based on participants' feedback.

2 Related Work

Grubert et al. [6] define the concept of PAR as opposed to Conventional Augmented Reality (CAR). The latter, representing the majority of work in AR research, is task and context related while also having a sporadic use. CAR applications are accessed one by one according to the user needs. In contrast, a complete PAR experience would be continuous and multipurpose oriented. Conceptually, various applications are opened simultaneously and never closed. In such environments, context-aware solutions must be adopted in complement of sporadic manual interactions to prevent the user from losing time managing all opened applications. To this end, Grubert et al. proposed a taxonomy of context sources that can be used to define passive interaction across PAR applications.

The emergence of PAR inside our society raises ethical, social, legal, political and technical issues. Gugenheimer et al. [7] organized a workshop on ethical, social and political impacts in Mixed Reality (MR) research. Unfortunately, the workshop was canceled due to the pandemic. Regenbrecht et al. [21] opened the discussion on the privacy, safety, belief and rights applied to the PAR. What stands out in particular is a careful modulation of what the user sees, proposing a control for managing the quantity of virtual elements displayed, and defining social and legal norms around the subject.

Beside ethical work done in the context of PAR, other works are more focused on view management techniques. Lu et al. [14] explore how AR applications can be presented and interacted with while being unobtrusive and with minimal cognitive effort. Their solution is called glanceable applications (i.e. applications such as Email, Calendar or Fitness minimized inside the user peripheral vision) with which the user can use gaze to expand their content. Their goal was, on the one hand, to compare applications with their equivalent in traditional devices (e.g. smartphones or computers), and, on the other hand, study user behaviors in this pervasive environment. Their results demonstrate a real interest for the use of pervasive applications. Furthermore, the experiment participants desired more interactions than just information access and also wanted to be able to turn on and off the AR to be relieved from the pressure of the digital world. Lindlbauer et al. [12] explore the view management problem of having multiple applications opened as windows for a continuous use of AR. They submit an optimization based approach of determining where, when and how applications should be displayed using interfaces with multiple levels of detail according to the user context and task. Others have also used context-awareness as a way to determine what and/or how information should be displayed, such as [2,5,9,11,15,18]. Another PAR related work was realized by Marques et al. [17]. In it, the authors test research and manipulation tasks in a PAR environment. They help the user in their task with the help of three navigation aids. Results showed good appreciation from the participants and interest in diverse daily life activities.

MacIntyre et al. [16] defined multiple requirements that must be met in order for a PAR ecosystem to exist. These are the following: "multiple sources (or channels of interactive information) must be able to be simultaneously displayed and interacted with, channels must be isolated from each other (for security and stability), channel authors must have the flexibility to design the content and interactivity of their channel, and the application must fluidly integrate with the ever-growing cloud of systems and services that define our digital lives." To our knowledge, no other work addresses issues arising from multiple contents producers in a PAR environment.

Most works focus on applications designed as we know them today on our smartphones, and do not fully exploit the potential of AR. Except for MacIntyre et al. [16], none of the works above explicitly address the problems that emerge from a world where multiple sources of information coexist. Most view management techniques are solving information clutter using context-aware approaches. In this work, we would like to proceed otherwise, by first trying to establish interaction strategies that can be applied to let the user keep control over a PAR environment.

3   Pilot Study

We conducted semi-structured interviews to better understand potential problems conveyed by the illustration of the street in the "Hyper-Reality" video of Matsuda [10]. Our hypotheses were that the high quantity of information, animations, and the weak coherence of the environment would make information irrelevant and the world oppressive, thus increasing cognitive load. For the interviews, we asked the participants to imagine themselves as pedestrians in an unknown augmented city (i.e. all streets are augmented like on Fig. 1). They were told to be visiting randomly the city or simply wanting to reach a specific place. Participants knew that they wore augmented glasses or contact lens that display virtual information. In order to verify our hypotheses, we had multiple research questions: 1) "How do users feel in this type of environment?", 2) "Is the separation between what is real and what is virtual clear?" and 3) "Is the virtual information understood and relevant?".

3.1   Participants

A total of five men and four women took part in the interviews. They were all volunteers, no remuneration was given. Five participants were between 25 and 30 years old, two were between 35 and 45 years old and two were 60 years old. All participants had a master degree, including four who had a PhD in computer science. However, no participants came from our laboratory team and none of them worked in the field of AR.

3.2   Protocol

The meeting was not audio or video recorded. The members of our team took notes. In the case where two interviewers were present, they were both allowed to ask questions, but one had the lead. The interviewees began by giving their agreements for the interview and the use of their answers. After that, their personal information described in Sect. 3.1 were collected and the context was exposed. Next, the photo in Fig. 1 was presented to the participants. They were requested to immerse themselves in the depicted environment. Then, the first question stated above was formulated. The interviewees were free to speak and never interrupted. The interviewers asked questions only for more details on a remark or to redirect the discussion through one of the research questions of the interview. When the participants said everything they had in mind and the interviewers had no more questions, the corresponding video part of the street was shown. At this moment, the question asked was: "Does the video change anything to your feelings?". The same procedure as the one for the photo was applied until the end of the interview. Beginning with a photo was a deliberate choice to help the participants analyze the details of the scene.

3.3   Outcomes

Results show that useful information is lost in the middle of the advertising and could even become useless due to the presence of information clutter. On the other hand, some participants mentioned the similarities of such a street with cities like Singapore or New York, noting that the difference with today's big cities is the possibility offered by AR to modify our perception of reality. According to six participants, the perception of what is real is deteriorated, and three participants feared for their physical safety, again due to information clutter. Other interesting observations not related to information clutter are the following. While some participants described a feeling of sickness, at least all agreed that this kind of environment was tiring. Two participants working in the medical field also noted that the environment as presented could greatly affect the health of the population. Either by "driving people crazy", or due to medical syndromes. To conclude, we want to highlight a remark from one of the participants: "This is about the future of cities, not the countryside.". Which raises the question of "what will be the limit of the intrusive advertising in front of these free spaces?".

4 Experimental Study

In this Section, we study the impact on cognitive load of four strategies aimed to solve the problem of information clutter highlighted in Sect. 3. To begin with, we use gaze based interaction to provide information on demand. Then, we allow the user to specify their desired level of information according to its nature. Afterwards, we develop the concept of situated applications. Finally, for specific information that cannot be reduced, we automate the management of their transparency according to their physical distance from the user. By applying these four strategies, we study their impact on the cognitive load of the user while evaluating their implementation in order to determine how to improve them, should they be effective.

4.1 Pervasive Environment and Constraints

(a)   (b)

Fig. 2. Chosen floor for the experimentation, with Fig. 2a and without Fig. 2b the virtual content. Note that the virtual elements appear more transparent in the screenshot than they appear to users.

To ensure a controlled environment, we realized the experiment on a building floor. We used its corridor as the main place for the experiment, mapping it to Matsuda's [10] vision of an augmented street. We matched the corridor to the street, the doors to shop windows, etc. Realizing the experiment in such an environment allowed us to keep control over weather condition, passers-by, privacy and social acceptance. It also enabled us to fully exploit the potential of the Hololens 2. Such headsets, being Optical See-through (OST) devices, are vulnerable to light variation, therefore controlling the light exposition of the environment solves the issue. In addition, OST devices have the advantage to reduce the possible phenomenon of motion sickness and are less intrusive than other types of AR headsets. However, it should be noted that the Hololens 2 suffers from a restrained Field of View (FOV), therefore users do not perceive holograms inside their peripheral vision.

In order to augment the floor, we designed five categories of virtual elements: 1) Decorations, 2) social norms, 3) navigation indications, 4) room information and 5) advertising. All these categories were inspired from the work of Matsuda [10] as illustrated in Fig. 1. Figure 3 shows the placement of the virtual elements on top of the physical layout of the floor. However, virtual pillars and roof as seen in Fig. 2a have not been represented for clarity reasons.

For the decoration category, we added pillars and a false roof to break the square red brick look of the corridor. While the virtual roof is higher than the real one, it is still visible and hides the physical roof. In addition to these architectural modifications, we added plants at multiple locations and flying paper planes in the corridor. Finally, we added a chirping birds sound in the background. For social norms, we consider any information considered to be cultural behavioral guidelines and expectations. In this experiment, this is expressed with animated arrows on the ground which indicate on which side to walk depending on the direction you want to go. These are not to be confused with navigation information. Those are either wayfinding signs indicating classroom names, or other visual elements such as the usual toilet sign placed on the dedicated doors or a bucket and a broom indicating the storage facility. We also placed a panel on the entry of the cafeteria to indicate that the access is for staff member only. Two other panels denying access were placed to prevent the user to enter a room always opened and to access the end of the corridor due to a lack of luminosity that makes the headset behave unexpectedly.

For room indications, we defined content depending on the use of the room. For professors' offices, their biography, agenda, last published paper or research domains were added as separate panels. We also added audio content in which the professors talk of their research area to attract passers-by. For classrooms, we added panels with agenda and classroom background noise to give the impression that the rooms were occupied. On the student open spaces, we placed panels with information on the usage of the room, rules of use and, if the room was named after a person, the biography of the corresponding personality.

For advertising, we added four bulletin boards (see Fig. 4f) with advertisements coming from students, faculty or university activities. Each panel is a square that takes the wall height. It rotates slightly towards the user to be more readable. The panels' content updates every ten seconds, and seven ads in aver-

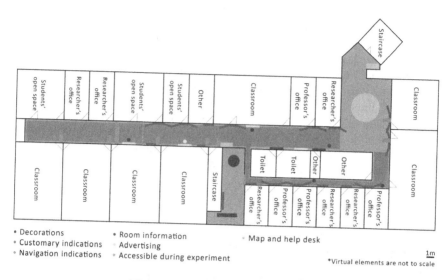

Fig. 3. Layout of the chosen floor.

age are presented simultaneously. We also added a teddy bear on one end of the corridor, moving up and down. When looked at for more than 0.8 s, an advertisement appears progressively towards the participant. Finally, in addition to these elements, we added two maps on opposite sides of the floor and a help desk at the floor entry near where the experiment would begin. The help desk holds a penguin in its center who asks the participant if they need any help when they get close to it.

4.2 Four Strategies to Control an Augmented Environment

Based on the results of the Pilot study presented in Sect. 3, we designed four strategies to help users keep control over their environment. Grubert et al. [6] argue that PAR environments need context-aware automation to reduce manual user interactions. Although we agree with them, context-aware approaches must support user interactions and not replace them. Therefore, users can keep control over the system. For this reason, we propose three strategies that are said to be active, meaning they make use of interactivity and solicit user actions, and one passive. These strategies are foundations on which context-aware automation could be applied. The first strategy uses the user gaze to let them situate and navigate regrouped information. The second strategy lets them specify their preference to filter the amount of information. The third one gives them access to situated applications that give dynamic content based on the context. Finally, the fourth strategy applies transparency to content that is considered too remote to be understood.

In an attempt to make the techniques accessible to the general user, we developed a User Interface (UI) that simulates a smartphone (see Fig. 4d). That virtual smartphone lets the user have access to the second and third strategies. While the latter resembles an actual smartphone app, the first has a direct influence over the surrounding world. Therefore, the virtual smartphone is an intrinsic part of the environment.

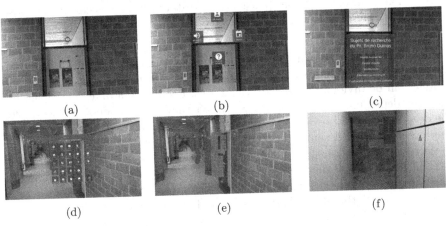

Fig. 4. Illustration of the 4 strategies. Figure 4a, 4b and 4c represent the succession of steps for the situated information on demand by gaze interaction. Figure 4d represents the smartphone with at the top the slider. Figure 4e represents the mini-map available as a situated application. Figure 4f represents the bulletin board with transparency due to the distance to the user.

Strategy 1: Situated Information on Demand with Gaze Interactions.
Room indications as described in Sect. 4.1 convey building related information. Since multiple types of information are available on a restricted area, we hide them inside a gaze based interactive menu. First, an eye icon (see Fig. 4a) is visible to the user. If the user wants to check available information, they can open the menu (see Fig. 4b) by focusing their gaze on the icon and then select the desired information. This technique has the advantage to keep information situated while still being visible from far away and reduce information clutter. As explained by Plopski et al. [19], using gaze as a mean of interaction is problematic. It is normally used as a mean of observation, and it is therefore difficult to distinguish a user intended interaction. This problem is more commonly known as the Midas-touch problem. According to Duchowski [4], there exist multiple solutions to get around the Midas-touch problem, such as eye gestures, multimodality, boundary crossing, etc. However, the most widely accepted solution being the use of a dwell time, our choice went to the latter with a time of 0.8 s.

Strategy 2: Transparency Management for Non-readable Content.
Advertising and university bulletin boards need further reflection. This kind of information is typically paid to be displayed, thus there exists a conflict of interest between the user needs to reduce information clutter and the needs of the entity paying for its advertisement to be displayed and visible. The solution considered is to play on the opacity of the information according to the user's distance from the advertisement (see Fig. 4f). That way, one can be aware that information is available at that place if their distance from it is considered close enough that the information is therefore readable.

Strategy 3: Reducing or Increasing the Amount of Virtual Elements in the User's Environment. As explained in the previous section, virtual content can be divided into several categories. Each have a different impact on the user depending on the context in which they are included. For example, the decorations could be appreciated by a new visitor but too distracting for an employee. Thus, we designed a slider included at the top of a virtual smartphone to decrease or increase the quantity of categories displayed (see Fig. 4d). Each level includes the elements of the lower levels. Five levels were available: 1) Absolutely no virtual elements except the virtual smartphone, 2) only the eye tracking icons for the situated information and bulletin boards, 3) the navigation indications, 4) the social norms and 5) the decorations with the ambient sound. This strategy was also proposed by Regenbrecht et al. [21] as discussed inside Sect. 2.

Strategy 4: Situated Applications. Some types of information offered by the building may not be situated. That is the case for the help desk answering visitors' questions or the maps placed in certain places as described in Sect. 4.1. They are however related to the building as a whole. Therefore, we decided to remove information from the virtual environment while still letting them accessible from the smartphone as applications, making them accessible as the user wishes. Here, we describe the concept of situated applications. These are available only when accessing the place they are associated with, and would be removed and replaced by others as the user moves by. We consider these applications and their installation secure.

4.3 Tasks

We asked the participants to find successively four hidden information inside the experiment corridor. This approach lets us explore, on the one hand, users' behavior in a street-like environment by exploring the virtual environment and, on the other hand, to force the participants to test the different interactions proposed by the strategies. An example of requested information was, for instance, the title of the course given at a specific time in a specific classroom, the name of a person, or a date for a specific event. The tasks were designed to force participants to explore and interact across all the virtual environment.

4.4   Variables

Our first objective is to study the evolution of users' mental load between an environment using no strategies, and an environment using the strategies described in Sect. 4.2. Hence, we chose the NASA TLX form [8] that has six scales to compute the overall workload score of a participant. The standard way of filling the NASA TLX form asks participants to complete the scales and give a weight for each. However, as we wanted to evaluate the impact of the entire environment on the cognitive load through a daily life task, the weight of each scale was predefined and communicated to the participants. Users had to walk around and observe the environment. We put the following order of importance on the scales, from most important to least important: Mental Demand, Frustration, Effort, Performance, Temporal Demand and Physical Demand. Finally, we performed a semi-structured interview to retrieve the participants' feedback. This allowed us to correctly understand the TLX reports and focus on our second goal, that is the ease of interaction and implementation of the four strategies. The questions that structured the interviews were: 1) How do strategies impact user feelings and their perception of reality?, 2) is each strategy useful and properly implemented?, 3) are there other useful strategies? and 4) what virtual elements were the most frustrating?

4.5   Pretests

We conducted pretests to refine the procedure described in the Sect. 4.7 and to check the concordance with the pilot study described in Sect. 3. Five members of the Computer Science department tested the experiment. Four of them were participants of the pilot study. They concluded that the virtual environment was oppressing and overwhelming if they must experiment it all day. In regard to the strategies, users considered them as of great interest. Note that they knew the corridor where the experiment took place, thus, they knew where to find some answers during the experimentation.

4.6   Participants

A total of eight men and eight women took part in the experimentation. None of them knew the floors of the building, and none previously participated within the Pilot Study or the Pretests. They were all volunteers, no remuneration was given. The age range was between 21 and 35 with an average of 27.31 years old. Three participants had their high school degree, four had a bachelor's degree, and nine had a master's degree. Ten participants had never tested AR or Virtual Reality (VR). Four played occasionally with VR, one played occasionally with AR and VR and one played regularly with VR. Finally, based on results from Sect. 3, we further asked each participant how they felt if they were on Time Square based on a photo (See Fig. 5). One answered they felt nauseous, one was uncomfortable, six were neutral, four were calm and four were comfortable.

Fig. 5. Picture of Time Square used to determine the participants' level of comfort in big cities (Photo taken by Tagger Yancey IV).

4.7 Procedure

We received each participant individually on the first floor of the building and accompanied them to a meeting room. To begin with, we explained how the experiment would be conducted. First, the participants would go through two experiments, each followed by a NASA TLX form. This part would last approximately 40 min. Then, participants would answer questions during a semi-structured interview, which would last about 20 min. Before the experiments would start, the participants were asked to sign a data processing agreement and complete a form with personal information (i.e. the information described within Sect. 4.6). Then, they performed the ocular calibration on the headset, also allowing them to discover how to interact with virtual content as the device displays a floating window with a button to click on to start the calibration.

After this setup phase, the first trial, with the strategies disabled, could start. Explanations were given to the participants as follows: They play the role of a staff member of the building, and they can walk anywhere on the floor except for some rooms. The participants had some time available to get used to the Hololens 2 device and the environment. Four successive questions were then asked to the participant, without any further indication. There was no time limitation, but the investigators would give some clues if a participant felt completely lost. The investigators would also ensure the participant security while also taking notes. Once the four questions were answered, the participant returned to the meeting room to complete the NASA TLX form. Next, the second trial with the four strategies enabled began following the same protocol. The investigators gave explanations on the three active strategies. During the adaptation time, the participant could explore the virtual smartphone capabilities. At the end of this second trial, the participant completed a second NASA TLX form and a semi-structured interview was conducted. Interviews were audio recorded. Not balancing the trials was a deliberate choice, as we did not want participants to have to apprehend the virtual environment simultaneously with the interactions required for trial 2.

4.8   Results

From the NASA TLX forms, we begin by computing the workload score of each participant. This is followed by a Wilcoxon signed-rank test to determine significant improvements in the second trial. Then, we test the dependence between the forms and the participants' familiarity with AR/VR and their comfort in big cities with a chi-square independence test. Finally, we finish with the results of the semi-structured interviews presented inside Sect. 4.4. Results were obtained with a thematic analysis of the audio recordings.

TLX Workload Score and Wilcoxon Signed-Rank Test. Figure 6 presents the distribution for each scale and for the overall workload score. With regard to the mean and median, we observe an improvement for the Mental Demand, the Performance and the Frustration. Conversely, we observe a deterioration of Temporal Demand. To verify the significance of these effects, we performed a Wilcoxon signed-rank test on all scales and on the workload score. No significant results were found, but the Mental Demand seems to tend to a significant improvement (Z = 85.0, p-value = 0.08).

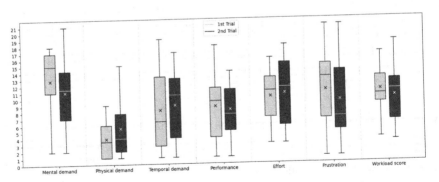

Fig. 6. Box plots of each subscale and of the workload scores of the TLX. First trial results are each time on the left, while second trial results are on the right.

Chi-Square Independence Test. We performed chi-square tests to determine the impact of AR/VR technology awareness and comfort level in big cities on each scale and on the workload score. For the former, we observe no significant results. However, we can observe a trend on the performance ($X^2 = 38.67$, p-value $= 0.07$, DoF $= 27$) of the first trial and on the temporal demand ($X^2 = 42.4$, p-value $= 0.03$, DoF $= 27$) and frustration ($X^2 = 41.47$, p-value $= 0.08$, DoF $= 30$) of the second trial. These results seem logical as a better control of these novel technologies reduces the learning time and thus, the frustration. For the latter, similarly no significant effects were found except a trend on the Mental Demand ($X^2 = 53.33$, p-value $= 0.08$, DoF $= 40$) of the first trial. Similarly, it might be acceptable to assume that if the participant feels good in overwhelming cities, they felt good in our experiment's environment.

Impact of the Strategies on Participants' Feelings and Perception of Reality. Finally, we describe the results of the semi-structured interviews. Relative to the first trial, participants felt mainly calm. Nevertheless, everyone described being overwhelmed by the amount of information, while one specified it as intrusive. The participants pointed out the sound within the environment as a major contributor to their feeling. Therefore, 12 participants considered the experience as unusable in their daily lives. 12 of the participants also considered their perception of reality to be deteriorated. In addition, 8 participants found themselves isolated from reality. Eventually, all participants considered the information to be well-placed. For the second trial, results are mixed. 14 participants found their perception of reality enhanced compared with the first trial. However, 8 participants considered the different strategies improved their experience.

Evaluating Strategy 1. As we expected, 15 participants said that this strategy reduced information clutter. 4 said that it is most useful when knowing where to find the information. This last statement is supported by 8 participants saying that it negatively hides the information when searching for it. 9 said it structured the information, allowing them to easily navigate and isolate the wanted information. Finally, 5 participants said the gaze interaction icon was placed too high, and two participants would have preferred another way of triggering the interaction than the dwell time.

Evaluating Strategy 2. 10 participants stated that they found bulletin board transparency useful, while 3 were against this strategy and 3 had no opinion. 12 participants explicitly said that it may trouble them not being able to see information availability while searching for it from far away. One participant stated that universities' bulletin boards are not equivalent to advertising panels, and 7 said the technique could benefit from an icon indicating available information when too far away from the user. Finally, 12 of the participants said that the moving bear drawing attention was not problematic, however the manner in which the advertisement is displayed was.

Evaluating Strategy 3. 9 participants mentioned that they had difficulties in interacting with the slider. During the experiment, we observed that most participants selected the third or fourth level of information because they did not see any difference between the two while experimenting. They however noticed that these levels mute the audio. 5 expressly wished for a separated way of muting the audio, while 2 participants stated that they kept a high level of information because they feared they would lose some otherwise. Also, 7 explicitly said they would have preferred an alternative way of interacting where they would be able to turn on and off the chosen information level as they pleased. All participants liked the concept and the control it gave them over the environment.

Evaluating Strategy 4. 13 of all participants found the idea behind situated applications useful. However, 5 were concerned about security issues and their privacy, even though we focused on security during the phrasing of the question. 7 stated that it was useful since it created a pattern to access and find available information. Finally, 2 participants said that the applications should stay installed and that only their content should be situated, thus users would know how to use the applications and what information would be available.

Ideas and Frustrations. Before finishing the interviews, we requested each participant to classify what were the three most frustrating things they experienced during the experiment. Moreover, we asked them if they had any ideas for improving such environment. Recurring answers for the former were 1) mute the ambient sound that they considered as noise, 2) remove advertisements occluding the view, and 3) improve the interaction for the different active techniques. For the latter, some expressed the need for more interaction with the situated information, as being able to grasp it, resize it or make it scroll. Others would have wanted the ability to access the desired information without having to walk or to save it for later inside the map application. Finally, a participant said that daytime could be used in order to filter out unneeded information.

5   Discussion and Future Works

Participants' feedback shows that an unmanaged and unconstrained augmented world is difficult to withstand, thus elaborating strategies to handle augmented information clutter is a vital need. The strategies proposed in this paper were appreciated. Participants' mental demand and perception of reality tend to be improved as expected. Decreasing the amount of virtual situated information frees the user's environment, while the slider allows them to specify their preferences depending on their needs. For instance, a participant said that, in a museum, they would typically set on the last level to fully experiment the virtual content but in their daily life set it on a lower level to prevent distractions. The slider allows each user to specify their preferences rather than sharing a common level across all users. In addition, situated applications offer users quick access to information specific to their location and an easy way to grasp its spatial organization. As for bulletin boards, as they are advertisements that are paid to be displayed, participants understood that the same technique as the gaze input could not be applied. Despite the majority of participants finding the transparency strategy useful, they were not fully convinced by the strategy. First, it hides information, and last, bulletin boards were not the most obtrusive elements.

Nevertheless, it is difficult to determine the strategies' efficiency, as no statistically significant effects were found. First, we observed frustration and mental fatigue for the participants who had difficulty with the interactions. A small training session outside the experiment could prevent this in future works. Second, the short duration of the experiment did not allow the participants to properly overcome the novelty effect of trying an AR headset. For instance, a participant said they selected the fourth level on the slider so that the sound could be stopped while keeping the maximum amount of virtual elements to get the most out of this innovative experience. As far as the authors know, the minimum adaptation time to correctly study users' behaviors in pervasive environments is unknown. We are planning to conduct a longer experiment once the strategies are refined to study the evolution of the participants' cognitive load. Last, while it was not prohibited to use physically available information to guide or to answer questions, participants prevented themselves from doing so. An explanation given by a participant is that they were not sure if the virtual information was associated with the real location.

We now discuss the implementation of the different strategies and their ease of interaction. For strategy 1, some participants recommended to directly display the different categories of information (as can be seen on Fig. 4b). The current state increases the necessary interaction time significantly. This suggestion raises the question of the right balance between information clutter and the number of interaction steps needed to access available information. For frequent use, two successive dwell times of 0.8 s seems to be too burdensome. An alternative would be to display a reduced level of information and then, let users keep and expand only what is desired. For strategy 3, participants wanted more freedom in the selection of what is displayed and what is not. Isolating visual and audio controls is also crucial. Thus, rather than a slider, a better solution would be a toggle for each different category of audio and visual content. Therefore, users would be able to select only the ones they want. A toggle to enable and disable augmented reality content without changing all the specified preferences would also be required. This result is consistent with Lu et al. [14] stating that participants want to be relieved at times. For strategy 4, some participants want standardized visuals and interactions, thus pushing for situated content rather than a situated application. The help application should be implemented as a chatbot (i.e. Siri, Alexia, ChatGPT, etc.). Depending on the location, the application should have access to a dataset of information specific to the place to help it answer users' questions. Answers presentation must be explored in future works, but should not be limited to oral answers. The map application must indicate information position relative to the world and let the user gain access to it without having to move. One participant mentioned that they felt like they were regressing back to a time before smartphones existed, when you always had to go to different places for information. Eventually, the map must guide users to locations, but only on demand. About strategy 2, participants asked only for adding an icon when the boards disappear. As said above, participants considered this strategy as not really mandatory, even if they understood the interest to free the view when unreadable. Some participants said they are accustomed to advertising panels and do not pay attention anymore.

Finally, while most works in PAR study context-aware approaches, as stated by Grubert et al. [6], manual sporadic user interactions are also needed. Therefore, our approach first tries to give control back to the user. It is essential to reduce the frustration and fears caused by unexpected changes by ensuring user control. PAR environments need to stay transparent, with user's agreement and acknowledgment, by mixing automated and interactive approaches.

6   Conclusion

In this paper, we presented information clutter techniques in case of a Pervasive Augmented Reality (PAR) environment. We began by conducting a pilot study to highlight potential problems conveyed by Matsuda's illustration of an augmented street inside his video called "Hyper-Reality" [10]. This pilot study led us to define four strategies to control information clutter in an augmented environment:

1. Using gaze direction to expand situated information panels;
2. Applying some transparency on virtual information depending on the distance to the user;
3. A slider letting users specify their preferences over the amount of virtual elements displayed;
4. Situated applications (help and map) integrated in a virtual smartphone.

Finally, we conducted an evaluation of these strategies in a street-like PAR environment where virtual information came from various sources. Results are the following: 1) The experience without any strategy to handle information clutter generated negative feelings with our participants, in particular regarding the prospect of living in such a world, 2) participants appreciate all the strategies except the second one to reduce the cognitive load and 3) some usability aspects of all different strategies presented in this paper would need to be refined further. A strong recommendation is the ability to make information available anywhere to the user. In the future, we wish to work on how to better design these interactions and how applying specific context-aware solutions can support these strategies.

Acknowledgments. Research for this article was carried out with the FLARA-CC and OPTIMIS projects funded by Pole MecaTech. We also thank all the participants from the pilot and experimental studies for their participation.

References

1. Azuma, R.T.: A survey of augmented reality. Presence Teleoper. Virtual Environ. **6**(4), 355–385 (1997). https://doi.org/10.1162/pres.1997.6.4.355
2. Caggianese, G., Gallo, L., Neroni, P.: User-driven view management for wearable augmented reality systems in the cultural heritage domain. In: 2015 10th International Conference on P2P, Parallel, Grid, Cloud and Internet Computing (3PGCIC). IEEE, November 2015. https://doi.org/10.1109/3pgcic.2015.90
3. Dey, A., Billinghurst, M., Lindeman, R.W., Swan, J.E.: A systematic review of 10 years of augmented reality usability studies: 2005 to 2014. Front. Robot. AI **5**, 37 (2018). https://doi.org/10.3389/frobt.2018.00037
4. Duchowski, A.T.: Gaze-based interaction: a 30 year retrospective. Comput. Graph. **73**, 59–69 (2018). https://doi.org/10.1016/j.cag.2018.04.002
5. Gebhardt, C., et al.: Learning cooperative personalized policies from gaze data. In: Proceedings of the 32nd Annual ACM Symposium on User Interface Software and Technology. ACM, October 2019. https://doi.org/10.1145/3332165.3347933
6. Grubert, J., Langlotz, T., Zollmann, S., Regenbrecht, H.: Towards pervasive augmented reality: context-awareness in augmented reality. IEEE Trans. Vis. Comput. Graph. **23**(6), 1706–1724 (2017). https://doi.org/10.1109/tvcg.2016.2543720
7. Gugenheimer, J., McGill, M., Huron, S., Mai, C., Williamson, J., Nebeling, M.: Exploring potentially abusive ethical, social and political implications of mixed reality research in HCI. In: Extended Abstracts of the 2020 CHI Conference on Human Factors in Computing Systems. ACM, April 2020. https://doi.org/10.1145/3334480.3375180
8. Human Performance Research Group: NASA Task Load Index. Technical report, NASA Ames Research Center, Moffett Field, California. https://humansystems.arc.nasa.gov/groups/tlx/tlxpaperpencil.php. Accessed 29 Nov 2022
9. Julier, S., et al.: Information filtering for mobile augmented reality. In: Proceedings IEEE and ACM International Symposium on Augmented Reality (ISAR 2000). IEEE (2000). https://doi.org/10.1109/isar.2000.880917
10. Keiichi Matsuda: Hyper-reality (2016). http://hyper-reality.co/. Accessed 7 July 2022
11. Lee, J.Y., Seo, D.W., Rhee, G.: Visualization and interaction of pervasive services using context-aware augmented reality. Expert Syst. Appl. **35**(4), 1873–1882 (2008). https://doi.org/10.1016/j.eswa.2007.08.092
12. Lindlbauer, D., Feit, A.M., Hilliges, O.: Context-aware online adaptation of mixed reality interfaces. In: Proceedings of the 32nd Annual ACM Symposium on User Interface Software and Technology. ACM, October 2019. https://doi.org/10.1145/3332165.3347945
13. Lu, F.: [DC] glanceable AR: towards an always-on augmented reality future. In: 2021 IEEE Conference on Virtual Reality and 3D User Interfaces Abstracts and Workshops (VRW). IEEE, March 2021. https://doi.org/10.1109/vrw52623.2021.00241
14. Lu, F., Bowman, D.A.: Evaluating the potential of glanceable AR interfaces for authentic everyday uses. In: 2021 IEEE Virtual Reality and 3D User Interfaces (VR). IEEE, March 2021. https://doi.org/10.1109/vr50410.2021.00104
15. Lu, F., Xu, Y.: Exploring spatial UI transition mechanisms with head-worn augmented reality. In: CHI Conference on Human Factors in Computing Systems. ACM, April 2022. https://doi.org/10.1145/3491102.3517723

16. MacIntyre, B., Hill, A., Rouzati, H., Gandy, M., Davidson, B.: The argon AR web browser and standards-based AR application environment. In: 2011 10th IEEE International Symposium on Mixed and Augmented Reality. IEEE, October 2011. https://doi.org/10.1109/ismar.2011.6092371
17. Marques, B., Carvalho, R., Dias, P., Santos, B.S.: Pervasive augmented reality for indoor uninterrupted experiences. In: Adjunct Proceedings of the 2019 ACM International Joint Conference on Pervasive and Ubiquitous Computing and Proceedings of the 2019 ACM International Symposium on Wearable Computers. ACM, September 2019. https://doi.org/10.1145/3341162.3343759
18. Orlosky, J., Kiyokawa, K., Toyama, T., Sonntag, D.: Halo Content: context-aware viewspace management for non-invasive augmented reality. In: Proceedings of the 20th International Conference on Intelligent User Interfaces. ACM, March 2015. https://doi.org/10.1145/2678025.2701375
19. Plopski, A., Hirzle, T., Norouzi, N., Qian, L., Bruder, G., Langlotz, T.: The eye in extended reality: a survey on gaze interaction and eye tracking in head-worn extended reality. ACM Comput. Surv. 55(3), 1–39 (2022). https://doi.org/10.1145/3491207
20. Prouzeau, A., Wang, Y., Ens, B., Willett, W., Dwyer, T.: Corsican Twin: authoring in situ augmented reality visualisations in virtual reality. In: Proceedings of the International Conference on Advanced Visual Interfaces, pp. 1–9 (2020). https://doi.org/10.1145/3399715.3399743
21. Regenbrecht, H., Zwanenburg, S., Langlotz, T.: Pervasive augmented reality–technology and ethics. IEEE Pervasive Comput. 21(3), 84–91 (2022). https://doi.org/10.1109/mprv.2022.3152993

Development of an Index for Evaluating VIMS Using Gaze Data of Young People

Kazuhiro Fujikake[1]($\boxtimes$) (ID), Nari Takahashi[2], Kohki Nakane[3], and Hiroki Takada[3] (ID)

[1] Chukyo University, 101-2, Yagotohonmachi, Showa-Ku, Nagoya 4668666, Aichi, Japan
fujikake@lets.chukyo-u.ac.jp
[2] Nagoya City University, 2-1-10, Kita Chikusa, Chikusa-Ku, Nagoya 4640083, Japan
[3] University of Fukui, 3-9-1 Bunkyo, Fukui-Shi, Fukui, Japan

Abstract. Driving simulators (DS) have been used in many studies of traffic scenes, and the risk of visually induced motion sickness (VIMS) has been highlighted. This study aimed to develop an index for evaluating VIMS in young people from gaze data using a non-contact gaze measurement device. Gaze data were collected before and after a DS run to develop an evaluation index that enables the early detection of VIMS using gaze data. Gaze data were measured using a non-contact eye-measuring device. The participants viewed a 5-min DS running video five times and gaze data were measured at rest and before and after viewing the DS video. The participants were instructed to gaze at the optotype displayed at the center of the screen for 60 s when at rest. The results of this study indicate the validity of total locus length and sparse density (S_5) as evaluation indicators for VIMS and other issues. The total locus length and sparse density (S_5) were valid evaluation indices for VIMS. However, it was also clear that further studies on evaluation indexes other than the total locus length and the sparse density (S_5) are needed for the early detection of VIMS. In addition, because the present study was conducted using resting gaze data, it is also necessary to develop an evaluation index using gaze data during video gazing.

Keywords: Visually induced motion sickness (VIMS) · Gaze data · Rotational eye movement · Driving simulator (DS) · Young people

1 Introduction

Although driving simulators (DS) have been used in many traffic scene studies, the risk of visually induced motion sickness (VIMS) has been highlighted. An advantage of experiments utilizing a DS is that the experimental conditions can be adjusted. No injuries occur from accidents because it is a simulated experience, and it is easy to set up and reproduce traffic scenarios. One disadvantage associated with using DS is the deviation from the sense of reality and the high costs incurred. In recent years, DS-related hardware has become more powerful and less expensive; thus, the issues of realism and cost are being resolved. However, VIMS has been identified as an unresolved problem associated with DS. Because the symptoms of VIMS worsen as the field of view is expanded, it has been pointed out that the risk of VIMS increases as the size of the display screen increases [1]. This increases the risk of VIMS caused by the use of a DS.

VIMS caused by DS is considered a type of motion sickness [1], and motion sickness caused by visual information is classified as visual motion sickness. VIMS is believed to be caused by a mismatch between the visual information and the vestibular system, such as the semicircular canals. Therefore, VIMS is thought to involve an oculomotor control system. The physical symptoms associated with VIMS include sickness, lightheadedness, dizziness, nausea, and upset stomach.

There are several indices for evaluating VIMS, such as the simulator sickness questionnaire (SSQ) and center of gravity sway while standing [2, 3]. In addition, methods to evaluate the urge to vomit (lethargy) by measuring gastrograms [4] and the rotational movements of the eyeballs by measuring the area around the eyeballs using electromyograms have also been studied [5].

Rotational eye movement, which refers to the eye movement as it rotates around the gaze axis, is a physical symptom of VIMS [1]. It is generated by two types of stimuli: those from the vestibule (especially the otolithic organs) and visual stimuli. Rotational eye movements generated by vestibular stimulation are referred to as vestibular counter-rolling (vestibular torsional counter-rolling). When the body (head) is tilted in either direction, the eyeball rotates in the direction opposite that of the body (head), preserving vision [6]. Rotational eye movements are also a reflection of linear acceleration from otolithic organs. It has been suggested that ocular torsional counter-rolling occurs during motion sickness, whereas postural wobble is a physical symptom of motion sickness [7].

The evaluation indices for VIMS are based on data on the center of gravity sway, total locus length, area of sway, trajectory length per unit area, and sparse density [8–11]. The total locus length indicates the total movement distance of the center of gravity, whose numerical value increases when the posture fluctuates. The sway area is the inner area enclosed by the outer contour of the trajectory of the moving center of gravity, which increases when the posture is wobbly. The trajectory length per unit area is the length of the total locus divided by the area of sway, and the value increases when the posture is stable and decreases when wobbling occurs. Sparse density is a quantification index that shows the variation in data in the planar view and is a numerical value calculated as the number of times the center of gravity passes through each division of the sway diagram separated by squares. The sparse density value is close to 1 if the posture is stable, which results in locally dense divisions. If the posture fluctuates, the sparse density value increases. These quantification indices of the center of gravity sway have been shown to be effective in evaluating VIMS, which occurs due to gazing at moving images [12, 13] and stereoscopic images [12–14].

Several issues must be resolved in evaluating VIMS, including the burden associated with measurement. The physiological indices of eye movement-induced sickness from electrogastrograms and electromyography require electrodes and special equipment; thus, their burden on the experimental participants is significant, and their use is limited. Another limitation is the limited number of such cases. For example, in the case of VIMS using DS, an evaluation based on the center of gravity sway is inappropriate because it involves pedal operation in a sitting position. Furthermore, with regard to the physiological indices of sickness caused by eye movements such as the center of gravity sway, gastric electrocardiograms, and electromyograms, no consistent results have been obtained for the complex changes in the progression of sickness [8, 9]. Although the SSQ allows for a high degree of freedom in evaluation, it is neither objective nor accurate. Additionally, the SSQ is not suitable for the early detection of VIMS. If symptoms progress to the point where VIMS can be subjectively perceived, the symptoms may last for approximately 24 h [15]. Therefore, it is necessary to detect signs of VIMS at an early stage in DS experiments before the symptoms become serious.

Measurement with a non-contact eye measurement device is a method of measuring physiological indices that is less burdensome for participants than conventional evaluation methods in the experiment. Because a non-contact gaze measurement device does not require electrodes to be attached, there is little burden on the participants in terms of data acquisition. The corneal reflection method is used as a measurement method for non-contact gaze measurement devices. The corneal reflection method irradiates a light source onto the cornea to distinguish between the reflection points of light on the cornea and pupil, and the direction of the eye is calculated based on the reflection points of light and other geometric features [16–18].

Studies on older adults have demonstrated the effectiveness of VIMS assessments using gaze data. The results of the evaluation of resting gaze data in older adults showed that the locus of gaze data was lengthened and more diffuse in the group in which VIMS occurred [19–21]. The results of the evaluation of gaze data during DS driving showed that the regularity in the gaze data increased when VIMS occurred [19–21]. Furthermore, based on the results of a machine learning analysis, the effectiveness of VIMS evaluation using the gaze data of elderly people was determined [22–24]. However, because both studies were conducted on elderly people, it is necessary to examine the results on young people.

Therefore, this study aimed to develop an index for evaluating VIMS in young people from gaze data using a non-contact gaze measurement device. Gaze data were collected before and after the DS was run. Develop an evaluation index that enables the early detection of VIMS using gaze data. Because rotational eye movement is caused by unsteadiness resulting from VIMS, the following hypotheses are proposed.

Hypothesis 1: The locus of gaze data is lengthened in the VIMS group.
Hypothesis 2: The locus of the gaze data is diffused in the VIMS group.

2 Method

2.1 Experimental Stimulus and Devices

The experiment participants viewed a 5-min DS running video five times. It is generally believed that VIMS associated with DS driving is induced by the screen display when decelerating by braking and turning right or left. Therefore, the driving course in the DS video was set at two temporary stop intersections and two right/left turn points. The participants were taught to gaze at the DS video as if they were driving themselves and to hold the steering wheel to make them aware that they were driving. In addition, the participants answered the SSQ before and at the start and end of the experiment.

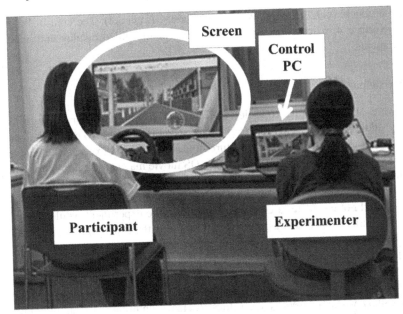

Fig. 1. Experimental setup.

Fig. 2. Experimental devices.

The experimental setup consisted of one screen (the viewing distance from the participant in the driver's seat to the front screen was approximately 57 cm), a steering wheel, and a control PC (Figs. 1 and 2). The screen was 31.5 inch (3840 × 2160-pixel resolution, EV3285-UNBK, EIZO Corporation). The steering wheel was composed of gaming products (G923 Racing Wheel and Pedals, Logicool). The control PC was a laptop (Surface 4, Microsoft), which was used for the video display and gaze data measurements.

2.2 Participants

There were 41 participants (16 males, 25 females), including university students and working adults (average, 21.22 y.o.; standard deviation, 1.00). Experimental participants were recruited after university lectures and introduced by experienced people. We explained to the participants that viewing the DS movie may cause symptoms similar to motion sickness, that they should indicate whether they felt sick or unwell, and that, if so, the experiment would be stopped immediately. Furthermore, we explained that if their symptoms did not ease after a certain break period, the experiment would be stopped, and there would be no penalty associated with stopping the experiment. Individuals who agreed to participate were selected for the experiment.

Regarding the VIMS symptoms associated with viewing the DS movie, the results of the SSQ responses were recorded along with the presence or absence of VIMS based on the internal reports of the participants themselves before and after the experiment.

This study was approved by the Ethics Review Committee of Chukyo University (Approval No. 21-023).

2.3 Measurement of Gaze Data

During the experiment, gaze data were measured at rest, before, and after viewing the DS movie. The experiment participants were instructed to pay attention to the safety of their surroundings while viewing the DS movie, as they would during a daily drive. The participants were instructed to gaze at the optotype displayed at the center of the screen for 60 s when at rest.

A Tobii Pro Fusion device (sampling rate of 250 Hz) was used as the gaze measurement device, and Tobii Pro Lab was used as the analysis software. The gaze measurement device measured eye movements using the corneal reflection method. It was placed at the bottom of the screen in front of the participants (Figs. 1 and 2). Gaze data were plotted at a resolution of 3840 (width) × 2160 (height) pixels on the screen. Because the resolution is the number of pixels contained in one inch (25.4 × 25.4 mm), the result of this experiment is approximately 150 pixels for 1 mm in the horizontal direction and 85 pixels for 1 mm in the vertical direction. In addition, gaze data were collected for both the left and right eyes. Therefore, the gaze data acquired by the eye measurement device were the values of the plane coordinates for each eye. The mean value calculated from the gaze data of each eye was analyzed as the gaze point of the corresponding eye.

2.4 Statistical Analyses

The statistical analysis of this study was performed a test of difference (t-test) between the corresponding/non-corresponding population. The results of each evaluation index in the pre- and post-conditions for the groups with/without VIMS were analyzed using a test of difference (t-test) between the corresponding population. In the post condition, the results of each evaluation index for the groups with/without VIMS were analyzed using a test of difference (t-test) between the non-corresponding population.

3 Results

Based on their SSQ results, the participants were classified into two groups, without VIMS (n = 21) and with VIMS (n = 20). The group without VIMS had SSQ values that did not change or decrease after the experiment. The VIMS group included patients whose SSQ values increased after the experiment.

Examples of the trajectories of the resting gaze data are shown in Figs. 3 and 4. Figure 3 presents the gaze data of person with and without VIMS before the experiment (pre). Comparing the trajectories of gaze data before the experiment, those of the VIMS person were slightly more diffuse than those without VIMS. Figure 4 shows the gaze data of person with and without VIMS after the experiment (post). Figure 4 shows the results for the same participants shown in Fig. 3. Comparing the trajectories of the gaze data after the experiment, the trajectory of a person with VIMS was more diffuse than a person without VIMS.

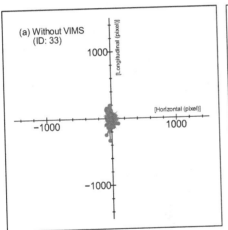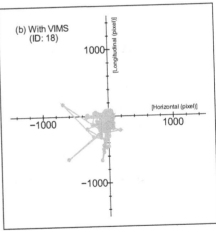

Fig. 3. Example of gaze data at rest time (pre). The left is the result of the participant (ID: 33) without VIMS. The right is the result of the participant (ID: 18) with VIMS. The vertical axis is the longitudinal movements of the gaze, and the horizontal axis is the right and left movements of the gaze.

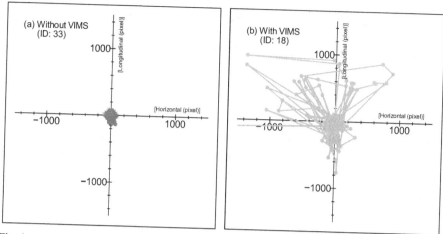

Fig. 4. Example of gaze data at rest time (post). The left is the result of the participant (ID: 33) without VIMS. The right is the result of the participant (ID: 18) with VIMS. The vertical axis is the longitudinal movements of the gaze, and the horizontal axis is the right and left movements of the gaze.

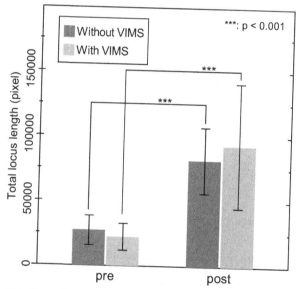

Fig. 5. Results of total locus length of gaze. As shown in Fig. 5, the mean total locus length is shown on the vertical axis and the pre/post-condition on the horizontal axis. The error bars indicate the standard deviation.

The mean total locus length was calculated from the resting gaze data for each group. Figure 5 shows that the total locus length was longer post-condition than pre-condition for both groups. A test of difference (t-test) between the corresponding populations pre- and post-VIMS showed significant differences in both groups, indicating that the total locus length post-VIMS was significantly longer than that pre-VIMS (p < 0.001 for both).

The mean area of the gaze was calculated from the resting gaze data for each group, with and without VIMS, as shown in Fig. 6. Figure 6 shows that the area of gaze was larger after than before for the group with VIMS. However, in the group without VIMS, the pre-VIMS value was wide. A test of difference (t-test) between the corresponding populations pre- and post-VIMS for each group showed significant differences in VIMS, indicating that the area of gaze post-VIMS was significantly larger than that pre-VIMS (p < 0.01). Furthermore, the results of the test of difference for the non-corresponding population (t-test) showed a trend toward a significant difference in the pre-test (p < 0.1), with the group with VIMS being smaller than that without VIMS.

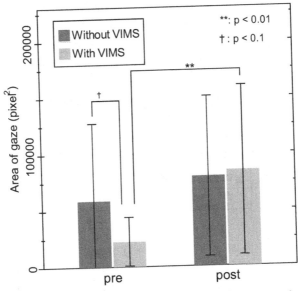

Fig. 6. Results of area of gaze. As shown in Fig. 6, the mean area of gaze on the vertical axis and pre/post-condition on the horizontal axis. The error bars indicate the standard deviation.

The mean trajectory length per unit area was calculated from the resting gaze data for each group, with and without VIMS, as shown in Fig. 7. The trajectory length per unit area was calculated as the total locus length divided by the gaze area. The values of the trajectory length per unit area for VIMS did not change significantly, whereas those without VIMS increased. A test of difference (t-test) between the corresponding populations pre/post for each group without/with VIMS showed significant differences without VIMS, indicating that the value of the trajectory length per unit area post-condition was significantly higher than that pre-condition (p < 0.01).

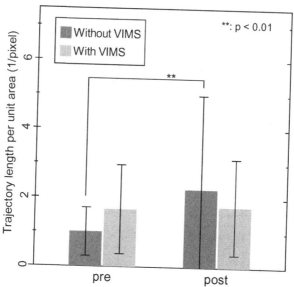

Fig. 7. Results of trajectory length per unit area. As shown in Fig. 7, the mean trajectory length per unit area on the vertical axis and pre/post-condition on the horizontal axis. The error bars indicate the standard deviation.

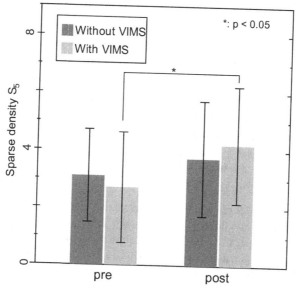

Fig. 8. Results of sparse density (S_5). As shown in Fig. 8, the mean sparse density (S_5) on the vertical axis and pre/post-condition on the horizontal axis. The error bars indicate the standard deviation.

The mean sparse density (S_5) was also calculated from the resting gaze data for each group, with and without VIMS, as shown in Fig. 8. Sparse density is a quantification index represented by a scatter plot of data on a plane, and the diffusion of data increases its value. Figure 8 shows that the sparse density (S_5) value was higher post-VIMS than pre-VIMS for both groups. A test of difference (t-test) between the corresponding populations pre/post for each group without/with VIMS showed significant differences in VIMS, indicating that the sparse density (S_5) post-condition was significantly higher than that pre-condition ($p < 0.05$).

4 Discussions

This study aimed to develop an index for evaluating VIMS in young people from gaze data using a non-contact gaze measurement device. The following hypotheses were tested in this study: In the VIMS group, the locus of the gaze data was lengthened (Hypothesis 1). Furthermore, in the VIMS group, the locus of gaze data was diffused (Hypothesis 2). Hypothesis 1 was partially supported by the results of this study, as the locus of gaze data was longer regardless of subjective VIMS. Hypothesis 2 was supported because the VIMS group had diffuse gaze data.

The total locus length was longer post-condition than pre-condition for both groups with and without VIMS (Fig. 3). These results were inconsistent with those of the subjective VIMS evaluation. One possible factor that caused the locus of gaze data to be longer, even for the group without VIMS, was that the symptoms of VIMS may have occurred even in the absence of subjective VIMS. This suggests that the total locus length may be able to detect the initial stages of VIMS.

The area of the gaze in the group with VIMS was larger post-condition than pre-condition (Fig. 4), which is a valid indicator for evaluating VIMS. However, the results of the pre-VIMS and VIMS groups were lower than those of the group without VIMS. Although the occurrence of VIMS is thought to be influenced by peripheral vision [25], the relationship between the two is not fully understood. The results of this study suggest that the group experiencing VIMS may be characterized by gaze behavior related to peripheral vision. However, a detailed verification of the influence of peripheral and central vision is required for VIMS.

The trajectory length per unit area in the group without VIMS was larger in the post-intervention group than in the pre-intervention group (Fig. 5), inconsistent with the subjective VIMS evaluation. The trajectory length per unit area was calculated as the total locus length divided by the gaze area. Therefore, it is possible that the VIMS features could no longer be extracted from the total locus length and the area of gaze. Thus, trajectory length per unit area is not an appropriate metric for evaluating VIMS.

The sparse density (S_5) in the VIMS group was higher post-condition than pre-condition (Fig. 6). Moreover, the sparse density (S_5) results were consistent with the subjective evaluation results. Therefore, the sparse density (S5) is an appropriate metric for evaluating VIMS. However, it is unclear whether sparse density (S_5) is effective for the early detection of VIMS, and further studies are needed.

The results of this study indicate the validity of total locus length and sparse density (S_5) as evaluation indicators for VIMS and future issues. The total locus length and sparse density (S_5) were valid evaluation indices for VIMS. However, it was also clear that further study on the evaluation indexes, the total locus length, and the sparse density (S_5) are needed for the early detection of VIMS. In addition, because the present study was conducted using resting gaze data, it was necessary to develop an evaluation index using gaze data during video gazing.

5 Conclusion

This study aimed to develop an index for evaluating VIMS in young people from gaze data using a non-contact gaze measurement device. The results of this study indicate the validity of total locus length and sparse density (S_5) as evaluation indicators for VIMS and future issues. The total locus length and sparse density (S_5) were valid evaluation indices for VIMS. However, it was also clear that further study on the evaluation indexes, the total locus length, and the sparse density (S_5) are needed for the early detection of VIMS. In addition, because the present study was conducted using resting gaze data, it was necessary to develop an evaluation index using gaze data during video gazing.

Acknowledgment. This work was supported by JSPS KAKENHI Grant Number 20K11905.

References

1. Ohmi, M., Ujike, H.: Eizou Jouhou ni yoru Jiko Teii to Eizou Yoi. Bio Med. Eng. **18**(1), 32–39 (2004). (in Japanese)
2. Golding, J.F.: Phasic skin conductance activity and motion sickness. Aviat. Space Environ. Med. **63**(3), 165–171 (1992)
3. Wan, H., Hu, S., Wang, J.: Correlation of phasic and motion sickness-conductance responses with severity of motion sickness induced by viewing an optokinetic rotating drum. Percept. Motor Skills **97**(3), 1051–1057 (2003)
4. Kinoshita, F., Fujita, K., Miyanaga, K., Touyama, H., Takada, M., Takada, H.: Analysis of electro-gastrograms during exercise loads. J. Sports Med. Doping Stud. **8**(2), 285–294 (2018)
5. Shackel, B.: Eye movement recording by electro-oculography. In: Venables, P.H., Martion, I. (eds.) A Manual of Psychophysiological Methods, pp. 300–334. North-Holland Publishing Co., Amsterdam (1967)
6. Howard, I.: Human Visual Orientation. John Wiley & Sons Ltd., New Jersey (1982)
7. Marg, E.: Development of electro-oculography; standing potential of the eye in registration of eye movement. A.M.A. Arch. Ophthalmol. **45**, 69–185 (1951)
8. Nakagawa, C., Ohsuga, M.: The present situation of the studies in VE-Sickness and its close field. Virt. Soc. Japan **3**(2), 31–39 (1998). (in Japanese)
9. Hirayanagi, K.: A present state and perspective of studies on motion sickness. Jpn. J. Ergon. **42**(3), 200–211 (2006). (in Japanese)
10. Fujikake, K., Miyao, M., Honda, R., Omori, M., Matuura, Y., Takada, H.: Evaluation of high quality LCDs displaying moving pictures, on the basis of the results obtained from statokinesigrams. Forma **22**(2), 199–206 (2007)
11. Fujikake, K., Takada, H., Omori, M., Hasegawa, S., Honda, R., Miyao, M.: Evaluation of moving picture image quality on LCDs using Stabilometer. Jpn. J. Ergon. **44**(4), 208–217 (2008). (in Japanese)

12. Kinoshita, F., Takada, H.: Numerical analysis of SDEs as a model for body sway while viewing 3D video clips. Mechatron. Syst. Control **47**(2), 98–105 (2019)
13. Miyao, M., Takada, M., Takada, H.: Visual issues on augmented reality using smart glasses with 3D stereoscopic images. In: Proceedings of the HCII 2019, Florida, vol. 11572, pp. 578–589 (2019)
14. Tanimura, T., Takada, H., Sugiura, A., Kinoshita, F., Takada, M.: Effects of the low-resolution 3D video clip on cerebrum blood flow dynamics. Adv. Sci. Tech. Eng. Syst. J. **4**(2), 380–386 (2019)
15. U.S. Navy. OPNAVINST, 3710.7T (2004)
16. Young, L.R., Sheena, D.: Methods and designs; survey of eye movement recording methods. Behav. Res. Methods Instrum. **7**, 397–429 (1975)
17. Cornsweet, T.N., Crane, H.D.: Accurate two-dimensional eye tracker using first and fourth Purkinje images. J. Opt. Soc. Am. **63**, 921–928 (1973)
18. Crane, H.D., Steele, C.M.: An accurate three-dimensional eye tracker. Appl. Opt. **17**, 691–705 (1978)
19. Fujikake, K.: Measurements for visual function, including gaze, and electrooculography (EOG). In: Takada, H., Yokoyama, K. (eds.) Bio-information for Hygiene, pp. 45–56. Springer, Berlin (2021)
20. Fujikake, K., Ono, R., Takada, H.: Development of an index for evaluating VIMS using gaze data. In: Proceedings of International Conference on Human-Computer Interaction 2021, pp. 545–554 (2021)
21. Fujikake, K., Ono, R., Takada, H.: Development of visually induced motion sickness evaluation index using gaze data of elderly people. Jpn. J. Hyg. **77**, 1–6 (2022). https://doi.org/10.1265/jjh.21001 (in Japanese)
22. Fujikake, K., Itadu, Y., Takada, H.: Development of evaluation system for VIMS by machine learning of eye movement data. IEEJ Trans. Electron. Inf. Syst. **142**, 1107–1114 (2022). https://doi.org/10.1541/ieejeiss.142.1107 (in Japanese)
23. Fujikake, K., Itadu, Y., Takada, H.: Analyzing gaze data during rest time/driving simulator operation using machine learning. In: Proceedings of the International Conference on Human-Computer Interaction 2022, pp. 420–434 (2022)
24. Fujikake, K., Itadu, Y., Takada, H.: Development of VIMS evaluation system by machine learning of gaze data during driving simulator operation. Bull. Sci. Form **37**, 59–71 (2023). (in Japanese)
25. Kim, G., Kim, B.: The effect of retinal eccentricity on visually induced motion sickness and postural control. Appl. Sci. **9**, 1919 (2019). https://doi.org/10.3390/app9091919

Meta-experience via VR and Telepresence Systems

Yasush Ikei[1]([✉])(ID), Vibol Yem[2](ID), Yusuke Kikuchi[3](ID), and Yukiya Ojima[3](ID)

[1] The University of Tokyo, Tokyo 1138656, Japan
ikei@vr.u-tokyo.ac.jp
[2] University of Tsukuba, Ibaraki 3058577, Japan
yem@iit.tsukuba.ac.jp
[3] Tokyo Metropolitan University, Tokyo 1910065, Japan
{kikuchi-yusuke4,ojima-yukiya}@ed.tmu.ac.jp

Abstract. This paper describes meta-experience creation by using a presentation system of a virtual reality space and a remote real space. The spatial experience is based on the simultaneous perception of the environment and the body, and since multiple senses are used for perception, the simultaneous presentation of multisensory information is required to realize appropriate integration. In active (voluntary) experiences, avatars are moved in the target space via physical movements and button operations, where the multisensory integration is also important. Passive experiences are the basic premise for reliving the viewpoint of others. The equivalent amount of motion stimulus to the body that is not actively driven should be less than 10%. We constructed a multisensory reliving device and a remote presence experience device, and we confirmed their functions. The metaverse is a new type of multiuser experience, which is an experience of an extended three-dimensional world that includes the perception of other people's bodies and conventional individual-centered experiences. These meta-experiences are expected to amplify our presence and capabilities in the future.

Keywords: Experience creation · Multisensory · Virtual reality

1 Introduction

Information and communication technologies have resulted in effective methods for encoding, communicating, and reproducing events in physical space. In recent years, such technologies have greatly expanded the domain of the human body and its own experiences.

The human experience is the result of comprehensive but subjective perception of the external world in its various aspects and its selective behaviors. It is at the prerogative discretion of each individual and changes in each moment. The goal and effect of virtual reality (VR) is to engage with these personal characteristics.

In a world where security and freedom are guaranteed, people tend to shift focus from the physical aspects of the external environment to events that involve complex changes in the environment. In other words, human needs are shifting to the aspects of the total context. This shift is a growing preference, and sympathy for diversification and synchronous change in the senses that constitute the context and the object of interest is moving toward the experience itself.

The experience is subjective and stems from the relationship between the individual and the world, and VR is a promising method to represent the entirety of that relationship. VR can be used to create various worlds by representing the environment or space around you arbitrarily. However, VR can also change the concept of a conventional form of experiences by creating a self-body (i.e., an avatar) in the VR space and the senses from the space, projecting thoughts, and giving the world behavior (interaction) that matches the user's senses, such as a collaborative structure closely coupled with the environment. Despite this potential to significantly change the future "experience scenario," VR that fully satisfies human perceptions and behaviors has not yet been achieved. Thus, the VR experience is expected to be taken as a meta-experience that comprehensively considers the perspective of the experience.

2 Multisensory and Space

VR, which reproduces space, makes us perceive the existence of another space around us. However, only by reproducing our physical (bodily) sensations simultaneously can we truly immerse ourselves in the VR world. There are different types of experiences in conventional VR methods because there are two spaces, i.e., the real space, where the experiencer is physically located, and the VR space of the object to be experienced. The avatar's body exists in the VR space separately from the experiencer's physical body, and there is diversity in the VR space composition depending on the content. The first form of VR was proposed in 1989. In this initial system, only the avatar's hands were visible while viewing a world synthesized using computer graphics from a first-person perspective using a head-mounted display (HMD) device. The viewpoint was shifted by performing hand gestures; thus, the user rarely walked in the real space[1]. In this case, moving in the VR space required caution, and in most cases, visually induced motion sickness (VIMS) occurred. VIMS occurs because the state of the user's vision and the physical sensations do not match when the sensation of the flow of images corresponding to physical movement are perceived without a sense of motion or movement in the user's body. This problem occurs frequently when using HMDs as VR devices, which are now widely used by the general public.

Human perception of space is based on the simultaneous perception of space and the body. For example, for the entire body's movement, we use visual, auditory, vestibular, proprioceptive (postural and motor senses), and cutaneous (plantar contact and airflow) senses. The state of the surrounding environment,

---

[1] The user could not walk due to the cable connecting the HMD and the DataGlove (gesture input gloves) device to the control computer.

which has the greatest influence on the person, and the state of the person's posture and movement in that environment are estimated simultaneously. In this process, a large amount of sensory information is typically used comprehensively without the user being aware of this process. If there is noise or inconsistency in such information, the estimation is primarily based on the information that is deemed to have high accuracy [1]. In addition, the weighting of sensory inputs [2] in the estimation process changes according to the state of the relationship between the environment and the body. A very elaborate processing system with multiple layers and interactions in the central nervous system learns integration strategies for unusual situations, including sports, as required, thereby making it quite difficult to discuss the entire aspect of multisensory spatial perceptions. Thus, it is difficult to predict how perceptions will be integrated when synthetic sensations are presented in VR, even more so when the body and environment are in a relationship that differs from the natural human perceptual experience.

3   Active Experience

Typically, human perception naturally takes place under the situation of a body in motion (changing) in space, which, characteristically, is the state in which a person is acting freely. This free motion is due to the free choice of the brain [3]. In other words, it is not limited to conscious movement and includes reflexive movement. This is typically referred to as an active movement; however, the internal functions of the human body, from life support to thinking, can be considered passive in the sense that short-term to long-term adaptations or reactions are generated by the inputs received from the external environment[2]. During extremely short periods, changes in physical stimuli are primarily based on the active movement of the individual; however, they are also brought about by natural phenomena in the external environment, including other living individuals. All of these are elements of the stimulus level of the experience, and to generate an experience in VR, we must generate these stimuli. However, the person's active movement requires careful consideration when generating the sensation for the movement in a VR device.

Typically, a three-dimensional (3D) avatar is used to experience the VR space, and the first typical example of a VR experience is when the avatar performs the same motions as the user's physical body. In this case, the user's motions are reproduced by the avatar in the VR space, and that physical sensation is interpreted as having occurred in the VR space. In this configuration, the relationship between the avatar and the user's body is clear. In addition, the motion of the user's body occurs in the VR space, and there are no buttons

---

[2] Active or passive are terms that describe the behavior of the central concept, defining its boundaries with the environment and the information and physical quantities that move between them. However, due to the diversity of control structures, conceptual hierarchies, and objects of human processing, strictly defined discussions of these concepts are required.

or other intervening objects; thus, there is little difference from the real experience. The advantage of this configuration is the consistency of the physical sensation; however, the disadvantage is that the actions in the VR space are restricted to the real space area, which is typically not wide enough for most users. For example, for a walking motion, the walking range can be limited by using a treadmill or the redirected walking method [4]; however, these methods require large equipment and a relatively large space. In addition, while the body motion is free, the position changes, thereby making it difficult to provide feedback other than the walking sensation. For example, it is currently not possible to reproduce the sensation of hands manipulating spatial objects at a high quality during or after walking. In other words, physical interactions with the external environment in this form are limited. In the metaverse, which will be the center of the future VR space, this configuration is expected to become one of many experience methods.

Another way to experience a VR space or the metaverse is to configure the avatar in a manner that does not directly correspond to the user's physical movements. In this case, the avatar can be moved in the VR space by manipulating buttons and sticks on a gamepad or keyboard. The advantages of this technique are that it is easy to move around in a large VR space, and the avatar can be operated while the user is seated, which reduces the user's physical burden. Seated operation is highly convenient for the general user population, and this is a significant benefit. However, while it is easy to move around, without bodily sensory feedback, the sensory inconsistency and VIMS problems may occur when moving the viewpoint.

4   Passive Experience

In contrast to the active configuration described above, a different type of synthetic experience can be considered by incorporating passivity. Current VR systems can be used for general user applications, e.g., entering and moving around in different spaces, playing games, attending concerts and exhibition events, conversing with other avatars, and purchasing products, and also for professional applications, e.g., training and work simulators. When the content of the world is viewed as educational or entertainment, these spatial experiences are frequently sufficiently passive or heteronomous experiences that are primarily just watching and listening. In other words, these experiences do not necessarily require all of the user's actions[3].

For example, watching a TV program is obviously a simple viewing experience; however, it is still useful as an experience of a distant space with a low requirement level. When VR is used, the experience is not the two-dimensional (2D) world of TV viewing, in which the viewer observes through a window at a world partitioned by a frame, but rather the experience of wearing an HMD, stepping into the scene of that world, looking around while immersed in the 3D

---

[3] Particularly for educational purposes, a passive position where the user is initially taught may be more efficient in terms of information transfer.

space, and being guided to see and hear while moving through the space. A similar real-world example is a guided tour. Such tours allow the viewer to look in any direction on-site; thus, they include a considerable amount of the sensation of an active on-site experience rather than an entirely passive experience, as is the case with TV viewing. In this case, it is important to provide the physical sensation of walking to ensure consistency between the senses to prevent VIMS.

In addition, in content that allows the user to experience body motion, the user's body is moved by the VR display, and the user is taught how to move their body passively. This attentive guidance represents instruction on how to use the body, including the position of the head. This is a way to convey information about physical movements, and, from a different perspective, the user is experiencing the experience of someone who has already mastered a given movement. When watching TV, we are rarely aware of this because the sense of presence is insufficient; however, the visual world shown in live coverage of a scene can be considered similar to experiencing the scene from the perspective of the cameraperson on the scene. In VR, by immersing oneself in the virtual space, one experiences actually standing in the same place as the cameraperson. If the body movements are linked to shifts in the cameraperson's viewpoint, it is equivalent to experiencing or reliving the cameraman's experience.

In this case, an interesting phenomenon that occurs. When giving the sensation of walking, the intensity of the walking motion stimulus presented to the lower limbs and head by the VR system must be much smaller than the force and displacement generated by the actual motion because there is a mechanism that attenuates the sensation generated from the motion during active human movement [5]. The sensation that occurs when a person utilizes their muscles during body motion is suppressed and perceived as small. However, when the body is driven passively by a VR device, this suppression does not occur, which means that the stimulus must be small to be perceived in the same manner. This allows the size of the device to be reduced, which is a design advantage of a reliving type VR. The device described in the next section creates a sensation that is compatible with real walking by presenting vestibular and proprioceptive stimuli that are 5%–10% of real motion depending on the conditions and type of sensation.

5   Multisensory Reliving Experience

In this study, using the example of walking in a sightseeing spot as the sensation of a passive on-site experience, we attempted to present the sensation using a five-sense reliving device. This project attempts to allow the users to relive the experience by actually walking around the site and capturing images of the scenery using an omnidirectional camera. The VR device can present stereoscopic images, stereophonic sound, swaying of the entire body while walking, swinging of the upper arms, air currents, aroma, the vibration caused by splashing water, the motion of the lower limbs, and vibration of the sole of the foot. Figure 1 shows the configuration of a multisensory presentation device (five-sense theater) [6]. Note that the phrase "five senses" generally refers to basic human senses including visual, auditory, olfactory, gustatory, and tactile sensations. Note that gustatory sensations are not included in this system. Instead, vestibular sensation (e.g., head translation and rotation acceleration) and proprioceptive sensation (e.g., arm and leg movements) are included, which effectively represent the sensation of walking.

A video (Fig. 2) from the academic exhibition (SIGGRAPH Asia 2018) was recorded while walking through the cities of Toronto and Niagara Falls from a tourist's perspective. To capture important visual information that is essential for a high sense of realism, six 4K GoPro cameras were used to record the entire scene, which was then combined to create an 8K omnidirectional image. In this case, the video is monocular in principle. The resolution was nearly equivalent to that of the HMD device (VIVE Pro; 1440×1600 pixels/monocular), and a high-quality video is presented. Note that VIMS did not occur because the walking sensation was presented to the entire body according to the walking movement present in the video.

In terms of information other than visual and auditory, it is possible to record and reproduce actual walking motion, acceleration, and various other environmental information. However, these data tend to contain a large amount of noise and are not very effective in practice. In the case of reliving type content, walking at a constant speed with a stable field of view is effective, and fluctuations in actual walking motion do not typically provide particularly useful information when recreating the scene. This is thought to be because the brain normally ignores information containing unwanted variability when integrating perceptual information [7].

Thus, as the experience content, we used kinesthetic stimuli obtained from long-term research as a representation of the walking sensation. For the other senses, if the event is synchronized with the local event, standard stimulus data and other appropriate stimuli are frequently sufficiently effective as long as further specificity is not an issue. Note that this depends on the content theme of the experience.

6   Remote Presence Experience

While the multisensory presentation described in the previous section allows the user to relive past travel experiences, experiencing a remote location at the present moment also has a configuration that is very similar to the VR experience. This configuration is called telexistence [8] or telepresence because the purpose is to have the user's presence in a remote real space. In this case, the user's avatar is placed in a remote location to realize the sensation of "being there." Ideally, information from all five basic senses is required to obtain a sense of presence; however, it is difficult to collect information about the entire body at a remote location because it is impossible to implement functions and forms similar to those of the human body in an avatar at a remote location using current robotics technology.

40   Y. Ikei et al.

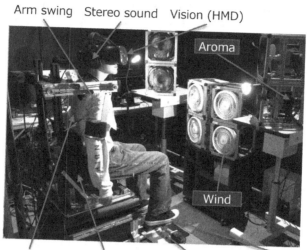

Fig. 1. Multisensory display (SIGGRAPH Asia 2018).

Fig. 2. 8K images of Toronto (upper) and Niagara Falls (lower)

In addition, acquiring and reproducing local information, which is important in terms of realizing a sense of presence in the remote areas, involves delays in the communication process, which is a difficult problem. This means that when the avatar acts actively, the resulting sensory (or scenic) change in the information transmission loop is too slow for accurate action, or when talking to a local person, there is a delay in the audio and visual response, which makes it difficult to speak. Tactile sensations are even more demanding when manipulating objects using the avatar's hand. In this case, a loop of 500–1000 Hz is required to realize an accurate tactile representation. If 5G and 6G communication environments are developed in the future, and ultrahigh-speed and ultra-low latency communication is realized, this problem will be alleviated rapidly. However, realizing these goals with the current communication environment is difficult.

We constructed a system that allows an avatar to move around while obtaining a 360° stereoscopic view of the local area, which is important in terms of achieving a sense of remote realism. Figure 3 shows the avatar robot we developed. Here, the avatar can be controlled by a user wearing an HMD. Here, motion instructions are provided using a controller and body movements. In addition, the user can manipulate the avatar's arms. Figure 4 shows a vestibular and proprioceptive display system designed by one of the coauthors. This display system allows the user to sit and experience the remote location while gaining a sense of the avatar's gait as it progresses. The audiovisual information is provided by a TwinCam system [9] equipped with two 360° cameras (THETA Z1, Ricoh), which enables stereoscopic viewing in all directions. This makes it possible to work with a sense of presence and grasp distance objects [10]. The avatar can deliver 4K (30 fps) omnidirectional stereoscopic images to a large number of viewpoint-sharing remote users (even overseas) via a high-speed 5G mobile network connection. We confirmed that live omnidirectional 3D images from New York (USA), Brisbane (Australia), Phnom Penh (Cambodia), and other cities can be received in Tokyo, Japan.

7   Meta-experience

Direct spatial or real-world experiences, such as those described above, have clear practical implications, and their utility is immediately apparent. However, the world of experience can generally be interpreted more broadly. Humans can view their own bodily experiences and the experiences of others, not simply as events in the external world, but as meta-experiences that are in some kind of continuity with their own experiences. This characteristic is likely due to the early evolutionary development of sociality and the subsequent development of language. These things are due to the need to understand others in order to survive, i.e., whether they are allies or enemies.

One of the foundations of understanding others is understanding their thoughts and intentions based on their actions and to infer them using the aspect of their bodies as a medium. This is done by observing the bodies and actions of others and interpreting them through the motor control system of one's own

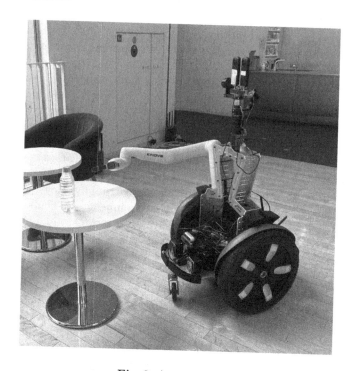

Fig. 3. Avatar robot.

body. In other words, this understanding mechanism is based on simulated computation, where the individual projects onto their own unique body model and its state control mechanism to understand the state of another person's body and analogize the results and intentions of the other person. This can be referred to as a meta-experience of experiencing others. This mechanism, which processes visual observations, is an extremely efficient real-time survival strategy. Thus, it is effective to accompany the experience of others with bodily images. In this case, the type of representation of others should be given and how to provide the actual body the sensation are governed by the overall past memory or perceptual integration mechanism. Therefore, a rendering method that conforms to the principles of experience is desirable.

Verbal descriptions of others are suitable for conveying long-term experiences that extend far beyond the relatively short time frame of immediate bodily actions. Although verbal expressions are insufficient for the purpose of physical motion transfer because they do not convey sufficient information about the body movements themselves, this process can be interpreted as a meta-experience in which the medium is different. However, future advances in artificial intelligence (AI) technologies will approach human capabilities in terms of both language and graphic pattern processing and will likely transcend human capabilities in some areas such that it will be easy to generate representations of physical-motor experiences from natural language.

Fig. 4. Walking sensation feedback device.

In addition, the metaverse, which is a virtual space with multiple participants that is expected to be developed in the future, will be very different from past experiences and will be incorporated into the meta-experience. The metaverse is a 3D virtual space in which users experience the virtual environment using an avatar.

However, unlike the experience of a real space described in the previous sections, this is an experience of a world in which the virtual object in the space have 3D data, and their appearance and physical behavior can be configured with an extremely high degree of freedom. Currently, the simplest form of use for ordinary metaverse participants is to view a self-avatar selected from the system from a third-person perspective on a 2D monitor and manipulate it using a mouse, keyboard, or game controller to move around a 3D space that is almost the same configuration as an online game space. This is a spatial experience; however, even though the external environment is reproduced, information about the body is missing, and there is no self to perceive the real space. In other words, the user's physical characteristics are not projected in any way. It is a simple simulated experience of space, and its spatiality is utilized to explain events and establish causality. The kinetic capabilities of the human body, which are extremely superior to any robotic mechanisms, are not utilized at all in this case. The focus of the metaverse experience is not on the self but on the other participants and communication among the participants. In other words, it is a social networking experience that uses a virtual 3D environment.

A metaverse that satisfies the spatial characteristics of humans who perform a wide range of motions and simultaneously execute information processing for external perception is a challenge for the future. When wearing an HMD and entering a 3D virtual space where virtual hand and body movements can be perceived as natural spatial objects, we feel the advanced coordination of both perception and motion, which is very different from the game space experience described above. Based on our discussions, it is evident that a spatial interface that can fully accommodate human spatiality does not yet exist. However, as mentioned above, there is a possibility that new ways to experience space will emerge with advances in AI technologies. We expect that, as AI sensory processing achieves performance that is equal to or better than that of humans, the metaverse space will provide new experiences that reflect the uniqueness and preferences of individuals and their thoughts.

8   Conclusion

In this paper, we have described a meta-experience created with a VR space and a remote space experience presentation system. Spatial experience will be the basis of human existence for the foreseeable future, and VR technologies and the metaverse are very useful technologies that can extend human existence because they are stage sets with the potential to freely construct spatial experiences. In the near future, we will be equipped with multisensory interfaces that implement the power of AI to create a virtual space that adapts to each person's sensibilities and amplifies human abilities.

Acknowledgment. In writing this paper, I have made use of the results of my previous research on physical reliving. The authors gratefully acknowledge the following research funding support. MIC/SCOPE #191603003, JSPS KAKENHI Grant Number 18H04118, 21K19785, 18H03283, TMU local-5G project.

References

1. Ernst, M.O., Banks, M.S.: Humans integrate visual and haptic information in a statistically optimal fashion. Nature **415**(6870), 429–33 (2002)
2. Hwang, S., Agada, P., Kiemel, T., Jeka, J.J.: Dynamic reweighting of three modalities for sensor fusion. PLoS ONE **9**(1), e88132 (2014)
3. Haggard, P.: Decision time for free will. Neuron **69**, 404–6 (2011)
4. Fan, L., Li, H., Shi, M.: Redirected walking for exploring immersive virtual spaces with HMD: a comprehensive review and recent advances. In: IEEE Transactions on Visualization and Computer Graphics (2022)
5. Blakemore, S.-J., Wolpert, D.M., Frith, C.D.: Central cancellation of self-produced tickle sensation. Nat. Neurosci. **1**, 635–640 (1998)

6. Shimizu, K., et al.: FiveStar VR: shareable travel experience through multisensory stimulation to the whole body. In: SIGGRAPH Asia 2018 Virtual & Augmented Reality (SA '18). ACM, NY (2018). Article 2
7. Sommer, M., Wurtz, R.: Brain circuits for the internal monitoring of movements. Annu. Rev. Neurosci. **31**, 317–338 (2008)
8. Telexistence. https://tachilab.org/jp/about/telexistence.html. Accessed 10 Feb 2023
9. Tashiro, K., Fujie, T., Ikei, Y., Amemiya, T., Hirota, K., Kitazaki, M.: TwinCam: omni-directional stereoscopic live viewing camera reducing motion blur during head rotation. In: Proceedings of SIGGRAPH 2017 Emerging Technologies (SIGGRAPH '17). ACM, NY (2017). Article 24. JP Patent 6752425. US Patent 11006028
10. Kikuchi, Y., et al.: Dual robot avatar: real-time multispace experience using telepresence robots and walk sensation feedback including viewpoint sharing for immersive virtual tours. In: ACM SIGGRAPH 2022 Emerging Technologies (SIGGRAPH '22). ACM, NY (2022). Article 3

AR and VR – A Review on Recent Progress and Applications

Jiachen Jiang[1], Guoyang Zhou[1], Brendan M. Duffy[2(✉)], and Vincent G. Duffy[1]

[1] School of Industrial Engineering, Purdue University, West Lafayette, IN 47906, USA
{jiang518,guoyang,duffy}@purdue.edu
[2] Elmore Family School of Electrical and Computer Engineering, Purdue University,
West Lafayette, IN 47906, USA
duffy45@purdue.edu

Abstract. The main theme of this report is a systematic literature review for the current states and future trends of virtual reality and augmented reality, especially in human factors related fields. Evidence shows that literature review is beneficial and essential for research, and there are numerous guides on how to accomplish that [15–17]. A number of academic databases will be searched, such as Google Scholar, Scopus, and Web of Science. Basic visualization and be performed, as well as trend analysis and content analysis. It can be seen from the results that VR/AR are two trending research topics in recent years. The applications are widely distributed all over society, from healthcare to gaming to engineering. It can thus be inferred that the future of AR/VR is limitless.

Keywords: augmented reality · AR · virtual reality · VR · human factors · ergonomics · Citespace · MAXQDA · VOS viewer

1 Introduction and Background

With the development of technology, it is no longer a dream to live in a simulation. The advancement of computation power, combined with the ability to shrink the physical dimensions of personal computers, offered a unique playground for virtual reality (VR) and augmented reality (AR) devices. According to a blog from Tulane University, AR transforms the mundane physical world to a more colorful and livelier one by projecting virtual images through a camera or video viewer. In other words, AR is simply adding to our real life experience. Virtual reality, on the other hand, brings it one level up. VR takes these elements into a whole new level by producing an entirely simulated alternate world generated by computers. Immersive simulations can bring humans into any place imaginable, as long as there is adequate equipment [1]. The key difference between the two being that AR builds on the real world, whereas VR is completely virtual. Generally speaking, AR can be accessed on personal devices, such as smartphones, whereas VR requires a headset device.

The practical applications of virtual reality and augmented reality can be endless. Let's begin with augmented reality. The famous game that made everyone running around, Pokémon Go, is a classical application of AR [2]. Pokémon Go overlays the images of Pokémons on top of real life through smartphones, and it allows users to engage with other people in augmented battles, of course, in smartphones. On a more serious application, Google Translate harnesses the power of AR to help people understand other languages better. In the figure below, Google Translate translates a Japanese flyer into English by overlaying the English words on top of the original Japanese words. This is beneficial than the traditional way of mobile translating where a user needs to type, or copy and paste, the original words into the app, and the app outputs the translated words. By overlaying the translated words, the original background and context are kept the same, which helps the user understand the meanings more easily. Virtual reality has its applications as well. One of the pioneers of virtual reality, Meta, has been promoting its VR product, Metaverse, for a long time. One of the most common applications of VR today is gaming. Games such as The Walking Dead, Among Us, and Iron Man are much more engaging and livelier when played on virtual reality headsets than in computers or mobile devices. It makes the user feel as if they were in the game world. VR can also be used to develop meeting platforms. With remote work becoming more and more common, regular meeting software, such as Zoom and WebEx, offer mundane experiences. Once VR is introduced to online meeting software, meeting attendees can all be in the same place, virtually. They can even interact with each other to make the meeting more engaging and effective (Fig. 1).

Fig. 1. Google Translate uses AR to translate Japanese to English

The above paragraph talks about the practical, consumer-level applications of AR and VR. In academia, there has been research done on these technologies as well. Way back in the early 2000s, there has been literature summarizing research on virtual reality. Schuemie et al. explored the use and effectiveness of virtual reality in psychology therapy [3]. At that time, there was not a complete understanding of why VR worked and what effect it had on humans. The paper acknowledged that there was a lack of knowledge in the field. Even before the 21st century, there had been publications on IEEE talking about VR. Zheng et al. provided an overview of VR and its applications in engineering and medicine from the perspective of a researcher in the late 1990s [4]. Fast forward to today, one of the popular research fields of VR is in medicine. Li et al. reviewed the progress in clinical medicine and reached a conclusion that both healthcare professionals and patients could benefit from VR [5]. VR can be effective in education as well, as

Elmqaddem has indicated in the publication exploring whether it's a myth of reality to use VR in education [6]. Zhang et al. proposed a virtual conference solution, VirtualCube [9], which goes hand-in-hand with the ever trendy remote work policy. Of course, VR and AR will inevitably revolutionize the way we teach and learn. In a more recent study by Oigara, it was shown that virtual reality could enhance the learners' experiences in classrooms [7]. In more advanced studies, such as one by Li et al., it was studied whether active parts of the brain are affected by the presence of VR and whether those brain signals can be used for user authentication using electroencephalography (EEG) signals [10]. In safety engineering, especially in construction fields, VR technologies are widely researched. Zhao et al. explored the possibility of using VR to train workers on safety related topics on construction sites [11]. The conclusion is positive – it is possible to improve workers' cognition and intervention of certain hazards using VR training. In the textbook of this class, Handbook of Human Factors and Ergonomics, there are a number of chapters including the use of virtual reality on the topic they are talking about, such as control theory, sensations, and training [8].

Just like any other technology, VR and AR have their own uniqueness. One of the examples, demonstrated by Bramley et al., is using virtual reality on surveys [13]. Although it is one of the most widely used data collection techniques, surveys are not always reliable. One of the main goals of conducting surveys is to collect information in a reliable and valid manner [14]. Unfortunately, it is not always the case. Using virtual reality can offer subjects a more vivid and lively feel about the target they are thinking about, which will likely increase the credibility of their survey answers. VR and AR together can also be uniquely used in some settings, such as education. Using these technologies will inevitably make the classroom livelier and more enjoyable.

As demonstrated in the above paragraphs, VR and AR have a lot of practical applications. Because of this, much of the research is devoted to practical applications, rather than purely for academia. Many studies focus on using these technologies in a new field, rather than how to make the technologies themselves better or dig more deeply into these technologies.

Since this is a project report for IE 556 class, there have been some mentioning of VR/AR and systematic review in some of the in-class assignments as well. Packback is one of the software used in class, and I added quite a few contents there. The first screenshot below is one of the assignments in Packback: using Scite.ai to further facilitate lab 3. The second screenshot below shows my declaration of semester project topic, which shows that I chose VR/AR as my topic, and I planned to complete the project alone. The class textbook is "Handbook of Human Factors and Ergonomics" [38], and some of the chapters are closely related to this topic as well, such as Chapter 7 on page 893 and Chapter 5 on page 685 (Figs. 2 and 3).

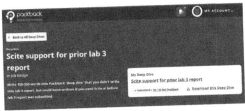

Fig. 2. One of the homework assignments in Packback - using Scite.ai to facilitate lab 3.

Fig. 3. My declaration of semester project topic in Packback

2 Procedures and Results

2.1 Databases and Initial Search

One of the key parts of data collection is searching for topic related areas in academic databases. For this project, I used 3 databases: Google Scholar, Scopus, and Web of Science. Access is provided through Purdue library [12]. To facilitate the goal of this course, I will search for four different terms: "virtual reality and safety", "augmented reality and safety", "augmented reality and human computer interaction", and "virtual reality and human computer interaction". The date range was set to the past ten years, from 2012 to 2022. At the time of writing this report, it is halfway through 2023, and there will likely be more publications during the next few months. Hence, only publications up to 2022 were considered. The table shows the search terms and number of articles returned from the search (Table 1).

To give a bigger picture, the figure below shows a visualization of the above table. It is clear that Google Scholar contains the greatest number of publications, whereas Scopus and Web of Science have much fewer publications. In addition, in any of the 3 databases, the blue bar and grey bar, which represent "virtual reality and safety" and "virtual reality and human computer interaction" respectively, both have a greater number of publications than the orange bar and the yellow bar, which represent "augmented reality and safety" and "augmented reality and human computer interaction". From

Table 1. Databases and number of publications returned from the search.

	Google Scholar	Scopus	Web of Science
virtual reality and safety	82500	4491	2618
augmented reality and safety	36600	1469	1163
virtual reality and human computer interaction	45600	5810	2347
augmented reality and human computer interaction	28700	2679	1402

this observation, we can tell that virtual reality related topics have more publications over augmented reality related topics, which implies that virtual reality may have more popularity over augmented reality over the last 10 years (Fig. 4).

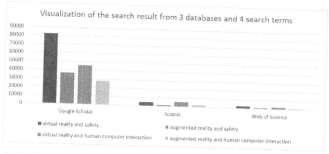

Fig. 4. A visualization of the initial search of the 4 search terms in 3 databases

The table below shows the list of most cited publications for each search term. An interesting observation is that a few of them appeared in more than one search. This suggests that the application areas of AR and VR are highly related (Table 2).

The word cloud from these articles is shown below. The word cloud includes 30 words with at least 4 occurrences in MAXQDA. Useless words such as "the", "a", "an" have been removed (Fig. 5).

Table 2. Summary of the most cited articles under the search terms

Title	Reference
A critical review of the use of virtual reality in construction engineering education and training	[18]
A critical review of virtual and augmented reality (VR/AR) applications in construction safety	[19]
A survey of 3D object selection techniques for virtual environments	[20]
Augmented reality: Research agenda for studying the impact of its media characteristics on consumer behaviour	[21]
Construction safety training using immersive virtual reality	[22]
Frontline service technology infusion: conceptual archetypes and future research directions	[23]
Immersive and collaborative data visualization using virtual reality platforms	[24]
Mobile augmented reality survey: From where we are to where we go	[25]
On human motion prediction using recurrent neural networks	[26]
Player experience of needs satisfaction (PENS) in an immersive virtual reality exercise platform describes motivation and enjoyment	[27]
Review on cyber sickness in applications and visual displays	[28]
Smart textile-integrated microelectronic systems for wearable applications	[29]
Survey on human–robot collaboration in industrial settings: Safety, intuitive interfaces and applications	[30]
Sustainable Industry 4.0 framework: A systematic literature review identifying the current trends and future perspectives	[31]
Systematic review of skills transfer after surgical simulation-based training	[32]
Virtual and remote labs in education: A bibliometric analysis	[33]
Virtual reality sickness: a review of causes and measurements	[34]
WiFinger: Leveraging commodity WiFi for fine-grained finger gesture recognition	[35]

2.2 Trend Diagram (Web of Science and Google nGram)

Trend diagram shows the number of publications per year over a period of time. This can show how the underlying topic's popularity varies over time. If the trend goes up, that means the topic is becoming more popular. On the other hand, if the trend goes down, it indicates that the topic is becoming less popular and may be dying soon. This feature is available in Web of Science in the form of bar chart. The figures below show the trend diagrams for the 4 aforementioned search terms (Figs. 6, 7, 8, and 9).

The trend diagrams show quite a few information. First and foremost, all four trend diagrams show positive trends. This means that in the last ten years, the popularity of augmented reality and virtual reality has kept increasing. However, subtle differences can be found between the diagrams. For example, the first two figures that are related to

Fig. 5. Word cloud generated from MAXQDA for the most cited articles.

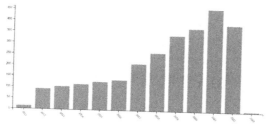

Fig. 6. Trend diagram for the search term "virtual reality and safety"

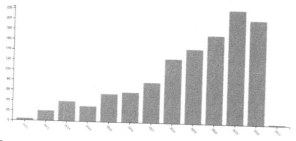

Fig. 7. Trend diagram for the search term "augmented reality and safety"

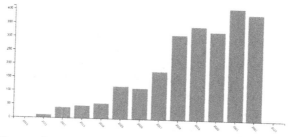

Fig. 8. Trend diagram for the search term "virtual reality and human computer interaction"

safety show relatively consistent trends throughout the ten years. The last two figures that are related to human computer interaction show a slight hesitation in the increasing trend

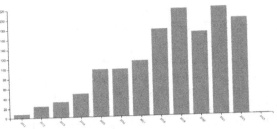

Fig. 9. Trend diagram for the search term "augmented reality and human computer interaction"

in the last few years. This phenomenon is especially obvious in the last trend diagram, the search results for "augmented reality and human computer interaction". From the trend diagrams here, we can infer that safety is a more popular field on research related to AR and VR, compared with human computer interaction.

Another measurement of trend is Google nGram. This is a search engine that charts the frequencies of any set of search strings using a yearly count of n-grams found in printed sources published between 1500 and 2019. It is clear that "safety" matures much earlier than the other three keywords, and AR is slightly more popular in books than the other two (Fig. 10).

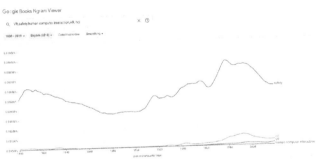

Fig. 10. Google nGram comparison between VR, AR, safety, and human computer interaction

2.3 Engagement (Vicinitas)

In the section "databases and initial search", it was shown that topics related to VR tend to have more popularity over the topics related to AR. This was a way of measuring engagement on these two technologies. Another relatively more modern way to measure engagement is through a platform called Vicinitas. Vicinitas uses Twitter to showcase in-depth analytics on how people are engaging with some user-defined topics in the fast-paced society. Its drawback is obvious – it only relies on Twitter, and not everyone uses Twitter to post their thoughts. In this part, I will search for these four search terms in Vicinitas. Vicinitas presents three useful exhibitions for the purpose of this report: a word cloud, an engagement timeline, and a posts timeline. Thus, the following 12 figures will be the outputs of Vicinitas. In the search, I will use VR and AR instead of virtual reality and augmented reality. This is because, compared to scientific literature, people on the internet tend to use abbreviations.

First, we look at the term "VR and safety". The word cloud returned several words that are worth looking at. Words such as "safety, safer, training, workplace, associate" imply that VR can be used for workplace safety training. Other words also imply a few applicable areas that VR and safety are related. Both the engagement timeline and posts timeline show positive slope, meaning that the engagement is high, and that the topic is popular (Figs. 11 and 12).

Fig. 11. Word cloud on "VR and safety"

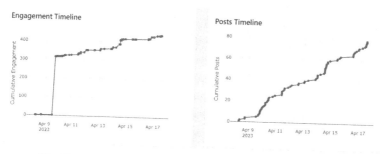

Fig. 12. Engagement timeline and post timeline for "VR and safety"

Next, we look at "VR and human computer interaction". For this topic, I have to abbreviate "human computer interaction to HCI", otherwise there is nothing returned at all. This further proves that people on the internet tend to use abbreviations. From the word cloud, it looks like nothing specific is shown. It is possible to suspect that the word HCI in here refers to a conference rather than "human computer interaction" due to the presence of the word "Germany". Again, the engagement timeline and the posts timeline are both positively sloped, showing increased interest in these topics (Figs. 13 and 14).

Next, we look at "AR and safety". For this search, I had to reverse my statement earlier about abbreviations. If I search for "AR and safety", it seems to be related to gun violence. It's not surprising because a lot of politicians talk about this issue openly on Twitter, and "AR15" is one of the more popular rifles. As a result, I needed to revise my search term to "augmented reality and safety". The word cloud presents a few interesting

Word Cloud

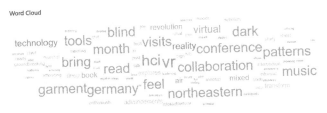

Fig. 13. Word cloud for "VR and HCI"

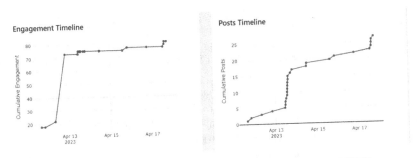

Fig. 14. Engagement timeline and post timeline for "VR and HCI"

discoveries, such as "simulating", "overlaying", "training", etc. It seems like augmented reality can be used for training as well. Although there are not as many datapoints as we'd like to have, the engagement timeline and post timeline both also show positive slopes, indicating an increase in interest in these topics (Figs. 15 and 16).

Word Cloud

Fig. 15. Word cloud for "augmented reality and safety"

Finally, we attempted to look at "augmented reality and HCI". Unfortunately, Vicinitas was only able to find one tweet related to this topic. As a result, it will not be shown, since it clearly is not one of the hot fields right now, at least on social media.

2.4 VOS Viewer and Citespace

VOS viewer and Citespace are two visualization tools introduced in class. Here, we will show the figures generated by VOS viewer and Citespace. Both of these platforms can

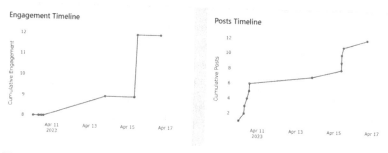

Fig. 16. Engagement timeline and posts timeline for "augmented reality and safety"

read bibliographic data exported from Web of Science. Thus, Web of Science serves as a data source in this task.

One of the limitations of VOS viewer is that it can only read one file as the input. As a result, it is impossible to export the data for all publications returned from the search result. Thus, to capture the most information, I sorted the publications from the most cited to the least cited and selected the top 1000 of them. The number of citations, in this case, serves as a measurement of impact.

First, we look at "virtual reality and safety". The figures below show the co-authorship diagram and the co-occurrence map. In creating the co-authorship diagram, I set a selection criterion a little bit higher than the default settings to get the most impactful authors. For example, I set the minimum number of documents per author to 10 from the default 5. For the same reason, I made the threshold of co-occurrence map stricter. The minimum number of occurrences of a term is set to 100. That means that if a word appears more than 100 times, it will then show up on the map. The co-authorship map identifies authors that are most connected together, and the co-occurrence map identified the most commonly occurring words (Figs. 17 and 18).

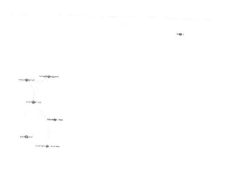

Fig. 17. Co-authorship diagram for "virtual reality and safety"

Next, we look at "virtual reality and human computer interaction". The co-authorship diagram is much more dispersed than the last one, meaning that there are more "smaller

Fig. 18. Co-occurrence map of "virtual reality and safety"

groups" formed within the top authors. For co-occurrence map, it is highly similar to the last one. The linked words represent the application areas of virtual reality and human computer interaction (Figs. 19 and 20).

Fig. 19. Co-authorship diagram for "virtual reality and human computer interaction"

Fig. 20. Co-occurrence map of "virtual reality and human computer interaction"

The next search term is "augmented reality and safety". The co-authorship diagram is almost as dispersed as the last one. This implies that fewer authors are studying similar topics, meaning that researchers are studying different areas of augmented reality and safety related topics. In the co-occurrence map, it is largely what I expected from the search result. One interesting observation is that one of the linked words is "virtual reality". It seems that these two topics are related in some ways (Figs. 21 and 22).

Fig. 21. Co-authorship diagram for "augmented reality and safety"

Fig. 22. Co-occurrence map for "augmented reality and safety"

Lastly, we look at the search term "augmented reality and human computer interaction". The co-authorship diagram is different from the other three. There seems to be a rather large author group separate from the rest of the authors. The co-occurrence map looks largely similar to the rest of the co-occurrence maps above (Figs. 23 and 24).

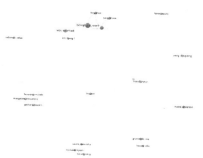

Fig. 23. Co-authorship map for "augmented reality and human computer interaction"

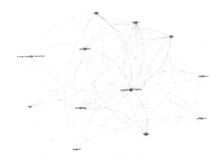

Fig. 24. Co-occurrence map for "augmented reality and human computer interaction"

Due to the length of this report, I will not show every search term's Citespace diagram. I will just show one of the Citespace diagram below as an example. The figure shows the "bursts" captured by Citespace. The bursts represent the time period that the articles were cited the most, marked in salmon color. These bursts can be seen on the map as well (Fig. 25).

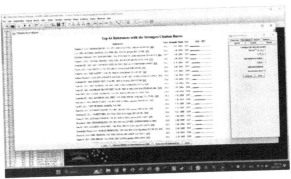

Fig. 25. The "bursts" generated from Citespace for "VR and safety."

2.5 Leading Tables

To form leading tables, I also used the help of Web of Science. The powerful visualization tools from Web of Science can show leading tables such as leading authors, keywords, institutions, and countries. I will show the leading country tables for each search term here. It is not difficult to see the general trend here. All four figures show the leading countries for these topics are the United States and China. Although not shown here, the leading institutions charts also show universities and research institutions in the United States or China. This information implies that both countries are leading the research and development of AR and VR technologies and applications today (Figs. 26, 27, 28, and 29).

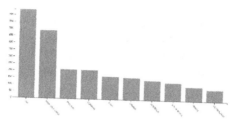

Fig. 26. Leading country table for "VR and safety"

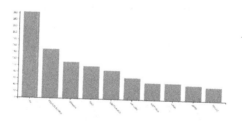

Fig. 27. Leading country table for "AR and safety"

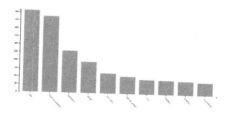

Fig. 28. Leading country table for "VR and HCI"

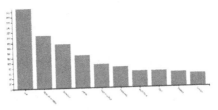

Fig. 29. Leading country table for "AR and HCI"

3 Discussion, Future Work, and Conclusion

The methods for bibliometric analysis follow prior literature [36–39]. Until now, we already have a relatively complete knowledge of VR and AR as well as their applications and research directions, both in the industry and academia. Starting from the initial literature search in Google Scholar, Scopus, and Web of Science over the last 10 years, we identified the general trend of VR and safety, VR and human computer interaction, AR and safety, and AR and human computer interaction. From a summary bar chart comparing the number of literatures from 3 databases across 4 search terms, we can tell that VR related topics have more publications over AR related topics, which implies that VR may have more popularity over AR over the last 10 years. Later, we created trend diagrams from Web of Science searches and gained additional insights. We can infer that safety is a more popular field on research related to AR and VR, compared with human computer interaction. Additional tools used include MAXQDA, Citespace, and VOS viewer. From this information, we can draw a clear conclusion that VR and AR are definitely future trends, and their applications can be limitless. National Science Foundation (NSF) continuously awards research grants and fundings to institutions and researchers. Carl Washburn from Greenville Technical College received a grant of $886,886.00 from NSF to investigate aviation maintenance related applications of VR in the grant "Virtual Simulated Inspection (ViSIns) Laboratory: Using Interactive 3D Knowledge Objects to Promote Learning for Non-Destructive Inspection in Aviation Maintenance Technology" [8]. Rajiv Dubey from University of South Florida was awarded a grant of $537,245.00 to conduct research on rehabilitation [40, 41]. This just further proved that there exists a lot of potential for VR and AR in our society.

References

1. What's the Difference Between AR and VR? Tulane School of Professional Advancement, 22 December 2020 (2020). https://sopa.tulane.edu/blog/whats-difference-between-ar-and-vr
2. Pokémon, G.O.: Pokémon GO (n.d.). https://pokemongolive.com/?hl=en. Accessed 8 Apr 2023
3. Schuemie, M.J., Van Der Straaten, P., Krijn, M., Van Der Mast, C.A.P.G.: Research on presence in virtual reality: a survey. Cyberpsychol. Behav. 4(2), 183–201 (2001)
4. Zheng, J.M., Chan, K.W., Gibson, I.: Virtual reality. IEEE Potentials 17(2), 20–23 (1998)
5. Li, L., et al.: Application of virtual reality technology in clinical medicine. Am. J. Transl. Res. 9(9), 3867 (2017)

6. Elmqaddem, N.: Augmented reality and virtual reality in education. Myth or reality? Int. J. Emerg. Technol. Learn. **14**(3), 234 (2019)
7. Oigara, J.N.: Integrating virtual reality tools into classroom instruction. In: Handbook of Research on Mobile Technology, Constructivism, and Meaningful Learning, pp. 147–159. IGI Global (2018)
8. Salvendy, G., Karwowski, W. (eds.): Handbook of Human Factors and Ergonomics. John Wiley & Sons (2021)
9. Zhang, Y., et al.: Virtualcube: an immersive 3d video communication system. IEEE Trans. Visual. Comput. Graph. **28**(5), 2146–2156 (2022)
10. Li, S., Savaliya, S., Marino, L., Leider, A.M., Tappert, C.C.: Brain signal authentication for human-computer interaction in virtual reality. In: 2019 IEEE International Conference on Computational Science and Engineering (CSE) and IEEE International Conference on Embedded and Ubiquitous Computing (EUC), pp. 115–120. IEEE (2019)
11. Zhao, D., Lucas, J.: Virtual reality simulation for construction safety promotion. Int. J. Inj. Contr. Saf. Promot. **22**(1), 57–67 (2015)
12. A-Z Databases. Purdue.edu. (n.d.) https://guides.lib.purdue.edu/az.php. Accessed 17 Apr 2023
13. Bramley, I., Goode, A., Anderson, L., Mary, E.: Researching in-store, at home: using virtual reality within quantitative surveys. Int. J. Mark. Res. **60**(4), 344–351 (2018)
14. Taherdoost, H.: Validity and reliability of the research instrument; how to test the validation of a questionnaire/survey in a research; How to test the validation of a questionnaire/survey in a research, 10 August 2016 (2016)
15. Boote, D.N., Beile, P.: Scholars before researchers: on the centrality of the dissertation literature review in research preparation. Educ. Res. **34**(6), 3–15 (2005)
16. Callahan, J.L.: Writing literature reviews: a reprise and update. Hum. Resour. Dev. Rev. **13**(3), 271–275 (2014)
17. Denney, A.S., Tewksbury, R.: How to write a literature review. J. Criminal Just. Educ. **24**(2), 218–234 (2013)
18. Wang, P., Peng, W., Wang, J., Chi, H.-L., Wang, X.: A critical review of the use of virtual reality in construction engineering education and training. Int. J. Environ. Res. Publ. Health **15**(6), 1204 (2018)
19. Li, X., Yi, W., Chi, H.-L., Wang, X., Chan, A.P.C.: A critical review of virtual and augmented reality (VR/AR) applications in construction safety. Automat. Construct. **86**, 150–162 (2018)
20. Argelaguet, F., Andujar, C.: A survey of 3D object selection techniques for virtual environments. Comput. Graph. **37**(3), 121–136 (2013)
21. Javornik, A.: Augmented reality: research agenda for studying the impact of its media characteristics on consumer behaviour. J. Retail. Consum. Serv. **30**, 252–261 (2016)
22. Sacks, R., Perlman, A., Barak, R.: Construction safety training using immersive virtual reality. Constr. Manag. Econ. **31**(9), 1005–1017 (2013)
23. De Keyser, A., Köcher, S., Alkire, L., Verbeeck, C., Kandampully, J.: Frontline service technology infusion: conceptual archetypes and future research directions. J. Serv. Manag. **30**(1), 156–183 (2019)
24. Donalek, C., et al.: Immersive and collaborative data visualization using virtual reality platforms. In: 2014 IEEE International Conference on Big Data (Big Data), pp. 609–614. IEEE (2014)
25. Chatzopoulos, D., Bermejo, C., Huang, Z., Hui, P.: Mobile augmented reality survey: from where we are to where we go. IEEE Access **5**, 6917–6950 (2017)
26. Martinez, J., Black, M.J., Romero, J.: On human motion prediction using recurrent neural networks. In: Proceedings of the IEEE Conference on Computer Vision and Pattern Recognition, pp. 2891–2900 (2017)

27. Ijaz, K., Ahmadpour, N., Wang, Y., Calvo, R.A.: Player experience of needs satisfaction (PENS) in an immersive virtual reality exercise platform describes motivation and enjoyment. Int. J. Hum. Comput. Interact. **36**(13), 1195–1204 (2020)
28. Rebenitsch, L., Owen, C.: Review on cybersickness in applications and visual displays. Virtual Reality **20**, 101–125 (2016)
29. Shi, J., et al.: Smart textile-integrated microelectronic systems for wearable applications. Adv. Mater. **32**(5), 1901958 (2020)
30. Villani, V., Pini, F., Leali, F., Secchi, C.: Survey on human–robot collaboration in industrial settings: safety, intuitive interfaces and applications. Mechatronics **55**, 248–266 (2018)
31. Kamble, S.S., Gunasekaran, A., Gawankar, S.A.: Sustainable Industry 4.0 framework: a systematic literature review identifying the current trends and future perspectives. Process Saf. Environ. Prot. **117**, 408–425 (2018)
32. Dawe, S.R., et al.: Systematic review of skills transfer after surgical simulation-based training. J. Br. Surg. **101**(9), 1063–1076 (2014)
33. Heradio, R., et al.: Virtual and remote labs in education: a bibliometric analysis. Comput. Educ. **98**, 14–38 (2016)
34. Chang, E., Kim, H.T., Yoo, B.: Virtual reality sickness: a review of causes and measurements. Int. J. Hum. Comput. Interact. **36**(17), 1658–1682 (2020)
35. Tan, S., Yang, J.: WiFinger: leveraging commodity WiFi for fine-grained finger gesture recognition. In: Proceedings of the 17th ACM International Symposium on Mobile Ad Hoc Networking and Computing, pp. 201–210 (2016)
36. Fahimnia, B., Sarkis, J., Davarzani, H.: Green supply chain management: a review and bibliometric analysis. Int. J. Prod. Econ. **162**, 101–114 (2015)
37. Jiang, J., Duffy, V.G.: Modern workplace ergonomics and productivity – a systematic literature review. In: Stephanidis, C., et al. (eds.) HCII 2021. LNCS, vol. 13097, pp. 509–524. Springer, Cham (2021). https://doi.org/10.1007/978-3-030-90966-6_35
38. Xu, J., Duffy, B.M., Duffy, V.G.: Data mining in systematic reviews: a bibliometric analysis of game-based learning and distance learning. In: Duffy, V.G. (ed.) HCII 2021. LNCS, vol. 12777, pp. 343–354. Springer, Cham (2021). https://doi.org/10.1007/978-3-030-77817-0_24
39. Duffy, B.M., Duffy, V.G.: Data mining methodology in support of a systematic review of human aspects of cybersecurity. In: Duffy, V.G. (ed.) HCII 2020. LNCS, vol. 12199, pp. 242–253. Springer, Cham (2020). https://doi.org/10.1007/978-3-030-49907-5_17
40. NSF Organization List. "NSF Award Search: Award # 1229561 - MRI: Acquisition of a CAREN Virtual Reality System for Collaborative Research in Assistive and Rehabilitation Technologies." Nsf.gov (n.d.). https://www.nsf.gov/awardsearch/showAward?AWD_ID=1229561&HistoricalAwards=false. Accessed 20 Apr 2023
41. NSF Organization List. "NSF Award Search: Award # 0703061 - Virtual Simulated Inspection (ViSIns) Laboratory: Using Interactive 3D Knowledge Objects to Promote Learning for Non-Destructive Inspection in Aviation Maintenance Technology." Nsf.gov (n.d.). https://www.nsf.gov/awardsearch/showAward?AWD_ID=0703061&HistoricalAwards=false. Accessed 20 Apr 2023

Exploring Hand Tracking and Controller-Based Interactions in a VR Object Manipulation Task

Cheryl I. Johnson[1]([✉]), Nicholas W. Fraulini[2], Eric K. Peterson[3], Jacob Entinger[3], and Daphne E. Whitmer[3]

[1] Quantum Improvements Consulting, LLC, Orlando, FL 32803, USA
cjohnson@quantumimprovements.net
[2] StraCon Services Group Fort Worth, LLC, Fort Worth, TX 76109, USA
nicholas.w.fraulini.ctr@us.navy.mil
[3] Naval Air Warfare Center Training Systems Division, Orlando, FL 32825, USA
{eric.k.peterson20.civ,jacob.w.entinger.civ}@us.navy.mil

Abstract. As the uses of virtual reality (VR) continue to expand, more systematic research on interaction design is needed to improve user performance and experience. Although hand tracking technology holds promise for being a more natural and intuitive interface, previous research has consistently shown that hand tracking has been rated as less usable and led to worse performance than controller-based interactions. In this experiment, we sought to explore why this might be the case, focusing on feelings of agency and perceived naturalness of the interaction. Specifically, twenty-one participants used two different interaction types that included a hand tracking condition and a controller-based condition with four variations that manipulated what participants saw (i.e., controllers, virtual hands, both, and animated virtual hands) in a ball sorting task. We found that hand tracking led to the lowest ratings of perceived naturalness and feelings of agency and the worst performance overall. Participants showed little preference among the controller conditions on overall experience or performance, with the exception of the animated hands condition, which was rated lower on some items than the other controller conditions. Participants overwhelmingly rated the hand tracking condition as their least favorite and many described tracking accuracy issues as a cause. Interestingly, they also described a lack of feedback and having nothing physical to touch as other reasons for disliking this condition. Implications for interaction design are discussed.

Keywords: Virtual Reality · Hand Tracking · Sense of Agency · Natural User Interaction

1 Introduction

Interest in using virtual reality (VR) has been soaring in the last decade as the price of commercial off-the-shelf equipment has become more affordable. Moreover, VR applications have been used for a variety of experiences, including marketing, entertainment, and medical and military training. In most of these experiences, users interact with the virtual environment (VE) by way of handheld controllers to move and manipulate objects within a scene. However, one of the characteristics that makes VR special is the capability to use more natural input methods, such as using one's hands, to interact directly with the VE rather than through a mediated interaction with a controller. Hand tracking is one example of a technology that supports natural user interactions in VR, although many studies have found that hand tracking does not necessarily lead to better performance in VR than traditional controller-based interactions [10, 13, 15]. Therefore, the main goal of the current experiment was to explore potential factors that may impact users' experience with controller-based and hand tracking interaction methods in VR, such as how these interactions are displayed in the VE (i.e., do users see a visual representation of their hands, their controllers, or both?) and how this affects the user's awareness of their body and actions in the VE (i.e., sense of embodiment).

1.1 Natural User Interactions

Advances in technology have driven the costs of motion-tracking systems down considerably, enabling the use of natural user interfaces (NUI) as a means to interact within a VE. NUIs refer to interfaces that reuse existing skills for interacting directly with content [3]. A distinguishing feature of a NUI is that it uses the body to directly interact with a computer system, rather than through an intermediary device, such as a controller or keyboard. Examples of NUIs include using hand tracking (i.e., gestures), speech, or touch to interact within the VE. NUIs have the potential to be more user-friendly and intuitive because they allow users to capitalize on their existing skills of physical interaction, rather than learning how to use a device [16]. Their ability to unlock this potential, however, depends on the degree to which users consider NUIs preferable and more intuitive compared to traditional interactions with familiar intermediary devices, such as controllers.

When considering how natural or intuitive an interaction is, one can apply the concept of natural mapping, which describes the extent to which an interaction matches its real-world action [21]. The natural mapping spectrum ranges from "arbitrary" (e.g., clicking a mouse button three times to select a paragraph) to "natural" (e.g., using your finger to highlight the paragraph). When interfaces are poorly designed or not intuitive, users may have a negative experience, and their performance may suffer. For example, Schwartz and Plass [19] found that naturally mapped interactions were more memorable than arbitrary interactions. Similarly, in a study by Bailey and colleagues [2], participants rated the system with naturally mapped gestures as more usable and reported higher feelings of presence (i.e., the sense of "being there") than the system with arbitrary gestures. Therefore, careful consideration of interaction design is needed to maximize performance and user experience.

To that end, the first goal of this experiment was to explore performance and user experience across different interaction methods (i.e., hand tracking and controller-based interactions) in a VR object manipulation task. The task that was used in this experiment was intentionally designed to be a simple task, with the purpose of determining how users prefer to interact in VR and whether their preferences also map to their performance. These results are intended to inform the design of future VR-based training systems, allowing for a data-driven approach to designing interactions rather than traditional system-driven approaches.

1.2 Hand Tracking

Hand tracking is one type of NUI in VEs that can be achieved in a few different ways. The most commonly used method incorporates cameras and depth-sensing technology to estimate the position and orientation of a user's palm and phalanges. One drawback of this approach is that no haptic feedback is provided to the user. Alternatively, wearable motion capture technologies (e.g., gloves, bodysuits), which have been used in film and video game production for decades, are being outfitted with small motors to provide users with vibrotactile stimulation. Currently, these wearable devices are sold at a significant premium and are often too fragile for frequent use, as would be required for military training applications. In the current study, we explored the first method, as it is most feasible for military training uses right now.

The current experiment is a follow-up to a previous study [12] that examined participants' ability to complete a button selection task using five different VR interaction methods. Participants were required to select highlighted squares in a 5x5 grid using a hand-held controller (i.e., in three different configurations), their gaze (Eyetracking), or their own hand (Handtracking). In the three controller conditions, participants interacted with a real-world controller and witnessed a controller in VR selecting chosen squares. The camera-based Handtracking condition required real-world hand movements that were mapped onto a VR hand that selected squares, and the Eye-tracking condition required participants to maintain their gaze on a square for 0.6 s to select it in VR. Overall, participants performed better when interacting with controllers compared to their own hands or gaze. Participants also rated the Handtracking method as the most physically demanding interaction method overall, as well as the least usable (along with the Eyetracking method). The negative outcomes from the Handtracking condition were consistent with previous research in object manipulation tasks [10, 13] as well as a data exploration task [15] that found that controller-based methods were superior to hand tracking; notably, each of these tasks required somewhat precise hand movements.

Considering these results, we sought to explore why the controller-based conditions led to better performance and user experience than hand tracking in tasks that require precise hand movements. Researchers have argued that what participants view while performing a task in VR influences their feelings of agency and embodiment [14, 22, 23]. For example, an experiment by Voigt-Antons and colleagues [23] included four conditions: participants could see their virtual hands holding the virtual controller, only the controller was visible, only their hands were visible, or they completed the task using hand tracking (i.e., no controllers). They found that participants were more positive about the hand tracking interaction than the controller-based interactions, but they also reported feeling less in control of the hand tracking interaction. However, when asked to rank the conditions, participants preferred being able to see their hands holding the controller. Given these mixed results, there is a need to improve our understanding of these conditions and how they may affect performance, which was not assessed in their experiment. To that end, the second goal of this experiment was to examine how the controller-based interaction was visually represented in the VE and how that impacted performance and feelings of control over their movements and actions (i.e., sense of agency). It may be important for users in the controller-based conditions to see their hand holding a controller (rather than just their hands or just the controllers) in the VE while completing the task.

1.3 Embodiment and Performance

One consideration when examining performance in VR is users' awareness of their own bodies and how that awareness affects their actions in the VE. Specifically, users' sense of embodiment may influence the perceived relationship between their real-world motions and motions presented in the VE. Kilteni and colleagues [14] defined *sense of embodiment* (SoE) as "the ensemble of sensations that arise in conjunction with being inside, having, and controlling a body, especially in relation to virtual reality applications (p. 375)." Conceptualizations of embodiment typically include senses of self-location, agency, and body ownership. *Self-location* generally refers to the relationship between oneself and one's body; this differs subtly from the concept of presence, which relates to the relationship between oneself and the environment. Research has shown that one's visuospatial perspective can influence their feeling of location [5, 8]). *Agency* has been referred to as "global motor control, including the subjective experience of action, control, intention, motor selection and the conscious experience of will" [5, p. 7]." Critically, agency can be negatively impacted by poor relationships between one's action and the visual feedback one receives for that action [4, 9, 18]. Sense of *body ownership* encompasses one's attribution of experienced sensations to their own body [14]. This sense can emanate from a combination of top-down (i.e., cognitive processing of sensory information) and bottom-up (i.e., visual or tactile inputs) processes. Several studies have examined body ownership as it relates to the movements of virtual hands specifically. These studies have found the feeling of body ownership can be induced in virtual hands when there is a morphological similarity to the real-life hands [17, 20].

Taken together, these findings emphasize the degree to which visual symmetry between one's real-life and virtual movements can enhance one's sense of embodiment. With this in mind, we examined how sense of embodiment facilitated by the visual information presented in VR affects task performance; in particular, we focused on sense of agency in the current experiment for two reasons. First, sense of agency was most relevant to our research questions (i.e., we manipulated the presence or absence of virtual hands not the characteristics of the virtual hands). Second, we wanted to limit the number of questions participants were asked (by limiting the number of subjective items assessed) after each interaction because they had to answer these questions five times. Specifically, we compared multiple controller-based conditions, in which users saw a combination of virtual hands and/or controllers in the VE while they performed the task to determine the impact of what they see on their sense of agency and their performance.

1.4 Current Experiment

This study sought to explore how different interaction methods (i.e., using a controller or camera-based hand tracking) and visual representations when using controllers affect performance and user perceptions. Participants completed a VR sorting task that involved grabbing balls and placing them in the appropriate bin as quickly as possible. Participants completed the task using five conditions. Four methods utilized controllers (i.e., Hands Only, Controllers Only, Hands and Controller, and Skeleton conditions), and we manipulated what participants saw in their head-mounted display (HMD; i.e., how these interactions were visually represented in the VE). Specifically, Hands Only saw their hands represented, Controller Only saw the controllers represented, and Hands and Controller saw both represented. The Skeleton condition was like Hands Only, except the VE showed a hand-grasping animation when the trigger button was pressed. Participants in these controller-based conditions moved the controller close to a ball to select it, pulled the trigger button on the controller to pick up the ball, and released the trigger button to drop the ball into the bin. The fifth condition was Handtracking, in which participants used their hands to perform the task without a controller and they saw virtual hands represented in the HMD.

We hypothesized that the condition in which participants saw their hands holding controllers would lead to higher feelings of agency and better performance compared to seeing just one or the other. We were also interested in comparing the Handtracking condition to the Hands Only and Skeleton conditions as these conditions presented similar visual information when participants interacted with the VE but required separate user actions to initiate grabbing and dropping. In theory, hand tracking would be hypothesized to lead to the highest feelings of agency and performance compared to the other conditions, since it is a direct NUI. Based on previous research, however, we anticipated that hand tracking would lead to the worst sense of agency and performance, which is likely driven by limitations in the technology (e.g., latency, difficulty recognizing hand positions). In addition, participants were asked to name their least favorite interaction, explain what they did not like about it, and describe how the interaction could be improved. We expected that participants' responses to these prompts would provide both additional context to their performance and insights about how to improve their experience while using VEs.

2   Method

2.1   Participants and Design

A total of 24 participants were recruited from a large southeastern university. Three participants were excluded due to technical issues with the testbed, leaving data from 21 participants used in the subsequent analyses. Participants' ages ranged from 18 to 28 (M = 20.62, SD = 2.20) and 52% of the sample identified as female. Eighty-five percent of participants reported having previous experience with VR systems, with 47% reporting that they used a VR system within the last month. Participants received $15 for their participation. To participate in the experiment, participants had to be at least 18 years old, have normal color vision, and have no history of seizures. In addition, to gain entry into the facility, participants were required to hold U.S. citizenship and complete a COVID-19 screening form.

The experimental design was within-subjects. Participants completed a ball-sorting task using five different interaction conditions in a randomized order (i.e., Hands & Controllers, Controllers Only, Hands Only, Skeleton, and Handtracking).

2.2 Materials

Testbed. The ball-sorting task was implemented in the Unity game engine. The VE included a welcome area where participants received instructions prior to the task and a primary testing area that included a table, red and blue colored balls, and their corresponding baskets required for the sorting task. The goal of the task was to pick up the balls and place them in the corresponding colored baskets before the time limit expired. Participants completed three trials for each condition: a familiarization period to get comfortable with VE while practicing the task and two tests, in which they completed the task, and their performance was measured. For each trial, participants stood in front of a virtual semi-circular table that would be filled with an equal number of red and blue balls (Fig. 1).

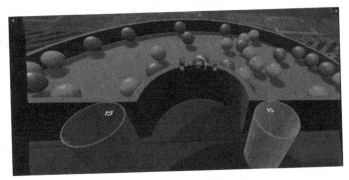

Fig. 1. Main Sorting Table & Bins

The number of balls required for sorting increased with each trial. Counters were present at the bottom of the table to inform participants how many of each color remained and only decreased when a ball was placed into the correct basket. If a ball was dropped or knocked off the table, a new ball would drop onto the table to replace it. The conditions were either controller-based or just hands. The controller-based methods included the Hand & Controller, Controller Only, Hands Only, and Skeleton conditions. Functionally, the Hand & Controller, Controller Only, and Hands Only conditions were the same. A field of effect placed in front of the visible or invisible controller would cause the nearest ball to snap to an attachment point, thereby allowing the participant to select and sort the ball. The Skeleton condition functioned similarly to the other controller-based conditions with the exception that this method included an animation of a virtual hand closing. The virtual hand was designed to close as though it was a real hand picking up a ball any time the trigger was pressed. When selecting a ball, the virtual hand would grasp the ball as if by a real hand. The Handtracking condition required participants to physically reach out and grab the balls with just their hands like they would in the real world. Importantly, the controller-based interactions (i.e., Hands & Controllers, Controllers Only, Hands Only, and Skeleton) provided haptic feedback to the participants in the form of vibration whenever a ball was picked up, whereas the Handtracking interaction did not provide any haptic feedback to the participant related to contact with the virtual ball. See Fig. 2 for an overview of the interaction methods.

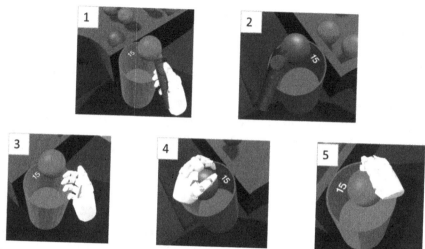

Fig. 2. Example screenshots from each condition. (1) Hands & Controllers (2) Controller Only (3) Hands Only (4) Skeleton (5) Handtracking

Three Valve Lighthouse base stations were used to track participants' movements in six degrees of freedom. Participants wore a Varjo XR-3 HMD. Participants used two handheld HTC Vive Controllers or empty hands depending on the requirements of the condition. Motion tracking for hands was implemented using Ultraleap Stereo IR 170, which was integrated into the HMD.

Questionnaires. Participants completed a demographic questionnaire to obtain biographical information, such as age, sex, handedness, and education level. Participants were asked questions about their video game experience, including how long they have played, how often they have played, and their skill level. They were also asked similar questions about their experiences with VR and augmented reality (AR) systems, including whether they have used these systems before, when they last used them, how often they use them, which systems they have used, and their level of expertise with these systems.

A nine-item post-task interaction questionnaire was constructed using individual items from the NASA Task Load Index (NASA-TLX) [11], preliminary embodiment short questionnaire (pESQ) [7], and user preference questions sampled from Kangas et al. [13]. We carefully selected a few items from these measures to keep the questionnaire to less than ten items, since participants would be required to answer the questions five times over the course of the experiment. From the NASA-TLX, participants rated how physically and mentally demanding the task was on a scale from 0 (very low) to 100 (very high). From the pESQ, we adapted items from the agency subscale (Note: we replaced the word "body" with the word "hand"), in which participants rated their agreement with the statements, "The movements of the virtual hand were caused by my movements," "I felt like my hand movements occurred within the environment," and "I felt like my hand affected the environment" on a scale from 1 (strongly disagree) to 7 (strongly agree). From Kangas et al. [13], participants rated the statements, "I felt confident in my ability to use this interaction method," "I believe this interaction method was easy to use," and "I believe this interaction method felt natural to use" on a scale from 1 (strongly disagree) to 7 (strongly agree). Lastly, participants were asked to rate their agreement with the statement, "I liked using this interaction method" on a scale from 1 (strongly disagree) to 7 (strongly agree).

A nine-item post-experiment feedback questionnaire was constructed using both qualitative and quantitative questions. Qualitative questions assessed the participants' preferences and overall feedback about their favorite and least favorite interactions. Sample questions included, "Which interaction was your least favorite? Why?" and "What could have improved the least preferred interaction?" Quantitative questions asked participants to rate various aspects of the testbed and interactions on a scale from 1 (very poor) to 5 (very good). Sample questions included, "In the interactions where you could see a virtual hand, how would you rate the appearance of the virtual hands relative to human hands?" and "In the interaction where you were NOT holding a controller, how would you rate the relationship between the movement of your hands and the movement of the virtual hands?" Participants also rated the difficulty of the sorting task, regardless of the interaction method, on a scale from 1 (very easy) to 5 (very difficult).

2.3 Procedure

After consenting to participate, each participant completed the demographic questionnaire and a short Powerpoint tutorial. The tutorial provided an overview of the sorting task, explained the overall procedure for the trials, and described each of the five conditions and how to use them. After the tutorial, participants were asked to put on the HMD. Instructions on how to adjust the HMD were provided, and once they felt it was secure and comfortable, participants were asked to calibrate the integrated eye tracking. The eye tracking calibration was a system-guided process in which participants had to follow a dot moving across their field of view with their eyes; this process typically lasted no more than 20 s. Once successfully calibrated, participants were given controllers when required by the condition (i.e., the Handtracking condition did not require controllers) and asked to read the onscreen instructions prior to beginning the training task; within each interaction condition, participants completed the trials at their own pace and could proceed to the next one when they were ready. Next, they began the familiarization trial in which they had to sort 12 balls in 15 s. In Test 1, participants had to sort 30 balls in 45 s. In Test 2, they sorted 60 balls in 45 s. Feedback was displayed at the end of each trial showing the number of correctly and incorrectly sorted balls. After all of the trials were completed, the post-task interaction questionnaire was displayed in VR one question at a time; participants responded out loud and the researcher recorded their responses. The virtual environment was then reset and configured for the next interaction condition. This process repeated until the participants completed the three trials with all five interaction methods. Once all interaction conditions were completed, participants chose their preferred interaction and completed the task again (i.e., Test 3). Similar to Test 2, this preferred interaction session required participants to sort 60 balls in 45 s Finally, participants completed a post-experiment feedback questionnaire and received a debrief. The experiment took less than one hour to complete.

3 Results

For each test, we used a repeated measures analysis of variance (ANOVA) with condition as the within-subjects variable, unless otherwise noted. Greenhouse-Geisser corrections were applied when assumptions of sphericity were violated.

3.1 Performance

We examined performance-based variables, including the number of balls sorted correctly, time to complete the task, and the number of sorting errors committed on Test 1 and Test 2. First, as depicted in Fig. 3, there was a significant main effect of condition for the number of balls sorted correctly during Test 1, $F(1.314, 24.974) = 21.819$, $p < .001$, $\eta_p^2 = .535$. Post-hoc analyses revealed participants in the Handtracking condition accounted for the fewest balls sorted during each trial ($ps < .001$) relative to the other four conditions. There were no significant differences between the four controller-based conditions. The same pattern of results was found for Test 2 number of balls sorted correctly [$F(2.621, 54.425) = 38.155$, $p < .001$, $\eta_p^2 = .656$] with participants in the Handtracking condition again sorting the fewest balls correctly compared to the four controller methods ($ps < .001$).

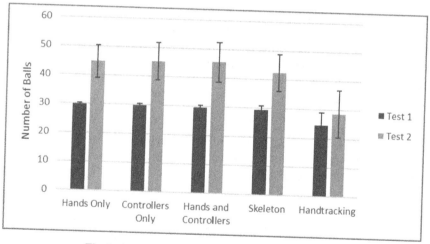

Fig. 3. Number of balls correctly sorted by condition.

Second, as depicted in Fig. 4, there was a significant main effect of condition for time taken to complete Test 1, $F(4, 76) = 21.540$, $p < .001$, $\eta_p^2 = .531$. Participants took longer to complete the task in the Handtracking condition than in any of the four controller conditions ($ps < .001$). Test 2 was designed to be challenging and we did not expect many participants to be able to complete the task in the time allotted. Consistent with our expectation, we found that all participants took the full 45 s to complete Test 2, so we did not run this analysis for Time 2.

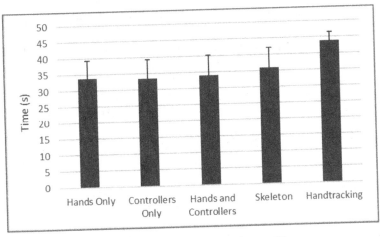

Fig. 4. Time to complete Test 1 by condition.

Third, analyses for both tests did not reveal differences in the number of sorting errors committed across conditions for Test 1 ($p = .49$) or Test 2 ($p = .38$). The average number of errors was low across conditions for Test 1 ($M = .07, SD = .06$) and Test 2 ($M = .16, SD = .10$), which indicated participants generally did not have issues identifying the correct bins.

Finally, we analyzed participants' choices for their preferred interactions, as well as their performance in a third test using their preferred condition. A one-way ANOVA revealed significant differences in the number of balls sorted correctly across preferred conditions, $F(4, 16) = 6.451, p = .003, \eta_p^2 = .617$. Post-hoc analyses revealed the Handtracking condition ($n = 2, M = 28.50, SD = 3.54$) accounted for the fewest balls sorted relative to the Hands Only ($n = 5, M = 52.20, SD = 4.76, p < .001$), Controllers Only ($n = 6, M = 47.00, SD = 6.69, p = .001$), Hands and Controllers ($n = 6, M = 46.83, SD = 54.42, p = .001$), and Skeleton ($n = 2, M = 49.50, SD = 6.36, p = .002$) conditions. Although the sample sizes for the Handtracking and Skeleton conditions were low, an inspection of the means shows that Handtracking performed markedly worse than the other groups and it is consistent with previous results for Tests 1 and 2. All participants took the full 45 s during the preferred interaction test, and the number of errors was again very low across all of the interaction methods.

3.2 User Perceptions

Post-task Interaction Questionnaire. We also examined differences in participants' experiences following their use of each condition (see Table 1). For the NASA-TLX items, analyses revealed no differences in participants' reported mental [$F(2.618, 52.352) = 2.272, p = .099$] or physical [$F(1.882, 37.636) = 1.242, p = .299$] effort across the five conditions.

Table 1. Means and Standard Deviations for Post-task Interaction Questionnaire by Condition

Item	Hands Only (1)	Controllers Only (2)	Hands and Controllers (3)	Skeleton (4)	Handtracking (5)
How mentally demanding was this task?	24.10 (23.65)	22.76 (21.51)	24.14 (21.87)	21.91 (21.92)	28.71 (22.58)
How physically demanding was this task?	28.71 (20.06)	29.38 (21.27)	29.52 (21.21)	27.38 (21.18)	34.10 (24.06)
I felt confident in my ability to use this interaction method[a]	6.52 (1.08)[5]	6.29 (1.01)[5]	6.33 (.0.73)[5]	6.05 (1.24)[5]	4.43 (1.50)[1,2,3,4]
I believe this interaction method was easy to use[a]	6.33 (0.80)[5]	6.38 (0.97)[5]	6.33 (0.97)[5]	5.71 (1.31)[5]	4.00 (1.52)[1,2,3,4]
I believe this interaction method felt natural to use[a]	5.95 (1.28)[4,5]	5.86 (1.39)[5]	5.95 (1.12)[5]	5.14 (1.53)[1]	4.52 (1.78)[1,2,3]
I liked using this interaction method[a]	6.10 (1.58)[5]	6.14 (1.15)[5]	6.05 (1.16)[5]	5.57 (1.50)[5]	4.10 (1.34)[1,2,3,4]
The movements of the virtual hand were caused by my movements[a]	6.52 (0.75)[4,5]	6.43 (0.93)[5]	6.48 (0.87)[5]	5.90 (1.34)[1,5]	5.14 (1.65)[1,2,3,4]
I felt like my hand movements occurred within the environment[a]	6.30 (0.80)[4,5]	6.05 (1.05)[5]	6.30 (0.80)[4,5]	5.65 (1.57)[1,3,5]	4.85 (1.76)[1,2,3,4]
I felt like my hand affected the environment[a]	6.00 (1.02)[5]	5.95 (1.52)[5]	5.80 (1.70)	5.70 (1.75)	4.85 (1.46)[1,2]

Note: [a]represent significant overall relationships ($p < .05$)
Superscripts show significant relationships between methods ($p < .05$)

Items relating to ease and naturalness of use revealed differences among the five conditions. Participants reported differences by condition in their confidence using each one $[F(4, 80) = 17.738, p < .001, \eta_p^2 = .470]$, ease of using each one $[F(8, 80) = 23.572, p < .001, \eta_p^2 = .541]$, and feeling of naturalness using each one $[F(4, 80) = 5.402, p = .001, \eta_p^2 = .213]$. Post-hoc analyses revealed these differences primarily related to participants' preference for the four controller conditions compared to the Handtracking condition. Participants also did report the Hands Only condition $(p = .018)$ felt more natural than the Skeleton condition.

Items relating to participants' real-world movements relating to movements in VR also revealed differences among the five conditions. Regarding the sense of agency questions, participants reported differences in their perception of their movements causing movements in the virtual hands $[F(2.708, 54.169) = 8.626, p < .001, \eta_p^2 = .301]$, their perception of their hand movements occurring within the VR environment $[F(2.408, 45.753) = 8.759, p < .001, \eta_p^2 = .316]$, and perception of their hand affecting the VR environment $[F(2.231, 42.382) = 3.684, p = .003, \eta_p^2 = .162]$. Again, post-hoc analyses revealed these differences primarily related to participants' preference for the four controller conditions compared to the Handtracking condition. Participants did rate the Hands Only condition higher than the Skeleton condition in terms of their real-world hand movements causing virtual hand movements $(p = .039)$; participants also responded more favorably for the Hands Only $(p = .019)$ and Hands and Controllers $(p = .05)$ conditions compared to the Skeleton condition for their real-world hand movements occurring in the VR environment. Participants rated Hands Only $(p = .012)$ and Controllers Only $(p = .009)$ higher for their hands affecting the VE than Handtracking.

Finally, participants did report differences in how much they liked each interaction method $[F(2.727, 54.544) = 12.762, p < .001, \eta_p^2 = .390]$. Specifically, participants reported liking the Handtracking condition less than the four controller conditions $(ps < .001)$.

Post-experiment Feedback Questionnaire. At the end of the experiment, we probed participants' perceptions of how their real-world movements affected the VR environment broadly as well as their favorite and least favorite conditions. Participants rated the relationship between their real-world hand movements and movements of the virtual hands higher for the four controller conditions (Hands Only, Controllers Only, Hands and Controllers, and Skeleton) than the Handtracking condition, $F(1, 20) = 40.698, p < .001, \eta_p^2 = .670$.

Regarding their favorite and least favorite conditions, participants overwhelmingly reported the Handtracking condition as their least favorite, whereas responses for their favorite were split among the Hands Only, Controllers Only, and Hands and Controllers conditions (see Fig. 5). To further explore why participants chose Handtracking as their least favorite, we coded their responses into themes. Table 2 shows the most common themes with an example of each; many participants' responses included multiple themes. Overall, participants found that the hand tracking method suffered from technical accuracy issues, including not being able to track their hands well, being unable to discern whether their hand was open or closed (i.e., difficult to recognize when picking up a ball or trying to drop it), and maintaining grip on the ball (i.e., user experienced that

the ball dropped out of their hand when they were trying to hold it). Several participants also noted that hand tracking was harder to use because they did not have haptic
feedback, and they found it awkward that they were grabbing at air and not something
tangible, which indicates that they wanted some sort of feedback to let them know
they had successfully picked up the ball (e.g., a vibration or pressing a button). Finally,
a few participants said that hand tracking was less efficient because it required more
hand movement. Interestingly, when participants explained why they liked using the
controller-based conditions best, they used words such as "easiest," "more natural," and
"realistic" in their descriptions.

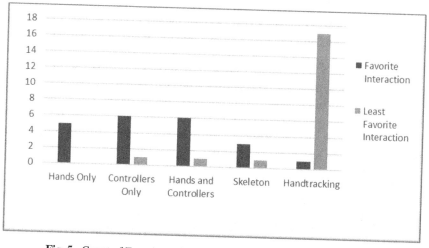

Fig. 5. Count of Favorite and Least Favorite Interactions by Condition.

Lastly, participants provided their opinions on how to improve their least favorite
interaction condition. Since participants overwhelmingly picked Handtracking as their
least favorite interaction, we coded their responses and a few clear themes emerged
again, which mirrored their responses as to why they did not like it. They suggested
that the tracking of their hand movements ($n = 6$) and hand positions ($n = 8$) could be
improved as well as providing feedback when they grip a ball ($n = 3$).

Table 2. Counts and Example Participant Reasons for Disliking the Hand Tracking Method

Reason	Count	Example Response
Tracking movement	6	It didn't respond well to my movements
Maintaining grip on ball	5	I was not confident in my ability to carry a ball from one location to another without it falling out of my hand
Recognizing open vs. closed hand	4	It was slightly more difficult to pick up and drop the balls in the bin because it sometimes wouldn't read my hands accurately
No feedback provided	3	Not having the haptic feedback of the controllers buzzing made it difficult to tell if I had successfully picked up the ball
Less efficient	3	I expected the controller free to be the easiest but due to more hand movement … it felt strenuous
Nothing tangible	3	The hands by themselves were already strange to use as you were trying to grab something that isn't there

4 Discussion

The goal of the current study was to examine different interaction methods and visual representations in a VR object manipulation task to understand how they influence users' feelings of agency and performance. First, we were interested in comparing hand tracking and controller-based interaction methods. Specific comparisons drawn between the Handtracking condition and the Hands Only and Skeleton conditions were of particular interest because of the visual similarities yet different input conditions. We found that the hand tracking consistently led to the lowest performance, ratings of naturalness and usability, and feelings of agency compared to the controller-based methods. The results support our hypothesis that although hand tracking should have led to higher performance and user perceptions, issues related to expected outcomes and latency led to lower performance and experience ratings. These results are consistent with research that has shown worse outcomes with hand tracking compared to controller-based conditions during tasks that use precise hand gestures [10, 13, 15, 23]. This result is also in line with Argelaguet and colleagues' [1] finding that more realistic and complex interactions were perceived as more difficult because the movements did not align with their expectations. For example, participants consistently rated hand tracking as less natural, less usable, and a poorer representation of their movements compared to the controller conditions.

Second, we were interested in comparing the four controller-based interactions to determine if what users see affects their feelings of agency and performance in the task. We manipulated the visual representation of the interface, such that participants saw virtual hands, a controller, or both. There also was a fourth condition (i.e., Skeleton) that animated a grasping motion when participants pressed the trigger button to pick up a ball. In terms of performance, there were no significant differences across the four groups. However, user perceptions of the controller conditions differed. Participants generally rated the Skeleton condition less favorably on most of the user perception items, and it was the second-least preferred interaction. Overall, participants seemed to prefer interactions that more closely mapped to their experience, and the grasping animation, which was meant to mimic the intent of their action, likely detracted from their experience rather than added to it.

Third, we sought to explore why participants favored different interactions over others. Participants overwhelmingly chose hand tracking as their least favorite interaction method and they provided insightful reasons why. The majority reported that the system lacked acceptable accuracy in tracking their hand movements and hand positions. This result suggests that these technical issues greatly impacted users' sense of agency and their perceptions of the interaction more generally, consistent with previous research [4, 9, 18]. Given the tracking issues, participants felt as though they had less control of their actions in the VE and reported a negative experience (see also [23]). In addition, participants listed a lack of feedback and grabbing at nothing tangible as detrimental to their experience as well. Anecdotally, experimenters noticed a distinct difference in the way participants interacted with virtual objects using controllers versus the gesture-based hand tracking condition. With a controller in their hands, participants performed confidently and their actions were deliberate. Conversely, when using hand tracking to interact, participants performed timidly and carefully, and they seemed uncomfortable with the fact that they were only interacting with air. Over time, participants seemed to gain confidence with the hand gestures and this behavior diminished. Thus, it is unclear if participants' lower ratings for naturalness for the hand tracking condition are due to technical issues, the lack of feedback, lacking something tangible to interact with, or some combination of these.

4.1 Limitations and Future Research

There were several limitations in the current study that may have impacted results and interpretations. First, optical hand tracking such as the Ultraleap device used in this experiment does not provide the user with any haptic feedback, whereas the controller conditions inherently provide audible and tactile clicks and optional vibrations. In this study, several participants pointed out that the Handtracking condition was missing haptic feedback, which could have helped them understand when the system recognized that they picked up an object. Future research should explore haptic-enabled wearable hand tracking technology, such as gloves, which may be able to provide sufficient feedback to improve users' perceptions of when their actions are recognized by the system.

Second, from a development perspective, controller-based grabs are determined explicitly, such that a button press indicates a grab and a button release indicates a drop. Conversely, gesture-based grabs in hand tracking are determined implicitly, such that the system guesses if a grab or drop gesture is being performed based on a number of variables (e.g., phalanx angle relative to other phalanges and collision detection). At times, the system was unsuccessful in determining the intent of the user which likely led to user frustration and a lower perception of the hand tracking condition. Improvements to the gesture determination algorithm, which would require significant work, may have an equally significant effect on user perception of hand tracking interaction. In addition, compared to the controller-based conditions, there was a perceptible amount of latency in the gesture-based conditions caused by the additional calculations involved in detecting and estimating hand and finger position and in updating and rendering the hands in real-time in the VE. Latency is an issue for many computer systems and advances in computing power and wireless technology may reduce latency and thus, user perception of gesture-based interactions.

Third, error rates across all interaction methods and tests were extremely low. As a result, we are unable to discuss participants' performance or user perceptions as they relate to overcoming actions that lead to mistakes. Performance errors across interaction methods may have led to differing user perceptions, as affective factors such as self-efficacy have been shown to moderate training system effectiveness [6]. Future studies examining user perceptions of VR interactions may consider implementing a task sufficiently difficult to elicit performance errors.

5 Conclusion

This experiment examined hand tracking and controller-based interaction methods and how different visual representations of controller interactions impact performance and user experience in a VR object manipulation task. Overall, participants rated hand tracking as less usable, it induced a lower sense of agency, and task performance was lower than controller-based methods. Participants' reasoning for disliking hand tracking included issues with tracking accuracy, a lack of feedback, and a lack of something tangible with which to interact. Meanwhile, for the controller-based conditions, participants performed similarly if they saw virtual hands, controllers, virtual hands and controllers, or animated hands and controllers. However, the animated hands condition was less preferred than the other controller conditions, indicating that participants prefer to see their actions closely mapped to their experience, rather than see their actions interpreted. These results suggest that considering perceived naturalness and feelings of agency are important when designing VR interactions, as they play a role in the users' overall experience. Furthermore, although hand tracking holds promise as a natural user interface, the provision of physical feedback and touch in the form of controllers seems to enhance performance and the user experience in VR. Also, technical issues, such as latency and tracking hand positions accurately, are still barriers that need to be overcome for this technology to be a viable interaction method for tasks that require precise hand movements. More research is needed to understand these effects and to determine the optimal VR interface design solutions that foster performance and user experience.

Acknowledgements. This work was funded by the Naval Innovative Science & Engineering (NISE) Basic and Applied Research (BAR) program. We gratefully acknowledge Cuong Nguyen for developing the testbed used in this experiment. Presentation of this material does not constitute or imply its endorsement, recommendation, or favoring by the U.S. Navy or Department of Defense (DoD). The opinions of the authors expressed herein do not necessarily reflect those of the U.S. Navy or DoD.

References

1. Argelaguet, F., Hoyet, L., Trico, M., Lécuyer, A.: The role of interaction in virtual embodiment: effects of the virtual hand representation. In: 2016 IEEE Virtual Reality (VR), pp. 3–10. IEEE, Greenville (2016)
2. Bailey, S.K.T., Johnson, C.I., Sims, V.K.: Using natural gesture interactions leads to higher usability and presence in a computer lesson. In: Bagnara, S., Tartaglia, R., Albolino, S., Alexander, T., Fujita, Y. (eds.) IEA 2018. AISC, vol. 826, pp. 663–671. Springer, Cham (2019)
3. Blake, J.: The natural user interface revolution. In: Natural User Interfaces in NET, pp. 4271–4335. Greenwich, Manning (2010)
4. Blakemore, S.J., Wolpert, D.M., Frith, C.D.: Abnormalities in the awareness of action. Trends Cogn. Sci. 6(6), 237–242 (2002)
5. Blanke, O., Metzinger, T.: Full-body illusions and minimal phenomenal selfhood. Trends Cogn. Sci. 13(1), 7–13 (2009)
6. Colquitt, J.A., LePine, J.A., Noe, R.A.: Toward an integrative theory of training motivation: a meta-analytic path analysis of 20 years of research. J. Appl. Psychol. 85(5), 678–707 (2000)
7. Eubanks, J.C., Moore, A.G., Fishwick, P.A., McMahan, R.P.: A preliminary embodiment short questionnaire. Front. Virtual Reality 2, 24 (2021)
8. Ehrsson, H.H.: The experimental induction of out-of-body experiences. Science 317(5841), 1048 (2007)
9. Franck, N., et al.: Defective recognition of one's own actions in patients with schizophrenia. Am. J. Psychiatry 158(3), 454–459 (2001)
10. Gusai, E., Bassano, C., Solari, F., Chessa, M.: Interaction in an immersive collaborative virtual reality environment: a comparison between leap motion and HTC controllers. In: Battiato, S., Farinella, G., Leo, M., Gallo, G. (eds.) New Trends in Image Analysis and Processing ICIAP 2017, pp. 290–300. Springer, Cham (2017)
11. Hart, S.G.: NASA-Task Load Index (NASA-TLX): 20 years later. Proc. Hum. Fact. Ergon. Soc. 50(9), 904–908 (2006)
12. Johnson, C.I., Whitmer, D.E., Entinger, J., Peterson, E.K., Sobel, B.M.: Interacting with virtual reality with a controller instead of the body benefits performance and perceptions. In: Proceedings of the Human Factors and Ergonomics Society Annual Meeting, pp. 1294–1298. Sage, Los Angeles (2022)
13. Kangas, J., Kumar, S.K., Mehtonen, H., Järnstedt, J., Raisamo, R.: Trade-off between task accuracy, task completion time and naturalness for direct object manipulation in virtual reality. Multim. Technol. Interact. 6(1), 6 (2022)
14. Kilteni, K., Groten, R., Slater, M.: The sense of embodiment in virtual reality. Presence: Teleoperat. Virt. Environ. 21(4), 373–387 (2012)
15. Reski, N., Alissandrakis, A.: Open data exploration in virtual reality: a comparative study of input technology. Virtual Reality 24, 1–22 (2020)
16. Roupé, M., Bosch-Sijtsema, P., Johansson, M.: Interactive navigation interface for virtual reality using the human body. Comput. Environ. Urban Syst. 43, 42–50 (2014)
17. Sanchez-Vives, M.V., Spanlang, B., Frisoli, A., Bergamasco, M., Slater, M.: Virtual hand illusion induced by visuomotor correlations. PLoS One 5(4) (2010)
18. Sato, A., Yasuda, A.: Illusion of sense of self-agency: discrepancy between the predicted and actual sensory consequences of actions modulates the sense of self-agency, but not the sense of self-ownership. Cognition 94(3), 241–255 (2005)
19. Schwartz, R.N., Plass, J.L.: Click versus drag: user-performed tasks and the enactment effect in an interactive multimedia environment. Comput. Hum. Behav. 33, 242–255 (2014). https://doi.org/10.1016/j.chb.2014.01.012

20. Slater, M., Pérez Marcos, D., Ehrsson, H., Sanchez-Vives, M.V.: Towards a digital body: the virtual arm illusion. Front. Hum. Neurosci. **2**(6), 1–8 (2008)
21. Steuer, J.S.: Defining virtual reality: dimensions determining telepresence. J. Commun. **42**, 73–93 (1992)
22. Tsakiris, M., Prabhu, G., Haggard, P.: Having a body versus moving your body: how agency structures body-ownership. Conscious. Cogn. **15**(2), 423–432 (2006)
23. Voigt-Antons, J.-N., Kojic, T., Ali, D., Moller, S.: Influence of hand tracking as a way of interaction in virtual reality on user experience. In: Twelfth International Conference on Quality of Multimedia Experience (QoMEX), pp. 1–4. IEEE (2020)

A Multimodal Virtual Reality Inventory System

Kenneth King L. Ko(✉) [iD], Dan Mark D. Restoles [iD], and Eric Cesar E. Vidal Jr. [iD]

Ateneo de Manila University, Katipunan Ave., 1108 Quezon City, Metro Manila, Philippines
{kenneth.ko,dan.restoles}@obf.ateneo.edu, evidal@ateneo.edu

Abstract. Applications involving virtual reality (VR), especially VR-based video games, integrate multiple gameplay mechanics. One such mechanic is an inventory system, which is a way for a player to manage their items in an easy and convenient manner. This study aims to iterate upon previous studies and implementations of inventory management to produce a new inventory system framework for use in VR adventure and serious games, with a primary focus on improving ease of use, convenience, and accessibility for a more refined and more immersive experience. The framework allows for different modalities, including control via vision-based hand tracking and traditional controllers. The study finds that the inventory systems implemented using the framework were able to satisfy essential user requirements criteria and improve upon existing implementations found in related literature, indicating that the framework is functional. Additionally, the study also finds that vision-based hand tracking provides a similar user experience as traditional controllers in terms of immersion, despite some tracking inaccuracies experienced when utilizing the former modality.

Keywords: Inventory · Multimodal · Improvement

1 Introduction

Virtual reality (VR) makes use of technologies such as eye displays and positional tracking to allow users to experience a simulated reality and to create immersion. VR is part of the extended reality (XR) umbrella term, which encompasses VR alongside other simulated reality technologies, such as augmented reality (AR) and mixed reality (MR) [8].

VR has seen use in multiple fields, most notably in the entertainment and leisure space, allowing creators and developers to further express their creativity [3]. This includes video games, movies, and social virtual spaces. Companies such as Meta, Oculus, HTC, Sony and Valve, alongside others have made it possible for consumers to enter the XR market by lowering entry price points into XR technologies such as head-mounted displays and full-body tracking equipment.

Such events have led to further development of the medium, especially in the video game market, where VR-related games have started to pop up. In each iteration, the medium has aimed to build upon the last [2]. These iterations may improve on certain game mechanics, or on the quality of life (QoL) features in the games in general. One

J. Y. C. Chen et al. (Eds.): HCII 2023, LNCS 14058, pp. 82–100, 2023.
https://doi.org/10.1007/978-3-031-48050-8_6

such improvement is in *inventory systems*. Inventory systems are implementations of certain mechanics in a video game or similar medium which allows players to store and manage certain items and freely take them around. Trying to improve these systems for users could potentially lead into a better immersive experience, and possibly become one of VR's selling points that will increase adoption and advance further development.

To further immerse users and improve the overall experience, it is imperative to explore and develop new ways of inventory management, and compare these with existing well-established systems. In attempting to create these new inventory systems, a framework was designed to help simplify their implementation, while allowing a level of flexibility and customization by modifying different parameters and settings.

In this paper, we first describe our inventory system framework and the design and compatibility considerations we took into account. Then, we describe a user test to validate the design decisions made for our framework, including the testing environment and methodologies used to gather information from our participants. Finally, we attempt to present and discuss the results gathered from the testing and present possible improvements and future work.

2 Inventory System Framework and Considerations

The following section outlines the basis and framework used for the creation of our new inventory system engine.

2.1 Interaction in Virtual Reality and Virtual Environments

Immersion in a virtual environment naturally requires interaction. Interaction in VR relies on the use of hardware that would allow the user to input data as well as experience immediate feedback upon inputting the said data. In general, most contemporary VR headsets make use of a head-mounted display alongside two motion-tracked controllers with six degrees of freedom, intended for use for each hand. However, it is possible to augment this with additional devices to potentially increase immersion – these devices include multi-sensory devices which also stimulate other bodily senses such as smell [1] and touch [12] as well as navigation and movement tracking devices which allow the user to "simulate" locomotion (e.g., full-body tracking through hardware such as SlimeVR, HaritoraX, base stations, or even through interpolated data) [4]. In addition, using vision-based bare-hand tracking in place of motion-tracked hand controllers could potentially increase immersion as well, although it may not provide the most ideal user experience [6].

For this study, the most general and convenient option is used, referring to the standalone head-mounted displays with standard motion controllers. This most general option allows the users to interact with the virtual environment and the objects within it in a myriad of ways. Traditional object interaction methods via motion controls include ray-casting – a method of selecting targets from a distance using a 'ray' emanating from the user's hand [11] – and direct grabbing, to name a few. Multiple studies testing different object selection and manipulation techniques have found that certain techniques will offer greater precision and speed over others, at the expense of naturalness or interaction fidelity. Depending on the needs of the application, the developer may decide to settle on specific types of object interaction and menu interaction, including how the user interacts with the inventory system. The technique which ends up being chosen by the developer will inevitably affect the immersion of the user in the virtual environment.

In this study, the virtual environment is built using Unity version 2021.3.16f1 for Windows alongside the following XR packages:

- XR Interaction Toolkit version 2.3.0
- XR Hands 1.1.0-pre3
- OpenXR Plugin version 1.6.0

These versions of the packages allow for better compatibility across multiple headsets with Unity using the OpenXR framework. Older versions of the API do not support certain features, such as Meta Quest 2's hand tracking feature, which were previously only available on Meta's own Oculus SDK.

2.2 User Requirements for Inventory Systems

A set of user requirements that will serve as the criteria for evaluating inventory systems will be used in the study. These user requirements, based on the study of Mussman et al. [10], are simplified to only the dominant ones (see Table 1), which still encompasses the majority of the expected functionality of an inventory system without being too complicated. The following user requirements are as follows:

Table 1. Simplified user requirements based on [10].

User requirement	Description
UR1	Item selection/manipulation
UR2	Item addition to inventory
UR3	Item removal from inventory
UR4	Presentation of items to user
UR5	Select one or more items in inventory
UR6	Perform action on selected item
UR7	Perform action on another item within inventory
UR8	Combine items to make new items
UR9	Receive feedback from actions/interactions

The most common types found in related literature, namely the *Flat Grid, Virtual Drawers,* and *Magnetic Surface,* all adhere partially to the user requirements criteria. These three inventory system types are described as follows [2]:

- *Flat Grid*: a "two-dimensional overlay placed at a static position from the player's eye when activated. Items are stored in a grid of a certain dimension. This is the modality typically used by many video game inventory systems.

- *Virtual Drawers:* a similar implementation to that of the *Flat Grid* but situated in a 3D space where the inventory is turned into a drawer or shelf where the player can place items.
- *Magnetic Surface*: a freely-movable plate which can accommodate multiple objects and such objects can be arranged in a relatively much more creative manner than the previous implementations.

An evaluation of the user requirements fulfilled by each inventory system type is shown in Table 2.

Table 2. Inventory system types evaluated using simplified user requirements criteria [10].

User requirement	Flat Grid	Virtual Grid	Magnetic Surface
UR1	✔	✔	✔
UR2	✔	✔	✔
UR3	✔	✔	✔
UR4	✔	✔	✔
UR5			
UR6			
UR7			
UR8			
UR9	✔		

It can be observed that the inventory system types only allow for basic inventory system interaction so far – it is not necessarily a disadvantage for an inventory system to not have certain criterion met, seeing that there may be interventions made to circumvent these problems, such as an overarching system implementation.

Nevertheless, the functionality of our designed inventory systems will take these user requirements into account and will generally use these requirements as a basis for all other possible improvements.

2.3 Inventory System Framework

Inventory systems typically implement the concept of "slots" where inventory objects are placed by the user. Our inventory system framework (see Fig. 1) facilitates the use of multiple types of inventory systems that implement the slots concept. The developed inventory system types could either be player-situated (where the inventory system is placed relative to the user, e.g., belt, wrist) or based on world space (where the inventory system is situated within the game environment, e.g., shelves, chests). All system types can be operated through interactions caused by a collision between a game object (designated as an inventory item) and an inventory slot. Furthermore, all these system types are managed by a master inventory runtime component, which is responsible for updating inventory parameters such as the current type of inventory, item ordering semantics, and what inputs from the player are recognized.

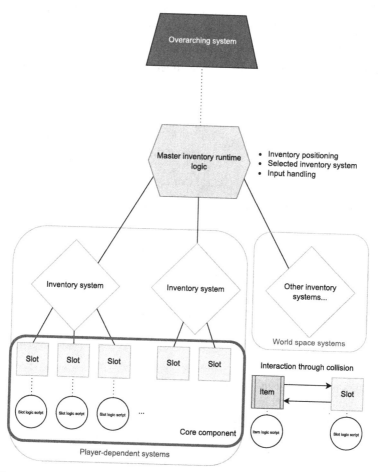

Fig. 1. Framework for the inventory system runtime, integrated into an overarching VR system.

The framework in its current iteration and the components involved are described in greater detail as follows:

Slot. In its essence, a Slot component takes an object designated as an Item and does multiple checks to see if an Item can be placed within the Slot. Additionally, the Slot component has two modes, namely the normal single-slot mode and the magnetic surface mode. The single-slot mode allows for one object within the slot at a time, while the magnetic surface mode allows for multiple objects in one slot at the same time.

It should be noted that in the current iteration of our engine, there are some limitations when using the magnetic surface mode. One limitation is that cross-inventory system item position and slotting is no longer preserved when using magnetic surface mode. Other functionalities work as intended, however.

The checks performed in the Slots component logic are summarized as follows, and depicted in Fig. 2:

1. Determine whether the Slot is in single-slot mode or magnetic surface mode (this setting can be modified by the developer).
   a. If the Slot setting is set to single-slot mode:
      (1) Check if there is an item already in the Slot. Proceed if none.
      (2) Check if the object being inserted is designated as an Item game object. Proceed if true.
      (3) Check if the object being inserted is colliding with two or more unoccupied Slots. If it is, get the closest slot to the object and proceed.
      (4) Insert item into the Slot.
   b. If the Slot setting is set to magnetic surface mode:
      (1) Check if the object being inserted is designated as an Item game object. Proceed if true.
      (2) Check if the Slot already contains the object being inserted. If not, proceed.
      (3) Insert item into the Slot.

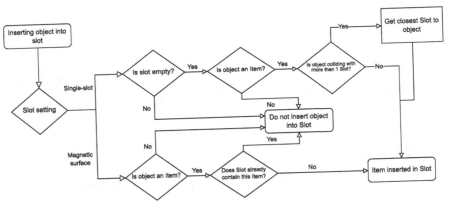

Fig. 2. Flowchart of the Slot component logic.

Furthermore, the Slot component also handles the logic for insertion and removal of Items, both of which differ slightly depending on which mode the Slot component is using.

Item. The Item component is inserted into a game object which allows the system to recognize that it is an object that can be interacted with by the player and subsequently be inserted into the inventory system. In the current iteration, the Item component presents three parameters to the developer: item rotation, default scale, and current slot.

Item rotation allows the developer to override the rotation of the item when it is within the slot. Note that this is only used when the Item is inserted into a Slot that is set to the single-slot mode. Default scale is automatically determined at runtime and allows the item to return to its original scale when removed from the inventory. Lastly, the current slot parameter shows which slot the item is currently slotted in.

Master Inventory Runtime. The master inventory runtime component is responsible for handling all the created inventory systems which make use of the Slot component. Generally, the master inventory runtime component handles the positioning and activating of the inventory system when the selected type is player-situated, selecting which type of inventory system to be used. This component is also responsible for inventory retention when switching between different inventory systems that make use of slots under the single-slot mode.

In the current iteration of the engine, each of the three specified inventory system implementations (or a close equivalent in terms of functionality) have been implemented using our framework (see Fig. 3). Slight variations of these systems have also been included, which we named as *Magic Box* and *Wrist-based Stack* (see Fig. 4), for a total of five (5) implemented inventory systems.

Magic Box and *Wrist-based Stack* can be described as follows:

- *Magic Box*: A modification of the *Magnetic Surface*, allowing for a larger area (a cube to put in items) instead of only a plane.
- *Wrist-based Stack*: An implementation of the Virtual Grid that implements a stack, emulating a Last-In-First-Out (LIFO) functionality.

Fig. 3. Inventory system types described in the user requirements criteria implemented using the aforementioned framework. These (from left to right) are the functional equivalents of *Flat Grid*, *Virtual Grid*, and *Magnetic Surface*.

Fig. 4. Modified inventory systems based on implementations in literature, named *Magic Box* (left) and *Wrist-based Stack* (right), respectively.

2.4 Vision-Based Hand Tracking and OpenXR Compatibility

Initial iterations which made use of the Meta Quest 2's native hand tracking support [9] posed potential limitations which needed to be immediately addressed. These potential limitations include requiring the need to build or deploy for only the Meta Quest 2, which come with limited hardware compared to desktop computers. This implies the need for optimization, which could either be turning down certain graphical settings, or outright removal of content. Depending on the use case of the developer, this may not be an option. Additionally, implementing only for the Meta Quest 2 would lock the system under the Meta/Oculus controller scheme, which may pose a problem for users of other headsets.

As such, the study opted to use OpenXR-compatible hand tracking APIs and modified them accordingly to accommodate the created inventory system framework. The latest release of the XR Hands package for Unity, at the time of writing, only allowed for limited interaction with objects and the environment, with only poke and pinch being the allowed actions at the moment. With our modification, it is possible to further interact with the system and the environment. An example is activating the inventory by performing a specific hand pose. In future iterations, it is expected to add more possible interactions for more hand poses, such as adding a specific pose to allow player movement while staying in place or seated.

In the latest build used for testing, a specific hand pose, which involves pinching the middle finger and thumb together, can be done to activate or deactivate the selected inventory system. Additionally, an unfinished mock-up of a console can be activated when the hand is detected to be rotated at a certain angle (see Fig. 5).

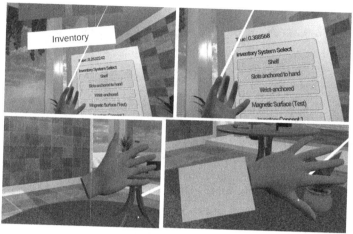

Fig. 5. Screenshots showing custom hand gestures and resulting functionalities.

3 User Testing

To evaluate our inventory system framework, a user test is designed that covers user interactions with the inventory, with a questionnaire inquiring users about the overall experience, testing whether or not certain user requirements are upheld, and collecting general feedback. Both modes of input – using traditional controllers and vision-based hand-tracking – will be tested.

For the testing, 16 participants were recruited. The participants consisted of men and women with an average age of 21.625 (±2.870). The testing procedure is described below.

3.1 Questionnaires

There are two questionnaires involved in the testing. One involves the self-evaluation questionnaire, and the other is for the inventory system questionnaire.

Self-evaluation Questionnaire. At the beginning of the testing, each participant is asked to answer the self-evaluation questionnaire about their experience and knowledge about VR in general (see Table 3). The questions use a 7-point Likert scale rating system ranging from 'Not familiar' to 'Expert at using'.

Briefing and Supervision. Afterwards, the participant receives a briefing on the procedure and a guide on how to operate the headset within the environment. The briefing tells participants to do the following actions for both modalities:

- Add items to all five (5) types of inventory systems available.
- Remove items from all five (5) types of inventory systems available.
- Toggle inventory systems for types that support it.
- Toggle ray casting on or off and interact with items, inventory system and the menu.

Table 3. Self-evaluation questionnaire.

No	Questions
1	How much experience have you had with Virtual Reality in general?
2	How much experience have you had with Virtual Reality Games?
3	How much experience have you had with adventure games in general?
4	How much experience have you had with the Meta Quest 2?

Then, they proceed to wear the headset (in this case, the Meta Quest 2) and interact with the inventory system using two modalities – traditional controllers and vision-based hand tracking for around 25–30 min. During this timeframe, the facilitator supervising the test will assist the participants, answer their questions, and note any comments or difficulties they encounter.

Inventory System Questionnaire. After the test, a second questionnaire (see Tables 4 and 5) is given to the participant to inquire about their overall impression and experience of the inventory systems. Participants were also specifically asked to distinguish between their experience of using traditional controllers and vision-based hand tracking.

Table 4. Open-ended questions included in the questionnaire.

No	Questions
1	What did you think about the different types of inventory systems?
2	What did you like about these inventory systems?
3	What did you dislike about these inventory systems?
4	What did you think of the vision-based hand tracking experience when interacting with the inventory system? Please describe your experience

Table 5. Questions in the questionnaire which utilize the Likert scale [5].

No	Questions
1	In terms of immersion, rate these inventory systems
2	In terms of convenience, rate these inventory systems
3	Compared to using actual controllers, how would you rate the overall vision-based hand tracking experience, with 1 being worse than controllers and 5 being better than controllers?
4	Rate your overall experience with the inventory systems (both traditional controllers and vision-based hand tracking)

A section of the questionnaire (see Table 6) asks participants whether or not they believe a specific inventory system implementation managed to satisfy user requirements criteria. This is included to test if the study's implementation of inventory systems found in related literature changed in certain ways. This section also asks the participants about our created inventory systems, namely the *Wrist-based Stack* and *Magic Box*.

However, since the inventory system implementations using our framework does not have some of the functionality yet (in particular, combining items together), we decided to omit the non-applicable criterion for this study and include it in future work.

Table 6. Checkbox questionnaire.

User requirement	*Shelf*	*Slots anchored to hand*	*Wrist-based Stack*	*Magnetic surface*	*Magic Box*
Item selection/manipulation					
Add item to inventory					
Remove item from inventory					
Present items to user					
Select more than 1 item in inventory simultaneously					
Perform action on selected item					
Perform action on another item within inventory					
Receive feedback from actions					

After gathering the results, they will be analyzed using a statistical hypothesis test. Aside from the tests, open-ended questions (qualitative responses) will be analyzed using thematic analysis.

3.2 Testing Environment

The study has taken steps to optimize both the process of user testing as well as receiving user feedback. Some of the steps taken include introducing an easy way to switch between inventory systems for testing while in runtime. This allows the participants and developers alike to easily exchange feedback about usability and reduce build times associated with testing multiple inventory types at once (see Fig. 6). Another step is to use a single type of headset for the testing, in which the Meta Quest 2 was used to allow for faster modality switching.

Additionally, a toggle for ray casting and the heads-up display (HUD) has been added for testing purposes. Having a toggle for ray casting allows the testers to try interacting with the inventory systems in a slightly different way.

Fig. 6. Selection between inventory system types and some options.

Meanwhile, having a toggle for the HUD allows users to see relevant information regarding their actions. Participants are able to see the following information in the testing environment (see Fig. 7):

- Currently selected inventory system
- Ray casting state (*ON* or *OFF*)
- Inventory active state (*ACTIVE* or *INACTIVE*)
- Status (e.g., added/removed an item, changed inventory system).

Fig. 7. Debug console displayed on HUD of user during testing.

4   Results and Discussion

This section presents the results of the user study, following the same order of presentation as the previous section. We also discuss some possible implications of the results.

4.1 Self-Evaluation Questionnaire Results

The results of the self-evaluation questionnaire indicate that almost all of the participants have little to no experience in VR in general. While a minority have indicated that they have some familiarity with the concept, only a single participant has had any actual experience with VR, and only two participants having some familiarity with the Meta Quest 2 headsets (but not necessarily using them).

However, the question regarding adventure games had more variety in the responses, indicating that games are recognized in general. (See Table 7).

Table 7. Self-evaluation questionnaire results.

Experience with:	Minimum	Maximum	Mean
Virtual reality in general	1	4	1.688
Virtual reality games	1	4	1.438
Adventure games	1	6	4.375
Using the Meta Quest 2	1	2	1.063

4.2 Briefing and Supervised Testing

All participants were able to successfully follow the instructions given during the briefing, and subsequently finish testing all of the inventory system with both vision-based hand tracking and traditional controllers despite their lack of familiarity with VR in general.

Vision-based Hand Tracking. The loss of hand tracking due to a variety of factors, such as one of the hands being moved outside of the visible range of the Meta Quest 2 headset, or due to sudden occlusion, has been observed in majority of the participants. This has resulted in the participants suddenly dropping the object when they are trying to interact with the inventory system. However, it has also been observed that the participants did not really mind the occasional loss of tracking, perhaps due to the resulting immersion or amazement with the hand tracking provided by the headset.

Another observation made was that despite earlier instructions regarding the importance of certain hand gestures to do different actions (in this case, pinching to grab an object versus pinching to toggle the inventory), a number of participants kept doing different gestures than what was instructed of them. Corrective instructions given by the facilitator allowed the participants to subsequently perform the gestures correctly and progress along the testing procedure more smoothly.

Traditional Controllers. Since the traditional controllers were given to the participants after they finish the vision-based hand tracking part, the participants already had an idea of what actions they had to perform, and as such, the procedure went much smoother. Aside from clarifications about the control scheme, the participants were generally able to grasp how to use the controllers almost immediately. We assume this is because having dedicated buttons for controllers are not that much different from controllers from other systems or game consoles, and that a majority of participants have experience with adventure games, which can be played on these game consoles or similar.

Ray Casting. When briefly asked about the ray casting, participants had mixed perspectives. Some preferred ray casting to be off as it provided better immersion and mimicked the feeling of having to grab the items, "just like in real life". Others preferred ray casting to be kept on as it was the most convenient way to interact with the objects and did not like having to move around the testing area as much. Some of them answered that their preference is dependent on the scenario or the use case.

4.3 Inventory System Questionnaire Results

To process the results from the inventory system questionnaire, we use Cnded questions and get the average scores for questions that involve the Likert scale [5].

Open-ended Questions. There were four open-ended questions in the questionnaire which will be discussed below:

General Comments on Inventory Systems. Participants' sentiments on the different types of inventory systems were generally positive, with a majority of participants liking the variety of implementations and how fun it was to interact with them. Other participants also responded with some of the inconveniences they found with some of the implementations, particularly the ones which are based on world space (e.g., *Shelf* and *Magic Box*). However, some participants had the opposite opinion, which implies that convenience may be a matter of preference.

Some participants also provided feedback with regards to the limitation of some inventory systems, such as the *Slots anchored to hand* implementation only having four slots. Such limitations are part of the current iteration and are intended to be improved upon in the future.

Positive Feedback on Inventory Systems. When asked about the participants liked about the inventory systems, the majority stated that the inventory systems were intuitive, easy to use, and straightforward. Additionally, some feedback indicated that certain inventory systems were immersive, convenient, or both.

Negative Feedback on Inventory Systems. When asked about what the participants disliked about the inventory systems, the majority did not provide any negative feedback. However, the participants that did provide negative feedback indicated cluttering and visibility problems for the *Magnetic Surface* and *Magic Box* inventory system types. Additionally, some have stated usability problems with the *Wrist-based Stack*, noting that it may be difficult to find a perfect scenario to use that certain implementation, at least in its current iteration.

Other negative feedback provided by the users were mainly related to the modality settings, such as ray casting. These problems are not necessarily related to the inventory systems themselves.

Interacting Using Vision-based Hand Tracking. Participant response towards vision-based hand tracking was mixed, with half of the participants stating at least some kind of problem or inconvenience they experienced during testing. Common problems reported regarding vision-based hand tracking include that while most of the time, hand tracking is accurate and enjoyable to use, gestures sometimes do not register, most commonly due to the hands moving out of the headset's field of vision. Furthermore, being only able to grab items by pinching was also seen as a problem (which is caused by a limitation of the API). Additionally, some participants did not like that they had to keep their hands in front of them or at least within the headset's field of vision at all times to keep the tracking accurate.

The rest of the feedback for vision-based hand tracking were positive, stating that they felt immersed, "mimicked reality", and was a fluid experience overall.

Likert Scale Questions. There were four questions which make use of the Likert scale, which will be discussed below:

Immersion. In terms of immersion, the participants were asked if they found certain inventory system types to be immersive. The analysis of variance (ANOVA) test [7] was used to compare the averages of the different types of inventory systems. The results are shown below (see Table 8).

Table 8. Immersion on different inventory system types.

Inventory system types:	Count	Sum	Mean	Variance
Shelf	16	68	**4.250**	1.267
Slots anchored to hand	16	76	**4.750**	0.200
Wrist-based Stack	16	71	4.438	0.396
Magnetic Surface	16	75	**4.688**	0.363
Magic Box	16	75	4.688	0.629
			P-value	*0.294 (P > 0.05)*

The results reveal that the participants did not find a significant difference (P = 0.294, P > 0.05) in terms of immersion across the different inventory system types. This implies that all inventory systems are immersive to some extent.

Convenience. Participants were also asked if they found certain inventory system types to be convenient. Again, the analysis of variance (ANOVA) test [7] was used to compare the averages of the different types of inventory systems. The results are shown below (see Table 9).

Similar to the results for the immersion question, the results reveal that the participants did not find a significant difference (P = 0.130, P > 0.05) in terms of convenience across the different inventory system types. The implication is that all inventory systems are convenient in a sense, perhaps depending on the use case or scenario the inventory system is implemented in.

Table 9. Immersion on different inventory system types.

Inventory system types:	Count	Sum	Mean	Variance
Shelf	16	60	**3.750**	**1.800**
Slots anchored to hand	16	75	**4.688**	**0.629**
Wrist-based Stack	16	62	**3.875**	**1.583**
Magnetic Surface	16	62	**3.875**	**1.050**
Magic Box	16	66	4.125	1.050
			P-value	***0.130* (P > 0.05)**

Vision-based Hand Tracking over Traditional Controllers. Participants were also asked about their experience with vision-based hand tracking, whether or not it was better, same, or worse than when using traditional controllers. Figure 8 shows the distribution of the scores, which range from 1 (worse than controllers) to 5 (better than controllers). The average score of 3.313 ($\pm$1.261) may indicate that the participants found the vision-based hand tracking to be similarly enjoyable, immersive, or convenient as traditional controllers; however, the high variance may indicate that the results may be a matter of specific users' compatibility/accuracy with the hand detection algorithm, or of users' preferences, or both.

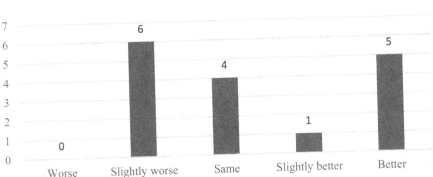

Vision-based hand tracking over traditional controllers

Fig. 8. Chart showing vision-based hand tracking scores compared to traditional controllers.

Overall Experience. The questionnaire also asked about the general experience of the participants after interacting with the different inventory system types. Figure 9 shows the distribution of the scores, which range from 1 (Very unsatisfactory) to 5 (Very satisfactory). The average score of 4.500 ($\pm$0.500) indicates that all participants found the overall testing experience to be satisfactory.

Checkbox Questionnaire. Table 10 shows percentage of users who believe a certain inventory system accomplished a specific user requirements criterion.

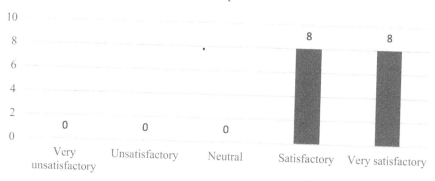

Fig. 9. Chart showing the overall experience of participants.

Table 10. Percentage of participants which observed the criteria for each inventory system.

User requirement	Shelf	Slots anchored to hand	Wrist-based Stack	Magnetic surface	Magic Box
Item selection/manipulation	93.75%	93.75%	75.00%	87.50%	87.50%
Add item to inventory	93.75%	93.75%	87.50%	93.75%	87.50%
Remove item from inventory	93.75%	93.75%	87.50%	93.75%	87.50%
Present items to user	100.00%	93.75%	50.00%	93.75%	87.50%
Select more than 1 item in inventory simultaneously	68.75%	31.25%	18.75%	75.00%	81.25%
Perform action on selected item	25.00%	50.00%	43.75%	56.25%	56.25%
Perform action on another item within inventory	12.50%	31.25%	18.75%	62.50%	56.25%
Receive feedback from actions	62.50%	68.75%	68.75%	62.50%	62.50%

While the questionnaire explicitly describes the user requirement criteria in concise and brief terms, perhaps due to misinterpretation by the participants, not all users believe that they observed certain user requirements (especially for the first four user requirements, which the facilitator found that all participants were able to correctly execute).

As such, we consider an observed rate of greater than 50% (consisting of the majority) to have satisfied the user requirements criterion. (Again, for this study, we exclude the 'combine new items' criterion [10] as it is not actually implemented yet in the current iteration of the inventory systems.) With this metric, our user testing results show that our framework's inventory system types compare favorably (at least in a controlled testing environment) to previously implemented inventory systems in related literature.

5 Conclusion and Future Work

The preceding study showcases the details and considerations taken in the development of a multimodal inventory system designed for virtual reality adventure and serious games. These considerations are then taken to implement both existing and new inventory system types using a simplified version of the user requirements criteria found in literature [10]. Five inventory system types, created through the use of our framework, were involved in the study: *Shelf*, *Slots anchored to hand*, *Wrist-based Stack*, *Magnetic Surface*, and *Magic Box*. Two modalities, namely, vision-based hand tracking and traditional controllers, were used to allow participants to interact with the aforementioned inventory system types.

The user testing conducted revealed that vision-based hand tracking was found to provide a functionally similar experience to traditional controllers in terms of usability, despite encountering some problems with regards to hand tracking accuracy. Furthermore, the testing revealed that the inventory systems implemented using the framework, at the very least, managed to pass certain criteria, indicating that the inventory systems are indeed functional and works as intended, and compares favorably to previous implementations found in literature.

Future studies may improve upon the inventory system implementations using this framework by adding more functionalities which address more user requirements criteria, including the aforementioned 'combining items' criterion. In addition, vision-based hand tracking could be improved by using newer versions of application programming interfaces or newer hardware. New functionalities that deal with specific hand poses or gestures may be implemented as well to improve the overall experience with vision-based hand tracking.

Finally, the inventory system framework developed in this paper is intended to support future VR adventure games for educational purposes, which are currently in development.

Acknowledgement. This research is part of a larger ongoing project of the Ateneo Laboratory for the Learning Sciences (ALLS) with grants provided by DOST-PCIEERD (through their Grants-In-Aid program, project no. 11169), Accenture Philippines, and Ateneo de Manila University. We would also like to thank Joan Dominique L. Lee, Dominique Marie Antoinette B. Manahan, laboratory head Maria Mercedes T. Rodrigo, and the rest of ALLS for providing invaluable support and assistance towards this study.

References

1. Archer, N.S., Bluff, A., Eddy, A., et al.: Odour enhances the sense of presence in a virtual reality environment. PLoS ONE **17**, 3 (2022). https://doi.org/10.1371/journal.pone.0265039
2. Cmentowski, S., Krekhov, A., Kruger, J.: "I Packed My Bag and in It I Put…": a taxonomy of inventory systems for virtual reality games. In: 2021 IEEE Conference on Games (CoG) (2021). https://doi.org/10.1109/cog52621.2021.9619153
3. Faisal, A.: Computer science: visionary of virtual reality. Nature **551**(7680), 298–299 (2017). https://doi.org/10.1038/551298a

4. Gu, L., Yin, L., Li, J., Wu, D.: A real-time full-body motion capture and reconstruction system for VR basic set. In: 2021 IEEE 5th Advanced Information Technology, Electronic and Automation Control Conference (IAEAC) (2021). https://doi.org/10.1109/iaeac50856.2021.9390617

5. Joshi, A., Kale, S., Chandel, S., Pal, D.: Likert scale: explored and explained. Brit. J. Appl. Sci. Technol. **7**(4), 396–403 (2015). https://doi.org/10.9734/bjast/2015/14975

6. Kim, A.: A Comparative study of the user experience of controller and hand-tracking interactions in a virtual environment. In: 2022 IEEE International Symposium on Mixed and Augmented Reality Adjunct (ISMAR-Adjunct) (2022). https://doi.org/10.1109/ismar-adjunct57072.2022.00157

7. MacKenzie, D.: The history of statistics: the measurement of uncertainty before 1900 by Stephen M. Stigler. Technol. Cult. **29**(2), 299–300 (1988). https://doi.org/10.1353/tech.1988.0165

8. Marr, B.: What Is Extended Reality Technology? A Simple Explanation For Anyone. https://forbes.com/sites/bernardmarr/2019/08/12/what-is-extended-reality-technology-a-simple-explanation-for-anyone/. Accessed 6 Apr 2023

9. Meta.: Getting started with Hand Tracking on Meta Quest headsets. https://www.meta.com/help/quest/articles/headsets-and-accessories/controllers-and-hand-tracking/hand-tracking-quest-2/. Accessed 6 June 2023

10. Mussmann, M., Truman, S., von Mammen, S: Game-ready inventory systems for virtual reality. In: 2021 IEEE Conference on Games (CoG) (2021). https://doi.org/10.1109/cog52621.2021.9619028

11. Pietroszek, K.: Raycasting in virtual reality. In: Lee, N. (ed.) Encyclopedia of Computer Graphics and Games (2018), pp. 1–3. Springer, Heidelberg (2018). https://doi.org/10.1007/978-3-319-08234-9_180-1

12. Ramsamy, P., Haffegee, A., Jamieson, R., Alexandrov, V.: Using haptics to improve immersion in virtual environments. In: Alexandrov, V.N., van Albada, G.D., Sloot, P.M.A., Dongarra, J. (eds.) ICCS 2006. LNCS, vol. 3992, pp. 603–609. Springer, Heidelberg (2006). https://doi.org/10.1007/11758525_81

Modulation of the Walking Speed by Moving Avatars with Age Stereotype Stimuli

Yusuke Koseki[1] and Tomohiro Amemiya[2,3]

[1] Faculty of Economics, The University of Tokyo, 2-11-16 Yayoi,
Bunkyo-ku, Tokyo 113-0032, Japan
koseki-yusuke551@g.ecc.u-tokyo.ac.jp
[2] Virtual Reality Educational Research Center, The University of Tokyo,
Bunkyo City, Japan
amemiya@vr.u-tokyo.ac.jp
[3] Information Technology Center, The University of Tokyo,
7-3-1 Hongo, Bunkyo-ku, Tokyo 113-8654, Japan
http://www.amelab.vr.u-tokyo.ac.jp/

Abstract. Human gait is typically influenced by the gait of other people and can be observed in real as well in virtual reality (VR) space. The projection of walking motion of various avatars on walls in VR space reveals that people's walking speed changes even when walking alongside moving point-light dots (i.e., biological motion), not just a full-body silhouette. However, the effect of the texture or motion of the avatar on the walking speed remains unclear. In this study, we examined the effects of the changes of the texture and walking motion of a human 3D avatar on the walking speed/gait sensation. Furthermore, we investigated the effect of the presence or absence of the priming stimuli of age stereotypes on the subjects' walking speed/gait sensation. The results revealed a significant interaction between the priming effect and avatar motion. Furthermore, gait sensation differed by motion and texture. These findings provide new insights into the control of human walking speed and the similarities and differences between psychological effects in real and VR spaces.

Keywords: Avatar · Cognitive · Elderly priming effect · Behavioral economics

1 Introduction

Improving walking techniques, such as avoiding crowded places to avoid the risk of spreading COVID-19 infection, for guiding pedestrians appropriately and effectively and encouraging pedestrians for safe evacuation in the event of a disaster are critical for ensuring their well-being. Human walking is mutually influenced by the walking of people around them. For example, when walking in a group, the walking speed is controlled such that an appropriate distance is maintained between individuals and the pedestrians in front of them [1]. Furthermore, the walking motion of virtual avatars around pedestrians influences

J. Y. C. Chen et al. (Eds.): HCII 2023, LNCS 14058, pp. 101–110, 2023.
https://doi.org/10.1007/978-3-031-48050-8_7

their walking speed, and the walking behavior of a group of virtual agents influences the walking behavior of humans [2]. The walking speed changes when the avatar is humanoid and exhibits a walking motion [3].

However, the effect of the texture and movement of the virtual avatar on the walking speed is yet to be studied comprehensively. Therefore, in this experiment, we examined the modulation of walking sensation and speed according to various textures and motions of an avatar walking alongside individuals. We focused on the walking motion of avatars with individual differences in gait as well as differences due to age. Therefore, in this study, we applied the gait of young and old people to the motion of a parallel avatar and compared the effects on the subject's walking speed. Studies have indicated that the effects of elderly priming affected behavior subconsciously. Although the effects of elderly priming are purported to be simply an experimenter effect [4], studies using elderly avatars [8,9] have revealed the Proteus effect [10], which refers to the tendency for people to be affected by their avatars. Because stereotypes play a critical role in the Proteus effect, we examined whether the combination of an avatar and elderly stereotypes by priming affects the walking speed of a walker.

Two aspects affect the elderly priming effect. First, in behavioral economics, people's subconscious and irrational behavior are analyzed to develop a method called nudging to influence subsequent behavior and decision making [5]. Progress in this field has enabled the use of this method in national policies. Second, to increase the sense of immersion in virtual spaces, psychological approaches that utilize human illusions have attracted considerable research attention for improving machine performance, such as increasing the resolution and viewing angle. For example, studies have combined VR and psychological effects to examine the psychological effects of using elderly avatars [7] to understand how the priming effect recalled by VR games affects cognitive processing [11].

We focused on the relationship between the elderly priming effect and walking in VR, which is yet to be studied based on combining the priming effect and VR (Fig. 1).

Fig. 1. Modulation of the walking speed by the virtual avatar moving alongside

2   Method

2.1   Participants

Eighteen participants (9 women and 9 men, aged 19–33) were considered in the study. The participants were unaware of the purpose of the experiment. Fourteen participants were acquaintances of the author, and four people unknown to the authors and recruited through social networking services. All participants had normal vision (including corrected), and no visual or vestibular sensory deficits were reported.

2.2   Apparatus

The experiment was conducted indoors (approximately $5\,\text{m}\times10\,\text{m}$) inside the Engineering Building #1, University of Tokyo. Participants wore a head-mounted display (HMD) (Oculus Quest2), held an Oculus Touch controller in their right hand, and walked in the experimental space. Head movements in the real space corresponded to head movements in the VR space, and the image was updated in conjunction with the movement in the real space, to simulate a sensation of walking in VR space.

2.3   Avatars Walking Alongside

In the experiment, avatars walked side by side with the participant as displayed in Fig. 2. The type of avatar (3D model) displayed was a combination of texture differences ("without texture" and "with texture") and motion differences ("young man walking" and "old man walking") (Fig. 3). The motions were selected from Adobe mixamo[1], and the motion data were attached to the 3D model of each avatar. The size of the 3D models, the number of pieces placed in the space, and the walking cycle were identical. We used an avatar with two patterns of "no texture" and "human" for texture, and two patterns of "young" and "old" for motion (Fig. 4). The sex of the avatar was matched to that of each participant.

2.4   Elderly Priming

Priming stimuli are of two types, namely direct or indirect priming. In the current experiment, the indirect priming stimulus was provided using the scrambled sentences test (SST), in which participants were asked to create sentences freely using multiple given words randomly. In accordance with the preceding study, we created 30 sets of SSTs in which five words were arranged in a row. Furthermore, we prepared two word-sets, one containing the geriatric stimulus and the other containing only neutral words. Of the 30 sets, 15 sets contained words that included geriatric stimuli. The words used for the geriatric stimuli were strict,

---

[1] https://www.mixamo.com/.

Fig. 2. Virtual space and avatars used in the experiment

Fig. 3. Motion of a young man walking (upper row) and the old man walking (lower row)

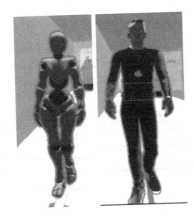

Fig. 4. Appearance of the 3D models used in the experiment. Without texture (left) and with texture (right)

bitter, obedient, conservative, knit, ancient, helpless, dependent, alone, withdrawn, traditional, retired, forgetful, bingo, polite, stubborn, wise, lonely, gray, sentimental, old, worried, cautious, selfish, and gullible, in accordance with previous research. For neutral words, we selected words that have not been applied to elderly stimuli in previous studies [6].

Table 1 details an example of the SST used in the experiment: each line has five words, and participants were asked to repeat the process of creating sentences freely using four of the five words, 30 times per set.

Table 1. Example of words for the scrambled sentences test (SST)

Work	I	Helpless	Always	Depend
Go	Strong	Charming	Ancient	She
Someday	Personal	You	Still	Work
Together	They	There	Conservative	Decisive
Obedient	Quick	He	Deceive	Understand
Food stalls	Anytime	Ramen	I	Sunny
Student	Knit	Not so much	Strict	Him
Up	Wrinkle	He	Often	Sea
Territorial	Alone	Already	I	Withdrawal
Traditional	Night	She	Bitter	Mountain
Cutting	Mass	Little	Desk	Paper
View	Eat	I	Sometimes	Like
Room	Clean	Early	Girlfriend	Sleep
Rare	Snowy	Crowd	Very	Exciting
Cool	They	River	Thirsty	Insects

2.5   Procedures

The experiments were performed in the following sequence. Elderly stimuli were included in the SST task in either Steps 1 or 6. The order of Steps 1 and 6 and that of the avatars were randomly assigned to each participant.

Step.1 Perform the SST task.

Step.2 Wear HMD and walk two round trips with no avatar displayed (just practice).

Step.3 Walk one round trip in each condition where the avatar is displayed (included condition under which no avatar displayed for measuring baseline)

Step.4 Respond to questionnaire answers.

Step.5 Repeat Steps 3–4.

Step.6 Remove the HMD and perform the SST task again.

Step.7 Put on the HMD.

Step.8 Repeat Steps 3–4.

2.6   Data

The walking speed and walking cycle were calculated from the elapsed time and the position coordinates obtained by the inside-out tracking system built into the HMD. The subjective scores for the sense of walking were collected using a Google Form questionnaire, which was answered for each one round of walking. The data were analyzed using Python and R. Significant differences were accepted if $p < 0.05$. The questionnaire items are presented in Table 2.

Table 2. Questionnaire items

Q1	How strongly were you aware of the avatar's presence while walking?	7: Strongly aware of avatar, 4: Neutral, 1: Not at all aware
Q2	Did the avatar's movements make it easier/more difficult to walk?	7: Felt easier, 4: Neutral, 1: Felt harder
Q3	How immersive was the avatar?	7: More immersive, 4: Neutral, 1: less immersive
Q4	Did you feel lighter/heavier when walking with the avatar?	7: Felt heavier, 4: Neutral, 1: Felt lighter
Q5	Did you feel the presence of people on either side?	7: Felt much, 4: Neutral, 1: Not at all

3   Result

Figure 5 displays the difference in the walking speed ratio due to parallel walking avatars. The walking speed of subjects increased from baseline in all conditions (Fig. 6).

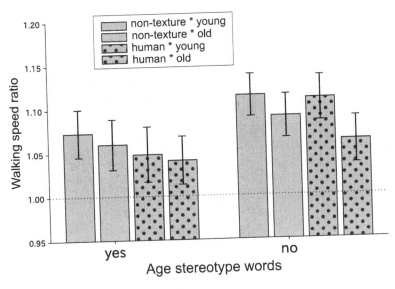

Fig. 5. Modulation in the walking speed ratio by the virtual avatar. Horizontal dotted lines indicate the baseline (walking speed without any avatars).

Data of eight groups were collected: two patterns of "yes" and "no" for the priming effect, two patterns of "nothing" and "human" for texture, and two patterns of "young" and "old" for motion.

Two assumptions regarding distribution (normality and homogeneity of variance) were tested as preconditions for multiple testing. First, a Shapiro–Wilk normality test was performed for each of the eight groups. Therefore, several groups were non-normal. Next, the equal variances of the eight groups were tested. Thus, several groups were non-normal in terms of the walking speed, and most groups were non-normal in terms of questionnaire responses. The Bartlett's test of equal variances was used to test for equal variances among multiple groups. The results revealed that there were no significant differences, no differences in distribution among the groups, and the assumption of equal variances was satisfied. First, we performed an aligned rank transform ANOVA to check for effects and interactions. Next, we performed multiple comparisons in this experiment using the Steel–Dwass test, which can be applied to nonparametric groups.

In terms of the walking speed, the one-way interaction between the motion and the priming was not significant but large effect size was observed ($F(1,11) = 4.00$, $p = 0.064$, $\eta_p^2 = 0.216$). No other possible interactions ($ps > 0.264$) were significant. No main effects were statistically significant ($ps > 0.099$). In terms of the questionnaire response, significant differences were observed in motion ($F(1,11) = 20.43$, $p = 0.0004$, $\eta_p^2 = 0.577$) for Q2, and motion ($F(1,11) = 6.50$, $p = 0.022$, $\eta_p^2 = 0.302$) for Q4, and texture ($F(1,11) = 4.83$, $p = 0.044$, $\eta_p^2 = 0.243$) for Q5.

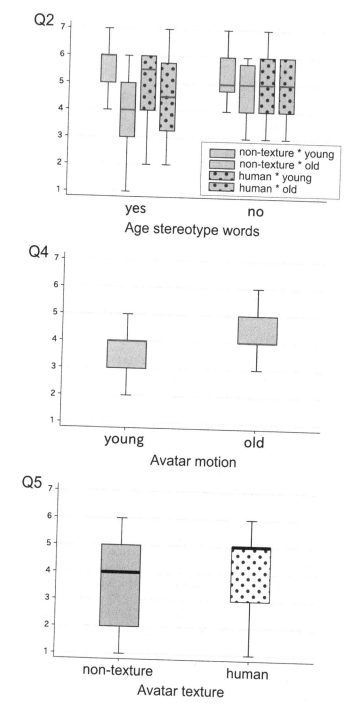

Fig. 6. Change in the sense of walking by the virtual avatar

4   Discussion

The results revealed that participants walked faster when walking with avatars than the baseline (i.e., walking without any avatars). This result is consistent with that of previous research [3].

A large effect size was observed for the interaction between the priming effect and the motion. When the motion of the avatar was young, participants were strongly affected by the age stereotype words. In terms of questionnaire, subjects exhibited significant conscious sensory changes, such as feeling lighter and easier to walk, depending on the difference in motion. These results indicate that just the motion of an old avatar has already affected the subject and induced emotions such as feeling heavy. However, even if the motion does not make the subject think of an elderly person, such as an avatar motion of the young, showing age stereotype words could induce such effects.

In this experiment, we tested the hypothesis that the results of the priming effect in the VR space are similar to the results of previous studies conducted in the physical world. The results of the priming effect revealed a difference in the walking speed as in the physical world, but the same results were not obtained because the VR space imitated the physical world. If we use a VR space whose appearance differs from the physical world, the effect may disappear.

In the VR space, an avatar embodiment of oneself can be obtained. The Proteus effect is a typical example of the effect of avatar embodiment on human attitudes and behavior [10]. Studies have combined the Proteus effect of elderly avatars embodiment and human exercise [8,9]. In the future, studies should focus on the effect of the walking speed and sensation when a young or old avatar is embodied and a mirror is placed so that the user can recognize his/her own body when walking.

5   Conclusion

This study examined the effects of various textures and movement of human avatars on the walking speed/sensation as well as the elderly priming effect. We could obtain results such as significant rate changes in priming effects and motion interactions. This study has the following limitations: The first limitation is the inadequate diversity in participants. For example, many of the subjects were experiencing VR world for the first time and the age range of the participants, who were mainly university students, was narrow. The results of this study can be used in pedestrian guidance technology using avatars in the real space and may contribute to the comparative study of differences in the psychological effects between real and VR spaces. In the future, studies should be conducted to investigate psychological effects by focusing on the VR space, rather than the real space.

Acknowledgement. This study was supported by JSPS Grant-in-Aid for Scientific Research (A) Grant Number 21H04883.

References

1. Rio, K.W., Rhea, C.K., Warren, W.H.: Follow the leader: visual control of speed in pedestrian following. J. Vis. **14**(2), 1–16 (2014)
2. Naoto Y., Wang C., Kazuki U., Kenji M., and Tomoko Y.: Proposal of attention guidance method based on induced behaviour of multiple virtual agents for pedestrians. Human-agent Interaction Symposium 2020. P-29, (2020) (in Japanese)
3. Tanizaki, M., Matsumoto, K., Narumi, T., Kuzuoka, H., Amemiya, T.: Modulation of walking speed by the change in motion and shape of the virtual avatar moving alongside. Trans. Virtual Reality Soc. Japan **26**(3), 208–218 (2021). (in Japanese)
4. Doyen, S., Klein, O., Pichon, C.L., Cleeremans, A.: Behavioral priming: it's all in the mind, but whose mind? PLoS ONE **7**(1), 1–7 (2012)
5. Richard, H.T.: Nudge, not sludge. Science **361**(6401), 431–431 (2018)
6. Perdue, C.W., Gurtman, M.B.: Evidence for the automaticity of ageism. J. Exp. Soc. Psychol. **26**(3), 199–216 (1990)
7. Beaudoin M., Barra J., Dupraz L., Mollier-Sabet P., Guerraz M.: The impact of embodying an "elderly" body avatar on motor imagery. Exp. Brain Res. **238**(6), 1467–1478 (2020)
8. Tammy Lin J.-H., and Wu D.-Y.: Exercising with embodied young avatars: how young vs. older avatars in virtual reality affect perceived exertion and physical activity among male and female elderly individuals. Front. Psychol. **12**, 693545 (2021)
9. Yee, N., and Bailenson, J.N.: Walk a mile in digital shoes: the impact of embodied perspective-taking on the reduction of negative stereotyping in immersive virtual environments. In: Proceeding of the 9th Annual International Workshop on Presence. Cleveland, Ohio, USA (2006)
10. Yee, N., Bailenson, J.N.: The proteus effect: the effect of transformed self-representation on behavior. Hum. Commun. Res. **33**, 271–290 (2007)
11. Wang, J., Wang, L.: Influence of affective priming effect of immersive virtual reality horror games on cognitive processing of college students. Revista Argentina de Clínica Psicológica. **29**, 1213–1222 (2020)

Flow State and Physiological Responses During Alternative Uses Task in Real and Virtual Working Environments

Hiroyuki Kuraoka(✉) , Mitsuo Hinoue , and Chie Kurosaka

University of Occupational and Environmental Health, Japan, Kitakyushu, Japan
h-kuraoka@health.uoeh-u.ac.jp

Abstract. This study investigated the flow state and physiological responses during an alternative use task (AUT) in a virtual reality (VR) environment among 15 healthy male undergraduate students. The experiment consisted of two conditions: a) conducting the task in a laboratory setting (REAL condition); b) performing the task in a VR environment replicating the laboratory setting (VR condition). Each session comprised a 5-min rest period and a 15-min task performance. Different task conditions were applied to two sets of conditions. This study compared subjective assessments (flow scores, subjective mental workload, and simulator sickness), task performance, and physiological responses between the conditions. The results showed no significant differences in the flow scores between the conditions. Conversely, subjective mental workload, physical demand, and frustration results in VR were significantly higher than those in the REAL condition. Furthermore, task performance was significantly lower in the VR condition, suggesting that increased eye fatigue may increase workload and lead to decreased performance. In terms of physiological response results, the heart rate increased significantly during task performance compared to the rest period, indicating heightened sympathetic nervous system activity. Additionally, during task performance, there was a significant decrease in the low-frequency (LF:0.04–0.15 Hz) and high-frequency components (HF:0.15–0.40 Hz) of heart rate variability, suggesting the inhibition of parasympathetic nervous system activity. Therefore, owing to the difficulty level of the task and the prominent negative effects of the HMD, the AUT used in this study may not induce a flow state, despite the immersive VR environment.

Keywords: Virtual Reality · Alternative Uses Task · Flow State

1 Introduction

Virtual reality (VR) is becoming an increasingly common technology and many studies have investigated the positive effects of using VR as a tool in daily life [1]. VR environments as head-mounted displays (HMDs) can induce a flow state easier than real-world work environments owing to their ability to enhance user productivity and immersion. Flow state "in the zone," refers to an optimal psychological state characterized by intense focus, effortless involvement, and a deep sense of enjoyment during an activity [2, 3]. A

J. Y. C. Chen et al. (Eds.): HCII 2023, LNCS 14058, pp. 111–121, 2023.
https://doi.org/10.1007/978-3-031-48050-8_8

previous study reported that playing a video game in a VR environment affects a user's time perception and immersion, leading to flow state more easily than in a real-world (REAL) environment [4]. Given the limited experimental research on flow states in virtual reality (VR) environments, fundamental investigations must be conducted on the influence of various stimuli and tasks on flow experiences within VR spaces.

In addition to subjective assessments such as the Flow State Scale [5], employing methods that allow for continuous evaluation, including physiological indices such as brainwaves and heart rate, is considered desirable for assessing the flow state. Previous experiments involving professional pianists demonstrated a correlation between flow and physiological indices, where the induction of flow through the repeated performance of challenging musical pieces resulted in an increased heart rate (HR) and heart rate variability (HRV) index, LF/HF, suggesting a link with sympathetic nervous system activity [6]. Tian et al. [7] noted an association between flow and sympathetic nervous system activity in an experiment using a personal computer (PC) environment, suggesting the potential of the heart rate as an index for detecting the state immediately before entering flow. Katahira [8] reported a relationship between flow and theta waves in the prefrontal region of the brain. However, simulator sickness is a well-known symptom of the physiological effects of VR using HMD; simulator sickness impacts autonomic nervous system activity, leading to increased heart rate [9], increased galvanic skin response [10], and changes in heart rate variability indices, such as increased LF and decreased HF [11, 12]. Therefore, because the existing knowledge of physiological indices associated with flow has been derived from studies conducted in real-world environments, the relationship between the flow state and physiological responses in VR environments must be investigated.

The alternative uses task (AUT) has been reported as a task for evaluating creativity [13], and several previous studies have used this task to investigate its impact on creativity in VR environments [14, 15]. A previous study reported improved task performance under VR conditions using an HMD [15]. However, because validation of the flow state during the AUT has not been reported, this study compared the flow state and physiological responses during task execution between real-world and VR environments.

2 Method

2.1 Participants

Fifteen healthy undergraduate students (mean age: 22.1 ± 3.8 years) participated in the study. This study was approved by the Ethics Committee of the University of Occupational and Environmental Health, Japan (Reception No. R4–024).

2.2 Experimental Procedure

After obtaining their informed consent, electrodes and sensors were attached to the participants upon their arrival at the laboratory. First, during the resting period (REST), the participants were asked to watch a video of a forest scene (Fig. 1) for 5 min while seated. Based on a previous study, there were no differences between the baseline and

Fig. 1. Forest scene in the video [17]

video conditions in terms of physiological responses [16, 17]. Therefore, we used the physiological data from REST as a baseline.

After 5-min resting, the participants performed the AUT for 15 min. The experimental procedure consisted of two sets, each comprising a 5-min rest period followed by the task. The experimental conditions for each set were as follow: REAL and VR conditions (Fig. 2). In REAL condition, the participants performed the tasks on a 49-inch monitor in the experimental laboratory. In VR condition, the participants performed the tasks in a simulated VR environment. The order of the task conditions was randomized for each participant. In this condition, participants wore an HMD (VIVE Pro Eye, HTC Corp.) during the experiment.

After completing the tasks under both conditions, the National Aeronautics and Space Administration Task Load Index (NASA-TLX) [18] and Flow Experience Checklist [19] were administered to the participants to evaluate their subjective experiences. In the VR condition, Simulator-sickness questionnaire [20] was administered after both the rest period and task performance. Additionally, physiological measurements were performed throughout the experiment.

Fig. 2. Experimental condition (Left: REAL condition; Right: VR condition)

2.3 Alternative Uses Task

The Alternative Uses Task (AUT) was used to assess divergent thinking in creative cognition [14]. In the AUT, participants were asked to respond to various ideas regarding alternative applications for everyday items (e.g., bricks and paper clips). In this experiment, three sets of illustrations, each consisting of four cards, were prepared (Set A: iron, water bottle, traffic cone, and scrub brush; Set B: cardboard box, baseball bat, inflatable ring, and slipper; and Set C: frying pan, hanger, beaker, and rain boots). Illustrations for each set were selected based on difficulty adjustments conducted in the preliminary experiment. The task involved initially presenting the participants with illustrations of familiar objects for 30 s, then allowing them 2.5 min to write as many ideas as possible on a response sheet. After completion of the writing task, a one-minute interval was provided, and four illustrations were presented for 15 min.

AUT responses were assessed based on the following four dimensions: fluency, flexibility, elaboration, and originality [21–23]. Fluency represents the total number of valid responses provided by the participants, excluding responses deemed unfeasible, excessively abstract, ambiguous, or too commonly used. Flexibility measures various response categories, disregarding responses that overlap in terms of categories. The elaboration was determined by calculating the number of words per response. Originality refers to responses that are statistically uncommon compared to those in the overall set of responses. One point was assigned to responses that accounted for less than 5% of the total responses, and all other responses were assigned zero. These points are summarized below:

2.4 Subjective Assessments

Flow experience checklist was used to evaluate the flow state [19]. The checklist employed a 7-point rating scale to collect responses and calculate scores for three items: the conscious experience through positive emotions and immersion (immersion), confidence in ability (ability), and goal challenge (challenge).

The Japanese version of the Simulator Sickness Questionnaire (SSQ) was used to evaluate VR sickness [24]. The participants responded to the questionnaire using a 4-point rating scale. The scores were calculated by applying Kennedy et al.'s scoring criteria, including sub-items, such as oculomotor function, disorientation, and nausea, with the total score representing the overall tendency.

Subjective mental workload (MWL) scores were obtained using NASA-TLX. This index contains six subscales: mental demand (MD), physical demand (PD), temporal demand (TD), performance (OP), effort (EF), and frustration (FR). The weighted mean (Adaptive Weighted Workload: AWWL) of these six subscales was calculated; it is the weighted average score of the six subscales calculated using the weighting coefficients defined by the rank order of the raw scores without paired comparisons [25].

2.5 Physiological Assessments

Electrocardiogram (ECG), tissue blood flow (TBF), tissue blood volume (TBV), and skin potential (SPL) were recorded throughout the experiment. ECG parameters, including RR interval and heart rate, were obtained from the waveform acquired through the CM5 leads placed on the chest. For heart rate variability analysis, power spectral analysis using autoregressive modeling was performed to extract the power spectrum in the low-frequency components (LF: 0.05–0.15 Hz) and high-frequency components (HF: 0.15–0.40 Hz). The LF/HF ratio was then calculated.

The TBF and TBV were measured by attaching a sensor from a laser doppler blood flow meter (OMEGAWAVE OMEGA FLOW FLO-C1) to the tip of the nose. The SPL was assessed using the forearm as the reference site, and the skin potential level of the thenar eminence of the left palm was measured using a DC amplifier (Nihon Kohden AD-641G).

2.6 Statistical Analysis

For statistical analysis, paired t-tests were conducted to compare the flow experience checklist and NASA-TLX between the different task conditions. For the SSQ, the mean values were computed for the VR condition during both the resting and task periods, and paired t-tests were performed. Task performance was evaluated by calculating the mean score for each item, followed by paired t-tests for comparisons between conditions. Regarding physiological responses, the latter half of the 3-min rest period (REST) was selected to examine temporal changes, while the task period was divided into four blocks (TASK1, TASK2, TASK3, TASK4) based on the questions, resulting in a total of five blocks for analysis. Standardized scores for the five blocks were obtained for each participant. Two-way repeated-measures analysis of variance with task conditions (2) × blocks (5) was used to analyze the differences between factors and interactions with task conditions and blocks. Degree of freedom was applied using the Greenhouse-Geisser correction. Tukey's post hoc tests were performed on all significant main effects.

3 Results and Discussion

3.1 AUT Scores

The AUT scores are shown in Fig. 3. All AUT scores for VR were significantly lower than those for REAL (fluency, $p < .01$, Flexibility, $p < .01$, Originality, $p < .01$, Elaboration, $p < .01$).

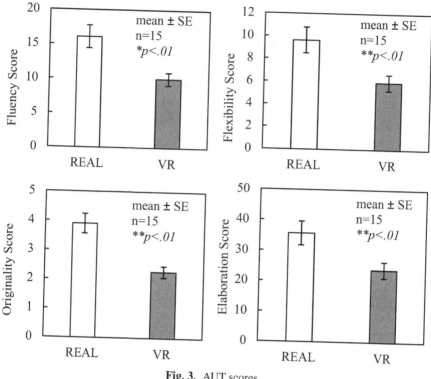

Fig. 3. AUT scores

3.2 Subjective Score

The FSS results showed no significant differences in any subscale or total score (Fig. 4). The SSQ scores showed that the oculomotor and overall scores in TASK were significantly higher than those in REST (Fig. 5). The NASA-TLX scores showed that the PD and FR subscales were significantly higher in the VR than in the REAL group (Fig. 6). However, there was no significant difference in the AWWL scores.

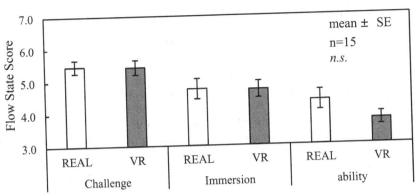

Fig. 4. Flow State Scores

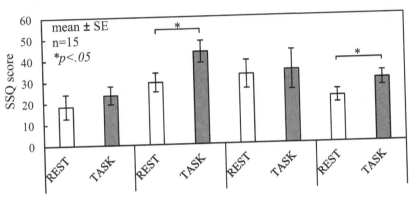

Fig. 5. SSQ scores

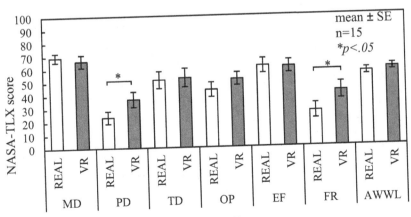

Fig. 6. NASA-TLX scores

3.3 Physiological Indices

Figures 7, 8 and 9 show the changes in the HR and HRV indices, respectively. Alphabet letters in each graph indicate homogenous subset results by Tukey's method. Regarding HR, no significant main effect of the condition was observed. However, a significant main effect of the block was found ($p < .01$). In both conditions, HR was significantly higher in all TASK blocks than in REST. For LF, no significant main effect of the condition was found. However, a significant main effect of the block was observed ($p < .01$). In the REAL condition, a significantly lower LF was observed in TASK1, TASK2, and TASK4 compared to REST. In the VR condition, a significantly lower LF was found in all blocks of TASKs compared to REST. Regarding HF, no significant main effect of the condition was found. However, a significant main effect of block was observed ($p < .01$). In the VR condition, a significantly lower HF was observed in all TASK blocks compared to REST, whereas in the REAL condition, there was a significant difference between REST and TASK3. No significant effects of the block or condition were observed for LF/HF.

Regarding TBV, TBF, and SPL, no significant main effects of the block or condition were observed. No interactions were observed for any of the indices.

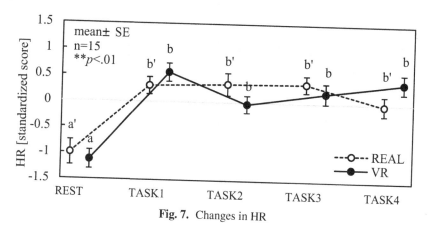

Fig. 7. Changes in HR

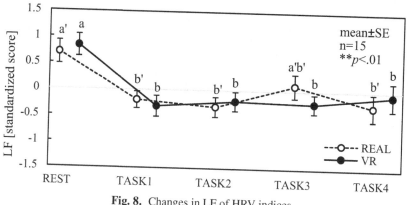

Fig. 8. Changes in LF of HRV indices

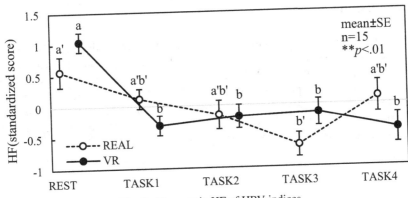

Fig. 9. Changes in HF of HRV indices

4   Discussions

Based on the results of the flow scores, the AUT used in this study could not induce a state of flow, despite the working environment. Lower scores on the ability factor indicated that the tasks were difficult and did not fulfill the prerequisites for entering a state of flow. To achieve flow, the difficulty level must be adjusted to encourage the generation of as many ideas as possible for the presented objects. Therefore, the difficulty settings considered in this study might be inappropriate. Furthermore, the results from other subjective measures indicated a significantly negative impact of working in VR environment. A previous VR study using AUT reported that visual stimulation through an HMD led to improved performance and immersion [15]. However, our study yielded results contrary to this finding. As aforementioned, simulator sickness, such as motion sickness, is a known negative side effect of HMD use [26, 27]. Our study also showed an increase in the oculomotor SSQ score and higher physical demand in NASA-TLX score during the task, suggesting an overall tendency towards simulator sickness. Furthermore, post-experiment introspection reports indicated that the negative effects may have outweighed the positive effects, such as enjoyment and deep immersion in the VR working environment, given that all eight participants were first-time HMD users.

Regarding physiological responses, an increase in heart rate from baseline was observed under both conditions, indicating increased sympathetic nervous system activity evoked by the mental tasks. However, no significant effects were observed owing to differences in the working environment. In contrast, the heart rate variability indices showed a significant decrease in LF and HF in the VR condition, suggesting inhibition of parasympathetic nervous system activity. These results were inconsistent with those of previous studies [11, 12]. A previous study reported that the unfamiliar use of an HMD increased tension and influenced autonomic nervous system activity [28]. Therefore, in studies involving the use of HMD, a longer adaptation to the experimental environment, such as a laboratory or office space, and a pre-investigation of the user burden is required.

5 Conclusion

This study compared the flow state and physiological responses during task execution between real-world and VR environments. The AUT used in this study failed to induce a state of flow despite the immersive VR environment. This may be because of the difficulty level of the task and the prominent negative effects of the HMD. To experimentally investigate the flow state using an HMD, participants must be carefully screened in terms of their frequency of VR device usage and years of experience to minimize negative effects such as eye fatigue in VR technology.

References

1. Clemente, M., Rodríguez, A., Rey, B., Alcañiz, M.: Assessment of the influence of navigation control and screen size on the sense of presence in virtual reality using EEG. Expert Syst. Appl. **41**, 1584–1592 (2014)
2. Csikszentmihalyi, M.: Beyond Boredom and Anxiety, pp. 38–43. Josey-Bass Publishers, San Francisco (1975)
3. Csikszentmihalyi, M.: Flow: the psychology of optimal experience. J. Leis. Res. **24**(1), 93–94 (1990)
4. Rutrecht, H., Wittman, M., Khoshnoud, S., Igarzabal, A.F: Time Speeds up during flow states: a study in virtual reality with the video game thumper. Timing Time Percept. **1**, 1–24 (2021)
5. Jackson, S.A., Ford, S.K., Kimiecik, J.C., Marsh, H.W.: Psychological correlates of flow in sport. J. Sport Exerc. Psychol. **20**, 358–378 (1998)
6. De Manzano, Ö., Theorell, T., Harmat, L., Ullén, F.: The psychophysiology of flow during piano playing. Emotion **10**(3), 301–311 (2010)
7. Tian, Y., Bian, Y., Han, P., Wang, P., Gao, F., Chen, Y.: Physiological signal analysis for evaluating flow during playing of computer games of varying difficulty. Front. Psychol **8**, 1–10 (2015)
8. Katahira, K., Yamazaki, Y., Yamaoka, C., Ozaki, H., Nakagawa, S., Nagata, N.: EEG correlates of the flow state: a combination of increased frontal theta and moderate frontocentral alpha rhythm in the mental arithmetic task. Front. Psychol. **9**, 1–11 (2018)
9. Nalivaiko, E., Davis, S.L., Blackmore, K.L., Vakulin, A., Nesbitt, K.V.: Cybersickness provoked by head-mounted display affects cutaneous vascular tone, heart rate and reaction time. Physiol. Behav. **151**, 583–590 (2015)
10. Kim, Y.Y., Kim, H.J., Kim, E.N., Ko, H.D., Kim, H.T.: Characteristic changes in the physiological components of cybersickness. Psychophysiol. **425**, 616–625 (2005)
11. Zuzewicz, K., Saulewicz, A., Konarska, M., Kaczorowski, Z.: Heart rate variability and motion sickness during forklift simulator driving. Int. J. Occup. Saf. Ergon. **17**(4), 403–410 (2011)
12. Malinska, M., Zuzewicz, K., Bugajska, J., Grabowski, A.: Heart rate variability (HRV) during virtual reality immersion. Int. J. Occup. Saf. Ergon. **21**, 47–54 (2015)
13. Guilford, J.P.: Creativity: Yesterday, today and tomorrow. J. Creat. Behav. **1**(1), 3–14 (1967)
14. Palanica, A., Lyons, A., Cooper, M., Lee, A., Fossat, Y.: A comparison of nature and urban environments on creative thinking across different levels of reality. J. Environ. Psychol. **63**, 44–51 (2019)
15. Ichimura, K.: Effects of virtual reality's viewing medium and the environment's spatial openness on divergent thinking. PLoS ONE **18**(3), 1–13 (2023)
16. Brown, D.K., Barton, J.L., Gladwell, V.F.: Viewing nature scenes positively affects recovery of autonomic function following acute-mental stress. Environ. Sci. Technol. **47**, 5562–5569 (2013)

17. Kurosaka, C., Kuraoka, H., Sakamoto, H., Miyake, S.: Physiological responses induced by mental workload simulating daily work. In: Book of HCI International 2020, pp. 359–366 (2020)
18. Hart, S.G., Staveland, L.E.: Development of NASA-TLX (Task Load Index): results of empirical and theoretical research. Adv. Psychol. **52**, 139–183 (1988)
19. Ishimura, I., Kodama, M.: Flow experiences in everyday activities of Japanese college students: Autotelic people and time management. Jpn. J. Psychol. Res. **51**, 47–54 (2009)
20. Kennedy, R.S., Lane, N.E., Berbaum, K.S., Lilienthal, M.G.: Simulator sickness questionnaire: an enhanced method for quantifying simulator sickness. Int. J. Aviat. Psychol. **3**(3), 203–220 (1993)
21. Lewis, C., Lovatt, P.J.: Breaking away from set patterns of thinking: improvisation and divergent thinking. Thinking Skills Creat. **9**, 46–58 (2013)
22. Milgram, R.M., Milgram, N.A.: Creative thinking and creative performance in Israeli students. J. Educ. Psychol. **68**, 255–259 (1976)
23. Palmon, R.R., Forthmann, B., Barbot, B.: Scoring divergent thinking tests: a review and systematic framework. Psychol. Aesthet. Creat. Arts **13**(2), 144–152 (2019)
24. Mishima, M., Ishida, T.: The subjective severity of simulator sickness induced by driving simulator and its correlation with the psychophysiological measurement results. Jpn. J. Ergon. **44**(5), 279–289 (2007)
25. Miyake, S., Kumashiro, M.: Subjective mental workload assessment technique -an introduction to NASA-TLX and SWAT and a proposal of simple scoring methods. Jpn. J. Ergon. **29**, 399–408 (1993)
26. Park, S., Kim, L., Kwon, J., et al.: Evaluation of visual-induced motion sickness from head-mounted display using heartbeat evoked potential: a cognitive load-focused approach. Virt. Real. **26**, 979–1000 (2022)
27. Mazloumi, G.A., Walker, F.R., Hodgson, D.M., Nalivaiko, E.: A comparative study of cyber-sickness during exposure to virtual reality and "classic" motion sickness: are they different? J. Appl. Physiol. **125**, 1670–1680 (2018)
28. Shima, A., Hamada, K., Nihei, M., Nakamura, T., Toshima, K., Hiyama, A.: Basic study of the influence on autonomic nervous activity of older people using virtual reality: validation experiment in young health participants with controlled baseline. In: 26th Proceedings of Virtual Reality Society of Japan, 2B2–6, VRSJ, Tokyo (2016)

A Virtual Reality Object Interaction System with Complex Hand Interactions

Joan Dominique L. Lee(✉) ⓘ, Dan Mark D. Restoles ⓘ, and Eric Cesar E. Vidal Jr. ⓘ

Ateneo de Manila University, Katipunan Ave., 1108 Quezon City, Metro Manila, Philippines
lee.joandominique@gmail.com, {drestoles,evidal}@ateneo.edu

Abstract. This study explores the use of complex hand interactions in virtual reality (VR) games. This paper presents a preliminary object interaction system that supports the combination of several accessory actions to develop more complex interactions. A proof-of-concept demo is built around this system, implementing three such complex interactions: twist, lever, and hit. Furthermore, a user test is conducted to evaluate users' experience of these interactions with varying levels of complexity. The study finds that most participants preferred the more complex versions of the interactions compared to their simpler counterparts.

Keywords: Object Interaction · Interaction Complexity

1 Introduction

With the input and output mechanisms afforded by head-mounted displays (HMDs) and hand tracked controllers, there are new opportunities and challenges for designing user interactions in virtual reality (VR) systems and games. With head-mounted displays (HMDs) having become commercialized and more affordable, much attention has been given to VR, especially by the gaming industry [3, 12]. HMDs act both as an input device and an output device; acting as a visual display while also performing head tracking, these devices present users with the virtual environment corresponding to their head movement [3]. Together with HMDs, VR setups often make use of additional input devices such as tracked hand-held controllers [3]. Hand tracking facilitated by these devices enables mid-air interactions that allow users to potentially interact with objects in the 3D virtual world in a manner similar to how they would interact with real world physical objects [6].

Vlahovic et al. [12] highlights the role of movement and motor skills in the gaming experience and how VR expands the possibilities of using movement in designing compelling games. While other VR systems may benefit from more straightforward interactions, VR games may benefit from more complex ones, the premise being that virtual actions that more closely mimic real-world actions may increase player immersion. Despite this, the preceding study identified that much of existing VR research focuses on optimizing interaction techniques, and there remains a gap for research on gaming-specific VR interaction design.

© The Author(s), under exclusive license to Springer Nature Switzerland AG 2023
J. Y. C. Chen et al. (Eds.): HCII 2023, LNCS 14058, pp. 122–134, 2023.
https://doi.org/10.1007/978-3-031-48050-8_9

One challenge in implementing complex user movements in VR is its inherent technical difficulty. Dodoo et al. [2], in developing a training VR simulation for assembling a mock aircraft wing, noted that it was challenging to accurately emulate the action of positioning virtual objects using Oculus Touch controllers, so they simplified the action by having objects snap into place. More generally, Ashtari et al. [1] identified that augmented reality (AR) and VR creators, across different levels of proficiency, experience difficulty in handling the technical implementation as well as the design for the physical aspect of these technologies.

This research attempts to address these challenges by developing an object interaction system which supports these complex movements in VR. More specifically, our research is interested in implementing actions which, in their execution, require users to orient virtual objects in certain configurations and perform additional or accessory actions (e.g., rotating the hand to perform a twisting motion). This research attempts to develop a range of complex interactions, supported by an object interaction system that allows developers to easily add accessory actions to an interaction, as well as provide a library of these developed actions which would make it easier to implement and develop more complex interactions.

The developed system and interactions are intended to be used in a larger VR system that will support several upcoming educational applications, in the form of breakout or escape-room styled adventure games. As such, while the object interaction system is intended to be general and adaptable to a wide range of interactions, the interactions developed in this study are intended to support common escape room mechanics as described by Nicholson [7] and Krekhov et al. [4] so that they may be used in upcoming escape room games. Moreover, this research hopes to investigate how users experience these actions in terms of whether it enhances or detracts from said users' overall immersion in a VR game.

The rest of this paper is structured as follows: the second section details the design and development of the object interaction system, describing the different considerations and elements of the system. The third section describes the user study investigating how users experience different levels of complex actions. The fourth section describes the results of the evaluation. Finally, the paper concludes with plans for further improvement and real-world usage of the developed system and interactions.

2   Object Interaction System for Complex Interactions

2.1   Complex Interaction Model

As mentioned earlier, this research is interested in complex hand interactions. These interactions require more from users than simply directing the controller to a target within the virtual world. This research defines these "complex interactions" as actions which, in their execution, require users to orient virtual objects in certain configurations and perform additional or accessory actions. In this section, we define the elements of these interactions using a hierarchical model, depicted in Fig. 1.

Actor and Receiver Objects. These are the main participants in an interaction. Actor objects are what the player uses to interact with the receiver objects. This can be tools

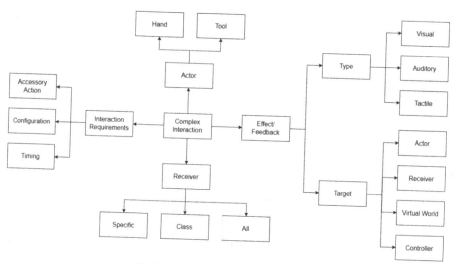

Fig. 1. Complex Interaction Elements

such as screwdrivers or even the players' (virtual) hand. Receiver objects are simply objects upon which an action is executed. Receivers can be a specific object (e.g., using a key for a specific lock), a class of objects (e.g., breaking a vase on hard objects), or all objects (e.g., using a marker to write on any surface).

Interaction Requirements. These define what must be done for an interaction to be completed. Their configuration has to do with the position of the actor and receiver objects in relation to each other, considering factors like distance and angle. Accessory actions are additional actions that must be performed in addition to positioning the actor and receiver objects within range of each other. A very simple example of this would be pressing a button, while a more complex example would be tracing a shape to fulfill an action.

Effect/Feedback. This is an important aspect of the interaction which allows the user to know whether their actions had any effect on the virtual world. The target defines what the interaction influences, whether this be the actors and receivers involved in the interaction, the objects in the virtual world around them, or the players' hardware (e.g., sound effects or haptic feedback).

2.2 System Design and Development

The following section outlines the preliminary design and framework of our object interaction system. Our developed object interaction system works by assigning virtual objects involved in a certain interaction as either actors or receivers. To manage the interaction between these objects, the system uses an object state manager and an action component system.

The object state manager handles the state of the actor objects. This state manager (see Fig. 2) is a generic state machine that can be modified depending on what interacting object or tool is needed, or what intermediary states are needed for interaction. For example, a screwdriver can have an object state manager that only interacts with screws containing a twisting action component only.

This state manager has internal checks for collision (angle and distance) which are computed mathematically, replacing the native collision reported by the underlying game physics engine. Due to this implementation, this state manager requires a position in the local space of the interacting object where the interaction starts, a direction of action, angle range, and distance of interaction. Along with this, the state manager makes an internal check whether the interacting object is interacting with the appropriate action component. The user must press the trigger button on the controller to put the actor object in the "interacting" state. This ensures that the intentionality of an action is preserved, preventing unwanted interaction of the tool with the action components. This works hand in hand with the action component system, which dictates what kind of actions can be performed on a receiver object.

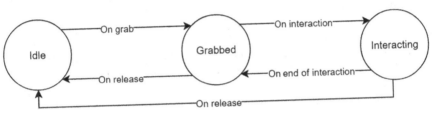

Fig. 2. State Transition Diagram of the Object State Manager

The action component system handles the computation and checks whether a certain action is completed or appropriate. This is another generic system that can be modified depending on what action is needed. These are implemented on certain parts of the receiver object—for example, a screw is a receiver object with the action component located at the screw's drive. The logic behind implementing this check on the receiver object is to allow internal verification and computation of the action, as long as the correct interacting object is used. This action component only has two states—incomplete or complete. Since this specifies the actions (e.g., twisting action to turn a screw) that are necessary to complete the interaction between the receiver object and its corresponding actor object, the same actor object can interact differently with different receiver objects.

This system was developed using Unity version 2021.3. This research also relies on the OpenXR Unity plug-in developed by Khronos which simplifies and supports development across different AR and VR devices [11]. Although there is an attempt to provide cross-compatibility, the current implementation is primarily targeted towards HTC Vive headset and handheld controllers. The OpenXR plug-in includes an XRGrabInteractable script that provides object-grabbing functionality; this is encapsulated and automatically initialized by our own state manager, removing the need to set up the same script multiple times during development. The state manager also interfaces with OpenXR's controls to allow checking and validation of button presses for interactions.

3   User Study Design

Other studies have implemented actions that require more than the simple approach of directing the controller to an intended target. Rogers et al. [8], in exploring interaction fidelity in VR, developed a VR shopkeeper game with two fidelity versions. In the low-fidelity version, players interacted with objects through widgets. In the high-fidelity version, players had to grab hold of objects and perform actions like pouring and turning book pages. Through their study, they found that object manipulation tasks benefited from high interaction fidelity. Lykke et al.[5], in attempting to simulate the weight of objects with VR controllers, created two interaction methods which they referred to as chasing and scooping. They performed a user study consisting of two test sessions, one with chasing and scooping and the other without it. They found that although they were able to successfully simulate the weight of objects with VR controllers and improve interaction realism, these only made small improvements in immersion. They even found that, due to strict implementation of interaction requirements, this may have led to a decrease in enjoyment.

This study hopes to add to this body of work, exploring users' experience of our developed interactions. In this user test, participants equipped the HTC Vive headset and controllers in a sitting position. They were then instructed to perform tasks within each of the developed virtual environments. Three versions of the environment (see Fig. 3) were implemented—low-level, mid-level, and high-level complexity. In each version, participants were instructed to perform the same tasks (see Fig. 4). However, for each version, this required performing the interactions with different levels of action complexity. Partial counterbalancing was used to determine the order of playing the versions for every participant. Our study differs significantly from previous studies in that our user test introduces an intermediate level of action complexity/fidelity (as opposed to just two levels—simple and complex). This is intended to hopefully get a better idea of the proper balance between challenge and ease.

3.1   Testing Environment

Fig. 3. Testing Environment

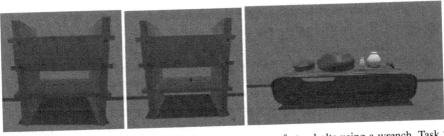

Fig. 4. From left to right: Task 1 (T1) requiring users to unfasten bolts using a wrench, Task 2 (T2) requiring users to remove screws using a screwdriver, and Task 3 (T3) requiring users to break objects on a table using a hammer

In the testing environment, there were three main stations and tasks. The first station consisted of a shelf with a panel bolted to it. The task (T1) in this station was to unfasten these bolts to remove the panel. In the station, a wrench was placed in the lower shelf for players to use. The second station was set up similarly, consisting of a shelf with a panel screwed to it. Here, the task (T2) was still to remove the panel, this time by using a screwdriver on the screws. The third station consisted of a table with varying sizes of rocks and vases. The task (T3) was to break these objects using the hammer also located on the table.

Each version of the virtual environment looked the same aside from the color of the rug in the center of the room, which is used to identify each version. This is to avoid referring to interactions as "complex" or "simple" in the questionnaires and thereby avoid priming or causing bias.

3.2 Test Interactions

To move and interact with the virtual world, participants had to make use of HTC Vive controllers. The trackpads were used to control movement, the grip button was used to grab hold of objects, and the trigger button was used to interact with objects. To complete the aforementioned tasks, participants had to use certain actions while holding onto the objects required for the task. For the low-level complexity version of the virtual environment, all interactions simply required holding the actor object and selecting the trigger button when the receiver object was within its range. Table 1 details the different versions of the said interactions.

Table 1. Testing tasks and their associated accessory actions.

Task	Low-Level Complexity	Mid-Level Complexity	High-Level Complexity
T1	While holding actor object (wrench), press trigger button when near receiver object (bolt)	While holding actor object (wrench), press trigger button while performing **lever action** near receiver object (bolt) until a small set angle is reached	While holding actor object (wrench), press trigger button while performing **lever action** near receiver object (bolt) until required number of rotations has occurred (depending on length of object)
T2	While holding actor object (screwdriver), press trigger button when near receiver object (screw)	While holding actor object (screwdriver), press trigger button while performing **twisting action** near receiver object (screw) until a small set angle is reached	While holding actor object (screwdriver), press trigger button while performing **twisting action** near receiver object (screw) until required number of rotations has occurred (depending on length of object)
T3	While holding actor object (hammer), press trigger button when near receiver object (objects on table)	While holding actor object (hammer), press trigger button while performing **hitting action** near receiver object (objects on table) for a specified number of times	While holding actor object (hammer), press trigger button while performing **hitting action** near receiver object (objects on table) depending on the set amount of strength for said object. Action's strength depends on distance of selecting trigger before striking object

The interactions, as well as how they were implemented in the mid- and high-level complexity versions of the virtual environment, are further explained as follows:

Twist. Requires a twisting action, such as when turning a doorknob or using a screwdriver (see Fig. 5). This was the action required to complete T1. To calculate this action, the z-component of the actor object was checked. In the mid-level complexity version of the interaction, players only had to perform this action until the accumulated angle they had turned on the object reached a low specified angle. In the high-level complexity version of the interaction, players had to perform this action depending on the length of the virtual receiver object.

Lever. Requires a wrench-like action where torque is applied in a class-two lever manner such as turning nuts and bolts (see Fig. 6). To calculate this action, the y-component of the actor object was checked. Like the twist action, in the mid-level complexity version of the interaction, players only had to perform this action until the accumulated angle they had turned on the object reached a low specified angle. In the high-level complexity

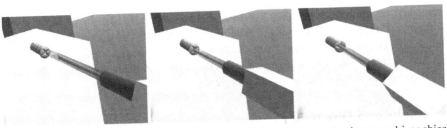

Fig. 5. From left to right: (1) Using controller (indicated by white box) to aim screwdriver object to screw object; (2–3) Gradually rotating screwdriver in a twisting movement.

version of the interaction, players had to perform this action depending on the length of the virtual receiver object.

Fig. 6. From left to right: (1) Using controller (indicated by white box) to aim wrench object to bolt object; (2–4) Gradually rotating wrench around the bolt pivot point.

Hit. Requires a hitting action, such as when swinging a hammer. In the mid-level complexity version of the interaction, players had to put the actor object within and outside the range of the receiver object while selecting the trigger button a certain number of times. In the high-level complexity version of this interaction, it accounted for how different objects would require different levels of strength to break and how hitting from further would cause a stronger strike; the strength was simplified and calculated by getting the distance player pulls trigger using the actor object from receiver object (if within range) until striking the object.

3.3 Research Procedure

Each user test session began with participants answering a demographics questionnaire asking them about their basic information (e.g., age, gender) as well as their prior experience with virtual reality and games. Participants were then instructed on how to use the HTC Vive controllers. The rest of the session was split into three parts: for each part, participants interacted with one game version, completed the three set tasks, and answered an interaction questionnaire for that game version. Testers were also asked to answer a final questionnaire after having played all three versions.

The questionnaires used in this study simplified those used by Rogers et al. [8]. For the questionnaire answered after playing each version, participants were asked to rate how much they liked the individual interactions in each task. In addition to this, they were asked which interactions they liked and disliked the most, along with the reasons for their preference. They were also asked to answer the INTUI questionnaire [10] to evaluate the overall intuitiveness of the actions they encountered in the game version they had tried. The final questionnaire asks participants to indicate the version that they preferred overall and the reason for their preference.

4   Results and Discussion

This section presents and discusses the results of the user study. Overall, 16 adult participants (12 male, 3 female, 1 preferred not to say) were recruited.

4.1   INTUI Questionnaire Results

Table 2. INTUI Questionnaire Results.

Complexity	Low-Level		Mid-Level		High-Level	
INTUI Factors	M	SD	M	SD	M	SD
Effortlessness	6	1.47	5.4	1.26	3.86	1.11
Gut Feeling	4.88	1.74	3.5	1.40	2.86	1.43
Verbalizability	5.83	1.36	6.44	0.76	5.98	0.95
Magical Experience	4.69	1.69	5.47	0.75	5.31	0.86

The INTUI questionnaire developed by Ullrich and Diefenbach [9, 10] has been used in VR to assess the intuitiveness of interactions [8]. The questionnaire assesses four components of intuitive interaction through 16 items on a 7-point semantic differential scale [10]. Ullrich and Diefenbach define those four components as follows:

- Gut feeling has to do with how an interaction is guided by feelings rather than reason; they note that many individuals perceive intuitiveness based on not having to consciously think about an action and instead following what "feels right."
- Verbalizability has to do with how users are able to describe the decisions and steps in an interaction; they note that in an intuitive interaction, users would not be able to easily describe the said interaction as a series of steps.
- Effortlessness has to do with how an interaction can be completed quickly and without strain.
- Magical Experience has to do with how special or extraordinary an interaction feels with intuitive interactions feeling magical; this component is supported when new technologies or interaction concepts are introduced.

Table 2 presents the mean INTUI component scores for each version of the virtual environment. As expected, the low-level version of the virtual environment had the highest scores for effortlessness and gut feeling. On the flipside, it had the lowest score for magical experience. The mid-level version scored the highest for magical experience, leading slightly more than the high-level version. This slight difference is reasonable considering how these actions for these versions were implemented similarly, with the high complexity version usually just requiring prolonged or repeated execution of the action. It is important to note, however, that the mid-level complexity version has considerably higher scores than the high-level complexity version for gut feeling and effortlessness.

4.2 Interaction Preference

Table 3. Interaction Preference

Complexity	Low-Level		Mid-Level		High-Level	
Action	M	SD	M	SD	M	SD
Lever	5.44	1.71	6.06	1.06	3.25	1.73
Screw	5.56	1.46	6.5	0.52	5.56	1.26
Hit	5.75	1.84	6.19	1.05	6.94	0.25

Table 3 presents the results of the questionnaire asking users to rate each action for each version of the virtual environment. From this, users seem to equally prefer the low-level and mid-level versions of the lever action, the mid-level version of the twist action, and the high-level version of the hitting action.

As the highest rated action, the high-complexity version of the hitting action was praised for being easy, satisfying, and easy to understand. A few participants pointed out that they liked the additional detail of how different receiver objects had different capacities for strikes. In contrast, as the lowest rated action, the high-complexity version of the wrench action received many complaints. Many participants mentioned that it was difficult, tedious, and time-consuming. Participants expressed frustration with the action both during the testing and in the open-ended portion of the questionnaires. Two participants noted that it felt as though the effect on the screw was not proportional to the effort they were exerting in real life and that outcomes weren't translating quickly enough. Some even mentioned that it caused their wrist to feel strained.

4.3 Overall Version Preference

Figure 7 depicts the participants' overall preference for each version of the test environment. Out of the 16 participants, only three (18.8%) preferred the simplest version of interactions. The majority preferred the more complex versions with eight (50%) preferring the mid-complexity version and five (31.3%) preferring the high-complexity version.

For those who chose the simplest version, their reasons mentioned that it was easy and convenient. One of them noted that they preferred it because it allowed outcomes to

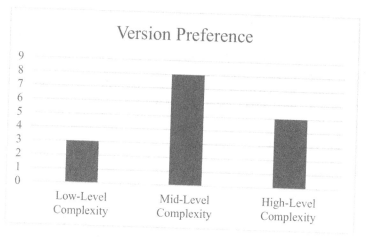

Fig. 7. Overall Version Preference

happen the fastest. Another noted that they had also liked the mid-complexity version similarly.

For those who chose the mid-level complexity version, five of them reasoned that it had a good balance in terms of difficulty and required amount of effort. Two mentioned how they appreciated the realism of actions without making the action require too much effort. Many participants, in reasoning their preference, compared this version to the other two, noting that the low-level version was too easy or dull while the high-level version was too mundane or tedious.

For those who preferred the high-complexity version, the majority mentioned that they appreciated the realism it provided, albeit acknowledging its difficulty. One of these participants preferred it because of its possible uses in therapy and training and another because of how this realism contributed to their immersion. Interestingly, contrary to many of the other participants, some participants perceived this version to be more intuitive than the mid-level complexity version. One participant even believed that this version was the one with milder difficulty. Like with those who preferred the mid-level complexity version, although they preferred this version overall, a participant mentioned wanting to switch out one of the actions (lever action) with its mid-complexity version.

4.4 Limitations

During testing, many participants were confused by the configuration requirements between the actor and receiver objects. The virtual world was set up such that successfully registering an action between two objects required both objects to either barely touch each other or be a minimal distance apart—it did not account for when objects were overlapping with each other. This may have caused some frustration for participants who were correctly executing the actions but not having these register. Still, it is interesting to note that some participants liked having to be more conscious of the configurations between the actor and receiver objects. One participant specified that, among the high-complexity actions, they liked the twist action the most precisely because it wouldn't allow the action to be executed when the screwdriver was overlapping too much with the screw.

5 Conclusion and Future Work

In this preliminary work, we designed and developed a system that supports the implementation of complex interactions. For our user test, we used this system to develop a virtual environment to perform the actions of hitting, twisting, and levering. Users tested these interactions with varying levels of complexity. Overall, most participants preferred the more complex versions of the interactions. To add complexity to actions, this study mostly made use of accessory actions with more complex versions requiring prolonged and/or multiple executions. However, it remains to be seen how other ways of adding complexity to actions can be implemented, while balancing such complexity with the need to maintain user engagement and minimize user frustration.

In upcoming work, we plan to further improve upon the system and these interactions. Thus far, the implemented system and interactions mainly support actor objects which take the form of tools. Effect and feedback have mostly been limited to visual ones, which mainly target receiver objects and the virtual world, but later versions of the system may implement auditory and tactile feedback as well. We plan to improve the system to better account for the various complex interaction factors we detailed earlier in the paper. We also plan to implement this interaction system in a simple VR escape room prototype, to better present the action possibilities provided by this system.

In another iteration of user study, we shall investigate how users respond to the use of our complex actions to complete more of what Vlahovic et al. [12] defines as magical tasks. Compared to the literal approach to implementing VR interactions which attempt to imitate real-life interactions, they define a so-called "magical approach" to implementing interactions as one that provides the player with abilities that go beyond the real world's constraints. User feedback on the more complex actions was often tied to how these added realism to actions. Other studies that have investigated implementing complex actions, as mentioned in the third section, focus on how such actions add to interaction fidelity or action realism; as a counterpoint, it would be interesting to investigate how added complexity affects users' experience regardless of whether such complexity actually increases interaction fidelity.

Acknowledgement. This research is part of a larger ongoing project of the Ateneo Laboratory for the Learning Sciences (ALLS) with grants provided by DOST-PCIEERD (through their Grants-In-Aid program, project no. 11169), Accenture Philippines, and Ateneo de Manila University. We would also like to thank Kenneth King L. Ko, Dominique Marie Antoinette B. Manahan, laboratory head Maria Mercedes T. Rodrigo, and the rest of ALLS for providing invaluable support and assistance with this study.

References

1. Ashtari, N., Bunt, A., McGrenere, J., Nebeling, M., Chilana, P.K.: Creating augmented and virtual reality applications: current practices, challenges, and opportunities. In: Proceedings

of the 2020 CHI Conference on Human Factors in Computing Systems, pp. 1–13. ACM (2020). https://doi.org/10.1145/3313831.3376722

2. Dodoo, E.R., et al.: Evaluating commodity hardware and software for virtual reality assembly training. Electron. Imaging **2018**(3), 468–471 (2018). https://doi.org/10.2352/ISSN.2470-1173.2018.03.ERVR-468

3. Kim, Y.M., Rhiu, I., Yun, M.H.: A systematic review of a virtual reality system from the perspective of user experience. Int. J. Hum.-Comput. Interact. **36**(10), 893–910 (2020). https://doi.org/10.1080/10447318.2019.1699746

4. Krekhov, A., Emmerich, K., Rotthaler, R., Krueger, J.: Puzzles unpuzzled: towards a unified taxonomy for analog and digital escape room games. In: Proceedings of the ACM on Human-Computer Interaction, CHI PLAY, vol. 5, pp. 1–24. ACM (2021). https://doi.org/10.1145/347 4696

5. Lykke, J.R., Olsen, A.A., Berman, P.C., Bærentzen, J.A., Frisvad, J.R.: Accounting for object weight in interaction design for virtual reality. J. WSCG **27**, 131–140 (2019). https://doi.org/10.24132/jwscg.2019.27.2.6

6. Mendes, D., Caputo, F.M., Giachetti, A., Ferreira, A., Jorge, J.: A survey on 3D virtual object manipulation: from the desktop to immersive virtual environments. Comput. Graph. Forum **38**(1), 21–45 (2019). https://doi.org/10.1111/cgf.13390

7. Nicholson, S.: Peeking behind the locked door: a survey of escape room facilities (2015)

8. Rogers, K., Funke, J., Frommel, J., Stamm, S., Weber, M.: Exploring interaction fidelity in virtual reality: object manipulation and whole-body movements. In: Proceedings of the 2019 CHI Conference on Human Factors in Computing Systems, pp. 1–14. ACM (2019). https://doi.org/10.1145/3290605.3300644

9. Ullrich, D. & Diefenbach, S.: INTUI: exploring the facets of intuitive interaction. In: Ziegler, J., Schmidt, A. (Eds.) Mensch & Computer 2010, pp. 251–260 (2010)

10. Measuring Intuitive Interaction. The INTUI Questionnaire. http://intuitiveinteraction.net/method/. Accessed 22 June 2023

11. OpenXR Plugin. https://docs.unity3d.com/Packages/com.unity.xr.openxr@1.6/manual/index.htmlAccessed 18 May 2023

12. Vlahovic, S., Suznjevic, M., Skorin-Kapov, L.: A framework for the classification and evaluation of game mechanics for virtual reality games. Electronics **11**(18), 2946 (2022). https://doi.org/10.3390/electronics11182946

Grip Comfort Study of Virtual Reality Handles

Yuxuan Liu[✉], Qijuan Yu, and Haining Wang

School of Design, Hunan University, Changsha 410082, China
liuyx1999@hnu.edu.cn

Abstract. Virtual reality (VR) devices are increasingly being utilized in a variety of scenarios. The aim of this study was to investigate the grip comfort of VR handles in different scenes. Thirty-two representative participants were recruited for the study, and three different VR handles, including the O-shaped, H-shaped and I-shaped, were evaluated. Four dimensions of grip comfort were subjectively rated by the participants in both dynamic and static scenes, and subjective interviews were conducted. A high-precision 3D scan was performed on the participants' grip posture, and the Average-Hand was determined from the scan results. The fit of the product was analyzed through a deviation analysis test, which was combined with the subjective rating method to obtain visualization of the human-product fit results. It was found that in the dynamic scene, larger handles such as the H-shaped handles provide better stability and grip comfort. In static scene, handles with a better distribution and smaller dimensions such as O-shaped and I-shaped handles provide less pressure and fatigue and thus better grip comfort.

Keywords: VR handles · Grip comfort · Subjective evaluation · Deviation analysis

1 Introduction

1.1 Background

Virtual Reality (VR) technology can provide immersive and interactive experiences and is being used in many fields such as gaming [1, 2], education [3–5], medicine [6, 7], travel [8] and so on, giving people a completely new experience. The VR handles are common controllers for existing VR devices and have a high frequency of use in various scenarios. It provides users with more impressive vibrations and more refined controls through which people can physically express themselves for a great interactive experience [9].

J. Y. C. Chen et al. (Eds.): HCII 2023, LNCS 14058, pp. 135–146, 2023.
https://doi.org/10.1007/978-3-031-48050-8_10

Most of the research on virtual reality devices has focused on their use in different scenarios and on headset or visual comfort [10, 11]. There are also studies on the development of VR input devices and how they affect user performance [12, 13]. However, there are few studies on VR handles comfort and this aspect has not been investigated in detail. According to questionnaire statistics, most people believe that VR handles are not yet comfortable enough to hold and may even cause muscle fatigue or even critical injuries due to their size, design and grip angle [9]. Therefore, grip comfort has a certain impact on the experience of VR devices.

Anthropometry plays an important role in the design and evaluation of handheld products. Research has shown that the shape of the handle of products is an essential determinant of user comfort and product usability [14], and has a significant impact on hand posture and upper limb discomfort [15]. Different handle shapes result in different grip force distributions and muscle loads, and can also strongly influence force distribution between the fingers, as well as affecting muscle coordination, which is important when designing handles to reduce specific tendonitis and muscle disorders [16]. In addition, hand pressure during grip use is strongly related to grip comfort, which is higher with a relatively balanced pressure distribution in the hand [17].

Digital simulation-based fit testing methods are widely used in wearable product comfort studies, as they can maintain realistic wear relationships with high accuracy and provide visualization results for qualitative analysis [18]. Thierry Ellena et al. applied it to the design and testing process of a bicycle helmet [19]. Haining Wang et al. used it to improve the fit of the facial interface of a VR headset [18]. Gregor Harih et al. employed it to the design of a handheld tool grip and experimentally demonstrated that the designed handles improved user comfort and reduced the risk of cumulative trauma disorder (CTD) [20]. However, to our knowledge, it has been less applied to the design and testing of gaming controllers.

The main purpose of this paper is to investigate the grip comfort of VR handles by recruiting representative participants and investigating the subjective and objective fit of different shapes of VR handles in different scenes. The structure of this paper is as follows: Sect. 2 introduces the participants and materials in the experiment and presents the subjective rating method and testing procedure. Section 3 presents the results of the suitability test. Section 4 contains a discussion and limitations, and Sect. 5 concludes with a summary.

2 Materials and Methods

2.1 Participants

The experiment involved 32 participants, including 17 males and 15 females, with ages ranging from 19 to 44 years old (mean = 28.94, SD = 7.39). Their hand length ranged from 161.48 to 199.78 mm (mean = 182.67, SD = 9.68) and hand width from 15.4 to 21.69 mm (mean = 18.77, SD = 1.43). For males the hand length range is 171.85 mm to 199.78 mm (mean = 187.12, SD = 8.73) and the hand width range is 17.93 mm to 21.69 mm (mean = 19.45, SD = 1.13). For females the hand length range is 161.48 mm to 195.91 mm (mean = 177.63, SD = 8.31) and the hand width range is 15.4 mm to 20.15 mm (mean = 17.99, SD = 1.35). Among all the participants, small, medium and large hands accounted for 21.7%, 58.0% and 20.3% respectively. Most of them had some experience with VR handles or gamepads. Prior to the test, all participants gave written informed consent to the experimental procedure. The study was conducted in accordance with the ethical principles for research involving human subjects expressed in the Declaration of Helsinki and its subsequent amendments, and was approved by the Institutional Review Board of Hunan University.

2.2 Apparatus

In this study, the VR handles were distinguished by the way in which the shape characteristics and dimensional proportions were defined as O-shaped, H-shaped and I-shaped handles, respectively (Fig. 1). The dimensions and dimensional proportions of the three handles used in the experiment are given in Table 1. The specific way in which the three types of handles were defined in this study is as follows:

O-shaped handles: These VR handles are shorter but very rounded, with a smooth curve to the overall shape and a large, rounded control area. Their aspect ratio is greater than 2.5 but less than 3, their length to thickness ratio is around 2, and their panel width to handle width ratio is greater than 2.

H-shaped handles: These VR handles have a longer, thicker grip and a more linear overall shape, with a rounded, medium sized control panel. Their aspect ratios are greater than 3, their length to thickness ratio is greater than 2.5, and their panel width to handle width ratio is greater than 2.

I-shaped handles: These VR handles are shorter and have a more compact overall shape, with a smaller control panel that is similar in width to the handle position. Their aspect ratio is greater than 2.5 but less than 3, the length to thickness ratio is around 2, and the control panel width to handle width ratio is less than 1.5.

Fig. 1. Experimental VR handles: (a) O-shaped handles, (b) H-shaped handles and (c) I-shaped handles.

Table 1. Specific dimensions and dimensional proportions of the different shapes of handles.

Specific dimension		O-shaped	H-shaped	I-shaped
Measurement content	A: Overall length (mm)	125.93	162.87	147.91
	B: Holding position length (mm)	82.32	108.63	80.73
	C: Width at widest point (mm)	30.65	32.42	32.06
	D: Thickness at thickest point (mm)	41.75	40.91	41.79
	E: Width of operating panel (mm)	73.08	67.50	42.79
Proportionality	B/C: Length/Width	2.66	3.35	2.52
	B/D: Length/Thickness	1.97	2.66	1.93
	E/C: Panel width/Grip width	2.38	2.08	1.33

2.3 Subjective Assessment Experiment

Participants were asked to subjectively evaluate the comfort of the VR handles during the experiment by completing a questionnaire with four dimensions: instability, pressure, fatigue and discomfort. It was emphasized to the participants that they should focus primarily on the shape of the handles. The subjective experiment procedure was as follows. Firstly, basic information about the participants was collected and they were given a brief introduction to the experiment. Secondly, participants performed a dynamic scene simulating a Beat Saber game in which they had to perform heavy arm swings and wrist movements. The duration of the game was ten minutes. They were then asked to rate instability, pressure, fatigue and discomfort, and an informal interview was conducted to understand their preferences. Thirdly, participants experienced static scene in which they were asked to perform certain button presses with their fingers while their arms remained largely stationary. This process also took ten minutes. Finally, they were asked to give subjective ratings and describe subjective feelings.

Subjective evaluations were recorded on a 10-point Likert scale (Fig. 2), including instability, pressure, fatigue and discomfort. Instability is a measure of the relative stability of the position of the hands in relation to the handles. Pressure is a measure of the partial or general stress on the hand caused by the handle. Fatigue is a measure of the tiredness of the muscles in the hand. Discomfort is used to measure the overall feelings of the handle during use.

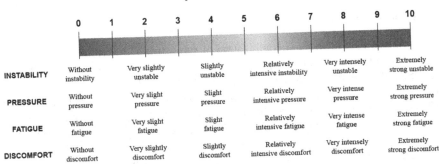

Fig. 2. 10-point Likert scale.

2.4 3D Scanning and Model Processing

Each participant was acquired the right-hand scan data by a non-contact Artec Spider 3D scanner. During the scanning process, participants were first plotted with hand feature points. In the second step, after the participant performed the handle, it was removed and the hand was scanned while the participant held the pose. The scanned mesh was then exported to Artec Studio software for further processing, where any redundant surfaces were removed and the surface was smoothed (Fig. 3). Hand feature points were then extracted and fitted to the hand models of the 32 participants to obtain representative Average-Hand. Finally, the three selected VR handles were digitized by 3D scanning to obtain their 3D models (Fig. 4).

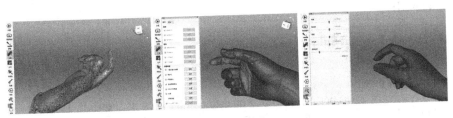

Fig. 3. Hand model handling process.

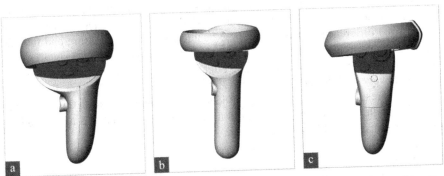

Fig. 4. VR handle models: (a) O-shaped handle, (b) H-shaped handle and (c) I-shaped handle.

2.5 Statistical Analysis

In the stage of data analysis, a combination of subjective and objective methods was used to obtain human-product adaptation results for different shapes of VR handles.

SPSS software version 26.0 (SPSS Inc., Chicago, IL, USA) was used to analyze the subjective rating data. Mean values and standard errors were presented. One-way ANOVA was applied to analyze differences in subjective ratings between different handles. An alpha level equal to or < 0.05 was accepted as significant for statistical tests.

The deviation analysis performed in CATIA V5R21 was used to calculate the results of an objective analysis of the fit between Average-Hand mesh and the calibrated VR handles of different shapes. Three parameters were used in this process: (i) Std Dev: the standard deviation of the total wear surface distance, a factor that reflects the overall fit of the fitting surface [19]; (ii) Pos Mean Dev: the statistical mean of the portion of the surface distance in the selected area that is positive, reflecting the gap status of the selected area; (iii) Neg Mean Dev: the statistical mean of the negative surface distance in the selected area, reflecting the interference status of the selected area [18]. The results of the deviation analysis can reflect the objective spatial relative position of the human-product adaptation [21]. In addition, the results can be analyzed qualitatively using deviation analysis maps. The interference region (blue) reflects a tight fit in a realistic grip relationship, the gap region (red) reflects a gap in a realistic grip relationship, and the region where the surface distance is close to zero (green) is a critical fit [19].

3 Results

3.1 Handle Use and Subjective Evaluation

Dynamic Scene

One-way ANOVA was performed based on different handles, as shown in Table 2.

For each of the four dimensions, the mean scores of the subjective ratings of the three handles in the dynamic scene are shown in Fig. 5. There is a significant difference in the perception of instability between the three handles, with the H-shaped handle being more stable, but the other two handles are also in the 'slightly unstable' category. There were no significant differences between the three handles in terms of pressure and fatigue, with participants rating the H-shaped and I-shaped better than the O-shaped in both dimensions. Handle shape had a significant effect on grip discomfort, with the H-shaped having relatively grip discomfort and the O-shaped having relatively high discomfort. Based on the results of the subjective interviews, participants felt that in this scene, the O-shaped handle was not long enough, did not fit well enough and was more tiring to use. The H-shaped handle was safer to hold.

Static Scene

One-way ANOVA was performed based on different handles, as shown in Table 3. For each of the four dimensions, the mean scores of the subjective ratings of the three handles in the static scene are shown in Fig. 6. There are no significant differences between the

Table 2. Descriptive statistics and ANOVA of different handles in dynamic scene.

Dimension	O-shaped		H-shaped		I-shaped		ANOVA	
	Mean	SD	Mean	SD	Mean	SD	F	p-values
Instability	3.81	1.839	2.52	0.918	3.34	1.599	4.976	0.002**
Pressure	3.78	1.362	3.31	1.476	3.47	1.481	0.888	0.405
Fatigue	4.31	1.401	3.84	1.393	3.97	1.534	0.909	0.407
Discomfort	4.38	1.497	3.33	1.167	4.03	1.534	3.691	0.029*

**Correlation is significant at the 0.01 level.
*Correlation is significant at the 0.05 level

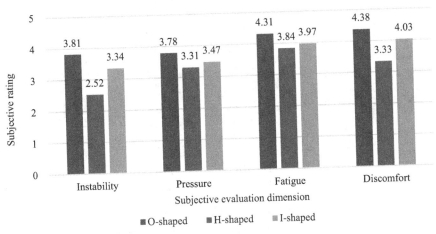

Fig. 5. Subjective evaluation results in dynamic scene.

three handles in terms of instability, with the H-shaped handles being slightly more unstable. Feelings of pressure, fatigue and discomfort differed significantly between them. Interestingly, the H-shaped handles perform the opposite way in static scene and in the dynamic scene mentioned above, being rated worse in all three dimensions compared to the other two. While the I-shaped handles had less pressure, the O-shaped handles had less fatigue and discomfort. Based on the results of the subjective interviews, participants found the O-shaped handles more comfortable to hold in the static scene. The H-shaped handle was too long and had a more obvious feeling of pressure on the hand muscles during use. For the I-shaped handle, participants generally felt that the grip area was too small.

Table 3. Descriptive statistics and ANOVA of different handles in static scene.

Dimension	O-shaped		H-shaped		I-shaped		ANOVA	
	Mean	SD	Mean	SD	Mean	SD	F	p-values
Instability	3.11	1.389	3.35	1.539	3.19	1.401	0.228	0.796
Pressure	3.52	1.262	4.36	1.393	3.25	1.032	5.666	0.005**
Fatigue	3.70	1.182	4.83	1.311	4.12	1.269	5.223	0.008**
Discomfort	3.64	1.136	4.52	0.975	4.29	1.233	3.990	0.023*

**Correlation is significant at the 0.01 level.
*Correlation is significant at the 0.05 level

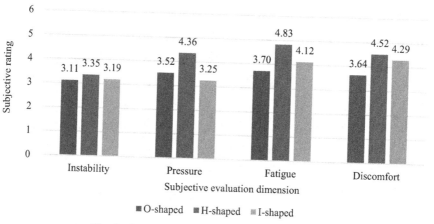

Fig. 6. Subjective evaluation results in static scene.

3.2 Objective Fitness Test

Figure 7 shows the results of the deviation analysis of the three VR handles by CATIA V5R21. The fitting statistics are shown in Table 4 and Fig. 8. From the distance maps and statistics, it can be seen that there is little difference in the mean values of Std Dev and Pos Mean Dev between the three grips. The Std Dev is slightly larger for the H-shaped handle and more uniform for the others. The Pos Mean Dev is slightly larger for the O-shaped handle and the smallest for the H-shaped handle. It is more obvious that there is more interference between the H-shaped handle and the Average-Hand mesh, especially in the lower part of it.

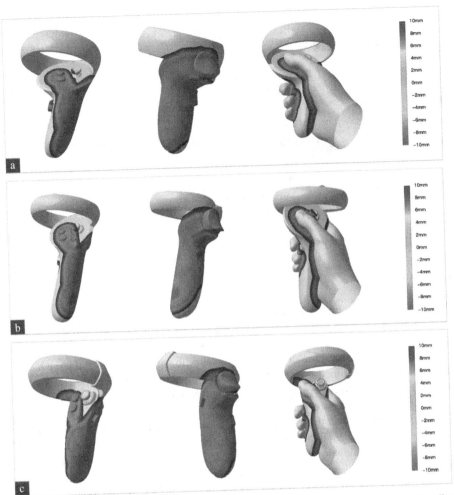

Fig. 7. Deviation analysis: (a) O-shaped handles, (b) H-shaped handles and (c) I-shaped handles. Green is within the allowed distance variation, yellow to red and blue is where the mesh has been expanded or retracted, respectively.

Table 4. Surface distance data for the three handles.

VR handles	Std Dev (mm)	Pos Mean Dev (mm)	Neg Mean Dev (mm)
O-shaped	3.59	4.31	-1.33
H-shaped	3.66	4.21	-2.23
I-shaped	3.58	4.25	-1.43

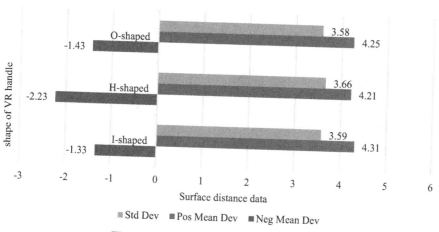

Fig. 8. Comparison of surface distance data.

4 Discussion

The main purpose of this study is to investigate the grip comfort of different shapes of VR handles in different scenes. This study focused on the use of O-shaped, H-shaped and I-shaped handles for gripping in dynamic and static scenes. A total of 32 participants were recruited, including 17 males and 15 females with small, medium and large hands. This experiment combined the results of the participants' subjective evaluations with the results of the objective evaluations conducted through deviation analysis to achieve a study of VR handle comfort.

In the dynamic scene, the H-shaped handles were more comfortable, mainly due to their relatively low instability. The analysis of the deviations of the H-shaped handles and the Average-Hand showed a slightly higher Std Dev and Neg Mean Dev than the other two handles, but a smaller Pos Mean Dev. The reason for the dominance of the H-shaped handles in the subjective evaluation may be that they have a larger volume and are easier to grip, therefore giving the user a greater sense of stability and security and reducing the concern and risk of the handles being thrown out during large movements. In this type of scenes, the shorter length of the handles may provide a relatively greater sense of instability.

In the static scene, the O-shaped handles provided a relatively good grip experience, mainly in terms of their relatively low levels of pressure, fatigue and discomfort. In this scene, the I-shaped handles also had a low level of pressure. The results of the deviation analysis showed that the O-shaped handles had a relatively good uniformity of distribution and a low Neg Mean Dev, so that the O-shaped handles were better adapted to the Average-Hand. Similarly, the I-shaped handles also had a good fitting effect. It can be seen that in the static scene, the better adapted handles give user a better experience. In these scenes there are no big motion, but only finger movements, and there is little risk of the grip being thrown out, so the need for stability is not as critical. However, because of the frequent movements of the finger muscles, handles with a larger contact area, more uniform fit, smaller operating range and less contact pressure on the hand can reduce pressure and fatigue in the hand, increasing subjective comfort and providing a better experience [20].

The study has several limitations. Firstly, this study only focused on the effect of VR handle shape on grip comfort, and further research can be conducted on other factors such as handle material and operating methods. Secondly, the three types of handles may not be representative of all products on the market.

5   Conclusion

This paper investigated the effect of VR handle shapes on grip comfort in different scenes. The results showed that in the dynamic scene, more stable and slightly larger handles like H-shaped handles can provide better grip comfort. In the static scene, handles with better distribution uniformity and slightly smaller size like O-shaped and I-shaped handles have less compression, less fatigue and thus better grip comfort. In conclusion, the results of this study can provide recommendations for the design of VR handles. The combination of subjective and objective evaluation can also provide a reference for the suitability study of handle-type products.

References

1. Theodoropoulos, A., Antoniou, A.: VR games in cultural heritage: a systematic review of the emerging fields of virtual reality and culture games. Appl. Sci. **12**(17), 8476 (2022)
2. Shoshani, A.: From virtual to prosocial reality: the effects of prosocial virtual reality games on preschool Children's prosocial tendencies in real life environments. Comput. Hum. Behav. **139**, 107546 (2023)
3. Wang, C., et al.: Application of VR technology in civil engineering education. Comput. Appl. Eng. Educ. **30**(2), 335–348 (2022)
4. Hui, J., et al.: Research on art teaching practice supported by Virtual Reality (VR) technology in the primary schools. Sustainability **14**(3), 1246 (2022)
5. Demitriadou, E., Stavroulia, K.-E., Lanitis, A.: Comparative evaluation of virtual and augmented reality for teaching mathematics in primary education. Educ. Inf. Technol. **25**, 381–401 (2020)
6. Paro, M.R., Hersh, D.S., Bulsara, K.R.: History of virtual reality and augmented reality in neurosurgical training. World Neurosurg. (2022)
7. Gustavsson, M., et al.: Virtual reality gaming in rehabilitation after stroke–user experiences and perceptions. Disabil. Rehabil. **44**(22), 6759–6765 (2022)
8. Godovykh, M., Baker, C., Fyall, A.: VR in tourism: A new call for virtual tourism experience amid and after the COVID-19 pandemic. Tour. Hosp. **3**(1), 265–275 (2022)
9. Wang, X.: The Research on a Design Approach to Grip Comfort of Handles. Yanshan University, Qinhuangdo (2021)
10. Yan, Y., Ke Chen, Y., Xie, Y.S., Liu, Y.: The effects of weight on comfort of virtual reality devices. In: Rebelo, F., Soares, M.M. (eds.) AHFE 2018. AISC, vol. 777, pp. 239–248. Springer, Cham (2019). https://doi.org/10.1007/978-3-319-94706-8_27
11. Lin, C.-H., et al.: Variations in intraocular pressure and visual parameters before and after using mobile virtual reality glasses and their effects on the eyes. Sci. Rep. **12**(1), 3176 (2022)
12. Lee, S., et al.: User study of VR basic controller and data glove as hand gesture inputs in VR games. In: 2017 International Symposium on Ubiquitous Virtual Reality (ISUVR). IEEE (2017)

13. Juan, M., et al.: Immersive virtual reality for upper limb rehabilitation: comparing hand and controller interaction. Virt. Real. **27**(2), 1157–1171 (2023)

14. Bisht, D.S., Khan, M.R.: Anatomically shaped tool handles designed for power grip. In: Chakrabarti, A., Chakrabarti, D. (eds.) ICoRD 2017. SIST, vol. 65, pp. 135–148. Springer, Singapore (2017). https://doi.org/10.1007/978-981-10-3518-0_12

15. Veisi, H., et al.: The effect of hand tools' handle shape on upper extremity comfort and postural discomfort among hand-woven shoemaking workers. Int. J. Ind. Ergon. **74**, 102833 (2019)

16. Rossi, J., et al.: Does handle shape influence prehensile capabilities and muscle coordination? Comput. Methods Biomech. Biomed. Engin. **17**(1), 172–173 (2014)

17. Kong, Y.-K., Lowe, B.D.: Evaluation of handle diameters and orientations in a maximum torque task. Int. J. Ind. Ergon. **35**(12), 1073–1084 (2005)

18. Wang, H., Chi, Z.: Fit test method study of wearable products by combining virtuality and reality. Packa. Eng. **42**(12), 84–90, 97 (2021)

19. Ellena, T., et al.: The helmet fit index–an intelligent tool for fit assessment and design customisation. Appl. Ergon. **55**, 194–207 (2016)

20. Harih, G., Dolšak, B.: Tool-handle design based on a digital human hand model. Int. J. Ind. Ergon. **43**(4), 288–295 (2013)

21. Wang, H., Chi, Z., He, R.: Fit improvement of facial interface for VR headset based on principal component analysis panel. J. Mach. Des. **37**(5), 117–124 (2020)

Effect of Electrical Stimulation Frequency on Vibratory Sensation Induced by Nerve Bundle Stimulation

Shuto Ogihara, Tomohiro Amemiya, and Kazuma Aoyama[✉]

The University of Tokyo, 7-3-1 Hongo, Bunkyo-Ku, Tokyo, Japan
ogihara@cyber.t.u-tokyo.ac.jp, {amemiya,aoyama}@vr.u-tokyo.ac.jp

Abstract. Transcutaneous electrical nerve stimulation is a technology for inducing various sensations by electrically stimulating sensory nervous systems. Nerve bundle electrical stimulation is a type of transcutaneous electrical nerve stimulation that can induce tactile sensations on the hand without attaching electrodes to the hand. Therefore, nerve bundle stimulation is expected to be applied in tactile displays and superimposition technologies for virtual and augmented reality. However, the quality of the induced tactile sensation has not been qualitatively evaluated. In this study, the relationship between the frequency of transcutaneous electrical nerve stimulation and that of the induced tactile sensation was investigated. The results indicated that the frequencies of transcutaneous electrical nerve stimulation and induced tactile sensation were approximately proportional at up to a 100-Hz transcutaneous electrical nerve stimulation frequency. This finding can be used to modify the vibration sensations in virtual and augmented reality systems.

Keywords: Electrical Stimulation · Haptic Display · Vibration Sensation

1 Introduction

Mixed reality (MR), which includes augmented reality (AR) and virtual reality, is a technology area for creating artificial experiences. In the field of MR, numerous haptic and tactile display technologies have been developed [1–3]. Herein, "tactile" means the sensations induced by skin responses such as vibration, pressure, thermal, and pain sensations, and "haptic" means a tactile sensation with a force sensation. In the MR area, the importance of research on tactile and haptic sensation display technologies is increasing because the visual and auditory display technologies have already been sufficiently developed.

In the field of MR, many types of tactile and haptic displays have been developed. Most conventional tactile and haptic display technologies require actuators to induce pressures, vibrations, and forces on the skin. For example, "SPIDAR" was developed with a grip pulled by wires using a motor to induce haptic sensations [4]. Although this device can output as much power as the motor will allow, users' motion is limited by the shifting range of the grip.

J. Y. C. Chen et al. (Eds.): HCII 2023, LNCS 14058, pp. 147–156, 2023.
https://doi.org/10.1007/978-3-031-48050-8_11

To resolve this problem, tactile displays consisting of wearable devices have been proposed. The simplest way to display vibration sensations is by using a vibrator. As a vibrator is a small and lightweight actuator, a method using this actuator can induce tactile sensations with only small limitations on motion. Such vibrator-based tactile displays are used in game controllers and smartphones and are currently the most widespread tactile display technology. Although vibration can induce vibro-tactile sensations, it cannot induce force sensations. Amemiya et al. proposed a method of using asymmetric vibration to induce a sense of force; however, the induced force was weak [5].

Although vibrator-based devices can induce tactile sensations, the only quality of the sensation is the vibration. Thus, other approaches to displaying tactile sensations are being studied. For example, Minamizawa et al. developed "GravityGrabber." This device uses a motor and belt to tighten and rub fingers to elicit tactile sensations [3]. Yoshida et al. proposed the pin array-type tactile display named "Pocopo" [2].

Because these devices require covering the display surface of the skin, the interaction between the hand and real environment is obstructed. Methods for superimposing tactile sensations on the hand without interfering with the interaction between the hand and real environment are being studied, as they are very important techniques for haptic AR systems, where exploration of the real environment is as important as that of the virtual environment.

With this background, Teng et al. developed "Touch&Fold," which induces vibration and pressure sensations. This device can present sensations when necessary by moving a vibration and pressure display part on the back of the finger to the surface of the finger only when it is necessary. However, it is not possible to superimpose tactile sensations while touching an object in the real world. Ando et al. developed a "smart finger," which superimposes the vibrations from an actuator on a nail when users track the surface of a real object [1]. Then, the user perceives the illusion of texture on the surface of the real object being traced. Maeda et al. proposed the "Fingeret" for reproducing various types of tactile sensations by placing roller-type vibrators on the sides of the fingers in addition to nails; these are responsible for high- and low-frequency stimulation, respectively [6].

Because the conventional tactile display technologies mentioned above rely on kinetic mechanisms such as vibrators and motors, they require a large and heavy mechanism to present a strong sensation.

Transcutaneous electrical nerve stimulation (TENS) has the potential to induce strong tactile sensations in a non-invasive manner with small and light weight devices. In this technology, weak electrical currents are applied from a gel and/or plate electrodes on the surface of the skin and stimulate the neural system of the human body. Kajimoto et al. applied an electrical current to a finger using an electrode array to induce tactile sensations [7]. They also developed a system called "SmartTouch" with an electrode array plate and texture sensor on the opposite side of the electrodes on the plate. In this system, the users trace an object while touching their fingers to the electrodes, and electrical stimulation is applied according to the texture patterns as measured by sensors [8]. Withana et al. demonstrated that a 35-um tattoo-like electrode sheet applied to the fingertip can superimpose tactile sensations with as little disruption to the interaction between the real object and finger as possible. Although electrical stimulation can induce tactile sensations using lightweight and compact devices, and the methods described above are designed to minimize the inhibition from interactions between the hand and real environment, these methods still inhibit the interaction [9]. Therefore, it is preferable that electrodes, even thin ones, not be placed in the position where the tactile sensation is intended to be presented.

It is known that when TENS is applied to nerve bundles such as the ulnar and median nerves in the arm, a tactile sensation (like vibration) is produced at a different position than where the electrodes are placed. This technique has been studied to provide tactile feedback for prosthetic hand users. For example, Chai et al. showed the results from drawing the areas of tactile sensation elicited by electrical stimulation of nerve bundles in a prosthetic hand user [10]. The results of their experiments show that the electrical stimulation of nerve bundles can present tactile sensations to a lost hand. A similar experiment was conducted by Shin et al. but targeting non-disabled participants. They demonstrated that ulnar and median nerve stimulation by an electrode matrix on the upper arm shifts the area of the induced tactile sensations on the hand and finger in the non-disabled participants. Moreover, Yoshimoto et al. developed a method for presenting tactile sensations to the fingertips by applying electrical stimulation near the second joint of the finger [11]. Ogihara et al. proposed a method for moving the tactile region of an finger based on an electrode position near the third joint of the finger [12]. Moreover, Ogihara et al. proposed the method to induce tactiles sensation on the hand only and shift the tactile sensation on the hand by attaching electrodes array on the wrist [13].

As stated above, electrical stimulation of nerve bundles has indicated that nerve bundle stimulation, such as that of the ulnar and median nerves, presents tactile sensations on the hand without attaching electrodes to the hand; moreover, the area of the tactile sensation can be changed based on the position(s) of the electrodes. However, the technology for controlling the quality of the sensation induced by the nerve bundle stimulation is lacking. A method for modifying the quality of tactile sensations is desired. In terms of the quality of the tactile sensations induced by nerve bundle stimulation, Chai et al. reported in their paper that nerve bundle electrical stimulation induced tactile, pressure, buzzing, vibration, and numbness sensations [10]. This report also indicated that vibratory sensations of various frequencies were being generated. In addition, Yoshimoto et al. indicated that the vibration sensation induced by a 25-Hz mechanical vibration can be modified by the frequency of the electrical nerve bundle stimulation [12]. Therefore, we hypothesized that the frequency of the vibration sensation induced by electrical nerve bundle stimulation can be modified by the frequency of the electrical stimulation.

To investigate the relation between the frequency of the vibration sensation and frequency of the electrical stimulation, an experiment was conducted.

2 Method

Twelve healthy adults participated in this experiment. All subjects agreed in a letter of consent that (1) they sufficiently understood the experimental procedures, including the risks of electrical stimulation; (2) they consented to the use of data from this experiment for publication of academic papers; and (3) they participated in this experiment voluntarily. The study protocol was approved by the local ethics research committee at The University of Tokyo.

This experiment was conducted in a silent room. The participants sat on a chair, and gel electrodes were attached for the cathode on the median nerve and for the anode above the ulnar styloid process of their wrist. Then, the participants confirmed whether a tactile sensation occurred on their hand when a 1-mA sinusoidal current stimulation was applied and memorized the area of their tactile sensation. When participants did not feel any tactile sensation on their hand, the positions of the electrodes were modified.

In this experiment the frequencies of the vibration sensation induced by mechanical vibration stimulation (MVS) were measured with equivalent frequencies of sensation induced by TENS to the median nerve. The experiment consisted of four phases (i.e., screening, measuring threshold, measuring equivalent frequency, and questioning).

2.1 Experimental Apparatus

This experiment required an electrical stimulator and a mechanical vibrator. The electrical stimulator in this experiment was an in-house constant-current circuit. This stimulator could output a current value according to the command from a PC, and the stimulation range was ±5 mA (Fig. 1).

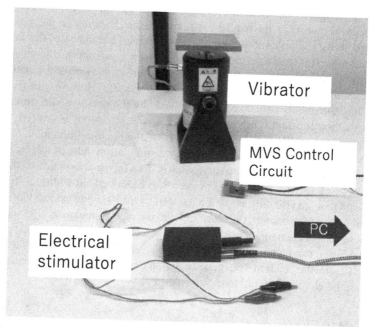

Fig. 1. Experimental devices such as a vibrator, a vibrator control circuit, and an electrical stimulator.

The vibrator (511-A, EMIC Co. Ltd) and aluminum plate was used for the MVS stimulator. This vibrator outputs a vibration according to the input voltage wave form. The input voltage was generated by a microcontroller (Seeeduino XIAO, Seeed Inc.). The output voltage from the microcontroller was modified by the custom-made circuit and amplified by a power amplifier (371-A, EMIC Co. Ltd.) before being input to the vibrator.

Based on a previous study [14], the intensity of the vibration sensation depends on the frequency. To keep the intensity of the vibration sensation constant at each frequency, the stroke of the vibrator was adjusted at each frequency. Bolanowski et al. indicated that the curve that shows the threshold stroke of the vibration sensation induced by the MVS against the frequency has a U-shape with a peak at approximately 250 Hz. From their report, we obtained an equation to determine the threshold value for each frequency, as shown in Eq. 2.1. Furthermore, during the experiment, the strokes were set to five times the threshold value (as shown in Eq. 2.2) to stimulate the participants at an intensity that would ensure tactile sensations during the experiment.

$$S_{threshold}[dB] = \begin{cases} -5\log_2\left(\frac{f[Hz]}{40}\right) + 12, & 3.0 \leq f \leq 40 \\ -12\log_2\left(\frac{f[Hz]}{40}\right) + 12, & 40 < f \leq 250 \\ 12\log_2\left(\frac{f[Hz]}{250}\right) - 20, & 250 < f \leq 400 \end{cases} \tag{2.1}$$

$$S_{objective}[\mu m] = 5 \cdot 10^{\frac{S_{threshold}[dB]}{20}} \tag{2.2}$$

In the actual experiment, instead of adjusting the stroke at all frequencies, the stroke was calculated at nine different frequencies, and between these frequencies, the signal intensity for determining the stroke was linearly complementary.

2.2 Screening Phase

To conduct this experiment, the Screening Phase was conducted first. In this experiment, the frequency of vibration sensation induced by TENS was measured by comparing it to that induced by MVS. Then, the participants were required to be able to recognize the differences in the frequencies of the vibration sensation. The purpose of this phase was to ensure that the participants in this experiment were able to discriminate between the frequencies of the mechanical vibration.

Participants received two MVSs with different frequencies and were asked which MVS had a higher frequency. Five combinations of MVS frequencies were used (i.e., 22 Hz vs 28 Hz, 45 Hz vs 56 Hz, 89 Hz vs 112 Hz, 178 Hz vs 224 Hz, and 269 Hz vs 339 Hz). These were determined to have a difference of 0.1 on a normal logarithmic scale around five frequencies (i.e., 25, 50, 100, 200, 300) based on a previous study [15]. Each condition was repeated 10 times, and 50 trials were conducted in total.

2.3 Measuring Threshold Phase

To decrease the effect of strength on the frequency sensation and ensure that participants could perceive the tactile sensations from the TENS, the threshold of the tactile sensation induced by the TENS was measured.

The threshold of the TENS was measured using the parameter estimation by sequential testing (PEST) method [16]. The initial step size was 0.125. The step size of the frequency was halved each time the evaluation of the frequency (higher or lower) was reversed, and the trial was terminated when the evaluation was reversed three times. In this phase, the step size did not increase no matter how many times the subject repeated the same evaluation.

In terms of safety, up to 5.0 mA of TENS was used for this experiment. In the next phase, the current intensity used was three times the threshold of the TENS. Consequently, if the current value of the threshold was higher than 1.6 mA, the experiment ended for that participant.

2.4 Measuring Equivalent Frequency Phase

Electrical current simulation was applied to the participant. The current strength was set at three times the threshold for each participant. There were five frequency conditions: 25, 50, 100, 200, and 300 Hz. After the TENS, the equivalent frequency of the vibration sensation induced by MVS was measured using the PEST method. The initial frequency of the MVS in this PEST method was determined randomly in the range of 10–400 Hz. The initial step size was 0.4. The step size of the frequency was halved each time the evaluation of the frequency (higher or lower) was reversed, and the trial was terminated when the step size became smaller than 0.1. In this phase, the step size doubled when participants repeated the same evaluation three times.

In total, 20 trials were conducted, consisting of four trials for each of the five frequency conditions.

3 Result

In the Measuring Threshold Phase, one participant did not feel any tactile sensation on the hand at up to a 1.6-mA condition; the data from this participant were completely removed.

Table 1. Result of the Screening Phase.

Condition Number	Combination of frequency	Averaged rate of correct answer (±standard deviation) [%]
1	22 Hz vs 28 Hz	80 ± 11
2	45 Hz vs 56 Hz	72 ± 22
3	89 Hz vs 112 Hz	84 ± 16
4	178 Hz vs 224 Hz	76 ± 14
5	269 Hz vs 339 Hz	67 ± 31

Table 1 shows the results from Screening Phase test. The third column shows the averaged rate of correct answer. Although all participants were not able to completely discriminate between high and low vibrations, the average percentage of correct responses was approximately 70% in all conditions. In addition, Table 2 shows the conditions under which the rate of correct answers was less than 70% for each participant. This table indicates that no participant failed to discriminate the frequency of MVS in all conditions, and there was no condition that no participant could discriminate.

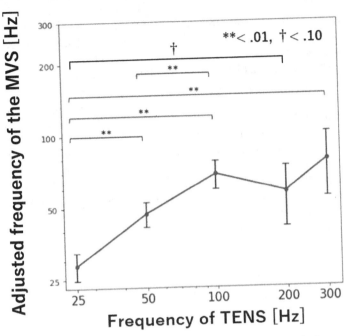

Fig. 2. Equivalence points between the frequency of transcutaneous electrical nerve stimulation (TENS) to the nerve bundle at the wrist and the frequency of the tactile sensation elicited by the TENS.

Table 2. Conditions that the rate of correct answer is less than 70%.

Participant ID	1	2	3	4	6	7	8	9	10	11	12
Condition Number that the rate of correct answer was less than 70%	2,5	–	-	5	–	2	4,5	2.4	5	3	2,5

Figure 2 depicts the relationship between the frequency of TENS (horizontal) and equivalent frequency of the MVS (vertical). The error bars show the standard error. The Freedman Test reveals the significant difference in the frequency of TENS ($p < 0.01$). A multiple comparison test (Wilcoxon signed-rank sum test) was also conducted. The multiple comparison test shows significant differences between 25 Hz and 50 Hz, 25 Hz and 100 Hz, 25 Hz and 300 Hz, and 50 Hz and 100 Hz ($p < 0.01$) and marginally significant differences are also shown between 25 Hz and 200 Hz ($p < 0.08$).

4 Discussion

Figure 2 indicates that the perceived frequency of MVS is approximately proportional to the frequency of TENS in the range of less than 100 Hz because the frequencies of the adjusted MVS under TENS conditions up to 100 Hz are approximately aligned in a straight line. In contrast, in high-frequency TENS conditions higher than 100 Hz, the frequency of the adjusted MVS is not proportional to the TENS frequency. This fact indicates that although the frequencies of tactile sensation induced by TENS were controllable up to 100 Hz, the tactile sensations at higher frequencies were not controllable by the method employed in this study.

The reason why the frequency of the tactile sensation elicited by TENS at frequencies higher than 100 Hz was lower is thought to be that the participant perceives both high-frequency and low-frequency tactile sensations simultaneously. Figure 3 shows the adjusted frequency of MVS against the frequency of TENS. Yellow crosses indicate data more than 1.5 times further away from the first and third quartiles of the quartile range in each condition, respectively. As shown in Fig. 3, in some trials, participants feel high-frequency vibration sensations similar to the TENS frequency in the 100-, 200-, and 300-Hz TENS conditions.

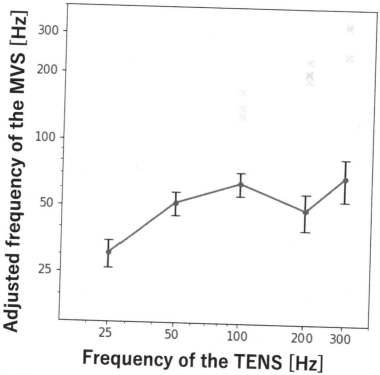

Fig. 3. Results of the Measuring Equivalent Frequency Phase with the data more than 1.5 times further away from the first and third quartiles of the quartile range in each condition (yellow crosses).

We considered that this phenomenon, i.e., that lower-frequency tactile sensations were induced in higher-frequency TENS conditions (higher than 100 Hz), is a limitation of the firing rate of the nerve. The high-frequency vibration sensation produced by the actual tactile experience is encoded by tactile receptors and transmitted through the nerves. Nerve bundle electrical stimulation may replicate this by changing the frequency of the nerve firing. However, the minimum interval required for a nerve to re-fire after it has fired once [17] limits its ability to fire at high frequencies.

5   Conclusion

In this study, we measured the equivalence point between the frequency of TENS applied to the nerve bundle at the wrist and the frequency of the tactile sensation elicited by the TENS. TENS, as applied to nerve bundles, is a technique that allows tactile sensations to be presented to the hand without the need to place electrodes on the hand. Therefore, it is expected to be used as a method for presenting and superimposing tactile sensations in MR and AR. This study has shown that TENS up to 100 Hz can induce vibration sensations of approximately equivalent frequencies, but the application of TENS at higher frequencies to nerve bundles at the wrist does not produce higher-frequency vibration sensations.

This method of controlling the frequency of the tactile sensations induced by TENS to nerve bundles may be used in the future for the superimposed presentation of a texture on the surface of an object, or to create the illusion of the material of an object by reproducing the vibration of the object when it collides with the hand.

Acknowledgement. This study supported by the JSPS KAKENHI Grant-in-Aid for Scientific Research(A) (21H04883) and JST PRESTO under Grant Number JPMJPR19J1.

References

1. Ando, H., Miki, T., Inami, M., Maeda, T.: Smartfinger: nail-mounted tactile display. In: ACM SIGGRAPH 2002 Conference Abstracts and Applications, p. 78 (2002)
2. Yoshida, S., Sun, Y., Kuzuoka, H.: Pocopo: handheld pin-based shape display for haptic rendering in virtual reality. In: Proceedings of the 2020 CHI Conference on Human Factors in Computing Systems, pp. 1–13 (2020)
3. Minamizawa, K., Fukamachi, S., Kajimoto, H., Kawakami, N., Tachi, S.: Gravity grabber: wearable haptic display to present virtual mass sensation. In: ACM SIGGRAPH 2007 Emerging Technologies, pp. 8–es (2007)
4. Nagai, K., Tanoue, S., Akahine, K., Sato, M.: A development of wearable wrist Haptic Device "SPI'AR-W". In: IPSJ SIG Technical Report, 2015-CG-159, vol. 13 (2015)
5. Amemiya, T., Gomi, H.: Buru-Navi3: behavioral navigations using illusory pulled sensation created by thumb-sized vibrator. In: Proceedings of ACM SIGGRAPH 2014 Emerging Technologies, Article 4, Vancouver, Canada (2014)
6. Maeda, T., Yoshida, S., Murakami, T., Matsuda, K., Tanikawa, T., Sakai, H.: Fingeret: a wearable fingerpad-free haptic device for mixed reality. In: Proceedings of the 2022 ACM Symposium on Spatial User Interaction, pp. 1–10 (2022)

7. Kajimoto, H., Kawakami, N., Maeda, T., Tachi, S.: Electro-tactile display with force feedback. In: World Multiconference on Systemics, Cybernetics and Informatics, pp. 95–99 (2001)
8. Kajimoto, H., Kawakami, N., Tachi, S., Inami, M.: Smarttouch: electric skin to touch the untouchable. IEEE Comput. Graphics Appl. 24(1), 36–43 (2004)
9. Withana, A., Groeger, D., Steimle, J.: Tacttoo: a thin and feel-through tattoo for on-skin tactile output. In: Proceedings of the 31st Annual ACM Symposium on User Interface Software and Technology, pp. 365–378 (2018)
10. Chai, G., Sui, X., Li, S., He, L., Lan, N.: Characterization of evoked tactile sensation in forearm amputees with transcutaneous electrical nerve stimulation. J. Neural Eng. 12(6), 066002 (2015)
11. Yoshimoto, S., Kuroda, Y., Imura, M., Oshiro, O.: Material roughness modulation via electrotactile augmentation. IEEE Trans. Haptics 8(2), 199–208 (2015)
12. Ogihara, S., Amemiya, T., Aoyama, K.: Transcutaneous electrical nerve stimulation along the base of the finger to modify the location of tactile sensation at the finger. In: IEEE International Symposium on Mixed and Augmented Reality (ISMAR) Poster Presentation, p. 10 (2022)
13. Ogihara, S., Amemiya, T., Kuzuoka, H., Narumi, T., Aoyama, K.: Multi surface electrodes nerve bundles stimulation on the wrist: modified location of tactile sensation on the palm. IEEE Access (Early Access) (2023). https://doi.org/10.1109/ACCESS.2023.3243175
14. Bolanowski, S.J., Jr., Gescheider, G.A., Verrillo, R.T., Checkosky, C.M.: Four channels mediate the mechanical aspects of touch. J. Acoust. Soc. Am. 84(5), 1680–1694 (1988)
15. Mahns, D.A., Perkins, N.M., Sahai, V., Robinson, L., Rowe, M.J.: Vibrotactile frequency discrimination in human hairy skin. J. Neurophysiol. 95(3), 1442–1450 (2006)
16. Taylor, M.M., Creelman, C.D.: PEST: efficient estimates on probability functions. J. Acoust. Soc. Am. 41, 782–787 (1967)
17. Brette, R.: Philosophy of the spike: rate-based vs. spike-based theories of the brain. Front. Syst. Neurosci. 9, 151 (2015)

3-D Mental Rotation Ability Testing with Mixed Reality

Zeynep Piri[1]([⊠]) [iD] and Kürşat Cagiltay[2] [iD]

[1] Faculty of Education, Department of Educational Sciences, Kastamonu University, Fakülte St., 37200 Kastamonu, Turkey
zeyneppiri@kastamonu.edu.tr
[2] Faculty of Engineering and Natural Sciences, Sabancı University, Orta St., 34956 İstanbul, Turkey
kursat.cagiltay@sabanciuniv.edu

Abstract. Mental Rotation ability is a key skill for success in many careers. Thus, accurate measurement of this ability is important. Three-dimensional holographic displays can help students process mental rotation stimuli easier and demonstrate their real performances without the limitations of two-dimensional representations. There are few studies measuring mental rotation ability in Mixed Reality environments. In this study, we transferred a mental rotation test, Purdue Spatial Visualization Test: Rotations (PSVT:R), into Mixed Reality. We compared the 2-D and 3-D versions of the test in terms of mental rotation performance and cognitive load with 47 participants. While the accuracy of 2-D and 3-D PSVT:R did not differ significantly, the 3-D test induced a lower cognitive load than the 2-D version. Gender difference was observed in the 2-D test but not in the 3-D test. 3-D PSVT:R is an authentic and reliable tool for measuring spatial ability. Moreover, it can be used for training purposes.

Keywords: mental rotation ability · three-dimensional environments · spatial ability tests · mixed reality

1 Introduction

Mental rotation is a sub-factor of spatial ability that involves visualizing the results of manipulating two and three-dimensional objects in the human mind. Mental rotation is especially an important ability for STEM-related careers such as engineering, medicine and architecture. Different people can use different strategies for solving mental rotation tasks. 'Holistic' and 'analytical' mental rotation strategies focus on different information in mental rotation tests. In holistic strategy, the object is handled as a whole while the rotation task is being performed in the mind. On the other hand, individuals who use the analytical strategy analyze the object first and refer to a part of the object for rotation [1]. The same individual can change their strategy depending on task characteristics or strategy learning as well.

Mixed Reality is an umbrella term that involves more than one type of technology including Virtual Reality (VR) and Augmented Reality (AR). Any environment that combines real and virtual information is referred to as mixed reality and can be anywhere within the real-virtual continuum depending on the dominant type of information it contains.

VR and AR-based immersive environments have been increasingly employed for cognitive ability testing in recent years with normal and diagnosed participants [2]. It is used for both evaluating executive functions of people from different age groups and rehabilitating the elderly for helping them manage activities of daily life. VR/AR is used to assess and enhance spatial ability by allowing interaction with virtual objects [3].

Literature in the last decade highlights the importance of measuring spatial ability in three-dimensional (3-D) environments. Up-to-date 3-D technologies may enhance quality or fidelity which can facilitate test performance in turn [4]. Mixed Reality, which allows overlaying virtual objects onto the real world [5], can be a suitable environment for spatial ability testing. Such 3-D environments are likely to be used for measuring the effectiveness of state-of-the-art cognitive training applications. Tests administered in traditional environments are not compatible with learning experiences in immersive environments. To provide tools for evaluating learning in immersive environments, we developed a test that can be administered in them. The test was converted to three-dimensional without any other alteration in the content.

2 Related Works

The primary distinction between 3-D and 2-D environments is the addition of depth information. Three-dimensional display with sufficient depth information is achieved by presenting slightly different images to each eye, a technology which is known as "stereoscopy". People mentally rotate stimuli presented with stereoscopic disparity faster and more accurately. This may result from the reduced ambiguity of stimuli [6]. Stereoscopy can influence cognitive processes entailed in the rotation as well as perceptual processes. Employing the eye-tracking method, [7] found that with increased familiarization with the three-dimensional environment, users become better at perceiving changes.

[8] used tasks designed by modifying existing items of spatial ability tests to compare performance in solving 2-D paper-based vs. 3-D Virtual-Reality based MR tasks. A 3-D display was prepared by projecting stimuli on a GeoWall. Participant performance was not influenced by the dimensionality of the stimuli. Processing depth cues is considered the most challenging aspect of three-dimensional representations. Therefore, research in this area expects the z-axis rotations to distinguish between two and three-dimensional environments.

[9] developed Immersive Mental Rotation Test (IMRT) to examine the effect of dimensionality and background complexity in the virtual environment on mental rotation performance. They conducted the study remotely whereby they presented MRT in Oculus Quest to participants who owned these particular goggles and watched the test session online. Importantly, they modified the original test choices by excluding the distractors to encourage mental rotation rather than piecemeal approaches. Both versions of MRT were delivered with the VR headset.

Few studies conducted mental rotation (MR) tests in 3-D environments and compared them to traditional 2-D tests. However, further studies are needed for understanding the characteristics of 3-D testing better. Typically, genders have a pronounced difference with regard to mental rotation ability. However, the evidence of gender difference is inconclusive because mental rotation ability in 3-D environments is not as sound as in traditional 2-D environments. Transferring the complete Mental Rotation Test (MRT) into Virtual Reality, [4] found that males scored higher than females in the test delivered on Oculus Rift. On the other hand, males outperformed females in the paper-based MRT but not in the Virtual Reality-delivered MRT [10]. In [11], the 3-D presentation of stimuli developed by the authors benefited females more than 2-D representations and narrowed the gap between male and female performance. Similarly, in [12] gender differences appeared in the 2-D screen while not occurring in the 3-D mental rotation task delivered with Augmented Reality. 2-D rotation tasks require participants to convert 2-D images into 3-D mental representations, carry out the necessary rotations on these representations and re-convert the resulting 3-D image to 2-D. These transformations are considered redundant for performing mental rotation and are referred to as the problem of "dimensionality crossing". The lack of gender difference in the 3-D mode in some studies may be a result of the elimination of this problem.

Cognitive load is another aspect of 3-D testing that requires further studies. Due to the high number of elements interacting with each other and the necessity to visualize the result in the mind, mental rotation tasks may expose the student to an excessive amount of cognitive load. When taking a 3-D test in novel technology, participants may become overwhelmed if they are not given sufficient time and practice to familiarize themselves with the environment. Additionally, depth cues should be used properly for mediating cognitive load in stereoscopic representations [8]. On the other hand, 3-D presentation of MR stimuli provides test-takers with additional visual information to make judgments and releases information processing load [12].

Immersion refers to the individual's subjective perception of having a realistic and comprehensive experience. The presence of depth stimuli can influence the feelings of the test-taker in immersive 3-D environments. For this reason, [13] investigated MR task performance in 2D non-immersive (flat screen), 3-D non-immersive (screen with shutter glasses), and 3-D immersive (HMD) environments. They indicated that 3-D immersive environments promote egocentric rather than the screen-based encoding of stimuli which can enable more realistic measurement of MR ability. Developing a VR-based spatial ability testing unit with three different spatial tests, [14] stated that the use of VR headset was found to positively affect spatial performance as opposed to using less immersive desktop VR. A correlation between mental rotation performance and feeling of presence was observed by [4].

Apart from visual authenticity, there are studies also highlighting the importance of interactional authenticity. [12] stated that their use of Augmented Reality was limited to the 3-D presentation of stimuli with no possibility of moving around objects or grasping them. For enabling more intuitive interaction, in some studies, virtual objects are rotated using hand gestures. [15] created a VR-based test unit that contained multiple-choice questions to be answered with hand gestures. They found a correlation between the scores in paper-based and VR-based MRT. A summary of the MR stimuli and display device used in 3-D mental rotation testing studies can be seen in Table 1.

Table 1. Works on 3-D MR Measurement

STUDY	Stimuli/Test	Display Platform
Parsons *et al.* (2004)	Mental Rotation Test	Virtual Reality Spatial Rotation
Neubauer *et al.* (2010)	Shepard & Metzler Figures	AR Projector
Price and Lee (2010)	Modified PSVT Figures	GeoWall Projector
Arendasy *et al.* (2011)	Self-developed Tasks	LCD + Shutter Glasses
Kozhevnikov and Dhond (2012)	Shepard & Metzler Figures	Head Mounted Display
Foroughi *et al.* (2015)	Mental Rotation Test	Oculus Rift (VR)
Burles (2019)	S&M type objects	LCD + Shutter Glasses
Ariali (2020)	Modified Mental Rotation Test	HTC Vive
Guzscvinez *et al.* (2020)	PSVT, MRT	Samsung GR
Lochhead *et al.* (2022)	IMRT	Oculus Quest

Studies in this area suggest the necessity of comparing a 3-D version of a mental rotation test delivered on a state-of-the-art visualization technology with a computer-delivered version. In this study, we investigated the following questions:

- What is the effect of the dimensionality of the test stimuli (2-D vs. 3-D) on students' mental rotation performance?
- What is the effect of the dimensionality of the test stimuli (2-D vs. 3-D) on students' cognitive load?
- Is gender difference observed in students' mental rotation performance in the 3-D test environment?

3 Methodology

The aim of this study is to compare the computer-based two-dimensional and the Mixed Reality-based three-dimensional versions of the Purdue Spatial Visualization Test: Rotations in terms of mental rotation performance, cognitive load, and gender. In this section, we outline the development of the MR-based PSVT:R and the process of the conducted study.

3.1 3-D Purdue Spatial Visualization Test: Rotations

The Rotations section of the Purdue Spatial Visualisation Test (PSVT) is a mental rotation ability test that consists of two-dimensional isometric drawings [16]. This test is one of the most heavily used mental rotation tests.

The original Purdue Spatial Visualization Test: Rotations (PSVT:R) has 30 questions and 2 practice questions. In the test, participants view the illustrations demonstrating one object rotated to a certain orientation. Then, they need to select the final orientation of another object to be rotated in the same way from among the five choices. It was suggested that PSVT:R is administered to individuals 13 years or older. This test was chosen from among other mental rotation tests because it contains various types of test objects with inclined, cylindrical, and oblique surfaces. PSVT:R is unbiased for gender comparison in mental rotation ability.

[17] revised the whole PSVT:R while transferring the PSVT figures to the computer environment to eliminate the errors she detected in the drawing of some items which might be confusing for students. We used the instructions of the test translated into Turkish by [18].

We measured the mental rotation ability of half of the participants in the 2-D computer environment. In this test, images from the paper-based test were used. Practice questions have written instructions. Test items were displayed on a monitor and participants used a mouse to answer the questions. An example test item from the 2-D computer-based PSVT:R can be seen in Fig. 1.

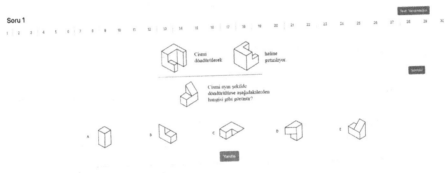

Fig. 1. 2-D PSVT:R Item

As its validity and reliability were established, the Revised PSVT:R by [17] was used in this study. The internal consistency coefficient of the test shows a good level of reliability (Cronbach's $\alpha = .862$). The Cronbach's alpha values of this test calculated in this study were .895 for the two-dimensional test and .749 for the three-dimensional test. These values are higher than .70, which is accepted as the threshold value by [19].

For measuring mental rotation ability in a more authentic environment, we developed a 3-D version of PSVT:R. 3-D test objects were created based on the original PSVT:R using the SketchUp modeling software. 3-D stimuli were attempted to resemble the 2-D drawings as closely as possible. We developed the test module by using Unity and delivered it on Microsoft HoloLens 2 (see Fig. 2). The development process was iterative with face-to-face and online meetings and MR headset tryout sessions whereby developers strived for ensuring that the orientation of the models in the 3-D test aligned with the original test, making size arrangements to use the field of view most effectively and shading in a way that minimizes uncertainty. As in the original 2-D drawings from the original test, holographic objects in the 3-D test were made clearer by drawing edges as well.

Fig. 2. Microsoft HoloLens 2

Microsoft HoloLens 2 employs the Windows 10 Holographic operating system. In addition to holographic imaging and spatial mapping, Microsoft HoloLens 2 can track hand and eye movements and recognize voice commands. Wearing the headset, participants are able to view the 3-D display illuminated using laser light. The headset has a 52-degree field of view. The test was displayed on a 53 × 105 panel 1.5 m from the user. The panel was fixed at this distance and the test items were displayed as if they were pinned on the air. It is possible to walk around the holographic objects and view them from different angles. However, for this study, these actions were not allowed during the test as they could give an unfair advantage to 3-D test-takers. For the same reason, we did not enable rotating objects to try answers.

Practice questions in the 3-D test involve written as well as audio instructions (with the same content as the 2-D group). Participants answer the questions using hand gestures recognized by the sensors capturing hand movements within a particular range of motion. The choice air-tapped by the participant turns to orange to show that it is selected. Then, the participant air-taps on the Next button to proceed to the next question.

In both versions of the test, participants can answer questions directly by clicking on the objects that contain the choices for the question. Participants are re-directed once to the questions they skipped. If they still do not answer these questions, they may finish the test. It was found that the tasks presented to the individual within a reference frame can affect mental rotation performance by changing how they perform the rotations [20]. Therefore, no frames were used for isolating separate test choices.

The two versions of the PSVT:R are identical in terms of the test content and question order. However, there were some extra considerations while developing the 3-D test module. Firstly, before taking the test in a new environment, the MR headset, participants need to be familiarized with the interaction method. Thus, we took them through a brief tutorial demonstrating the basic hand gestures used with HoloLens. An eye calibration was carried out for accurate hologram representation and hand tracking. Secondly, we adjusted the lighting carefully for achieving an accurate representation of the 3-D test stimuli for all participants. An example test item from the 3-D HMD-based PSVT:R can be seen in the Fig. 3. Test data was stored as text files that can be accessed through Windows Device Portal.

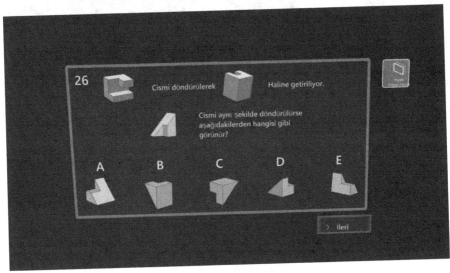

Fig. 3. 3-D PSVT:R Test Item

3.2 Procedure

For investigating the effect of test dimensionality on mental rotation performance and cognitive load, we compared the two versions of the PSVT:R (2-D computer-based and 3-D HMD-based).

Participants are 47 undergraduate students aged between 18 and 22 from a university in Turkey (F = 30, M = 17). We administered a demographic questionnaire to the sample for collecting information about individuals including gender, eye conditions, gaming experience, and previous AR and VR exposure. We explained the flow of the session to the participants.

22 of the participants used the 2-D version while 25 participants used the 3-D version. To control for gender, we arranged 2-D and 3-D test groups to include equal numbers of female participants (n = 15). We tested each participant in an individual session. Figure 4 shows a participant taking the 3-D PSVT:R.

Fig. 4. 3-D PSVT:R on HoloLens 2

Since the 3-D group took the test in a new environment, they were engaged in activities to familiarize themselves with the MR Headset before taking the test. We demonstrated Click and airtap hand gestures that are used to interact with the headset to the students. Airtap involves pointing the index finger to the ceiling and tapping it down quickly rising back again (Fig. 5). We showed participants how to position their arms and elbows for airtap without feeling fatigued.

Tasks such as pressing holographic buttons closely and remotely, moving resizing, and rotating objects, and navigating and calibrating the holographic operating system were carried out using the Microsoft Tips application. Only when they are confident with the technology, students proceeded to the test.

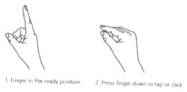

1. Finger in the ready position   2. Press finger down to tap or click

Fig. 5. Airtap Gesture (https://docs.microsoft.com/th-th/dynamics365/mixed-reality/guides/hl1)

Participants were given 20 min for completing the test. For measuring cognitive load, we employed the four-item cognitive load scale used by Lee et al. [21]. After finishing the test, students in both groups received this scale. The flow of the study can be seen in Fig. 6.

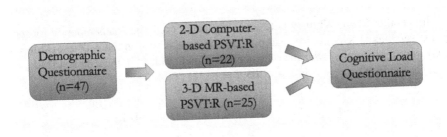

Fig. 6. Flow of the study

4 Results

The descriptive statistics about the 2-D and 3-D mental rotation scores are presented in Table 2. The participants in the 2-D test group ($M = 15.95$, $SD = 5.51$) and the 3-D test group ($M = 15.24$, $SD = 3.83$) showed equal performance in mental rotation ability.

Table 2. Descriptive Statistics of 2-D and 3-D Test Groups

	n	M	SD	Min	Max
2-D PSVT:R	22	15.95	5.51	10	29
3-D PSVT:R	25	15.24	3.83	9	25

Due to non-normal distribution, we used a Mann-Whitney U test for comparing mental rotation scores of 2-D and 3-D versions of PSVT:R. There was no significant difference between the three-dimensional mental rotation test scores (Mdn = 14.00) and the two-dimensional rotation test scores (Mdn = 14.00) (U = 271.50, z = −.075, p < .05, r = −.11) (Table 3).

Table 3. Score Difference Between 2-D And 3-D Tests

Mental Rotation Ability	2-D Test (n = 22)	3-D Test (n = 25)	
	Mean Rank	Mean Rank	z value
	23.84	24.14	−.075

With another Mann-Whitney U test, we compared cognitive loads reported for the two test versions. The cognitive load participants experienced in the 3-D test (Mdn = 10.00) was significantly lower than the cognitive load induced in the 2-D test (Mdn = 16.00) (U = 156.00, z = −2.546, p < .05, r = −.37) (Table 4).

Table 4. Cognitive Load Difference in 2-D and 2-D Tests

Cognitive Load	2-D Test (n = 22)	3-D Test (n = 25)	
	Mean Rank	Mean Rank	z value
	29.41	19.24	−2.546*

We compared female and male participants' test scores for investigating gender differences in the testing environment.

We examined gender differences separately for the two-dimensional and three-dimensional groups with Mann-Whitney U tests (Table 5).

Table 5. Gender Difference in Two Test Versions

Mental Rotation Ability	Female (n = 30)	Male (n = 17)	
	Mean Rank	Mean Rank	z value
2-D Test	9.15	14.89	−2.045*
3-D Test	11.76	15.63	1.235

Men's mental rotation ability (Mdn = 18) was higher than that of women (Mdn = 13.00) in the two-dimensional test (U = 28.00, z = −2.04, p < .05, r = −.434). In the three-dimensional test, there was no difference between the mental rotation skills of women (Mdn = 14.00) and men (Mdn = 16.50) (U = 47.00, z = −1.23, p > .05, r = −.25).

5 Discussion

This study found no difference in mental rotation performance between two-dimensional computer-based and three-dimensional Mixed Reality-based PSVT:R we created. Equal mental rotation accuracy was measured by the two versions of the test. [9] found that participants score higher in MRT using 3-D stimuli than MRT using 2-D stimuli when they are both displayed on a headset. This difference may be explained with the use of a different mental rotation ability test in the two studies. Additionally, although time for familiarization with the headset was allocated, the performance of the 3-D group may be hindered due to having to wear some accessory during the test. [9] studied the effect of dimensionality on 2-D and 3-D MR tests with a paired-sample design. Their procedure involved participants taking the two versions of IMRT successively. As we thought that this type of design may result in a learning/practice effect, the 2-D and 3-D test scores in this study are obtained from different groups.

Expectedly, we observed gender difference in the two-dimensional test. However, men and women performed equally in the three-dimensional test. No gender difference in mental rotation ability measured in three-dimensional environments was reported also in [10, 12]. The authors commented that women's disadvantage may not be due to the mental rotation process itself, but having to extract a three-dimensional image from a two-dimensional image. According to [22], as a result of women's increasing interaction with new technologies, it is expected that gender differences in mental rotation tasks given in such environments may not be so underlined.

We know that three-dimensional virtual environments create less cognitive load than two-dimensional video in a spatial task [23]. In previous studies, concerns have been expressed that three-dimensional technologies such as Augmented Reality may create high cognitive load due to the use of intense sensory cues for fidelity. However, if these clues contain information necessary for problem-solving and removing uncertainty, they can alleviate the cognitive load. Similar to Dan and Reiner, when the two-dimensional test and the three-dimensional test were compared in terms of cognitive load in this study, it was seen that the two-dimensional test gave more cognitive load than the three-dimensional test. In the three-dimensional test environment where all participants are not accustomed to both the display device (Augmented Reality headset) and the inter-action type (gesture-based), the cognitive load of the users was lower than in the two-dimensional test environment using a computer screen and a mouse which they are familiar with. As in [12], this finding can be interpreted that three-dimensional repre-sentation reduces the information processing load. Similarly, body movements may be used for offloading some of the cognitive load to the body parts.

In this study, participants in both groups were commonly seen as performing hand gestures to find answers to the test items, which is considered to be more typical of low spatial ability individuals. Some participants in the 3-D test-takers noted that walking around the holographic objects would make the test easier; however, this was restricted in this particular study as we think this would give them an unfair advantage against the 2-D test-takers. [24] used marker-based AR to understand the effect of this tool on paper-based MR test performance. They noted that such visual aid especially benefits low spatial ability participants. We believe that some participants in our study felt that the test would be easier if they could wander around the test objects. As we were interested in the actual performances of individuals without unlikely boosts, the 3-D group was not allowed to look at test items from multiple angles. Nevertheless, the visual properties of the holographic display enabled them to perceive the virtual objects in three dimensions like tangible objects.

Cognitive load can also be considered in terms of redundant visual information. [9] investigated the effect of the background used in IMRT by comparing a "clean" background that is simple and similar to previous MR measurement environments and a "cluttered" background that contains a furnished virtual living room. The furniture in this case is not necessary for solving the mental rotation problems. However, background complexity did not influence MRT scores. In the present study, the 3-D test was displayed on a holographic panel outside of which they could see the physical world. Although the panel can be switched off, experimenting with the background was not within the scope of this study. Nevertheless, it would be interesting to compare versions of PSVT:R with and without a panel framing the test items to look further into the effect of the background.

As it does not hinder test-takers in terms of cognitive load and measures three-dimensional thinking skills in a three-dimensional environment, the 3-D PSVT:R can be used instead of the two-dimensional version and can be integrated into future spatial training in three-dimensional environments. This test can be used for screening in places where spatial ability is critical for success. Additionally, it can be used as a mental rotation exercise simply by allowing participants to move around the holographic objects or making them rotatable for answering the questions. Another spatial ability test can then be used for investigating the effectiveness of such immersive training.

6 Conclusion

We devised a reliable and realistic mental rotation ability measurement tool in this study using three-dimensional models and a Mixed Reality headset. Like 3-D environments for general spatial ability testing, most 3-D platforms for MR ability measurement were developed within the last decade. According to these works, MR ability testing in 3-D is more authentic as it allows a clearer presentation of stimuli. Furthermore, it affects the cognitive processes entailed in mental rotation and frames of reference used for rotation. Especially immersive environments facilitate the use of more effective strategies and allow more valid measurement of MR ability. This study found a difference between 2-D and 3-D mental rotation tests not in accuracy but in cognitive load. The 3-D testing environment induced a lower cognitive load than the 2-D computer-based environment. Furthermore, male and female participants performed equally in 3-D.

Future studies should look for investigating the relative features of 2-D and 3-D spatial tests with larger samples and different age levels. As educational practices using Mixed Reality technologies increase, traditional measurement tools will not be sufficient to measure learning, and measurements will be made in these three-dimensional environments. Practitioners can benefit from immersive testing tools to enable valid measurement in immersive learning environments. In this respect, in a future study, the authors will use the 3-D MR-based PSVT:R for examining the effectiveness of an MR-based spatial ability training module they created. Also, we plan to explore mental rotation strategies being used in tests in two-dimensional and three-dimensional environments using the think-aloud method. Cognitive processes in these two conditions can be better understood with this scope. In the future, new tests can be developed specifically for these environments apart from transferring standard tests to the Mixed Reality environment. Such tests can be embedded in personalized spatial ability training that meets the needs and interests of individual learners [25]. While the interest in virtual universes is growing, we should be open to finding practical ways of carrying out various cognitive tasks in 3-D environments. Specific design guidelines for immersive platforms should be elucidated through evidence-based studies. Perceptions in and about such environments should be investigated.

Acknowledgments. This study is partially supported by the Scientific and Technological Research Council of Turkey under the 1002 Fast Support Program 121E293.

References

1. Sorby, S.: Educational research in developing 3-D spatial skills for engineering students. Int. J. Sci. Educ. **31**(3), 459–480 (2009). https://doi.org/10.1080/09500690802595839
2. Kim, E., et al.: Examining the academic trends in neuropsychological tests for executive functions using virtual reality: systematic literature review. JMIR Ser. Games **9**(4), e30249 (2021). https://doi.org/10.2196/30249
3. Bilgin, C.U., Anteneh, M.R., Thompson, M.: What's so special about spatial? A review study joining virtual reality and spatial ability. In: Implementing Augmented Reality Into Immersive Virtual Learning Environments, pp. 56–73 (2021)
4. Foroughi, C.K., Wren, W.C., Barragán, D., Mead, P.R., Boehm-Davis, D.A.: Assessing mental rotation ability in a virtual environment with an oculus rift. In: Proceedings of the Human Factors and Ergonomics Society Annual Meeting, vol. 59, no. 1, pp. 1849–1852. Sage Publications, Los Angeles (2015). https://doi.org/10.1177/154193121559139
5. Allcoat, D., Hatchard, T., Azmat, F., Stansfield, K., Watson, D., von Mühlenen, A.: Education in the digital age: learning experience in virtual and mixed realities. J. Educ. Comput. Res. **59**(5), 795–816 (2021). https://doi.org/10.1177/0735633120985120
6. Burles, F., Lu, J., Slone, E., Cortese, F., Iaria, G., Protzner, A.B.: Revisiting mental rotation with stereoscopic disparity: a new spin for a classic paradigm. Brain Cogn. **136**, 103600 (2019). https://doi.org/10.1016/j.bandc.2019.103600
7. Karacan, H.U., Cagiltay, K., Tekman, H.G.: Change detection in desktop virtual environments: an eye-tracking study. Comput. Hum. Behav. **26**(6), 1305–1313 (2010). https://doi.org/10.1016/j.chb.2010.04.002
8. Price, A., Lee, H.S.: The effect of two-dimensional and stereoscopic presentation on middle school students' performance of spatial cognition tasks. J. Sci. Educ. Technol. **19**(1), 90–103 (2010). https://doi.org/10.1007/s10956-009-9182-2
9. Lochhead, I., Hedley, N., Çöltekin, A., Fisher, B.: The immersive mental rotations test: evaluating spatial ability in virtual reality. Frontiers Virtual Reality **5** (2022). https://doi.org/10.3389/frvir.2022.820237
10. Parsons, T.D., et al.: Sex differences in mental rotation and spatial rotation in a virtual environment. Neuropsychologia **42**(4), 555–562 (2004). https://doi.org/10.1016/j.neuropsychologia.2003.08.014
11. Arendasy, M., Sommer, M., Hergovich, A., Feldhammer, M.: Evaluating the impact of depth cue salience in working three-dimensional mental rotation tasks by means of psychometric experiments. Learn. Individ. Differ. **21**(4), 403–408 (2011). https://doi.org/10.1016/j.lindif.2011.04.002
12. Neubauer, A.C., Bergner, S., Schatz, M.: Two- vs. three-dimensional presentation of mental rotation tasks: sex differences and effects of training on performance and brain activation. Intelligence **38**(5), 529–539 (2010). https://doi.org/10.1016/j.intell.2010.06.001

13. Kozhevnikov, M., Dhond, R.P.: Understanding immersivity: image generation and transformation processes in 3D immersive environments. Front. Psychol. **3**, 284 (2012). https://doi.org/10.3389/fpsyg.2012.00284
14. Guzsvinecz, T., Orbán-Mihálykó, É., Perge, E., Sik-Lányi, C.: Analyzing the spatial skills of university students with a virtual reality application using a desktop display and the Gear VR. Acta Polytechnica Hungarica **17**(2), 35–56 (2020)
15. Ariali, S.: Training of mental rotation ability in virtual spaces. J. Tech. Educ. (JOTED) **8**(2), 46–63 (2020). https://doi.org/10.48513/joted.v8i2.207
16. Guay, R.: Purdue spatial vizualization test. Educ. Test. Serv. (1976)
17. Yoon, S.Y.: Psychometric properties of the revised Purdue spatial visualization tests: visualization of rotations (The Revised PSVT: R). Purdue University (2011)
18. Turgut, M., Uygan, C.: Spatial ability training for undergraduate mathematics education students: designing tasks with SketchUp®?. Electron. J. Math. Technol. **8**(1) (2014)
19. Cohen, J.: Statistical Power Analysis for the Behavioral Sciences, 2nd edn. Lawrence Erlbaum Associates, Mahwah, NJ (1988)
20. Bilge, A.R., Taylor, H.A.: Framing the figure: mental rotation revisited in light of cognitive strategies. Mem. Cognit. **45**(1), 63–80 (2017). https://doi.org/10.3758/s13421-016-0648-1
21. Lee, I.J., Chen, C.H., Chang, K.P.: Augmented reality technology combined with three-dimensional holography to train the mental rotation ability of older adults. Comput. Hum. Behav. **65**, 488–500 (2016). https://doi.org/10.1016/j.chb.2016.09.014
22. Rodán, A., Contreras, M.J., Elosúa, M.R., Gimeno, P.: Experimental but not sex differences of a mental rotation training program on adolescents. Front. Psychol. **7**, 1050 (2016). https://doi.org/10.3389/fpsyg.2016.01050
23. Dan, A., Reiner, M.: EEG-based cognitive load of processing events in 3D virtual worlds is lower than processing events in 2D displays. Int. J. Psychophysiol. **122**, 75–84 (2017). https://doi.org/10.1016/j.ijpsycho.2016.08.013
24. Connolly, P., Beeler, J., Connaughton, P., Price, J., Trefz, B.: Spatial ability testing with augmented reality. In: 2010 Annual Conference & Exposition (2010). https://doi.org/10.18260/1-2-15987
25. Papakostas, C., Troussas, C., Krouska, A., Sgouropoulou, C.: Exploration of augmented reality in spatial abilities training: a systematic literature review for the last decade. Inf. Educ. **20**(1), 107–130 (2021)

Design of a Mixed Reality Approach to Enhance Understanding of Reverse Total Shoulder Arthroplasty

Alireza Sadeghi Milani[1], Joe Cecil[1(✉)], Miguel Pirela-Cruz[2], and Shelia Kennison[3]

[1] Center for Cyber-Physical Systems, Department of Computer Science, Oklahoma State University, Stillwater, USA
j.cecil@okstate.edu
[2] Department of Orthopedic Surgery, Texas Tech University, El Paso, USA
[3] Department of Psychology, Oklahoma State University, Stillwater, USA

Abstract. This paper focuses on the design of a mixed reality-based (MR) simulation environment to train health care personnel in reverse total shoulder arthroplasty (RTSA) procedure. Information-centric models involving interaction with orthopedic surgeons were created as part of a participatory design approach. These information models provided a structural foundation for the design and development of the environments. This paper concludes with a discussion of the preliminary assessment activities which includes studying the impact of such a MR approach on understanding and knowledge acquisition of the targeted surgical procedure.

Keywords: Reverse Total Shoulder Arthroplasty · Mixed Reality · Participatory Design

1 Introduction

Extended reality tools and environments are being increasingly used to support learning and education [1]. The term Extended reality (XR) encompasses three categories: virtual reality (VR), augmented reality (AR), and mixed reality (MR). These technologies extend various levels of reality by blending real and virtual worlds to support effective immersive experiences [2]. By integrating XR into training, learners can be immersed in a multisensory environment that is more interactive, engaging, and effective. XRs can be used to support the design of Virtual Learning Environments (VLEs) which can be described as a special type of XR environment designed to support learning and training [3].

MR combines the use of AR and VR to seamlessly merge the physical and digital realms, creating an interactive environment for users. This environment can either consist of real surroundings enhanced with virtual elements (known as augmented reality) or virtual environments enriched with physical objects (known as augmented virtuality). By leveraging cutting-edge computer technology, graphics, and input systems, MR enables learners to actively engage with both physical and digital components in real-time. With the integration of mixed reality, learners can immerse themselves in lifelike interactions with objects and individuals, blurring the boundaries between the real and virtual worlds. They are empowered to manipulate and engage with digital assets, as well as interact with real-life objects and people within the same environment. This technology opens up new possibilities for realistic and dynamic learning experiences [3].

Glenohumeral arthritis and complicated proximal fractures can be treated surgically with reverse total shoulder arthroplasty (RTSA). The humeral and glenoid stages are the two key steps in this surgery [4]. In standard total shoulder arthroplasty (TSA) the implants (ball and cap) resemble the natural shape of the humerus and scapula however, in RTSA the implants are reversed. The ball is attached to the scapula and the cap is attached to the humerus (Fig. 1).

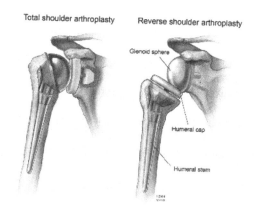

Fig. 1. TSA (on the left), RTSA (on the right) [5]

In RTSA, the proper positioning of the glenoid component helps to increase the survival rate and prevent premature loosening which is one of the procedure's key considerations [6]. Surgeons are required to have a good amount of working knowledge of these bones and surgery steps to be able to plan and perform safe RTSA. However, even after planning a complex surgery such as RTSA, its realization is challenging. Therefore, the level of experience of surgeons plays a crucial role in this process. In medical universities, the usage of XR simulators for training surgeons and residents has grown in recent years. Residents in surgical training are typically instructed to use cadavers, animals, and artificial replicas [7]. These conventional techniques have some shortcomings. Animals being used for surgical training has drawn criticism from animal rights activists. The use of cadavers increases the danger of infection. Training with synthetic mockups is expensive and impersonal when it comes to people [8]. Other methods involve residents watching a skilled surgeon perform the surgery before gradually transitioning to assist them. In this context, new technologies, such as MR, provide surgeons and residents with less expertise to catch up to those with more experience which result in reduced surgical risks and errors caused by insufficient information about anatomical variations. MR utilizes both AR and VR to blend the physical and digital worlds, with the user situated in an interactive environment that could be either real with virtual assets, or virtual with physical objects [9]. Hence, MR provides interaction with real-world information and better training as trainees do not feel completely alone because of a collaborative learning environment, and trainers do not have to be represented as virtual avatars because students are still aware of the real world [10]. Therefore, our research focuses on designing MR-based simulation environments to train residents in RTSA by creating information-centric process models. The proposed approach dealing with the MR simulator for RTSA is outlined as follows:

1. Expert surgeons' knowledge for comprehending specific surgical procedures has not been prioritized in prior research efforts; in the strategy outlined in this study, the simulator was conceived and built in close collaboration with expert surgeons.
2. Other earlier research initiatives have not investigated the development of advanced information-centric models of target surgical processes (as a basis to comprehend a surgical process) before developing training simulators. A few previous initiatives have investigated information-centric methodologies, but they have not gone as far as the information-centric modeling strategy used in this paper. In this work, the effect of employing such a strategy is also discussed.

Thus far, some of the key terms and concepts have been defined and described. Next, a review of the literature provided. The rest of this article is structured as follows. The research methodology is provided in Sect. 2. Subsequently, Sect. 3 maps out knowledge assessment results. In Sect. 4, a discussion of the results is provided. Further, Sect. 4 provides a presentation of the taxonomy and a comparison of the results. In Sect. 5, Comprehension assessment is included. Finally, the conclusion and future work is presented in Sect. 6.

1.1 Related Works

In recent years, the role of XR in medical training simulators has been covered in a number of studies. However, there is a lack of proper utilization of the participatory design approach during the creation of information models. Prior research efforts have not emphasized the role of expert surgeons as knowledge sources for understanding target surgical processes; in the approach discussed in this paper, the simulator was designed and developed in close interaction with expert surgeons.

A study was conducted by [11] involving a group of older adults in which they engaged in creating a VR-based ATM training simulation by using a participatory design approach. The results from the study demonstrate that VR is an effective way to directly gain valuable insights related to the design from the participants. Few studies have investigated the role of using XR-based medical training environments by conducting pre and post-test questionaries. In [12] a VR module was used for training an advanced temporal bone procedure. Their results indicate that the environment is effective in training surgical residents for the surgery. In [13] an assessment method based on cyber-humans was created for a virtual reality orthopedic surgery training simulator. Their strategy was based on the evaluation of three perspectives: knowledge, skills, and mental stability. A Mixed Reality-based surgical navigation system for orthopedic surgical navigation has been discussed by [14]. The MR-based navigation system consists of a HoloLens display, a magnetic launcher, a passenger sensor, and a processor. The MR-based system is useful in providing real-time 3D visualization. Using the MR-based system, the 3D reconstructed virtual model generated using a CT scan or MRI can be integrated with the body of the patient which can help guide the operating procedure. Such a system provides additional visual information related to the internal organ of the patient which is not visible to the naked eye. The MR-based navigation system has several advantages over the conventional image-guided surgical system such as intuitive and detailed imaging information, less time spent and mental load, and low risk of errors among others. [15] utilized VR simulation for teaching orthopedic surgery residents to see it is beneficial for their performance in cadaver Total Hip Arthroplasty (THA) surgical skills. They compared the improvement in cadaver THA performance, specific aspects of surgical skills, and knowledge and perception of surgical anatomy and indications. Participants first completed a written pretest and a single THA for establishing their baseline knowledge, then half of them randomly interacted with VR simulation. They utilized the OramaVR software platform and Oculus Rift CV1 headset for their simulation. Their results showed that VR improves surgical and technical skills but has no effect on medical knowledge. [16] presented initial outcomes of using an immersive VR-based preoperative planning tool for laparoscopic donor nephrectomy. The author stated that it was challenging to understand more than 2500 CT images hence they developed 3D models using a 3D slicer which allowed an interactive and comprehensive anatomy when viewed through an immersive headset. The CT images of seven patients were used for a study in which two surgeons assessed the preoperative understanding using CT alone and CT on the immersive headset. The results from the study indicated that immersive models enhanced the surgeons' understanding of the patient's arterial and venous anatomy. Moreover, the surgeons' overall confidence regarding the operation improved while interacting with the 3D image on the immersive headset. [17] proposed two teaching modules for their prototype 3D first Aid VR. A teaching module that described the cause and symptoms of seizure and a training module was utilized to train first aid instructions in a VR simulation. Wang and Wang [18] proposed a VR simulation for the entire chest anatomy to perform the anatomical operation with experimental steps. They divided the process into three modules: scene construction, result determination, and UI interface. [19] Created 3D-printed glenoid models with a B2 defect. Then, they used Unity to build and program 3D models for the same prints with a guide pin for installation on Microsoft HoloLens2. Their study focused on comparing the accuracy of MR holographic model–assisted glenoid guidewire placement to FreeHand (FH) and patient-specific instrumentation (PSI) methods. In all participants, the accuracy of MR was very similar to PSI and FH for the start point, and there was no statistically significant difference in version between MR/PSI and MR/FH. [20] simulated guide wire insertion procedure during dynamic hip screw surgery to depict the training potential of AR and VR. They devised a digital fluoroscopic imaging simulator that tracked colored markers tied to a guide wire using orthogonal cameras. They demonstrated that the AR overlay has a 0.4 mm precision for projecting tip apex distance. They also demonstrated that with more repetitions, the trainee's accuracy improved. [21] tracked 24 medical students who were randomly assigned to four sessions of either one-on-one instruction from a hip replacement surgeon or augmented reality instruction using the Microsoft HoloLens headgear. The accuracy, trainee perceptions, and potential training role of the AR headset were compared to hands-on, expert instruction by a surgeon. Participants underwent surgical training to position an acetabular cup on an opaque hip model in 6 distinct orientations. [22] developed a system for surgical planning and evaluated the results of unilateral, mono-segmental cervical foraminal stenosis using 3D Slicer software on a VR workstation coupled to an HTC Vive and the SteamVR tracking and controller system. The paper comprised 73 patients who used the VR system, and the surgery was planned to use traditional imaging techniques like radiography, CT, and MRI. The authors proposed that designing surgical strategies can benefit from employing VR systems to rebuild preoperative and postoperative images.

Based on the related works discussed in this section there is a need to create information-centric process models to gain better understanding of the target surgical procedures. In this research the role of creating such information-centric process models to better understand RTSA was explored. The preliminary design and implementation of our approach are based on our group's previous simulator for orthopedic surgical training [23]. The creation of information-centric models of target surgical processes is based on that work, although in a more extensive way. Also, the scope of training and assessments are more focused on MR-based simulators and by building various models under different phases to expand training sessions.

2 Research Methodology

In virtual environments, virtual reality technologies are used to create a three-dimensional artificial or synthetic environment that allows users to do "what-if" analyses, comprehend target problems, and compare different solutions for a variety of fields. The overall project objective is to create and assess the impact of an MR-based simulation environment to train medical residents in orthopedic surgery. The benefits of creating such an MR simulator for training include:

- Better Preparation of medical residents for RTSA.
- Avoiding the use of human cadavers as there is the risk of infection.
- Avoiding the use of small animals such as rodents (as they are opposed from animal rights groups, which is part of the changing societal values).
- Opportunity to practice repetitively without additional costs when compared to using physical models.

An information model can be described as a model that captures either the functional or process-oriented relationships between sub-activities that comprise a higher-level activity. In some situations, they can represent both the functional and process dependencies. Such an information Centric model is necessary for a formal foundation before creating VR or MR-based simulation environments. Functional relationships can enable a target process to be better understood using attributes such as information inputs controlling criteria performing agents and decision outcomes. Creation of information models to support design of software systems in engineering activities was originally proposed in [24]. In that research, a functional model of the fixture design activities was created and used as the basis to develop an automated fixture design approach, which resulted in a software tool to accomplish the same. In this research activity, the use of an engineering Enterprise modeling language (eEML) has been adopted which is used to understand the target surgical activities from the perspective of an expert surgeon [25, 26]. The importance of developing a formal modeling foundation for the participatory design approach is discussed in this study. In this study, this strategy has been used with a focus on using participatory design to build information models that help people comprehend the complexity of the surgical procedure.

2.1 Participatory Design

Participatory Design is a method to involve the people who are going to be affected to have their input during the design process [27]. It is a democratic design process for the design of social and technological systems based on the argument that users should be involved in the design and all stakeholders should have input during the design process [28]. The participatory design method was first used in Scandinavia [29].

One of the key perspectives that emphasizes the role of participatory design involves the creation of information intensive function models involving human experts. The importance of the creation of such information models needs to be underscored as it provides a strong foundation for understanding the various relationships of a target function or process. Such an understanding can be captured in an information model which in turn provides a structured basis for designing and building software systems to accomplish various engineering and medical activities. One of the origins of such an approach in creating software-based systems based on participatory design involves the field of automated fixture design. In [25, 30], multiple experts served as knowledge sources to create an advanced information-rich function model of the target manual fixture design process. This information model was created based on the IDEF-0 function methodology and used as the foundational basis to design and build an automated fixture design system [25, 26, 31]. By identifying various relationships involving four key attributes (information inputs, control factors, decision outcomes and Performing mechanisms) and capturing this relationships in a function model, a better understanding of decision-making process involving the fixture design engineering approach was obtained [30]. This in turn was the basis to create an automated fixture design approach and system to support the manufacturing of prismatic parts.

A key aspect of this project involves collaborating with a leading group of medical surgeons at Dignity Regional Medical Center (Phoenix, AZ). One of the innovative aspects is the creation of an information model capturing the overall steps of the surgical procedures as well as identifying the functional and process relationships of the sub-activities and tasks within these surgical procedures. As the surgical process itself is complex, having such a representation was important for the team to understand the process and then design/build the simulator.

In the domain of medical surgery, an information-centric process model was created of a less invasive stabilization system (LISS) plating surgical procedure which is typically used to treat fractures of the femur bone [23]. This information model was used as the basis to understand the target surgical procedure (LISS plating) which in term was used to design and build an immersive VR and haptic-based simulation environment to train orthopedic surgery residents [32]. In this paper the same approach was followed; An experienced surgeon served as the knowledge source for this information model. As the 3D environments were being created, feedback was obtained from surgeons who interacted with the training simulation modules and provided changes/suggestions for the content and the manner of providing the cues /training assistance to the trainees.

2.2 Creation of Surgical Training Modules

The use of MR (Fig. 2) in the simulator offers a potential way to increase the precision of glenoid pin insertion while simultaneously reducing substantial practical restrictions. For this module a realistic 3d printed model of the humerus and glenoid bones used as a physical set-up, then an exact CAD model of the same bone was created by Maxon ZBrush and Autodesk Maya and imported to Unity3D for MR simulator design and to be scripted in C#.

The glenohumeral joint is a synovial joint that attaches the upper limb to the axial skeleton. It is a ball-and-socket joint, formed between the glenoid fossa of the scapula and the head of the humerus. The anatomical plane that passes vertically through the inferior angle is named the scapular body line. The Friedman line is drawn along the long axis of the scapula from the tip of the medial border to the center of the glenoid fossa. The Friedman or scapular line can be used to determine the glenoid version and glenoid bone loss. It is useful for non-navigation surgeries to detect the proper angle for positioning the k-wire into the glenoid.

In order to train residents and improve glenoid positioning, the simulation incorporated the visualization of the Friedman line, intermediate joint line, and Scapula body line. These visual cues were provided to assist residents in achieving more accurate glenoid positioning compared to freehand placement. Additionally, the simulation included the depiction of commonly observed incorrect positioning scenarios during RTSA. By highlighting these repeated incorrect positions, the simulation aimed to help learners recognize and avoid these errors, ultimately enhancing their understanding and skill in glenoid positioning during the surgical procedure. The main steps for RTSA are as below:

1. The first step is to remove soft tissue to expose the glenoid and then use the correct anatomical guide size to determine the proper spot for inserting the central guide pin.
2. Ream the glenoid fossa to remove the cartilage by Sliding the glenoid resurfacing reamer onto the central guide pin and smoothing the surface.
3. Connect the cannulated stop drill to the power tool and drill the central hole over the guide pin.
4. Assemble the internal rod of the metagene holder in the holder's main body. Insert in the final metagene implant central hole. Make the sure metagene is fully seated on the bone and screw it in. Baseplate should have good contact with the bone.
5. Attach Glenosphere.

The Physical Environment: A core part of our innovative approach is to explore training using an integrated cyber-physical approach. For this, a physical surgical setup has been created. 3D-printed bones have been created and a platform has been built in which trainees can rotate the bones and position them to have a better understanding of the anatomy and surgery process. For this purpose, an inline joint linkage with steel

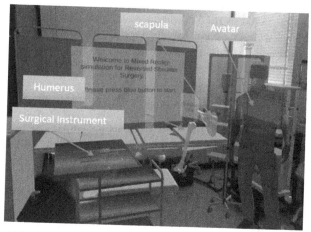

Fig. 2. A view inside the Mixed Reality environment for RTSA (Glenoid steps)

threaded rods was used. Also, an acrylic sheet was used as a base for the setup to make it lightweight regarding the interactions.

2.3 Validity of Simulation

Simulators offer the potential for comprehensive training, gaining surgical skills, and the assessment and certification of surgical proficiency. To confirm their suitability as testing and certification modalities, these simulators must first undergo validation investigations. The validity of a simulator must be thoroughly and objectively assessed before it can be used to measure skill. Validity assesses whether the simulator or training tool is really imparting or measuring what it is supposed to [33].

First, the realism of the simulator is typically evaluated informally by non-experts, to examine the simulator accurately weather represents what it is meant to portray, this is called Face Validity [33]. Validity of simulations in this paper was examined in such a way. Next, a formal review by an expert on the subject of the training should be performed, this is referring to content validity. It is the judgment of the simulator's suitability as a teaching tool [33]. To ensure the validity of the simulation, multiple meetings were conducted with our head surgeon. During these meetings, held at Dignity Regional Medical Center in Phoenix, Arizona, our head surgeon meticulously examined the simulation step by step and provided feedback on various aspects of it. In order to enhance the realism of the simulation, more accurate 3D models were created for the bones (scapula and humerus). Corrections were made to the angles and positions of instruments for each step of the procedure, including the Friedman line angle and the angle and position for performing the k-wire procedure. Taking into account the feedback from surgeons on each main step of the surgery, we incorporated more detailed animations and instructions to further enhance the simulation's accuracy and instructional value.

3 Knowledge Assessment Results

To understand how and to what extent computers may aid learning, as well as how learning could be made more useful, engaging, effective, and approachable, assessments are necessary to throw light on how humans interact with virtual environments including VR/MR based simulation environments [1, 34–36].

Interactions were conducted with two distinct participant groups: first responders and nurses, as well as non-medical students. These participants were randomly assigned to either the text-based cues group or the voice cues group with a 3D medical avatar. Throughout the interaction, participants were provided with instruction on the positioning of k-wires and were given the opportunity to practice this technique on a physical setup. At the conclusion of the simulation, participants were tasked with picking up a drill and correctly indicating the direction for performing the k-wire procedure on the Glenoid. Due to the unfamiliarity of most nurses and students with the drilling process, they were not asked to perform the drilling.

Hypothesis for First Responders and Nurses. MR simulation of RTSA has a significant impact on the learning process of our participants. The assessment activities focusing on the understanding correctness of our hypothesis were performed at Dignity hospital, Prescott, Arizona. The expert surgeon involved in the participatory design approach also facilitated the assessment activities.

To evaluate the knowledge acquisition of first responders at Dignity Prescott and Northern Oklahoma College (NOC) following their interaction with the MR environment, a questionnaire-based pre- and post-test methodology was employed. This method involved administering a pre-test to assess participants' understanding of the RTSA concept through a series of questions. Subsequently, participants engaged in training activities within one of the MR environments featuring HL2, enabling them to learn and interact with a physical setup to determine the optimal positioning of the Glenoid. After the training session, participants completed a post-test consisting of the same set of questions from the pre-test, allowing for an assessment of knowledge gained by comparing the results of the pre- and post-tests. This knowledge assessment served as the basis for a comparative study. A total of 17 participants took part in the study, with 8 from Dignity Prescott and 9 from NOC (refer to Fig. 3 for details). Participant selection was conducted randomly to ensure unbiased representation. Welch's t-test was performed to compare the results of the pre-and post-tests (which are scored from zero to hundred points); paired-samples t-test [37] was used as it is designed for repeated measures as the pre-and post-tests are performed by same participants which is a repeated measures test.

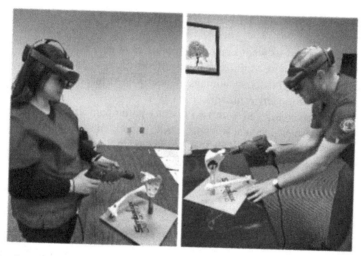

Fig. 3. Mixed Reality RTSA Interaction at Dignity hospital – Prescott and NOC

t-test to determine critical value for t with degrees of freedom = 16 and a = 0.05 was performed for participants to further analyze the results and to test if there was a significant difference in the means of answers. The absolute value of the calculated t exceeds the critical value (13.6292 > 2.12) with M = 13.7094, SD = 16.3967 for pre-tests and M = 63.7024, SD = 18.2863 for post-tests, so the means are significantly different.

The experimental results comparing the means of the pre-test and post-test scores are depicted in Fig. 4 and Fig. 5. It is evident from the figures that there is a significant difference in scores between the two tests. This observation leads to the conclusion that the participants' test scores improved significantly as a result of their interaction with the simulation. Consequently, our hypothesis regarding the effectiveness of the MR simulation is confirmed.

Hypothesis for Non-medical Students. MR simulation of RTSA has a significant effect on the learning process of the student participants. Additionally, it is expected that they would perform the simulation either equally as well or slightly less well compared to first responders and nurses. The assessment activities to evaluate the validity of this hypothesis were carried out at Oklahoma State University, located in Stillwater, Oklahoma. The assessment process was facilitated by an expert surgeon who was involved in the participatory design approach.

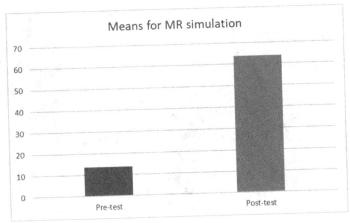

Fig. 4. Result of knowledge assessment for MR environment for first responders and nurses

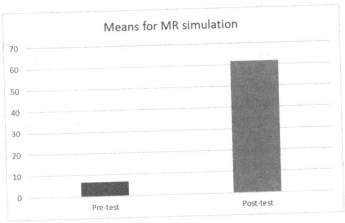

Fig. 5. Result of knowledge assessment for MR environment for non-medical students

To assess the knowledge acquisition of non-medical students at Oklahoma State University following their interaction with the MR environment, the same questionnaire-based pre and post-test methodology was employed. A total of 10 participants engaged with the MR environment as part of this study (refer to Fig. 6 for details). The selection of participants was conducted randomly to ensure unbiased representation. The pre-test and post-test questionnaires were administered to assess the participants' knowledge, and the results were scored on a scale from zero to one hundred points. To analyze the data and determine the significance of any observed differences, Welch's t-test was conducted. The paired-samples t-test, which is specifically designed for repeated measures, was utilized as the pre-test and post-test were performed by the same group of participants, constituting a repeated measures design.

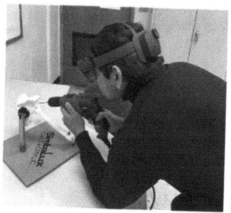

Fig. 6. Mixed Reality RTSA Interaction at Oklahoma State University.

t-test to determine the critical value for t with degrees of freedom = 18 and a = 0.05 was performed for participants to further analyze the results and to test if there was a significant difference in the means of answers. The absolute value of the calculated t exceeds the critical value (8.6614 > 2.101) with M = 6.652, SD = 11.0402 for pre-tests and M = 61.63, SD = 16.7634 for post-tests, so the means are significantly different.

The experimental results comparing the means of the pre-test and post-test scores for the non-medical student participants are presented in Fig. 6. The figures indicate a significant difference in scores between the two tests. From these findings, it can be concluded that the participants' test scores improved significantly as a result of their interaction with the MR simulation. This supports the hypothesis that the MR simulation has a positive impact on the learning process of non-medical students.

4   Results and Discussion

Through collaborations with surgeons, residents, and medical students at Dignity Hospital in Arizona, and non-medical students at Oklahoma State University the effectiveness and impact of employing MR simulation for RTSA as a teaching and training resource was investigated. The learning exercises were conducted with the following two objectives in mind:

1. The first focus was on making sure the simulator environments were accurate; this was done by senior surgeons interacting with the different training environments and giving thorough feedback on changes to the content of the simulation environments.
2. The second focus was on researching the learning impact on medical residents and students, which will be done in stages. With the assistance of a skilled surgeon, the simulation's material was continuously revised and improved. 8 medical participants and 10 non-medical participants took part in the activity for phase 1 once these adjustments had been made and validated. Following the pre-test, the participants used the MR simulator to practice glenoid steps and learn about the surgery procedures. The individuals were then assessed using a post-test. The pre-test and post-test each

took 20 min to complete for the participants. The participants were only required to complete the training once during the 20 min of allowed interaction with the MR simulation. Every activity was carried out on the same day, and a 5-min break was given after the pre-test and after all interactions with the MR simulation for glenoid processes were finished. Scores for each participant are shown on the Y-axis in Fig. 7 and Fig. 8 on a scale from 0 to 100. (Participants are on the X-axis). If participants improved by at least 40 points, the lead surgeon involved in the learning designated the improvement as "substantial". "Moderate" improvement was defined as a change of 10 to 40 points. The outcomes of the evaluation activity are as follows:

- A majority of medical participants (13 of 17 for medical and 8 of 10 for non-medical) demonstrated an improved understanding of the glenoid process.
- 13 medical participants and 8 non-medical participants showed significant improvement, and 4 medical and 2 non-medical participants performed at a level termed moderate improvement.
- 9 medical and 7 non-medical participants received a score of 0 in the pre-test as they had no prior understanding of the surgical process (Fig. 7 and Fig. 8). After interacting with the VSE, 8 participants showed an improvement of 50 points, respectively (as shown in Fig. 7 and Fig. 8). Zero scores for non-medical participants are relatively high regarding medical participants which seems logical as non-medical participants have no prior knowledge of surgery procedures. The reason that a few non-medical participants answered the pre-test question is either they have prior experience with this surgery, or they know someone that experienced it, and they have some basic knowledge about the procedure.
- Non-medical and medical participants were randomly assigned to two various groups. Group 1 with text cues for instructions and group 2 with voice cues and a 3d medical avatar for training instructions. Based on the results participants in group 2 gained slightly better knowledge during simulation. For the next phase, the plan is to have more participants from each group to examine if voice cues and Avatar roles could have a significant impact on the learning process for simulation.

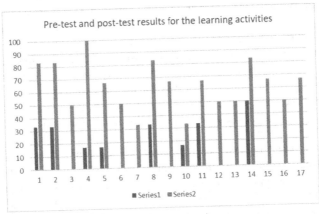

Fig. 7. Pre-test and post-test results for the learning activities for first responders and nurses

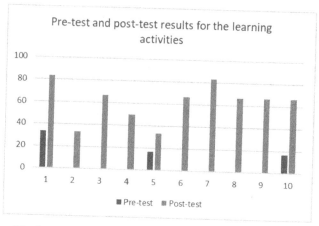

Fig. 8. Pre-test and post-test results for non-medical students

5 Comprehension Assessment

Comprehension measures whether a participant can understand the intended meaning of a step (label or voice) and can draw the correct conclusions from the instructions [38]. Participants in the study were also assessed on their ability to perform the intended actions following the learning process through the simulation. Two different scenarios were conducted for the comprehension test. Non-medical students were randomly divided into two groups.

In Group 1, students underwent training using the first simulation under normal circumstances in a relatively quiet room. Following the training session, they were asked to complete pre- and post-tests to assess their understanding. Subsequently, they engaged in a second simulation, referred to as the challenge test, where they were observed to determine if they could identify any incorrect steps during the simulation. In Group 2, additional auditory distractors were introduced during the training simulation. These distractors included ambient sounds from a surgery room, random intensive care unit sounds, and random voices related to various surgical processes. Similar to Group 1, participants in Group 2 completed pre- and post-tests after the training session. They were then asked to perform a second simulation and observe if they could recognize any incorrect steps during the simulation, despite the presence of distractors. These allowed for a comparison of performance between the two groups, assessing the impact of the added auditory distractors on the participants' ability to recognize and execute the correct steps during the simulation.

For Phase 1 of the study involved 10 students in each group. To evaluate the results, the Mann-Whitney test [39] was utilized. Unlike the t-test that compares the means, the Mann-Whitney U test compares a randomly selected value from group 1 to a randomly selected value from group 2. A maximum of 100 scores for pre/post-tests and a maximum of 100 scores for challenge tests were assigned. For the second phase 10 new students randomly assigned in these two groups. In order to perform a more in-depth study of distractors and stressors, also assessment of training simulation this time there were more challenge tests.

For Phase 2, a new set of 10 students was randomly assigned to the two groups. This phase aimed to conduct a more comprehensive examination of distractors, stressors, and the assessment of the training simulation. Additionally, more challenging tests were introduced for both new groups to further evaluate their performance. In this phase, a maximum score of 100 was considered as the criterion for evaluation.

Phase 1 Hypothesis: H0: The distractors don't have any effect on participants' learning process in group 2 versus H1: The distractors affect the learning process of group 2.

Since p-value < α, H0 is rejected. The difference between the randomly selected value of Group 1 and the Group 2 populations is big enough to be statistically significant. The p-value equals 0.04387, (p (x ≤ Z) = 0.9781). It means that the chance of a type I error (rejecting a correct H0) is small: 0.04387 (4.39%). The test statistic Z equals 2.0154, which is not in the 95% region of acceptance: [−1.96: 1.96]. U = 77, is not in the 95% region of acceptance: [24.2285: 75.7715]. The observed results suggest that there is a medium-level difference between the values obtained from Group 1 and Group 2. This indicates a significant distinction in the performance between the two groups. The histograms for both groups are presented in Fig. 9, providing a visual representation of the distribution of scores or values within each group. These histograms offer further insights into the performance characteristics of the participants in each group.

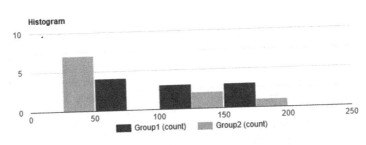

Fig. 9. Histogram for two groups in phase 1

Phase 2 hypothesis: H0: The distractors don't have any effect on participants' learning process in group 2 versus H1: The distractors affect the learning process of group 2.

Since p-value < α, H0 is rejected. The difference between the randomly selected value of Group1 and the Group2 populations is big enough to be statistically significant. The p-value equals 0.04344, (p(x ≤ Z) = 0.9783). It means that the chance of type I error (rejecting a correct H0) is small: 0.04344 (4.34%). The test statistic Z equals 2.0195, which is not in the 95% region of acceptance: [−1.96: 1.96]. U = 22, is not in the 95% region of acceptance: [3.7653: 21.2347]. The observed standardized effect size, $Z/\sqrt{(n1 + n2)}$, is large (0.64). The observed results suggest that there is a medium-level difference between the values obtained from Group 1 and Group 2. This indicates a significant distinction in the performance between the two groups. The histograms for both groups are presented in Fig. 10, providing a visual representation of the distribution of scores or values within each group. These histograms offer further insights into the performance characteristics of the participants in each group.

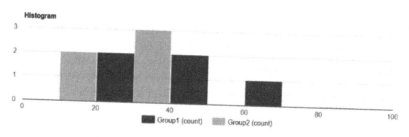

Fig. 10. Histogram for two groups in phase 2

While the sample size in this study may be limited, the results obtained provide initial evidence supporting the conclusion that the modeled distractors, based on real-life stressors, have an impact on the performance of both non-medical and medical students. These findings suggest that when designing training applications for surgical procedures, it is crucial to consider the inclusion of realistic stressors. However, further research with larger sample sizes would be necessary to draw more comprehensive and robust conclusions. These initial results highlight the importance of incorporating realistic stressors in training simulations to enhance the preparation and performance of students in real-life surgical scenarios.

6   Conclusion and Future Work

In this paper the design process for a distinct module that serves as a training simulator for RTSA has been explained. Using the engineering Enterprise Modeling Language (eEML), an information-centric modeling approach was suggested for developing this simulator. Detailed information-centric models of the surgical process were also built using eEML, providing a structural foundation for designing and developing this simulator. Validity of MR simulation has been performed and through interactions with medical and non-medical students, the usefulness of this simulator-based training technique was investigated. The majority of participants demonstrated improvement in their comprehension of the RTSA process after interaction activities. Also, it indicated how various types of affordances affect the users' comprehension and skills and knowledge acquisition. Assessment of distractors and impact of MR simulation for learning of complex processes studied in the simulation. Future plan is to create 3D surgical skills challenge tests within the VR as well as MR environments to study the role of various factors in affecting the acquisition of surgical skills.

Acknowledgment. The authors would like to acknowledge funding for the research activities discussed in this paper through grants from the National Science Foundation (2050960 and 2106901), and the Oklahoma Center for Advanced Science and Technology (OCAST). We also wanted to thank the collaborators at Dignity Regional Medical Center (Phoenix, AZ), Dignity Health, Yavapai Regional (Prescott Valley, AZ) and Northern Oklahoma College (NOC) (Enid and Tonkawa campuses). We also wanted to express our thanks to Vern McKinney (head ER nurse at Dignity Health, Yavapai Regional) and Dr. Nikole Hicks (Nursing Division Chair at Northern Oklahoma College) for interacting with us as part of these research activities.

References

1. Cecil, J., Kauffman, S., Gupta, A., McKinney, V., Pirela-Cruz, M.M.: Design of a human centered computing (HCC) based virtual reality simulator to train first responders involved in the Covid-19 pandemic. In: 2021 IEEE International Systems Conference (SysCon), pp. 1–7. IEEE (2021)
2. Cecil, J., Albuhamood, S., Ramanathan, P., Gupta, A.: An Internet-of-Things (IoT) based cyber manufacturing framework for the assembly of microdevices. Int. J. Comput. Integr. Manuf. 32(4–5), 430–440 (2019)
3. Sadeghi Milani, A., Cecil-Xavier, A., Gupta, A., Cecil, J., Kennison, S.: A systematic review of human–computer interaction (HCI) research in medical and other engineering fields. Int. J. Hum. Comput. Interact., 1–22 (2022)
4. Walker, M., Brooks, J., Willis, M., Frankle, M.: How reverse shoulder arthroplasty works. Clin. Orthop. Related Res.® 469, 2440–2451 (2011)
5. drgordongroh. https://www.drgordongroh.com/orthopaedic-injuriestreatment/shoulder/standard-total-shoulder-replacement/
6. Singhal, K., Rammohan, R.: Going forward with reverse shoulder arthroplasty. J. Clin. Orthop. Trauma 9(1), 87–93 (2018). (in Eng.). https://doi.org/10.1016/j.jcot.2017.10.002
7. Gertsch, K.R., et al.: Description and validation of a structured simulation curriculum for strabismus surgery. J. Am. Assoc. Pediatr. Ophthalmol. Strabismus 19(1), 3–5. e3 (2015)
8. Kunkler, K.: The role of medical simulation: an overview. Int. J. Med. Rob. Comput. Assist. Surg. 2(3), 203–210 (2006)
9. Gupta, A., Cecil, J., Pirela-Cruz, M., Ramanathan, P.: A virtual reality enhanced cyber-human framework for orthopedic surgical training. IEEE Syst. J. 13(3), 3501–3512 (2019)
10. Hughes, C.E., Stapleton, C.B., Hughes, D.E., Smith, E.M.: Mixed reality in education, entertainment, and training. IEEE Comput. Graphics Appl. 25(6), 24–30 (2005)
11. Kopeć, W., et al.: VR with older adults: participatory design of a virtual ATM training simulation. IFAC-PapersOnLine 52(19), 277–281 (2019)
12. Wijewickrema, S., et al.: Design and evaluation of a virtual reality simulation module for training advanced temporal bone surgery. In: 2017 IEEE 30th International Symposium on Computer-Based Medical Systems (CBMS), pp. 7–12. IEEE (2017)
13. Gupta, A., Cecil, J., Pirela-Cruz, M.: A cyber-human based integrated assessment approach for orthopedic surgical training. In: 2020 IEEE 8th International Conference on Serious Games and Applications for Health (SeGAH), pp. 1–8. IEEE (2020)
14. Wu, X., et al.: Mixed reality technology-assisted orthopedics surgery navigation. Surg. Innov. 25(3), 304–305 (2018)
15. Hooper, J., et al.: Virtual reality simulation facilitates resident training in total hip arthroplasty: a randomized controlled trial. J. Arthroplasty 34(10), 2278–2283 (2019)
16. Jefferson, F., et al.: MP35-08 immersive virtual reality (IVR) renal models as an educational and preoperative planning tool for laparoscopic donor nephrectomy: initial experience. J. Urology 201, e508 (2019)
17. Al-Hiyari, N.N., Jusoh, S.S.: Healthcare training application: 3D first aid virtual reality. In: International Conference on Data Science, E-learning and Information Systems 2021, pp. 107–116 (2021)

18. Wang, X., Wang, X.: Virtual Reality training system for surgical anatomy. In: Proceedings of the 2018 International Conference on Artificial Intelligence and Virtual Reality, pp. 30–34 (2018)
19. Erickson, J., et al.: Mixed-reality holographic-assisted placement of glenoid guidewire in shoulder arthroplasty: preliminary comparison to patient-specific instrumentation in B2 glenoid model. Semin. Arthroplasty JSES 32(4), 688–696 (2022)
20. Van Duren, B., Sugand, K., Wescott, R., Carrington, R., Hart, A.: Augmented reality fluoroscopy simulation of the guide-wire insertion in DHS surgery: a proof of concept study. Med. Eng. Phys. 55, 52–59 (2018)
21. Logishetty, K., Western, L., Morgan, R., Iranpour, F., Cobb, J.P., Auvinet, E.: Can an augmented reality headset improve accuracy of acetabular cup orientation in simulated THA? A randomized trial. Clin. Orthop. Relat. Res. 477(5), 1190 (2019)
22. Alsofy, S.Z., et al.: Virtual reality-based evaluation of surgical planning and outcome of monosegmental, unilateral cervical foraminal stenosis. World Neurosurgery 129, e857–e865 (2019)
23. Cecil, J., Gupta, A., Pirela-Cruz, M.: An advanced simulator for orthopedic surgical training. Int. J. Comput. Assist. Radiol. Surg. 13(2), 305–319 (2018)
24. Cecil, J.: Computer aided fixture design: using information intensive function models in the development of automated fixture design systems. J. Manuf. Syst. 21(1), 58–71 (2002)
25. Cecil, J.A.: Fixture design in a computer-integrated manufacturing (CIM) environment. Texas A&M University (1995)
26. Cecil, J.: A clamping design approach for automated fixture design. Int. J. Adv. Manuf. Technol. 18(11), 784–789 (2001)
27. Ehn, P., et al.: The envisionment workshop-from visions to practice. In: Proceedings of the Participatory Design conference, pp. 141–152. MIT Boston (1996)
28. Muller, M.J., Kuhn, S.: Participatory design. Commun. ACM 36(6), 24–28 (1993)
29. Jensen, P.L.: The Scandinavian approach in participatory ergonomics. In: 13th Triennial Congress of the International Ergonomics Association, pp. 13–15. Finnish Institute of Occupational Health (1997)
30. Cecil, J.: A functional model of fixture design to aid in the design and development of automated fixture design systems'. J. Manuf. Syst. 21(1), 58–72 (2002)
31. Cecil, J.: TAMIL: an integrated fixture design system for prismatic parts. Int. J. Comput. Integr. Manuf. 17(5), 421–434 (2004)
32. Gupta, A.: Investigation of a holistic human-computer interaction (HCI) framework to support the design of extended reality (XR) based training simulators. Ph.D., Computer Science, Oklahoma State University (2021)
33. McDougall, E.M.: Validation of surgical simulators. J. Endourol. 21(3), 244–247 (2007)
34. Cecil, J., Kauffman, S., Cecil-Xavier, A., Gupta, A., McKinney, V., Sweet-Darter, M.: Exploring human-computer interaction (HCI) criteria in the design and assessment of next generation VR based education and training environments. In: 2021 IEEE Conference on Virtual Reality and 3D User Interfaces Abstracts and Workshops (VRW), pp. 524–525. IEEE (2021)
35. Gupta, A., Cecil, J., Pirela-Cruz, M.: Role of dynamic affordance and cognitive load in the design of extended reality based simulation environments for surgical contexts. In: 2022 IEEE Conference on Virtual Reality and 3D User Interfaces Abstracts and Workshops (VRW), pp. 652–653. IEEE (2022)
36. Gupta, A., Cecil, J., Pirela-Cruz, M., Shamsuddin, R., Kennison, S., Crick, C.: An investigation on the role of affordance in the design of extended reality based environments for surgical training. In: 2022 IEEE International Systems Conference (SysCon), pp. 1–7. IEEE (2022)
37. Tergas, A.I., Sheth, S.B., Green, I.C., Giuntoli, R.L., Winder, A.D., Fader, A.N.: A pilot study of surgical training using a virtual robotic surgery simulator. JSLS J. Soc. Laparoendoscopic Surg. 17(2), 219 (2013)

38. Gernsbacher, M.A., Varner, K.R., Faust, M.E.: Investigating differences in general comprehension skill. J. Exp. Psychol. Learn. Mem. Cogn. **16**(3), 430 (1990)
39. Nachar, N.: The Mann-Whitney U: a test for assessing whether two independent samples come from the same distribution. Tutorials Quant. Methods Psychol. **4**(1), 13–20 (2008)

Emotional Experience in Real and Virtual Environments – Does Prior VR Experience Matter?

Ramona Schmid and Verena Wagner-Hartl(✉)

Faculty Industrial Technologies, Furtwangen University, Campus Tuttlingen, Kronenstraße 16, 78532 Tuttlingen, Germany
{ramona.schmid,verena.wagner-hartl}@hs-furtwangen.de

Abstract. Virtual reality (VR) has a great potential to induce emotions effectively and naturally. There are already existing concepts to use this technology, e.g., for the therapy of anxiety disorders or to train emotional and social skills for different user groups. Some research results show that visual stimuli are experienced emotionally different in a virtual environment than in a real environment. The aim of the study was therefore, to investigate whether a person's emotional experience (induced by affective pictures) differs between real and virtual environments. Additionally, the influence of prior experience with VR on the emotional reactions was investigated. Furthermore, in an exploratory part the effect of immersive 360° videos in VR was studied. The results indicate an effect of VR on the psychophysiological responses. The subjective assessments show that the affective pictures were able to induce significantly different emotional responses in VR. In addition, significantly different emotional responses are evident in both, the subjective and psychophysiological parameters regarding the 360° VR-videos. Overall, prior VR experience did not show a significant effect.

Keywords: Virtual Reality · Emotion Induction · Emotion Recognition · Psychophysiology

1 Introduction

The continuous development of virtual reality (VR) technologies is leading to more and more realistic, experienceable simulations [1]. Furthermore, VR has a great potential to induce emotions effectively and naturally [2]. Due to this, the technology is also increasingly used in emotion research. There are already concepts to use VR within this field of research, e.g., for the therapy of anxiety disorders [1] or to train emotional and social skills for people with ASD [3] or for managers and teams [4].

A major advantage of VR is that users focus entirely on the VR content without being distracted by visual stimuli from the real ("outside") environment [1]. This results in a VR experience with a high degree of immersion for the user. A high degree of immersion in the VR environment also leads to a higher sense of presence in VR. Presence is defined as a user's subjective feeling of actually being in the virtual environment while physically being in another environment [5]. Several studies show that the feeling of presence in VR has an influence on the emotional reactions of the users [6–8]. To ensure this sense of presence in the simulation, it is crucial that the stimuli are perceived as natural [9].

1.1 Prior Experience with Virtual Reality

A study of Sagnier et al. [10] shows that prior experience with virtual reality can have an impact on a person's VR experience. Users with prior VR experience perceived significant more presence in VR and also assessed their performance regarding a virtual assembly task significantly better than novice users. Furthermore, users with prior VR experience rated the user experience in VR, both in terms of pragmatic quality and hedonic quality stimulation, significantly higher. These results suggest that users who have prior VR experience, feel more connected to the virtual environment than users without prior VR experience.

1.2 Emotion Induction

In order to investigate emotional responses, independent of the environment, emotions have to be induced. A review by Siedlecka and Denson [11] shows that a variety of methods have been established for emotion induction. Following the authors, using visual stimuli is the most effective method for inducing the six basic emotions anger, disgust, surprise, happiness, fear, and sadness. Since they are commonly used in emotion research, standardized databases of emotionally stimulating pictures with the corresponding valence and arousal values have been established, e.g. [12–14]. Mostly, they have been investigated by presenting the pictures in a real environment on a computer screen.

Recent research shows that VR can effectively be used for emotion induction [8]. The pictures from the standardized databases can also be integrated easily into VR [2]. However, there is a dearth of studies that have investigated the use of visual stimuli as an emotion induction method in VR. It must also be considered that the static presentation of the stimuli can lead to a lower emotional intensity compared to other induction methods in VR, such as games or videos. Dynamic stimuli can create a higher immersion than static stimuli and therefore create a more natural emotional experience. Suitable dynamic stimuli for VR are 360° videos. The use of 360° media in VR provides the possibility to view the scene in full rotation without visual distraction, providing a high level of immersion for the users. According to Somarathna et al. [2] there are only a few studies that use 360° media in VR, which can be attributed to the lack of standardised material for emotion research in VR. A first public database with immersive VR videos was published by Li et al. [15] (Virtual Human Interaction Lab of Stanford University). They provide free available 360° videos with the corresponding ratings of arousal and valence.

1.3 Emotional Experience in Real and Virtual Environments

A pilot study by Estupiñán et al. [16] gives first indications that visual stimuli are experienced emotionally different in virtual than in real environments. Affective pictures (picture categories: snakes, spiders, human concerns, animal mistreatments, positive) from the GAPED database [17] were integrated into the VR environment. The descriptive results reported by the authors, show that compared with the valence and arousal ratings provided by the standardized database, the arousal was rated higher in the virtual environment for all pictures [16]. In terms of valence, the pictures of the negative emotional categories in VR showed higher values than reported in the database.

1.4 Emotion Recognition

Measuring a person's emotional reaction is a major challenge in emotion research [18]. Therefore, various measurement methods have been established. The subjective emotional state can be assessed using interviews and questionnaires, e.g. by participants assessing their perceived valence and arousal of an emotion [12]. Psychophysiological parameters [19], such as electrodermal activity, cortisol or pupillary diameter, as well as the analysis of facial expressions [20], can be used as objective methods for emotion recognition. According to Boucsein and colleagues [21, 22], it is useful to combine subjective and objective parameters to obtain a comprehensive assessment of a person's emotional state. Therefore, our research group has developed a multidimensional measurement environment that combines subjective and psychophysiological measurements [23] and conducted a first validation study [24]. For emotion induction, different emotional pictures were shown on a computer screen. The results showed significantly different emotional responses in the subjective assessments of valence, but no evidence in the psychophysiological parameters. Another study [25] using autobiographical recall as a method for emotion induction resulted in significant responses in the subjective and psychophysiological parameters for different emotions. Nonetheless, it is important to investigate further emotion induction methods, such as virtual reality, to analyse whether a stronger emotional involvement of the participants can be evoked.

1.5 Aim of the Study

As presented before, VR can be seen as an effective medium to induce and recognize emotions [8]. Furthermore, prior VR experience and their impact on the emotional responses of the participants needs to be considered. However, to use the advantages of the possibilities of the medium "VR", dynamic stimuli with "lower" and "higher" immersive content like 360° videos should be included in the research. Also, it is necessary to include a multidimensional approach that includes also psychophysiological parameters.

Therefore, the aim of the presented study was to investigate whether a person's emotional experience differs between real and virtual environments when emotions are induced by affective pictures. Additionally, the influence of prior experience with VR on the emotional reactions was investigated. Furthermore, an exploratory part was investigated within this study, which aims to examine the effect of immersive 360° videos in a virtual environment on the emotional experience.

2   Method

A laboratory experiment with repeated measurements was chosen for this study. The study was conducted at Campus Tuttlingen of Furtwangen University. The experiment presented in this paper was part of an overall study with two different parts. In the first part of the overall study (not presented within this paper; see [25]), the influence of two different emotion induction methods, visual stimuli and autobiographical recall, on six emotional categories (anger, disgust, fear, joy, sadness, surprise) and a neutral category were investigated in real environments.

The second part of the overall study is presented within this paper. This part of the study consisted of an experimental part and an exploratory one. In the experimental part the emotional experience of four emotional categories (disgust, happiness, fear and sadness) induced by pictures was investigated in different environments. For this purpose, four of the six conditions examined in real environments in the first section of the study (see [25]) were investigated in the virtual environment as well. In the exploratory part of the study, the emotional responses to immersive 360° VR-videos were examined.

2.1 Participants

Overall, 14 women and 10 men ($N = 24$) aged between 19 and 59 years ($M = 29.25$, $SD = 11.46$) participated in the study. Grouped by the independent variable prior VR experience, 11 persons reported no prior experience with virtual reality and 13 persons reported partial or a lot of experience with VR. For the prior VR experience groups, no significant effects regarding gender, $\chi^2(1) = .24$, $p = .628$, age, $r = -.30$, $p = .157$, and affinity for technology interaction [26], $r = .26$, $p = .229$, can be shown. Informed consent was provided by all participants at the beginning of the study. The study was approved by the ethics committee of Furtwangen University.

2.2 Material

As described before, the study consists of different parts (see Sect. 2). In the experimental part the independent variables prior VR experience (with, without), environment (real, virtual) and the measurement repetition factor emotional category (disgust, happiness, fear and sadness) were examined. Within the exploratory part the prior VR experience (with, without) and the emotional category (neutral, happiness, fear; measurement repetition factor) were analysed. Following a multidimensional approach, subjective assessments and psychophysiological parameters were used as dependent variables.

Emotion Induction. Visual stimuli were used to induce the different emotions in the participants. In the experimental part, affective pictures (databases: International Affective Picture System (IAPS) [12], Emotional Picture Set (EmoPicS) [13] and Open Affective Standardized Image Set (OASIS) [14]) were used to induce the four target emotions: happiness, fear, disgust and sadness. For each emotional category, four appropriate pictures were selected from the databases. In the real environment condition the pictures were presented on a 23-in. HP screen placed on a table at a distance of 50 cm. For the virtual environment condition the laboratory room was replicated in the VR environment to provide comparability between the real and virtual environments. The same pictures as in the real environment were displayed on a wall in the virtual room. Unity [27] was used to develop the VR environment. The used VR headset was the HTC Vive Pro [28].

In the exploratory part of the study, 360° videos were investigated to induce the following three target emotions in VR: neutral, happiness and fear (see Table 1). Due to the 360° format of the video material, it could only be presented in the VR environment and not in the real environment condition. The video material was selected from the 360° VR video database from Stanford University [15] for the emotional categories neutral and happiness. Following [15], there is a lack of material with negative valence and high arousal in the database. Therefore, an additional free available video was selected for the emotional category fear. To ensure comparability of the videos, they were all shortened to a duration of 60 s.

Table 1. Description of the 360° video material used in the exploratory part of the study.

Emotional category	Video	Description
Neutral	Sunrise [29]	Beach where the sun rises over the horizon
Happiness	Dog puppies [30]	Puppies beaming in a football match
Fear	Terrifying Sea Creatures [31]	Underwater scenario with various terrifying sea creatures

Subjective Measurements. The subjective emotional state of the participants was assessed with the Self-Assessment Manikin (SAM) [32] using the two dimensions, valence and arousal (9-point scale based on the pictograms). In addition, an emotion characterization according to Ozawa [33] was used to characterize the emotions actually felt by the participants. Therefore, the participants were asked to rate the extent to which they felt each of the six basic emotions (anger, disgust, fear, happiness, sadness, surprise), and the neutral condition using a 6-point scale ranging from "not at all" (1) to "very" (6). There was also the possibility to choose the option "other emotions" and shortly describe them. The subjective assessments were completed on a *Samsung Galaxy Tab A* tablet using the online survey tool Unipark [34]. During the virtual environment condition participants gave their assessment verbally to the experimenter.

Psychophysiological Measurements. Cardiovascular (ECG) and electrodermal activity (EDA) were recorded using sensors from Movisens [35, 36]. The ECG-sensor was placed with the use of a chest strap. The EDA-sensor was attached on the inner palm (thenar and hypothenar) of the participants' non-dominant hand. For the statistical analysis the following parameters were used: ECG: Heart rate (HR) in beats per minute and heart rate variability (HRV RMSSD); EDA: Skin conductance level (SCL), amplitude of non-specific skin conductance responses (NS.SCR amp), frequency of non-specific skin conductance responses (NS.SCR freq) and mean sum amplitude (NS.SCR amp/NS.SCR freq).

2.3 Procedure

The study was conducted in a laboratory room at Campus Tuttlingen of Furtwangen University. The lighting conditions were kept constant by blinds during the whole experiment. Participants sat on a rotatable office chair in the real and the virtual environment conditions.

After a short briefing, the participants provided their informed consent and their sociodemographic data. Then, they assessed their affinity for technology with the Affinity for Technology Interaction Short Scale (ATI-S) [26], their current well-being as well as their subjectively perceived prior VR experience. Subsequently, the electrodes for the psychophysiological measurements were attached and their functionality checked, followed by a four-minute baseline measurement.

Afterwards, the first part of the overall study (affective pictures, autobiographical recall; see [25]) was examined in the real environment. Therefore, the participants' chair was placed in front of a table with a computer screen. Four affective pictures of each emotional category were presented for a total of 30 s (7.5 s each). After each emotional category, the participants rated their emotional state in terms of valence and arousal using the Self-Assessment Manikin (SAM) [32] and the items for emotion characterization. The duration of the subjective assessments was individually determined by the participants. Afterwards, a one-minute rest measurement was performed. This was followed by the investigation of the same emotional category, using the second induction method, autobiographical recall. The emotion categories were presented in permuted order. A total of seven emotional categories (anger, disgust, fear, joy, sadness, surprise, neutral) were examined, of which the four emotional categories, disgust, happiness, fear and sadness induced with affective pictures are part of the presented paper. After examining all emotional categories in front of the screen, a break of about 10 min followed.

The second part of the study started with a second measurement of the participants' current well-being. Afterwards, the chair was placed in the center of the room, giving the participants more space within the VR environment. Subsequently, the participants were instructed in the use of the VR equipment and could familiarize themselves with the virtual environment which represents a simulation of the real examination room. The investigation in the VR environment started with the emotion induction of the four emotional categories disgust, happiness, fear and sadness by using pictures [12–14]. The emotional categories were therefore presented in permuted order. The pictures and the procedure were exactly the same as in the screen condition in the real environment. The presentation of the affective pictures (30 s.) was followed by the subjective assessments and a subsequent one-minute rest measurement, which were also performed in the VR environment. Afterwards, the 360° videos [29–31] for emotion induction were examined (exploratory part). Before the first 360° video condition started, the participants were told that they could rotate their chair while watching the videos in order to look around completely in the 360° VR environment. Each of the 360° VR-videos of the three emotional categories, neutral, happiness and fear, were presented for 60 s followed by the subjective assessments and a resting measurement. The video of the neutral category was shown first to each participant. After that, the VR videos of the categories happiness and fear were presented in permuted order.

After the last resting measurement, the VR equipment was removed from the participants and they had to answer final questions regarding how they perceived their emotions in the VR environment compared to the real environment (sitting in front of the screen) and to which extent, they perceived the VR environment as suitable for evoking emotions. In addition, a third measurement of the participants' current well-being was conducted. Finally, the sensors of the psychophysiological measurements were taken off the participants. In total, the overall study lasted about 90 min for each participant.

2.4 Statistical Analysis

The psychophysiological parameters were analyzed with the software DataAnalyzer [37] from Movisens. The mean values of the psychophysiological measures were baseline-corrected. For the statistical analyses the software IBM SPSS statistics was used. The statistical procedures used were analyses of variance with repeated measures. The statistical analyses were based on a significance level of 5%.

3 Results

3.1 Experimental Part: Real and Virtual Environments

Subjective Measures

Valence. For the dimension valence, an analysis of variance with repeated measures shows significant differences of the emotional categories, $F_{HF}(2.80, 56.05) = 146.28, p < .001, \eta^2_{part.} = .880$. All other effects did not reach the level of significance (environment: $F(1, 20) = .77, p = .392, \eta^2_{part.} = .037$, prior VR experience: $F(1, 20) = 1.59, p = .222, \eta^2_{part.} = .074$, interaction emotional category x environment: $F(3, 18) = 1.22, p = .330, \eta^2_{part.} = .169$, interaction emotional category x prior VR experience: $F(3, 18) = .64, p = .597, \eta^2_{part.} = .097$, interaction environment x prior VR experience, $F(1, 20) = .77, p = .392, \eta^2_{part.} = .037$, interaction emotional category x environment x prior VR experience, $F(3, 18) = 1.83, p = .178, \eta^2_{part.} = .233$).

Post-hoc analyses (Sidak) show that the emotional category happiness was assessed significantly more positive than disgust, fear and sadness (all $p < .001$). Also, the emotional category sadness was assessed significantly more negative than disgust ($p = .010$) and fear ($p = .019$; see Fig. 1).

Arousal. An analysis of variance with repeated measures shows for the dimension arousal no significant effect of the emotional categories, $F(3, 18) = 2.41, p = .101, \eta^2_{part.} = .286$, the environment, $F(1, 20) = 1.16, p = .294, \eta^2_{part.} = .055$, nor the prior VR experience, $F(1, 20) = .67, p = .424, \eta^2_{part.} = .032$, or the interactions of them (emotional category x environment: $F(3, 18) = .83, p = .496, \eta^2_{part.} = .121$, emotional category x prior VR experience: $F(3, 18) = .25, p = .858, \eta^2_{part.} = .040$, environment x prior VR experience: $F(1, 20) = .375, p = .547, \eta^2_{part.} = .018$, emotional category x environment x prior VR experience: $F(3, 18) = .45, p = .721, \eta^2_{part.} = .070$).

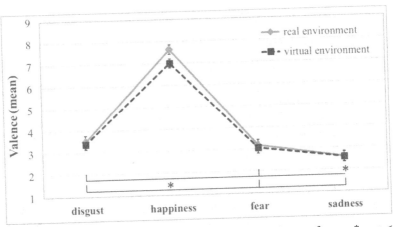

Note. 9-point-scale: Negative (1) – positive (9); I … standard error of mean; * … $p < .05$

Fig. 1. Mean subjectively perceived valence of the four different emotional categories induced in real and virtual environments.

Psychophysiological Measures

Cardiovascular Activity. Table 2 shows the results of the analyses of variance with repeated measures for the parameters of the cardiovascular activity.

Following the results presented in Table 2, a significant effect of environment was shown for the heart rate (HR). The HR was significantly higher during stimuli presentation within the real environment than in the virtual environment (see Fig. 2).

For the heart rate variability (HRV RMSSD), the results of an ANOVA with repeated measures show a significant interaction emotional category x environment. Following the results of post-hoc analyses (Sidak), the HRV was significantly higher when presenting affective pictures of the category happiness ($p = .030$) as well as of the category fear ($p = .031$) in the real than in the virtual environment (see also Fig. 3).

Table 2. Results of the analyses of variance with repeated measures for the parameters of the cardiovascular activity.

		F	df	df_{error}	p	$\eta^2_{part.}$
HR	Emotional category	1.20	3	17	.340	.175
	Environment	19.43	1	19	<.001	.506
	Prior VR experience	.09	1	19	.773	.004
	Emotional category x Environment	.10	1	19	.755	.005
	Emotional category x Prior VR experience	1.31	3	17	.303	.188
	Environment x Prior VR experience	.10	1	19	.755	.005
	Emotional category x Environment x Prior VR experience	2.12	3	17	.135	.273
HRV (RMSSD)	Emotional category	.76	3	17	.530	.119
	Environment	3.87	1	19	.064	.169
	Prior VR experience	.00	1	19	.957	.000
	Emotional category x Environment	3.22	3	17	.049	.362
	Emotional category x Prior VR experience	.23	3	17	.875	.039
	Environment x Prior VR experience	.09	1	19	.765	.005
	Emotional category x Environment x Prior VR experience	1.02	3	1	.409	.152

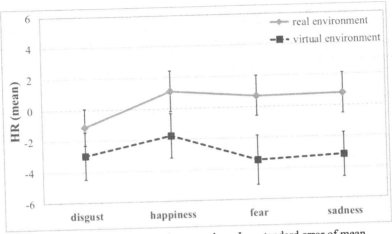

Note. Baseline-corrected mean values; I ... standard error of mean

Fig. 2. Mean heart rate (HR): Four different emotional categories induced in real and virtual environments.

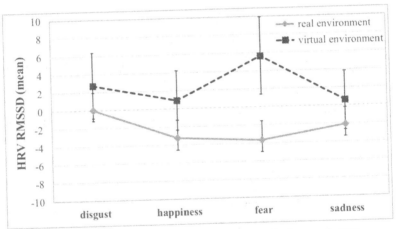

Note. Baseline-corrected mean values; I ... standard error of mean

Fig. 3. Mean heart rate variability (HRV RMSSD): Four different emotional categories induced in real and virtual environments.

Electrodermal Activity. Table 3 shows the results of the analyses of variance with repeated measures for the parameters of the electrodermal activity.

As presented in Table 3 a significant effect of the environment can be shown for the skin conductance level (SCL). The SCL was significantly higher during the presentation of the affective pictures in the virtual environment than during the presentation in the real environment (see Fig. 4).

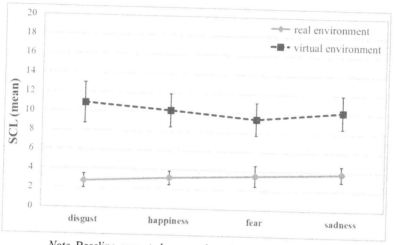

Note. Baseline-corrected mean values; I ... standard error of mean

Fig. 4. Mean skin conductance level (SCL): Four different emotional categories induced in real and virtual environments.

Table 3. Results of the analyses of variance with repeated measures for the parameters of the electrodermal activity.

		F	df	df_{error}	p	$\eta^2_{part.}$
SCL	Emotional category	.14	3	17	.932	.025
	Environment	41.82	1	19	< .001	.688
	Prior VR experience	.23	1	19	.639	.012
	Emotional category x Environment	.36	3	17	.783	.060
	Emotional category x Prior VR experience	1.82	3	17	.181	.244
	Environment x Prior VR experience	.17	1	19	.687	.009
	Emotional category x Environment x Prior VR experience	2.44	3	17	.100	.301

(continued)

Table 3. (*continued*)

		F	df	df_{error}	p	$\eta^2_{part.}$
NS.SCR freq	Emotional category	1.20[a]	1.19	22.58	.294	.060
	Environment	.65	1	19	.429	.033
	Prior VR experience	1.79	1	19	.196	.086
	Emotional category x Environment	1.08[a]	1.27	24.08	.327	.054
	Emotional category x Prior VR experience	2.63	3	17	.083	.317
	Environment x Prior VR experience	1.74	1	19	.203	.084
	Emotional category x Environment x Prior VR experience	2.36	3	17	.108	.294
NS.SCR amp	Emotional category	1.98	3	17	.156	.259
	Environment	1.19	1	19	.289	.059
	Prior VR experience	.10	1	19	.755	.005
	Emotional category x Environment	1.96	3	17	.158	.257
	Emotional category x Prior VR experience	.46	3	17	.713	.075
	Environment x Prior VR experience	.04	1	19	.850	.002
	Emotional category x Environment x Prior VR experience	.07	3	17	.977	.012
NS.SCR amp/NS.SCR freq	Emotional category	1.19	3	17	.342	.174
	Environment	1.03	1	19	.322	.052
	Prior VR experience	1.15	1	19	.298	.057
	Emotional category x Environment	1.81[b]	2.71	51.55	.161	.087
	Emotional category x Prior VR experience	.55	3	17	.655	.088
	Environment x Prior VR experience	.41	1	19	.529	.021
	Emotional category x Environment x Prior VR experience	1.59	3	17	.228	.219

Note. [a]Greenhouse-Geisser correction, [b]Huynh-Feldt correction

Emotion Characterization

As described in 2.2, the participants rated the extent to which they felt each of the six basic emotions (anger, disgust, fear, happiness, sadness, surprise), and the "neutral" condition. Figure 5 shows the mean values of the emotion characterization, i.e. to what extent the affective visual material for emotion induction was actually able to induce the target emotions of disgust, happiness, fear and sadness in the participants.

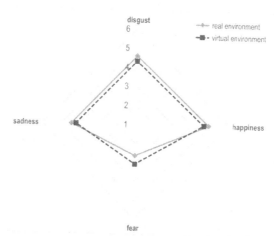

Note. Mean values, 6-point scale: Not at all (1) – very (6)

Fig. 5. Emotion characterization of the target emotion for each emotional category induced by pictures in real and virtual environment.

The results of the statistical analyses (ANOVAs with repeated measures) are shown in Table 4.

Table 4. Results of the ANOVAs with repeated measures for the subjective emotion characterization of the four different emotional categories.

		F	df	df_{error}	p	$\eta^2_{part.}$
Disgust	Environment	1.42	1	21	.248	.063
	Prior VR experience	.00	1	21	.958	.000
	Environment x Prior VR experience	3.00	1	21	.098	.125
Happiness	Environment	.62	1	20	.441	.030
	Prior VR experience	.23	1	20	.634	.012
	Environment x Prior VR experience	2.80	1	20	.110	.123
Fear	Environment	1.17	1	19	.292	.058

(*continued*)

Table 4. (*continued*)

		F	df	df error	p	$\eta^2_{part.}$
	Prior VR experience	.02	1	19	.889	.001
	Environment x Prior VR experience	1.17	1	19	.292	.058
Sadness	Environment	1.75	1	21	.200	.077
	Prior VR experience	.40	1	21	.849	.002
	Environment x Prior VR experience	1.75	1	21	.200	.077

As shown in Table 4, a tendency towards a significant interaction emotional category x prior VR experience can be shown regarding disgust. Post-hoc analyses (Sidak) show that participants with prior VR experience assessed disgusting pictures in the real environment as significantly more disgusting than in VR ($p = .038$; see Fig. 6).

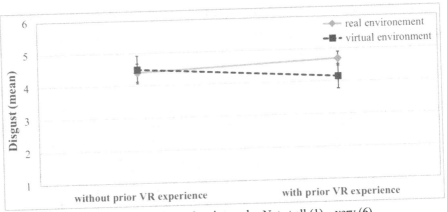

Note. Mean values, 6-point scale: Not at all (1) – very (6)

Fig. 6. Mean subjective assessments of the emotion disgust of the two prior VR experience groups in real and virtual environment.

3.2 Exploratory Part: 360° Videos in Virtual Environments

Subjective Measures

Valence. The results of an analysis of variance with repeated measures shows significant differences for the subjectively perceived valence of the emotional categories induced by the 360° videos in VR, $F(2, 21) = 21.53$, $p < .001$, $\eta^2_{part.} = .672$. All other effects did not reach the level of significance (prior VR experience: $F(1, 22) = 2.05$, $p = .166$, $\eta^2_{part.} = .085$, interaction emotional category x prior VR experience: $F(2, 21) = 3.01$, $p = .071$, $\eta^2_{part.} = .223$).

Post-hoc analyses (Sidak) show that the emotional category fear (M = 4.92, SD = 1.84) was assessed significantly more negative than the categories neutral (M = 7.63, SD = .97; p < .001) and happiness (M = 6.88, SD = 1.92; p = .001; see also Fig. 7).

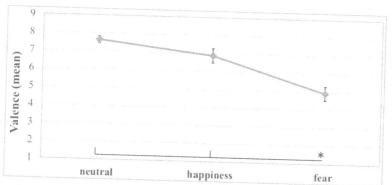

Note. 9-point-scale: Negative (1) – positive (9); I ... standard error of mean; * ... p < .05

Fig. 7. Mean subjectively perceived valence of the three different emotional categories induced by 360° videos in VR.

Arousal. Regarding the subjectively perceived arousal, the results of an ANOVA with repeated measures indicate a significant effect emotional categories, $F(2, 21)$ = 7.20, p = .004, $\eta^2_{part.}$ = .407. Furthermore, no significant effect of the prior VR experience, $F(1, 22)$ = .03, p = .861, $\eta^2_{part.}$ = .001, and the interaction emotional category x prior VR experience, $F(2, 21)$ = .99, p = .388, $\eta^2_{part.}$ = .086, can be shown. Following the results of post-hoc analyses (Sidak) the subjectively perceived arousal was significantly higher for the emotional category fear (M = 6.37, SD = 2.08) than for the

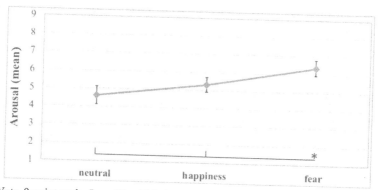

Note. 9-point-scale: Low (1) – high (9); I ... standard error of mean; * ... p < .05

Fig. 8. Mean subjectively perceived arousal of the three different emotional categories induced by 360° videos in VR.

categories neutral ($M = 4.62, SD = 2.48; p = .004$) and happiness ($M = 5.33, SD = 1.99$; $p = .044$; see also Fig. 8).

Psychophysiological Measures

Cardiovascular Activity. Table 5 shows the results of the analyses of variance with repeated measures for the parameters of the cardiovascular activity.

Table 5. Results of the analyses of variance with repeated measures for the parameters of the cardiovascular activity.

		F	df	df_{error}	p	$\eta^2_{part.}$
HR	Emotional category	2.56^b	1.48	35.81	.101	.104
	Prior VR experience	.00	1	22	.998	.000
	Emotional category x Prior VR experience	.12	2	21	.886	.011
HRV (RMSSD)	Emotional category	4.98	2	21	.017	.322
	Prior VR experience	.08	1	22	.779	.004
	Emotional category x Prior VR experience	.22	2	21	.804	.021

Note. ^{b}Huynh-Feldt correction

As presented in Table 5, the results of an ANOVA with repeated measures showed a significant effect of the emotional categories for the HRV (RMSSD). Post-hoc analyses (Sidak) show significantly lower HRV (RMSSD) for the emotional category happiness ($M = -.28, SD = 12.41$) than for the emotional category fear ($M = 3.60, SD = 13.51$; $p = .033$; see also Fig. 9).

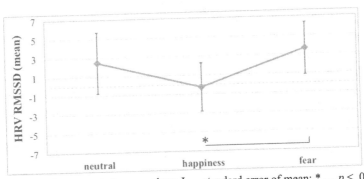

Note. Baseline-corrected mean values; I ... standard error of mean; * ... $p < .05$

Fig. 9. Mean heart rate variability (HRV RMSSD): Three different emotional categories induced by 360° videos in VR.

Electrodermal Activity. Table 6 shows the results of the analyses of variance with repeated measures for the parameters of the electrodermal activity.

Following the results presented in Table 6, a significant effect of the emotional categories can be shown regarding the skin conductance level (SCL). Post-hoc analyses (Sidak) show a significantly lower SCL for the the neutral category ($M = 12.61$, $SD = 11.57$) than the emotional category happiness ($M = 14.68$, $SD = 10.58$; $p = .049$) as well as fear ($M = 15.35$, $SD = 12.07$; $p = .016$; see also Fig. 10).

Table 6. Results of the analyses of variance with repeated measures for the parameters of the electrodermal activity.

		F	df	df_{error}	p	$\eta^2_{part.}$
SCL	Emotional category	5.42	2	21	.013	.340
	Prior VR experience	1.39	1	22	.251	.060
	Emotional category x Prior VR experience	.83	2	21	.449	.074
NS.SCR freq	Emotional category	2.88	2	21	.079	.215
	Prior VR experience	.77	1	22	.391	.034
	Emotional category x Prior VR experience	.41	2	21	.667	.038
NS.SCR amp	Emotional category	.90	2	21	.421	.079
	Prior VR experience	.05	1	22	.824	.002
	Emotional category x Prior VR experience	1.14	2	21	.340	.098
NS.SCR amp/NS.SCR freq	Emotional category	.22	2	21	.801	.021
	Prior VR experience	.49	1	22	.491	.022
	Emotional category x Prior VR experience	.33	2	21	.720	.031

Emotion Characterization

Figure 11 shows the results of the emotion characterization for the emotion induction of the two emotions happiness and fear and the neutral category with 360° videos in VR. For each of the three categories, the assessments for the subjectively perceived emotional impression assessed with the emotions happiness, fear, disgust, sadness, anger, surprise, and the categories neutral and others are presented.

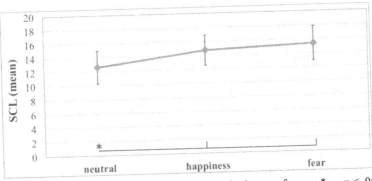

Note. Baseline-corrected mean values; I ... standard error of mean; * ... $p < .05$

Fig. 10. Mean skin conductance level (SCL): Three different emotional categories induced by 360° videos in VR.

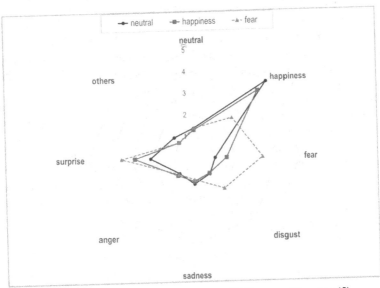

Note. Mean values, 6-point scale: Not at all (1) – very (6), cut at (5)

Fig. 11. Emotion characterization of the three different emotional categories induced by 360° videos in VR.

4   Discussion

The presented paper focusses on two different parts of the study: An experimental and an exploratory one. In the first, experimental part, it was investigated whether a person's emotional experience induced with affective pictures of four emotional categories (disgust, happiness, fear and sadness), differs when presented in a real or virtual environment. Furthermore, the influence of prior experience with VR was of interest. The results indicate that the affective pictures were able to induce significantly different emotional responses. Hence, the emotional category happiness was assessed significantly more positive than the used categories disgust, fear and sadness. Sadness induced by affective pictures was assessed significantly more negative than disgust and fear. Furthermore, the results reveal significant differences in emotional responses between virtual and real environments, while prior VR experience does not significantly affect emotions. Thus, regarding the measured cardiovascular responses of the participants, the heart rate (HR) was significantly higher during the stimuli presentation in the real environment than in the virtual environment. Furthermore, the HRV was significantly higher during the presentation of affective pictures in the virtual environment than in the real environment for the categories happiness and fear. Regarding the electrodermal reactions of the participants the results show that the skin conductance level (SCL) was significantly higher during the presentation of the affective pictures in the virtual environment than during the presentation in the real environment. The psychophysiological responses give a further indication that the use of VR environments have their advantages for emotion research [cf. 2, 8]. The presentation of the affective pictures used, seems to evoke stronger emotional responses in VR than on a computer screen (real environment). At the same time, stimuli presentation in the real environment may be more mental demanding when presented on the computer screen than when presented in VR. Following the results of HRV this seems to be especially relevant for the two emotional categories happiness and fear. This is also in line with [16] who showed that visual stimuli are experienced emotionally different in virtual than in real environments.

Whereas VR-experience did not significantly affect emotions in the experimental part of the study, a tendency towards a significant interaction emotional category x prior VR experience can be shown for the emotional characterization of disgust. Here, participants with prior VR experience assessed disgusting pictures in the real environment as significantly more disgusting than in VR. One explanation for this could be that the presentation order could not be permuted due to the circumstance of being a part of an overall study (see also [25]) – the participants experienced the affective pictures first in the real environment and afterwards in the VR environment. Interestingly, the effect was only shown for participants with prior VR experience. Maybe the "novelty" of experiencing VR, masked this effect for novices. This should be further investigated in future studies.

The second, exploratory part of the study aims to examine the effect of immersive 360° videos in a virtual environment on the emotional experience (categories: happiness, fear, neutral). The results show that significantly different emotional responses are evident in both, the subjective and psychophysiological parameters. Again, VR-experience did not show a significant effect. Subjectively, the emotional category fear was assessed significantly more negative and significantly more arousing than the categories neutral and happiness. This result is also supported by the participants' emotion characterization of the three 360° videos used. The psychophysiological responses of the participants point partly in the same direction. Hence, they indicate lower emotional responses regarding the neutral category than for the emotional categories happiness and fear. Interestingly, at the same time mental strain was significantly higher during stimuli of the category happiness than while experiencing stimuli of the category fear. This can possibly be explained with the visual stimuli (360° videos) used (see also emotion characterization) and should be included in future research.

Nonetheless, the study has some limitations. As mentioned before, sequence effects could not be excluded due to the embedding in a larger (overall) study, and should therefore become part of subsequent research. Furthermore, the authors suggest to include more resting measurements during the different experimental parts for future research. Although the subjective assessments of the subjective well-being before, during and after the experiment did not show any adverse effect, it cannot be completely excluded, that the sequence of the stimuli or the duration of the experiment influenced the results. Additional resting measurements between the different experimental blocks should help to control such possible effects even better. Furthermore, according to [2], there is a lack of standardized VR video material. As the results suggest, especially the video representing the emotional category fear, could therefore be improved. Unfortunately, some data from the psychophysiological recordings were missing due to technical problems. This should be further improved for future research. Finally, the presentation via the computer screen was used to present the stimuli in a real environment. The use of this medium might not have been perceived as different enough from the presentation in VR. From our point of view, further research is needed regarding emotional reactions on "real" scenarios and virtual scenarios.

To sum it up, the results show an effect of the environment (real or virtual) on the emotional responses in the psychophysiological parameters and the subjective assessments of the participants. On this matter, VR-experienced persons do not significantly differ from VR-inexperienced persons, but a tendency towards a significance can be shown for the emotional characterization of disgust.

References

1. Dörner, R., Broll, W., Grimm, P., Jung, B. (eds.): Virtual und Augmented Reality (VR/AR). Grundlagen und Methoden der Virtuellen und Augmentierten Realität [Virtual and Augmented Reality (VR/AR). Basics and methods of virtual and augmented reality]. 2nd edn. Springer, Heidelberg (2019). https://doi.org/10.1007/978-3-662-58861-1
2. Somarathna, R., Bednarz, T., Mohammadi, G.: Virtual reality for emotion elicitation - a review. IEEE Trans. Affect. Comput. (2021)
3. Yuan, S.N.V., Ip, H.H.S.: Using virtual reality to train emotional and social skills in children with autism spectrum disorder. Lond. J. Prim. Care 10(4), 110–112 (2018)
4. Schlegel, K., Vicaria, I.M., Isaacowitz, D.M., Hall, J.A.: Effectiveness of a short audiovisual emotion recognition training program in adults. Motiv. Emot. 41(5), 646–660 (2017)
5. Witmer, B.G., Singer, M.J.: Measuring presence in virtual environments: a presence questionnaire. Presence Teleoperators Virtual Environ. 7(3), 225–240 (1998)
6. Diemer, J., Alpers, G.W., Peperkorn, H.M., Shiban, Y., Mühlberger, A.: The impact of perception and presence on emotional reactions: a review of research in virtual reality. Front. Psychol. 6, 26 (2015)
7. Price, M., Mehta, N., Tone, E.B., Anderson, P.L.: Does engagement with exposure yield better outcomes? Components of presence as a predictor of treatment response for virtual reality exposure therapy for social phobia. J. Anxiety Disord. 25(6), 763–770 (2011)
8. Riva, G., et al.: Affective interactions using virtual reality: the link between presence and emotions. Cyberpsychol. Behav. 10(1), 45–56 (2007)

9. Sherman, W.R.: VR Developer Gems, 1st edn. CRC Press, Boca Raton (2019)
10. Sagnier, C., Loup-Escande, E., Valléry, G.: Effects of gender and prior experience in immersive user experience with virtual reality. In: Ahram, T., Falcão, C. (eds.) Advances in Usability and User Experience. AISC, vol. 972, pp. 305–314. Springer, Cham (2020). https://doi.org/10.1007/978-3-030-19135-1_30
11. Siedlecka, E., Denson, T.F.: Experimental methods for inducing basic emotions: a qualitative review. Emot. Rev. 11(1), 87–97 (2019)
12. Lang, P.J., Bradley, M.M., Cuthbert, B.N.: International affective picture system (IAPS): technical manual and affective ratings. NIMH Center for the Study of Emotion and Attention (1997)
13. Wessa, M., Kanske, P., Neumeister, P., Bode, K., Heissler, J., Schönfelder, S.: EmoPics: Subjektive und psychophysiologische Evaluation neuen Bildmaterials für die klinisch-bio-psychologische Forschung [Subjective and psychophysiological evaluation of new picture material for clinical-bio-psychological research]. Z. fur Klin. Psychol. Psychother. 39, 77 (2010)
14. Kurdi, B., Lozano, S., Banaji, M.R.: Introducing the open affective standardized image set (OASIS). Behav. Res. Methods 49(2), 457–470 (2017)
15. Li, B.J., Bailenson, J.N., Pines, A., Greenleaf, W.J., Williams, L.M.: A public database of immersive VR videos with corresponding ratings of arousal, valence, and correlations between head movements and self report measures. Front. Psychol. 8, 2116 (2017)
16. Estupiñán, S., Rebelo, F., Noriega, P., Ferreira, C., Duarte, E.: Can virtual reality increase emotional responses (arousal and valence)? A pilot study. In: Marcus, A. (ed.) Design, User experience, and Usability. User Experience Design for Diverse Interaction Platforms and Environments. LNCS, vol. 8518, pp. 541–549. Springer, Cham (2014). https://doi.org/10.1007/978-3-319-07626-3_51
17. Dan-Glauser, E.S., Scherer, K.R.: The Geneva affective picture database (GAPED): a new 730-picture database focusing on valence and normative significance. Behav. Res. 43(2), 468–477 (2011)
18. Frenzel, A.C., Götz, T., Pekrun, R.: Emotionen [Emotions]. In: Wild, E., Möller, J. (eds.) Pädagogische Psychologie, 2nd edn., pp. 205–231. Springer, Berlin Heidelberg (2009). https://doi.org/10.1007/978-3-540-88573-3_9
19. Boucsein, W., Backs, R.W.: Engineering psychophysiology as a discipline: historical and theoretical aspects. In: Backs, R.W., Boucsein, W. (eds.) Engineering Psychophysiology. Issues and Applications, pp. 3–30. Erlbaum, Mahwah, NJ (2000)
20. Arabian, H., Wagner-Hartl, V., Moeller, K.: Transfer learning in facial emotion recognition: useful or misleading? Curr. Dir. Biomed. Eng. 8(2), 668–671 (2022)
21. Boucsein, W., Schaefer, F., Kefel, M., Busch, P., Eisfeld, W.: Objective emotional assessment of tactile hair properties and their modulation by different product worlds. Int. J. Cosmet. Sci. 24(3), 135–150 (2002)
22. Boucsein, W., Schaefer, F.: Objective emotional assessment of industrial products. In: Westerink, J.H.D.M., Ouwerkerk, M., Overbeek, T.J.M., Pasveer, W.F., de Ruyter, B. (eds.) Probing Experience, 8th edn., pp. 69–76. Springer, Dordrecht (2008). https://doi.org/10.1007/978-1-4020-6593-4_6
23. Birkle, J., Weber, R., Möller, K., Wagner-Hartl, V.: Psychophysiological parameters for emotion recognition – conception and first evaluation of a measurement environment. In: Intelligent Human Systems Integration (IHSI 2022), vol. 22 (2022)
24. Schmid, R., Braunmiller, L., Hansen, L., Schonert, C., Möller, K., Wagner-Hartl, V.: Emotion recognition – validation of a measurement environment based on psychophysiological parameters. In: Intelligent Human Systems Integration (IHSI 2022), vol. 22 (2022)

25. Schmid, R., Saat, S.M., Möller, K., Wagner-Hartl, V.: Induction method influence on emotion recognition based on psychophysiological parameters. In: Intelligent Human Systems Integration (IHSI 2023), vol. 69, pp. 319–329 (2023)
26. Wessel, D., Attig, C., Franke, T.: ATI-S - an ultra-short scale for assessing affinity for technology interaction in user studies. In: Alt, F., Bulling, A., Döring, T. (eds.) Proceedings of Mensch und Computer 2019, pp. 147–154. ACM, New York, NY, USA (2019)
27. Unity. https://unity.com
28. HTC Vive Pro. https://www.vive.com/de/product/vive-pro/
29. Realidyne: Malaekahana Sunrise. YouTube (2015)
30. Animal Planet: Puppy Bowl XII. Highlight Reel. YouTube (2016)
31. MVR: Terrifying Sea Creatures. Deep Ocean Horror. YouTube (2022)
32. Bradley, M.M., Lang, P.J.: Measuring emotion: the self-assessment manikin and the semantic differential. J. Behav. Ther. Exp. Psychiatry 25(1), 49–59 (1994)
33. Ozawa, S.: Emotions induced by recalling memories about interpersonal stress. Front. Psychol. 12, 618676 (2021)
34. Unipark, Survey-Software. Tivian XI GmbH (2022)
35. Movisens GmbH: EcgMove 4 – ECG and Activity Sensor
36. Movisens GmbH: EdaMove 4 – EDA and Activity Sensor
37. Movisens GmbH: DataAnalyzer – Sensor Data Analysis

Predictive Indicators of Virtual Reality Sickness: A Look into Skin Temperature Disturbance

Kojiro Totsuka and Takehiko Yamaguchi[✉]

Suwa University of Science, Toyohira, Chino-shi 5000-1, Japan
tk-ymgch@rs.sus.ac.jp

Abstract. With the evolution of Virtual Reality (VR) technology in recent years, VR has been used in various applications such as medicine and education, and the market is expanding. However, VR contents may cause VR sickness, a side effect that causes discomfort to users.

Although content and device-based methods are often used to mitigate VR sickness in existing research, they have not yet completely prevented sickness. Recently, approaches to detect VR sickness in advance have been studied. However, these pre-detection methods require a large number of sensors to be attached to the body, which greatly impairs the VR experience. In this study, we focused on body temperature, which can be measured without contact, and investigated the relationship between facial skin temperature and the spatiotemporal characteristics of VR sickness.

Four out of six subjects who subjectively claimed to be intoxicated were able to detect a temperature difference of 0.15 °C-0.35 °C or more between the left and right cheeks 20–100 s before the subjective claim of intoxication, suggesting that it is possible to detect signs of intoxication even in situations where subjective perception of intoxication is not possible.

Keywords: VR Sickness · VR · Predict

1 Background

1.1 About Virtual Reality

Virtual Reality (VR) technology uses computer-generated virtual spaces to provide humans with real-world-like experiences. The basic components of VR are sensory presentation through displays as an output system, operation through devices as an input system, and a computer system that interactively simulates sensory presentation and operation. For example, a head-mounted display (HMD), which is often used in VR, converts visual and auditory information into information corresponding to each sensory organ and presents the converted information. The input system conveys motion information from a user through their motor systems, such as the hands. The simulation system generates a VR environment through the computer and applies it to the output system, which is simulated in the VR environment based on the information from the input system.

J. Y. C. Chen et al. (Eds.): HCII 2023, LNCS 14058, pp. 212–223, 2023.
https://doi.org/10.1007/978-3-031-48050-8_15

A VR environment consists of three elements: three-dimensional spatiality, real-time interactivity, and self-projection. Three-dimensional spatiality refers to the computer-generated three-dimensional visual and auditory space that spreads around humans; it is a natural three-dimensional space for humans. Real-time interactivity is a feature that enables a user to act freely in an artificial three-dimensional space that humans perceive as natural, while interacting with the environment in real-time. Self-projection means realizing them in a computer-generated artificial environment and a real environment such that no conflict occurs between senses, such as somatosensory and presuppositional senses, and different sensory modalities, such as audiovisual information from the eyes and ears [1].

1.2 Expansion of VR Market

In recent years, advances in VR devices have enabled the creation of more realistic experiences. VR technology is adopted not only for games and entertainment but also in various fields, such as education, medicine, and the military, and its market continues to expand. The metaverse is currently a focus of attention, as evidenced by Facebook's name change to Meta. According to a document published by the Ministry of Economy, Trade, and Industry of Japan, the metaverse is a place where producers provide services and content in various domains to consumers in a single virtual space; the market size of the metaverse will be approximately $828.95 billion by 2028 [2].

1.3 About VR Sickness

Although VR is expected to grow, VR activities continue to cause many users to suffer from a side effect: VR sickness.

The main symptoms of VR sickness include vomiting, nausea, headache, facial pallor, sweating, fatigue, and loss of sense of direction. Moreover, 60%–70% of users experience VR sickness when performing a task that involves a 30 min interaction in a VR environment [3]. The longer the exposure of a user to an HMD, the likelier they are to experience VR sickness [4]. Therefore, although the metaverse is expected to enable social activities in virtual spaces, VR sickness is a major barrier.

1.4 Existing Research on VR Sickness

Subjective evaluation and mitigation methods for VR sickness are being actively studied. The simulator sickness questionnaire (SSQ) is the most widely used questionnaire for the subjective evaluation of VR sickness [5]. In the SSQ, 16 questions are rated on a four-point scale (from 0 to 3); three sub-scores (eye movement discomfort, disorientation, and nausea) and a total score, which indicates the degree of sickness, are calculated.

Studies have been published on reducing VR sickness by dynamically changing the viewing angle [6] and blurring the surroundings of the field of vision [7].

1.5 Previous Research on Pre-detection of VR Sickness

VR sickness detection systems have been studied by Dennison et al. [8] and others, and various physiological indicators have been discussed, such as heart rate, respiration, and galvanic skin response data. However, the detection of VR sickness symptoms before they occur has been insufficiently discussed.

In a VR sickness pre-detection study, Lee et al. collected heart rate, respiration rate, heart rate variability, and galvanic skin response data by attaching sensors to the chest and fingertips of a user immersed in a VR roller coaster simulation. Using these data, the authors predicted the severity of VR sickness based on physiological signals obtained 2 min before the prediction, with an accuracy of 87.38% [9].

1.6 Current VR Pre-detection Problems

In conventional research on the pre-detection of VR sickness, physiological indicators, such as galvanic skin response data and heart rate variability, are used to predict and detect VR sickness. However, the sensors used by researchers are directly attached to the body. Participants can experience stress due to the limitation of movement caused by the attachment of sensors to their joints and the discomfort of the attachment; their sense of immersion may also be reduced. In particular, a reduced sense of immersion leads to a reduced sense of presence and makes the wearer more susceptible to VR sickness [10]. Therefore, a new measurement method that addresses these factors is needed.

1.7 Noncontact VR Sickness Detection Index

Based on the above background, this study focuses on surface body temperature, which can be measured in a noncontact manner using a thermal imaging camera.

VR sickness produces an autonomic nervous system flow due to psychological changes [11]. When the autonomic nervous system is disturbed and the sympathetic nervous system is dominant, the blood vessels constrict and blood flow is inhibited. This decreases the blood volume and body temperature. Conversely, when the parasympathetic nervous system is dominant, the blood vessels dilate and the blood volume and body temperature increase.

1.8 Previous Research on VR Sickness Detection Using Body Temperature

Yanaka et al. experimentally investigated the relationship between VR sickness and body temperature [12]. In this study, nasal skin temperature was measured in the environment of an HMD and a 55-inch display Their subjective evaluation suggested that body temperature decreases during sickness in an HMD environment and can thus be utilized as an indicator of immediate sickness.

Many existing studies focus on a single nasal skin temperature point, but no experiments have been conducted to focus on the temperature of the entire face and investigate the relative temperatures of the two sides of the face. In this study, we use a thermal imaging camera to measure the thermal patterns of these wide areas in a noncontact manner.

2 Objective

We investigated the Difference in temperature of both cheeks during VR sickness using a thermal imaging camera and conducted basic research on the relationship between VR sickness and the spatiotemporal characteristics of facial skin temperature.

3 Methods

3.1 Research Policy

The temperature of both cheeks during the VR experience was measured using a thermal imaging camera. These data were combined with the time data of sickness reporting, and the relationship between them was investigated.

3.2 Experiment Environment

The experiment was conducted in a seated position, and the temperature of the experimental environment was 23 °C. The room was kept at a constant temperature by closing the windows. During the experiment, each participant wore a Meta Quest 2, and their chin was placed on a chin rest. A tripod was placed 30 cm away from the front of the chin rest. The participant held the Meta Quest 2 controller in his right hand. The experiment in real space is shown in Fig. 1.

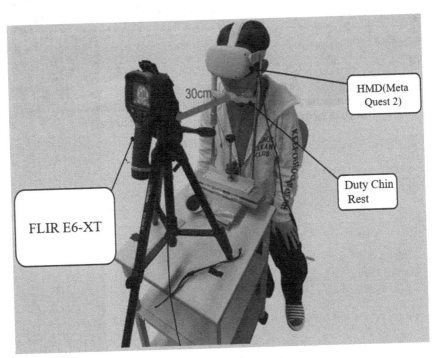

Fig. 1. Real environment

The virtual environment is shown in Fig. 2. Each participant was asked to run the course shown in the figure from the viewpoint of a car. Running the virtual car in a sitting position satisfied the condition that sickness occurs when the preconditioned sensation and visual information are inconsistent. The course was equipped with humps at regular intervals (Fig. 2), and transparent walls were placed on both sides of the course to prevent sudden motion sickness due to the drastic shaking of the viewpoint when the participant stepped off the course. The controller is shown in Fig. 3. The A button brought the car back to the course after being disabled (respawn), the B button recorded the time of symptom occurrence, the joystick controlled the car direction, the main trigger on the rear panel was the accelerator, and the grip button was the reverse function.

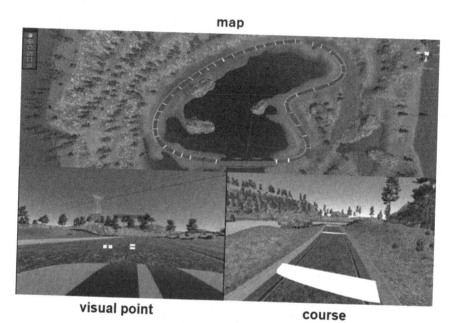

Fig. 2. Virtual environment

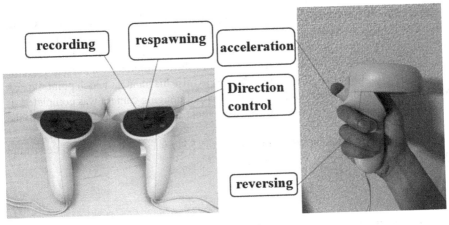

Fig. 3. Controller

3.3 Measurement Environment

A thermal imaging camera (FLIR E6-XT, which has built-in Wi-Fi) was used in this experiment to determine the differences in the temperature changes on the cheeks.

3.4 Participant Selection

The experiment was conducted on 12 male university students (Age M = 21.67, SD = 0.89).

3.5 Measurement of Nasal Area Temperature Using Thermal Imaging Camera During HMD Use

When a person wears a Meta Quest 2, which is a popular HMD, a thermal imaging camera can only capture images of the nasal wings and nasal bridge, which are easily affected by nasal breathing. Therefore, the imaging of the nasal area requires further miniaturization of the HMD, and this experiment focused on changes in the temperature balance between the left and right sides of the face.

3.6 Experimental Procedure

First, we checked whether each participant had any symptom of motion sickness or physical discomfort. He was then asked to assume a sitting position that was easy for him to maintain while wearing the HMD, and the thermal imaging camera was adjusted to his height. After the body temperature was maintained at a constant level, the participant's chin was placed on the chin rest. The baseline body temperature was measured, and temperature changes were measured every 5 min. Next, we explained the experimental procedure and the manipulation method to the participant. The task was to complete six laps of the course (Fig. 2) as quickly as possible. If the car became impossible to drive during the task, the participant was to press the A button to return to the beginning of the course. If subjectively perceived symptoms of VR sickness, such as headache, nausea, vomiting, sweating, and loss of sense of direction, occurred during the task, the participant was to press B to record the time and then maintain his posture by meditating and avoiding looking at the VR environment until the symptoms disappeared. Once he felt that the symptoms had disappeared, he was to raise his hand, at which point the task was terminated and the measurement of the thermal imaging camera was completed. If no symptoms of sickness occurred, the measurement was terminated after six laps of the course.

After the measurements were completed, the SSQ was administered to determine the sickness score.

3.7 SSQ

The SSQ was used to investigate the sickness score. The contents of the questionnaire are shown in Table 1. The questionnaire was designed to obtain a uniform sickness score regardless of the participant's claims of sickness and to maintain consistency between their subjective claims.

Table 1. SSQ

Q1	General discomfort
Q2	Fatigue
Q3	Headache
Q4	Eyestrain
Q5	Focusing difficulty
Q6	Increase in salivation
Q7	Sweating
Q8	Nausea
Q9	Concentration difficulty
Q10	Fullness of the head
Q11	Vision blurring
Q12	Dizziness with eyes open
Q13	Dizziness with eyes closed
Q14	Vertigo
Q15	Stomach awareness
Q16	Burping

3.8 Analysis Method

The data of the six participants who reported sickness during the task were compared with those of the participants who completed the task without reporting sickness. The temperature difference between the two cheeks and the changes in the absolute temperatures of the cheeks due to the temperature imbalance were analyzed.

The lower limit of the cheek analysis area was set at the corners of the mouth, the width was set to cover the left and right sides of the face, and the upper limit was set at the height where the temperature of the HMD could not be read. The measurement range was set to be large enough to allow for a relative investigation (Fig. 4). Data were measured at 10 frames per second, and the average temperature per frame was extracted. Analysis was performed using FLIR Thermal Studio.

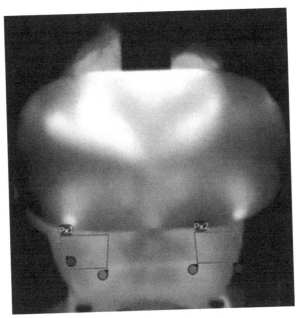

Fig. 4. Facial skin temperature measurement area

4 Results and Discussions

4.1 Analysis Results for Each Participant

The Difference in temperature of both cheeks of participant 001 is shown in Fig. 5.

The upper left graph in Fig. 5 shows the movement of the temperatures of both cheeks during the baseline measurement, and the lower left graph shows the temperature difference between the right and left cheeks during the baseline measurement. The upper right graph shows the movement of the temperatures of both cheeks during the task. The red line indicates the time the participant reported sickness. Therefore, for participants who did not report sickness, the lower right of the red line is the difference obtained by subtracting the temperature of the left cheek from that of the right cheek. The 0.1 °C error is attributed to the experimental apparatus used in this study.

The temperature waveform during the task, as seen in Fig. 5, drops by 0.35 °C from approximately 50 s before the reporting of sickness to the reporting, and the temperature balance begins to fluctuate.

In Table 2, the SSQ scores are divided into those of the participants with and without reports of sickness. The mean and standard deviation are summarized for each of the three subscores and the total score.

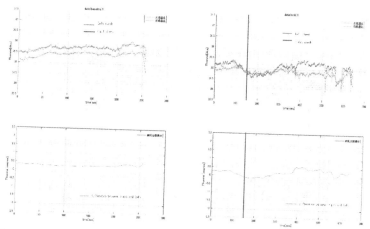

Fig. 5. Transition of change in temperature balance of participant 001 (Data001)

Table 2. SSQ scores of participants

	With VR sickness		Without VR sickness	
	Average	Standard deviation	Average	Standard deviation
Disorientation	76.32	29.67	38.16	17.07
Oculomotor discomfort	36.63	18.78	22.74	17.29
Nausea	104.4	51.30	19.49	20.83
Total score	76.05	26.42	31.42	20.15

4.2 Relationship Between VR Sickness and Body Temperature Transition

The total SSQ score of the group that reported sickness is higher than that of the group that did not report sickness.

The data suggested that a temperature imbalance of 0.15 °C–0.35 °C occurs 20–80 s before the onset report.

Table 3 shows the correlation coefficients between the time from the start of the temperature balance change to the reporting of sickness, the temperature change, and the SSQ subscores and total scores of the four participants who reported sickness and showed temperature imbalance.

This table suggests that the time from the start of the temperature balance change to the reporting of sickness has a negative correlation with the oculomotor discomfort subscore, nausea subscore, and total score (degree of sickness). Furthermore, temperature change has a negative correlation with the nausea subscore and total score (degree of sickness).

Table 3. Correlation between SSQ scores, time from start of temperature balance change to reporting of sickness, and temperature change

	Time from start of temperature balance change to reporting of sickness	Temperature change
Disorientation subscore	0.145	− 0.358
Oculomotor discomfort subscore	− 0.907	− 0.322
Nausea subscore	− 0.640	− 0.701
Total score	− 0.576	− 0.649

A temperature imbalance is observed in the participants who did not report sickness. However, since their total SSQ score (degree of sickness) is comparable to that of the participants who reported sickness, the participants who did not report sickness may have felt mildly sick.

Some participants did not show any temperature disturbance despite reporting sickness, and there are two possible reasons for this.

The first reason is that sickness was evaluated subjectively. The absence of temperature change may have been because of the differences in how people feel sick. Moreover, these participants reported discomfort caused by vection.

The second reason is the differences in people's driving experiences in real spaces and their ease of experiencing symptoms.

5 Conclusion and Future Works

5.1 Conclusion

In this study, we focused on the effect of autonomic disturbance on the temperature balance between the right and left cheeks. The results suggested that a 0.15 °C–0.35 °C disturbance in temperature balance occurred 20–80 s before the reporting of symptoms. The results also indicated a correlation between the SSQ scores, time from the start of the temperature change to the reporting of sickness, and temperature change. However, the results were not uniform across all participants, suggesting that the SSQ score may be easily influenced by individual differences.

222 K. Totsuka and T. Yamaguchi

5.2 Future Works

In this experiment, the chin was placed on a chin rest during the temperature measurement of the face. Although the face was fixed in place, the effect of measuring a location other than the measurement area was considered for some left–right movement of the face. Figure 6 shows an image of the measurement area during the experiment. The jump stand and HMD weighed the head down, resulting in a slight shift in the measurement area. The right image shows the high-temperature area around the nose. Data accuracy can be improved by eliminating this effect.

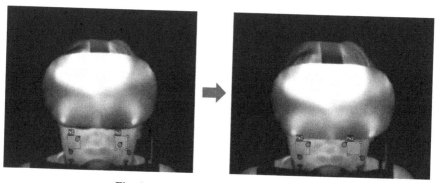

Fig. 6. Misalignment of measurement area

In the future, the temperature change and time of temperature change can be studied more accurately by increasing the number of data. Solving these problems will enable the creation of a system that uses machine learning for VR sickness pre-detection based on temperature changes.

References

1. Tachi, S., Sato, M., Hirose, M.: Virtual Reality Gaku, p. 6–7. Corona Publishing Co. Ltd. (2019)
2. Emergen Research Homepage. https://www.emergenresearch.com/industry-report/metaverse-market. Accessed 23 May 2023
3. Cobb, S.: Virtual reality induced symptoms and effects (VRISE): comparison of head mounted display (HMD), desktop and projection display systems. Displays **29**, 58-69 (2008)
4. Dużmańska, N., Strojny, P., Strojny, A.: Can simulator sickness be avoided? A review on temporal aspects of simulator sickness. Front. Psychol. **9**, 02132 (2018)
5. Kennedy, R.S., Lane, N.E., Berbaum, K.S., Lilienthal, M.G.: Simulator sickness questionnaire: an enhanced method for quantifying simulator sickness. Int. J. Aviat. Psychol. **3**, 203–220 (1993). https://doi.org/10.1207/s15327108ijap0303_3
6. Fernandes, A.S., Feiner, S.K.: Combating VR sickness through subtle dynamic field-of-view modification. In: 2016 IEEE Symposium on 3D User Interfaces (3DUI), pp. 201–210 (2016). https://doi.org/10.1109/3DUI.2016.7460053
7. Nie, G.-Y., Duh, H.B.-L., Liu, Y., Wang, Y.: Analysis on mitigation of visually induced motion sickness by applying dynamical blurring on a user's retina. IEEE Trans. Visual Comput. Graphics **26**, 2535–2545 (2020). https://doi.org/10.1109/TVCG.2019.2893668

8. Dennison, M.S., Wisti, A.Z., D'Zmura, M.: Use of physiological signals to predict cybersickness. Displays **44**, 42–52 (2016). https://doi.org/10.1016/j.displa.2016.07.002
9. Islam, R., et al.: Automatic detection and prediction of cybersickness severity using deep neural networks from user's physiological signals. In: 2020 IEEE International Symposium on Mixed and Augmented Reality (ISMAR), pp. 400–411 (2020). https://doi.org/10.1109/ISMAR50242.2020.00066
10. Lin, J.J.-W., Duh, H.B.L., Parker, D.E., Abi-Rached, H., Furness, T.A.: Effects of field of view on presence, enjoyment, memory, and simulator sickness in a virtual environment. In: Proceedings IEEE Virtual Reality 2002, pp. 164–171 (2002). https://doi.org/10.1109/VR.2002.996519
11. Yanaka, S., Kosaka, T.: Detection of visually induced motion sickness while watching a video using variation in autonomic nervous activity, Entertainment Computing. Symposium 2016 collection of papers, pp. 285–286 (2016)
12. Yanaka, S., Kosaka, T.: Detection of visually induced motion sickness while watching a video using variation in autonomic nervous activity, entertainment computing. Symposium 2016 collection of papers, pp. 287–288 (2016)

Temporal Aspects of Self-rotation Perception and Nystagmus: A Study on Disappearance and Onset Time

Ryosuke Urata and Takehiko Yamaguchi(✉)

Suwa University of Science, Toyohira, Chino-Shi 5000-1, Japan
tk-ymgch@rs.sus.ac.jp

Abstract. The purpose of this study was the objective evaluation of the self-rotation perception that occurs during real-space body turns in virtual reality (VR) activities. This phenomenon is a problem with a previously proposed method that enables natural walking in VR spaces using a turntable. We also investigated the time consumed until the disappearance of the self-rotation perception and eye movements. Experiments were conducted under three conditions: one 60 s normal rotation for visual and somatosensory stimulation and one 60 s rotation and one 30 s rotation for somatosensory stimulation only (proposed method). Nystagmus, which occurs during rotation, was observed during normal rotation but not under the proposed method. The time to the disappearance of the self-rotation perception was shorter at slower rotation speeds. Therefore, the self-rotation perception may be related not only to velocity but also to acceleration. Future research should focus on turntable speed and acceleration to mitigate the self-rotation perception.

Keywords: Virtual Reality · Turntable · Nystagmus

1 Introduction

1.1 Virtual Reality (VR) Technology

VR technology can artificially generate a sense of reality and reproduce the actions we perform in our daily lives. When we perceive reality, we receive information about the world through our five senses, and this information changes according to our movements in real time. To reproduce this system through engineering, VR uses motion in real space as input and information corresponding to the five senses as output, which is controlled in real time [1]. In this way, VR generates an equivalent experience of reality and reproduces walking as it is performed daily.

1.2 Walking Technology in VR Space

A method allowing users to walk in limited real spaces should be devised to enable them to walk in vast VR spaces. As seen in Fig. 1, researchers have proposed methods allowing users to move forward in VR spaces by attaching sensors to the feet and requiring the user to step on a spot [2], requiring the user to walk on a conveyor belt in a way that cancels the user's forward movement [3], and adjusting the walking trajectory in the real space by shifting the VR space image as the user blinks while walking [4]. Thus, a user can move in a vast VR space despite being in a limited real space by adjusting the walking trajectory in the real space.

However, in existing studies, the walking trajectory is adjusted in the real space, so the sensations presented to the visual and vestibular senses are not the same as those in reality, and the walking experience in the VR space is unnatural. Stepping on a spot [2] or walking on a conveyor belt [3] means walking in the VR space while staying at a single point in the real space. As for shifting the VR space image [4], the walking trajectories in the real and VR spaces differ because the user appears to be walking straight in the VR space despite walking diagonally in the real space. These technologies cannot correctly present vestibular sensory information corresponding to visual information. A natural walking experience cannot be obtained due to the discrepancy between the walking trajectories in real and VR spaces.

Fig. 1. Examples of existing VR walking techniques

1.3 Proposed Method

To solve the abovementioned problem with previous studies, we studied a method of infinitely connecting and expanding a closed real space [5]. Specifically, as shown in Fig. 2, we prepared a VR space consisting of several rooms that were each of the same size as the real space and placed a turntable in front of a wall in the real space. The walking trajectories in the real space and the VR space matched, so the user could only walk as far as the size of the real space. After walking to the wall, the user stepped on the turntable and turned their real body while the VR space image remained fixed. Therefore, the user turned their back to the wall of the real space while still facing the room ahead in the VR space and could proceed to this virtual room. Through repetition of this action, the closed real space could be infinitely expanded, allowing the user to move through the vast VR space without adjusting their walking trajectory.

In a previous study, we performed an object search task in multiple connected rooms in a VR space and evaluated the naturalness of the walking sensation during the task. The experiment was conducted in a VR space consisting of multiple connected rooms that were each of the same size as the real space, and the task was to move within these rooms to locate objects. In addition to the previously proposed method [5], we used three methods of moving in the space: foot stomping, which is a typical method of moving in a VR space, and the use of a controller stick. After the task, we administered a questionnaire about the walking sensation, calculated the average score for each item, and compared the scores between the different conditions. The score of the proposed method was significantly higher, indicating that it enabled the user to walk most naturally [5].

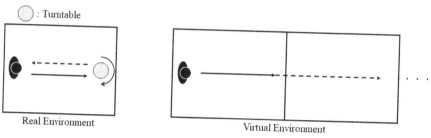

Fig. 2. Proposed method

1.4 Problems with Previously Proposed Method

The previously proposed method causes a self-rotation perception; the user perceives that their body is rotating when moving from one room to another in the VR space. When moving to the next VR room, the user's body is inverted by the turntable while the VR space image remains fixed, so the user visually feels as if they are standing still. However, because the user feels the rotation acceleration of the turntable at the start of the rotation, they perceive the direction change with their vestibular senses, which reduces the sensation of moving forward.

Previous studies on rotation suggest that the self-rotation perception decreases with time after the presentation of a rotation stimulus in the dark to a seated user. During rotation, eye movements called nystagmus are induced by the angular acceleration of rotation. The nystagmus slow-phase velocity decreases and approaches zero when a constant-velocity rotation stimulus is presented [6]. Thus, nystagmus may cease over time, and the self-rotation perception may decrease.

Different visual stimuli are used in our previous study and the present study. In the previous study, the experiment was conducted in a dark room, so the information seen was not distinctive, and it was difficult for the eyeballs to stay in a certain position. Since the present study is conducted in a room in a VR space, a participant may gaze at objects in the room, and the eyeballs may stay in a fixed position. If the eyeballs stay at a certain position, nystagmus may no longer occur. Therefore, whether nystagmus is generated, or reduced under the conditions of this study should be clarified.

The self-rotation perception caused by the previously proposed method increases rapidly at the start of rotation and decreases with time [5]. Figure 3 illustrates the temporal variation in the subjective assessment of the self-rotation perception and turntable acceleration based on previous findings. At the start of rotation, the turntable accelerates, and the self-rotation perception of the user increases rapidly as they feel the acceleration. Over time, acceleration decreases to zero, and the user's self-rotation perception is thought to decrease gradually along with acceleration. However, this self-rotation perception disappearance model (Fig. 3) is based on users' subjective assessment, and the time needed for the self-rotation perception to disappear varies from person to person. The relationship between the subjective assessment of the self-rotation perception and nystagmus has not been clarified.

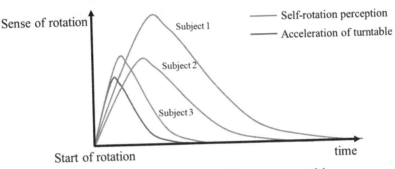

Fig. 3. Self-rotation perception disappearance model

1.5 Objectives

The purpose of this paper is the objective evaluation of the self-rotation perception that occurs during real body turns, which is a problem with the previously proposed method. The following research questions are formulated to evaluate the self-rotation perception:

- What is the relationship between the disappearance of the self-rotation perception and rotation velocity?
- What is the relationship between the self-rotation perception and nystagmus?

The disappearance of the self-rotation perception may be related to rotation speed. Stimulation of somatosensory perception changes with rotation speed. Slow rotation weakens somatosensory stimulation and thus may eliminate the self-rotation perception.

During rotation, the eyeballs undergo oculomotor movements called nystagmus. This condition is caused by the sensation of acceleration in the somatosensory system. In our previously proposed method, acceleration is felt only at the start of rotation, after which the rotation proceeds at a constant speed. Therefore, nystagmus may occur only at the start of rotation.

2 Methods

2.1 Vestibulo-Ocular Reflex

We focused on the vestibulo-ocular reflex, which is induced by body acceleration, to evaluate the self-rotation perception objectively. The vestibulo-ocular reflex prevents vision blurring by moving the eyeballs in the opposite direction of head movement. During body rotation, the slow phase, in which the eyeballs move slowly in the opposite direction of rotation, and the rapid phase, in which the eyeballs move rapidly in the direction of rotation, are repeated as shown in Fig. 4. The self-rotation perception can be evaluated from the eyes by observing the continuous motion of the slow and rapid phases.

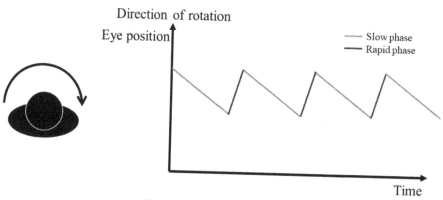

Fig. 4. Vestibular motile reflex

2.2 Experimental Environment

The experiment was conducted with each participant wearing a head-mounted display that can measure eye movements, as shown in Fig. 5, while standing on a turntable. The position of the eyeballs for each frame was recorded to measure eye movements. A turntable with an arbitrarily adjustable speed was used to compare eye movements at different rotation speeds. A controller was used to record the time of disappearance of the self-rotation perception based on the participant's subjective assessment.

2.3 Experimental Task

In the experiment (Fig. 6), eye movements were measured at rest and then during rotation. After the start of the experiment, each participant was asked to look at a gaze point, and measurements were made for 30 s after the eye movements stabilized. Afterward, the participant was asked to erase the gaze point and start the rotation, and their eye movements during rotation were measured. The participants were asked to press a button

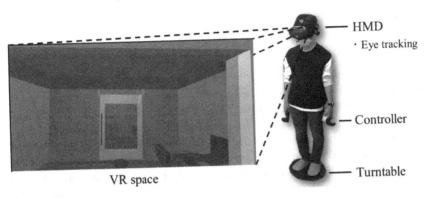

Fig. 5. Experimental environment

when they thought the self-rotation perception had disappeared. The participants were instructed to face the front as much as possible during the task.

The eye movements under three conditions were compared: one 60 s rotation for visual and vestibular and one 60 s rotation and one 30 s rotation for somatosensory stimulation only. In the previously proposed method, an image that continuously faces a door during rotation is presented. In the experiment, eye movements up to half a rotation were recorded.

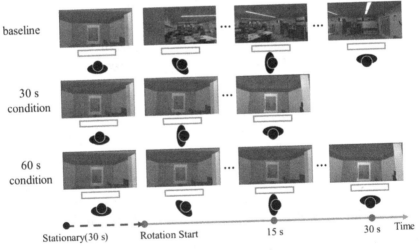

Fig. 6. Experimental procedure

2.4 Participants

Eleven students from the Suwa University of Science, Japan, were recruited for the experiment. Only males were selected to eliminate gender differences, and the mean age was 21.5 years ($SD = 0.96$).

3 Results

3.1 Time to Disappearance of Self-rotation Perception

Table 1 shows the time it took for the self-rotation perception to disappear. The 30 and 60 s conditions refer to the rotation stimulation of the somatosensory system for 30 and 60 s, respectively. The "-" sign indicates that the self-rotation perception did not disappear. Five out of the 11 participants felt the disappearance of the self-rotation perception under the 30 s condition, whereas seven participants felt the disappearance of the self-rotation perception under the 60 s condition. Under both conditions, the self-rotation perception did not disappear. Four of the five participants who felt the disappearance of the self-rotation perception experienced the disappearance earlier under the 60 s condition than under the 30 s condition.

Table 1. Time to disappearance of self-rotation perception (unit: s)

Participant number	30 s condition	60 s condition
1	-	14.1784
2	7.3409	12.2692
3	4.0154	3.0400
4	-	16.1478
5	-	-
6	4.9756	3.0501
7	5.6551	4.9965
8	-	-
9	11.3363	9.4740
10	-	-
11	-	-

3.2 Relationship Between Self-rotation Perception and Nystagmus

We focused on temporal eye position data to evaluate eye movements during rotation. In observing nystagmus, we focused on the rapid phase, in which the eyeballs move in the direction of rotation, and the slow phase, in which the eyeballs move in the opposite direction of rotation. The hypotheses are that (1) the rotation stimulation of the visual and vestibular systems will cause the continuous motion of the slow and rapid phases and (2) the rotation stimulation of only the vestibular system will cause the continuous motion of the slow and rapid phases immediately after the start of rotation only. Figure 7 shows the temporal variation in eye movements under each condition. The eyeball position is marked 0 to 1, with 0 representing the left-eye direction and

1 representing the right-eye direction. Since the right-eye direction is the direction of rotation, the closer the value is to 1, the more closely the eye moves in the direction of rotation. The eye movements during the rotation stimulation (baseline) of the visual and somatosensory systems were continuous in the slow and rapid phases. Therefore, nystagmus was observed during visual and somatosensory rotation stimulation. In the rotation stimulation of the somatosensory system (30 and 60 s conditions), no such movements were observed, indicating that the eye movements were almost constant.

Next, we focused on the nystagmus slow-phase velocity, which has been the focus of previous studies. The nystagmus slow-phase velocity decreases and approaches zero. In the case of somatosensory rotation stimulation, a certain slow-phase velocity may be generated at the start of rotation and approach zero with time. Figure 8 shows a graph of the temporal variation in the extracted slow-phase velocity. In the case of the rotation stimulation of the visual and somatosensory systems (baseline), a constant velocity was generated in the opposite direction of rotation. In the case of the rotation stimulation of the somatosensory system only (30 and 60 s conditions), the eye velocity quickly approached zero after the start of rotation.

Finally, we focused on the absolute value of the difference between the left- and right-eye positions. In the experiment, eye movements at rest were measured by requiring the participants to look at a gaze point. Then, eye movements were measured after erasing the gaze point at the start of rotation. While a participant gazed at the gaze point, the eyeballs were in the leaning state. Figure 9 shows a graph of the absolute positions of the left and right eyeballs over time. In the rotation stimulation of the visual and somatosensory systems, the difference between the left- and right-eye positions decreased after the start of rotation, increased, and decreased again, maintaining a constant difference. In the case of somatosensory-only rotation stimulation, the difference between the left- and right-eye positions decreased after the start of rotation and remained constant.

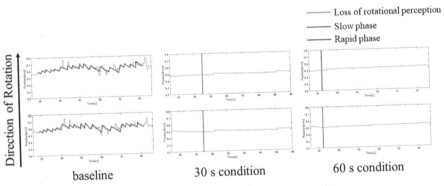

Fig. 7. Temporal variation in eye movements

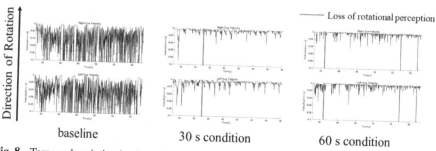

——— Loss of rotational perception

baseline   30 s condition   60 s condition

Fig. 8. Temporal variation in slow-phase eye velocity in rotation direction and opposite direction

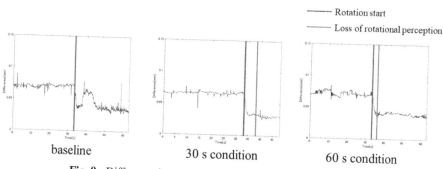

——— Rotation start
——— Loss of rotational perception

baseline   30 s condition   60 s condition

Fig. 9. Difference in absolute positions of left and right eyeballs

4 Discussion

The results validate the research questions. First, we examined the relationship between the perceived disappearance of the self-rotation perception and rotation speed. We compared the time to the disappearance of the self-rotation perception during somatosensory-only rotation stimulation. It was shorter under the 60 s condition than under the 30 s condition. The participants who did not experience the disappearance of the self-rotation perception during the 60 s rotation also indicated that they did not feel the disappearance during the 30 s rotation. However, they reported feeling that the self-rotation perception was about to disappear during the 60 s rotation. This indicates that the self-rotation perception was more likely to disappear during one 60 s rotation. Therefore, the self-rotation perception is more likely to disappear at slower rotation speeds.

The relationship between the self-rotation perception and nystagmus was examined next. Slow and rapid movements were observed under visual and somatosensory rotation stimulation but not under somatosensory-only rotation stimulation. This result indicates that the previously proposed method is unlikely to induce nystagmus. Next, the slow-phase velocity under visual and somatosensory rotation stimulation was above a certain level, but it increased at the start of rotation and then decreased quickly under somatosensory-only rotation stimulation. The slow-phase velocity was close to zero at the time of self-rotation perception disappearance, suggesting that the self-rotation perception disappears when the slow-phase velocity is close to zero.

We then studied the difference between the left- and right-eye positions. Findings showed that the self-rotation perception disappeared when the difference between the left- and right-eye positions was small. This may have been due to the change in user gaze from the gaze point to the frontal plane and the stabilization of focus. In other words, focus stability may be necessary to eliminate the self-rotation perception. However, since some participants did not experience a decrease in the self-rotation perception despite a decrease in the difference between the eye positions, additional conditions may be necessary for the disappearance of the self-rotation perception.

Figure 10 shows the temporal variation in turntable acceleration and eye movements. The upper graphs show the positions of the left and right eyeballs, and the lower graphs show the acceleration of the turntable, with 30 s being the highest acceleration. The difference in the time until the disappearance of the self-rotation perception may have been because the time until the disappearance differed between the participants depending on the acceleration magnitude. Thus, minimizing acceleration may make participants less sensitive to the self-rotation perception.

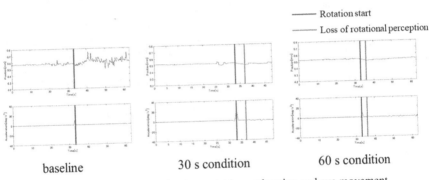

baseline   30 s condition   60 s condition

Fig. 10. Temporal variation in turntable acceleration and eye movement

5 Conclusion

We recorded eye movements during rotation and determined the time until the disappearance of the self-rotation perception for an objective evaluation of the self-rotation perception, which is a problem with our previously proposed method. The relationship between the self-rotation perception and rotation speed was examined. The self-rotation perception more easily disappeared after 60 s of rotation than after 30 s of rotation, suggesting that the self-rotation perception more easily disappears at slower rotation speeds. The relationship between eye movements and the self-rotation perception revealed that the self-rotation perception disappeared as the slow-phase velocity approached zero. Moreover, the self-rotation perception may disappear after the eye focus stabilizes after the start of rotation. However, some participants did not lose the self-rotation perception even when these conditions were met. This result may be related to the acceleration at the start of rotation. Therefore, in future research, we will modify the turntable speed and acceleration to reduce the self-rotation perception. In this study, the participants had to stand in front of a door in the VR space and wait until the end of rotation. As there was almost no waiting time in the real space, the turntable had to be rotated quickly to approximate the experience in the real space. However, findings revealed that a user is less likely to lose their self-rotation perception at higher rotation speeds.

References

1. Tachi, S., Satou, M., Hirose, M.: Virtual Reality-Gaku, p. 10. Corona Publishing Co. Ltd. (2019)
2. Feasel, J., Whitton, M.C., Wendt, J.D.: LLCM-WIP: low-latency, continuous-motion walking-in-place. In: 2008 IEEE Symposium on 3D User Interfaces, pp. 97–104. IEEE, Reno, NV, USA (2008)
3. Feasel, J., Whitton, M.C., Kassler, L., Brooks, F.P., Lewek, M.D.: The integrated virtual environment rehabilitation treadmill system. IEEE Trans. Neural Syst. Rehabil. Eng. **19**, 290–297 (2011)
4. Bolte, B., Lappe, M.: Subliminal reorientation and repositioning in immersive virtual environments using saccadic suppression. IEEE Trans. Visual Comput. Graphics **21**, 545–552 (2015)
5. Chen, J.Y.C., Fragomeni, G., Degen, H., Ntoa, S. (eds.): HCI International 2022 – Late Breaking Papers: Interacting with eXtended Reality and Artificial Intelligence: 24th International Conference on Human-Computer Interaction, HCII 2022, Virtual Event, June 26 – July 1, 2022, Proceedings. Springer, Cham, pp. 188–196 (2022). https://doi.org/10.1007/978-3-031-21707-4
6. Koizuka, I.: Rotational test, off-vertical axis rotation. Equilibrium Res. **70**, 47–56 (2011)

An Immersive Media Recognition Method Using Depth Information of Multi-View Videos

Injae Yoo[1] , Jaechung Lee[2] , Seyoung Jang[1] , Byeongchan Park[1] ,
Cheong Ghil Kim[3] , Seok-Yoon Kim[1] , and Youngmo Kim[1(✉)]

[1] Soongsil University, Seoul 06978L, Republic of Korea
halo8024@beyondtech.co.kr, seyjang216@soongsil.ac.kr, {ksy, ymkim828}@ssu.ac.kr
[2] Beyondtech Inc., Seoul 08503, Republic of Korea
jclee@beyondtech.co.kr
[3] Namseoul University, Chungnam 31020, Republic of Korea
cgkim@nsu.ac.kr

Abstract. In the case of multi-view videos, since they are transmitted in a file format in which the basic view and the depth information screen(additional view) are combined, the file capacity of the original video and query video is larger than that of a general stereo type video, which results in a problem of slow transmission to identify the video. This paper proposes a video recognition method which first extracts multiple frames from the input original multi-view video, extracts multiple basic view feature information from the basic view of each extracted frame, and stores it in the original database. Afterwards, when a query about a video happens, multiple frame and depth information screens are extracted from the multi-view video and recognized by comparing them with the basic screen feature information of the original multi-view video. The proposed method has the advantage of reducing memory capacity and communication load in that it can quickly determine whether the query multi-view video is the same as the original multi-view video, and use depth information with a small data capacity as feature information.

Keywords: Metaverse · MIV · Immersive Media · Recognition · Copyright

1 Introduction

Metaverse is a compound word of meta, which means artificial or abstract, and universe, which is the real world, and means a three-dimensional virtual world. Metaverse can provide another content within the content with merged immersive technology applied such as augmented reality and virtual reality technology so that users can be more immersed in the content. In the metaverse where such immersive content is provided, illegal copying and distribution may occur by applying geometric deformation such as cutting off a part of the screen or lowering the resolution to the video, resulting in copyright infringement on the video [1–4]. In addition, since a special type of online service provider (OSP), such as P2P and webhard, include a mandatory provision for technical measures (filtering) to block the transmission of pirated videos, so research is needed to identify whether the images provided to users in the metaverse are the same videos as those of others [5].

However, since the filtering technology for determining whether a work is illegal is mainly researched and used to determine whether a 2D video is illegally copied, there is a limit in that it cannot be applied to an immersive video. In addition, in the multi-view image used in the metaverse environment, since the image is transmitted in a form in which the basic view is combined with the additional view, so the size of the original video and the query video to determine whether it is illegally reproduced is larger than the normal video, there is a problem of slow transmission speed in receiving videos for identifying as the original [6].

In this paper, we propose an immersive media recognition method using the depth information of multi-view video, which is a method for determining illegal copying of immersive media containing multi-view information used in the metaverse environment. After MIV(MEPG Immersive Video) standard technology for immersive video encoding/decoding of MEPG, which is currently being standardized, is applied to generate additional views from multi-view videos to extract SURF-based feature points, and feature points are extracted from a query video, which may be an illegally copied video and various geometric transformations may have been applied, the proposed method determines whether or not it can be recognized as the same original video through similarity comparison with the original video.

The structure of this paper is as follows. Section 2 describes feature-based filtering technology and MIV technology, which is currently being researched as a standard technology, as related research. Section 3 describes the immersive media recognition method using the depth information of multi-view videos proposed in this paper. In Sect. 4, the experiments and results are reviewed, and Sect. 5 concludes this paper.

2 Related Research

2.1 Feature-Based Filtering Technology

Feature-based filtering technology [7] is a technology that extracts unique feature information from original content such as image, audio, and video to establish an original feature information database, extracts feature information from the content to be checked, and then compares it with the original feature information data to determine whether it is original or not, as shown in Fig. 1.

The performance indicators for these feature-based filtering technologies for determining the original for query content include toughness, consistency, feature information volume, extraction speed, and search comparison speed. In particular, video feature-based content filtering technology requires much more complex technology due to the video characteristics with a lot of information, as shown in Table 1.

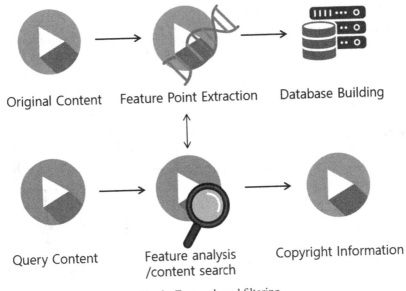

Fig. 1. Feature-based filtering

Table 1. Video information for applying feature-based filtering technology

Category	Contents
Use video filtering	Using color information, motion information, scene change information, original information, feature point information in the screen, etc
Video Transformation Type	In the case of a movie, a modification to create a text area at the bottom of the screen to process subtitles
	Transformation in the form of cutting the screen in the process of converting a 16:9 aspect ratio movie to a 4:3 aspect ratio video
	Variation in the form of inserting one's initials, logo, or specific phrase in the corner of the video
	Modify frame rate or resolution to reduce file size
	Transformation of color or brightness when video format is changed when video is re-encoded
	Rotation and tilting of the image when the movie is re-recorded using a camcorder
	Deleting or inserting commercial advertisements inserted in the middle of the video

238   I. Yoo et al.

2.2 MPEG-I/MIV Standardization

Figure 2 shows the MIV-based architecture for the encryption/decryption of immersive video that supports 6 DoF(Degree of Freedom) as a standard MIV technology [8, 9].

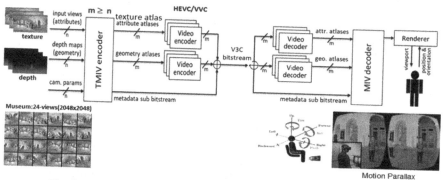

Fig. 2. Video information for applying feature-based filtering technology

Looking at the MIV-based immersive video encoding/decoding architecture, MIV uses multiple textures and geometric information obtained through omnidirectional cameras to remove spatial redundancy and then compresses it through a small number of video codecs. Pruner, a key algorithm used at this time, is implemented by extracting the area seen from the additional point of view video, although it is shielded from the basic point of view video to eliminate redundancy between point of view videos. At the decoder stage, metadata is required to play viewport videos dynamically and encode control information according to the viewer's movement through post-processing and mid-point video synthesis, and these metadata and bitstream structures are standardized.

2.3 SURF

SURF(Speed Up Robust Features) [10] is an algorithm based on multi-scale space theory and was proposed by H. Bay et al. in 2006, and its extracted feature points have four components. First, it consists of the coordinates of the feature point, which is the rotation of the feature point, second, the scale of the feature point proportional to the sigma value used for Gaussian smoothing, third, orientation, a value calculated using slope information, and finally, a 64-dimensional descriptor vector that summarizes information around the feature point.

3 Immersive Media Recognition Method Using Depth Information of Multi-View Videos

Immersive videos played on the metaverse contain multi-point information, which requires solving the problem of processing speed and low recognition rate because the capacity of the video is large. The first step of immersive emergent video recognition method using depth information of multi-view videos proposed in this paper is the extracting process of feature points and constructing them as feature information using depth information of videos by obtaining video space differences. The second, recognition process extracts the feature points of the query-immersive video and determines whether it is recognized as the original by comparing the similarity with the stored feature information of the original.

First, the method of extracting feature points using spatial differences using depth information of immersive media is a process of extracting feature points by generating additional views from images taken from multiple cameras (e.g., 24 cameras consisting of 4 x 6 types) used to produce immersive media, as shown in Fig. 3.

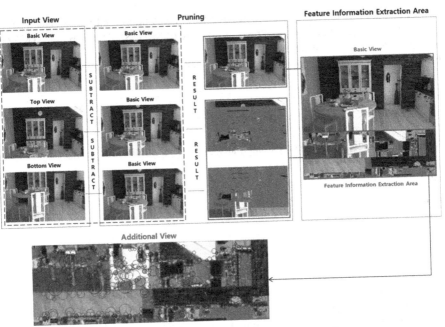

Fig. 3. Additional View creation and feature point extraction process

In order to reduce the pixel rate to be processed by the video codec, an additional view with the spatial difference subtracted is created using the depth information of the multi-point view containing multi-point information in the basic view of the immersive media. A basic view can be created by selecting the original time point as it is or by projecting it through the synthesis of emerging media at a specific time point. All multi-view view videos generate additional views that eliminate space redundancy between basic views, multi-view videos, and multi-view views through the Pruner. Frame information including video frame information and depth information is extracted from an video including depth information for generating an additional view. The immersive media includes depth information in the video media to provide a sense of reality to the user. As an ultra-realistic medium suitable for the metaverse environment, a number of spatial information is included in the video to have a 3DoF + degree of freedom in all directions, as shown in Fig. 4.

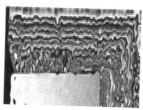

Fig. 4. Video with depth information

In this paper, feature points are extracted from these additional views. The performance of the recognition speed and recognition rate of SIFT, SURF, ORB, and AKAZE have been compared as a feature point extraction algorithm to determine the original through feature point extraction and similarity comparison process, and their results are shown in Table 2.

Table 2. Performance Comparison Using Feature Point Extraction Algorithms

Algorithm	Speed(s)	Feature Point Matching Rate(%)	Speed TOP	Matching Rate TOP
SIFT	0.712096	91.90	SURF	SIFT
SURF	0.173199	81.47		
ORB	0.340624	57.60		
AKAZE	0.462762	86.52		

As a result of the comparison, SURF has the best recognition speed of 0.17 s and SIFT has the best recognition rate of 91.9, but SIFT's recognition speed has been very slow to SURF, so in this paper, feature points are extracted using SURF.

As explained above, the feature information of the original immersive media is extracted and built as the original dataset, and the feature information of the query immersive media is extracted and compared to the original dataset. In the process of extracting a feature point of the query video using the spatial difference, a plurality of frames are extracted from the input immersive video. The depth information extraction process of the multi-view video can extract the depth information screen in the form of combining the generated depth information screen with the basic screen by calculating the difference between basic views in query videos taken from multiple cameras at different locations [11].

4   Experiments and Results

An experimental environment, as shown in Table 2, has been set up and tested to experiment with the immersive media recognition method using depth information of multi-view videos proposed in this paper.

Table 3. Experimental Environment

	Spec
CPU	Intel Core i9 12900K
RAM	64GB
GPU	NVIDA Geforce RTX 3090Ti
Dataset	1,000 Immersive Content

As an experiment proposed in this paper, the feature information has been extracted through FE Immersive for 1,000 videos containing depth information, and the extracted feature information has been inquired to a feature information comparison search server to verify that the recognition rate is more than 70%.

First, for the test, a video including depth information has been played, and it is shown in Fig. 5.

The test screen of the video including the reproduced depth information is shown in Fig. 6.

The similarity determination process has been performed by comparing a video (A) that does not include depth information and a video (B) that includes depth information, and their results are shown in Table 4.

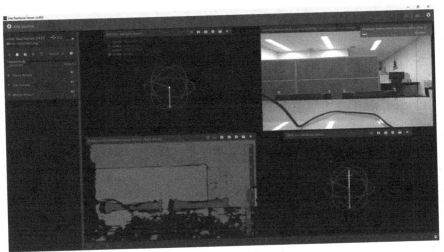

Fig. 5. Video playback with depth information

Feature information has been extracted from 1,000 videos with depth information, and the extracted feature information has been queried to the comparison search server to confirm that the recognition rate of recognizing the same video was 77%, which is over 70%.

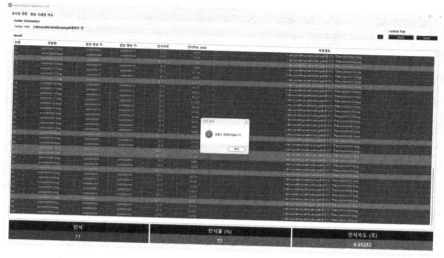

Fig. 6. Captured screen for results

Table 4. Experiment result

	(A)	(B)
Number of Dataset	1,000	1,000
Recognition Rate	50%	77%
False Recognition Rate	50%	23%
Recognition Speed	7.45122s	6.35252s

5 Conclusion

In this paper, we have proposed a technique for identifying multi-view videos mainly used in the metaverse environment. Since the multi-view video is transmitted in a file format in which the basic view and the depth information screen (additional view) are combined, the file capacity of the original video and query video is larger than that of a general stereo type video. Therefore, there is a problem that the speed of transmitting and receiving files to identify videos is slow.

In order to solve this problem, we have proposed a video recognition method which first extracts multiple frames from the input original multi-view video, extracts a plurality of base screen feature information from the base screen for each extracted frame, and stores them in the original database for each frame. Afterwards, if query about a video comes in, multiple frame and depth information screens are extracted from the multi-view video and recognized by comparing them with the basic screen feature information of the original multi-view video.

Through experiments, we have confirmed that the proposed method has the recognition rate of 77% and the recognition speed of about 6 s, which is more exact and faster than the recognition rate of 50% and the recognition speed of about 7 s when using a video that does not include depth information. In addition, it is also confirmed that the amount of communication used for recognition as an original can be reduced in that it can determine whether it is the same as a multi-view video and can use the feature information of an additional view with a small data capacity.

In the future, the proposed method can be used to prevent and monitor infringement of multi-view videos used in the metaverse environment and can be used as a technical measure. For this purpose, however, further research to extract feature points that are robust to transformation and variations on multi-view videos of various genres may be necessary.

Acknowledgment. This research project supported by Ministry of Science, ICT and Future Planning(MSIP) and IInstitute for Information & Communication Technology Planning & Evaluation(IITP) in 2023(2022–0-00699).
This work was supported by the National Research Foundation of Korea Grant funded by the Korean Government (NRF-2021R1I1A4A01049755).

References

1. Chun, H., Han, M., Jang, J.: Application trends in virtual reality. In: 2017 Electronics and Telecommunications Trends (2017)
2. Chen, S.: Quicktime VR: an video-based approach to virtual environment navigation. In: Proceedings of the 22nd Annual Conference on Computer Graphics and Interactive Techniques, pp. 29–38 (1995)
3. Kim, J.: Design of 360 degree video and VR contents. In: Communication Books (2017)
4. Kijima, R., Yamaguchi, K.: VR device time Hi-precision time management by synchronizing times between devices and host PC through USB. IEEE Virtual Reality(VR). pp. 201–202 (2016)
5. Jung, H., Yoo, J.: Feature matching algorithm robust to viewpoint change. J. Korean Instit. Commun. Inf. Sci. **40**(12), 2363–2371 (2015). https://doi.org/10.7840/kics.2015.40.12.2363
6. Ha, W., Sohn, K.: Image classification approach for Improving CBIR system performance. In: 2016 KICS Conference Winter, pp. 308–309 (2016)
7. Korea Copyright Commission: feature point filtering tech. https://www.copyright.or.kr/business/tmis/performance/filtering/init.do
8. Ho, Y.: MPEG-I standard and 360 degree video content generation. J. Electr. Eng. (2017)
9. W16824.: Text of ISO/IEC DIS 23090–2 Omnidirectional MediA Format (OMAF)
10. Lowe, D.: Distinctive image features from scale-invariant keypoints. IJCV (2004)
11. Park, B., Kim, J., Won, Y., Kim, Y., Kim, S.: An efficient feature point extraction and comparison method through distorted region correction in 360-degree realistic contents. J. Korea Soc. Comput. Inf., 93–100 (2019)

Gaming and Gamification Experiences

Effects of Heart Rate Based Potential Color Environment Stimuli on Users in VR Games

Hirotoshi Asano[1]([⊠])[ID], Junko Ichino[2][ID], Takumi Miyazaki[1], Yuka Makihata[2], and Masahiro Ide[2,3][ID]

[1] Kogakuin University, 1-24-2 Nishi-shinjuku, Shinjuku-ku, Tokyo 163-8677, Japan
hirotoshi@cc.kogakuin.ac.jp
[2] Tokyo City University, 3-3-1 Ushikubo-Nishi, Tsuzuki-Ku, Yokohama, Kanagawa 224-8551, Japan
[3] TIS Inc., Sumitomo Fudosan Shinjuku Grand Tower, 17-1, Nishi-shinjuku 8-chome, Shinjuku-ku, Tokyo 160-0023, Japan

Abstract. Most of the previous studies utilizing physiological data have investigated the effects on users' behavior, psychology, and physiology when users are presented with overt (conscious or subjective) auditory or visual stimuli. On the other hand, recent studies have shown that users' behavior, psychology, and physiology can also be affected by the presentation of latent (unconscious, unaware) stimuli. In this study, we focused on visual information that can be easily manipulated in a VR environment, and investigated the effects of latent color stimuli based on the user's heart rate on the user's sense of immersion during a VR game from the physiological and psychological aspects. The results showed that latent color stimuli had an effect on physiological indices to increase the user's sense of immersion, but had no effect on psychological indices. Therefore, it was found that physiological and psychological indices did not necessarily coincide. As for the physiological indices, there were significant trends and differences in nasal skin temperature (an index of sympathetic nervous system) and heart rate potential (an index of stress state), indicating a certain degree of consistency.

Keywords: Virtual reality · Physio-psychological measurement · Potential environment stimuli

1 Introduction

Appropriate use of physiological data such as heart rate and electroencephalogram (EEG) has the potential to control users' emotions [1,2]. For example, Houzangbe et al. [3] showed that users voluntarily controlled their heart rate. They conducted an experiment in which users were allowed to achieve each level of an escape game, and they found that controlling heart rate increased immersion. Most of the previous studies utilizing physiological data have studied the effects on users' behavior, psychology, and physiology by presenting users with explicit (conscious and subjective) auditory and visual stimuli. In contrast, in recent years, findings have emerged that users' behavior, psychology, and physiology can also be affected by the presentation of latent (unconscious and unaware) stimuli [4]. Since VR environments are easier to manipulate than real environments, they are suitable for the study of such effects or such studies are limited. In this study, we focus on visual information, which is particularly easy to manipulate in a VR environment, and investigate the effects of latent color stimuli based on the user's heart rate on the user's sense of immersion during VR games from the physiological and psychological aspects. If latent stimuli can draw in the user's physiological and psychological states, they can be applied to a wide range of applications, including VR games, because of their advantage of being stimuli that do not cause discomfort for the user.

2 Related Work

There are several studies that utilize physiological data to improve user immersion and motivation during game experiences. Many of these previous studies have used heart rate [1,2,5,6]. For example, Houzangbe et al. [3] showed that the user's own control of heart rate and the completion of each stage of the escape game increased the immersion and motivation of the game experience. Nenonen et al. [5] proposed a method to control a physically interactive biathlon (skiing and shooting) computer game using real-time heart rate information. In this method, the player's heart rate determines the speed of the skis, and the player can try different tactics, such as slow runs and sharp shooting, or fast runs and random shooting. Sra et al. [6] proposed a method to control the movement of the ball by manipulating the player's own breathing. The player can perform four breathing actions. We conducted experiments under two conditions, with and without the breathing motion, and confirmed that the breathing motion was more effective in increasing game score, fun, and satisfaction. In most of these previous studies, users were made conscious and aware of physiological movements such as their own or false heartbeats and breathing (manifest), and auditory and visual stimuli were linked to them. However, making users aware of physiological motion is not always natural, and the range of application of the method is limited. If the physiological motion is false, the discomfort caused to the user is even greater. On the other hand, there is a growing body of evidence that physiological motion or stimuli that change in conjunction with physiological motion can have some positive effects on users without making them conscious or aware of them. For example, Kajiwara et al. [4] suppressed a decrease in arousal level without making the driver conscious or aware of it by applying a weak external stimulus to skin temperature, which reflects sympathetic nerve activity. However, such studies are limited and their effects have not been fully confirmed.

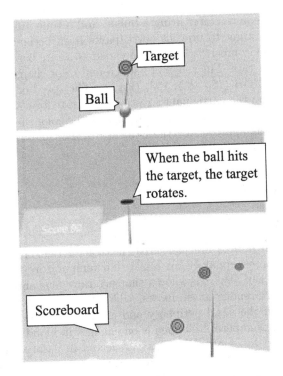

Fig. 1. Experimental task (Shooting game)

Fig. 2. In the condition using heart rate, the shading of the color of background changes with the heart rate

3   Procedure

3.1   Experiment Schedule

The experimental design was a one-factor design (within-participant factor) in which the presence or absence (two levels: change color, no change color) of a potential chromatic environmental stimulus was a factor using the color green. The total number of participants was 34 (22 males and 12 females, aged 20–23). The experimental system was implemented on Unity, and an Oculus Quest HMD was used. The participants played a shooting game for 6 min as the experimental task (Fig. 1). In this study, the difficulty level was adjusted so that the game would not be too easy and the participants would not become bored. Specifically, a 0.5-s pause was required after firing a bullet, and a time limit was set for the appearance of the target to prevent participants from becoming bored by the game. The color environment stimuli were varied at a rate based on the participant's resting heart rate. The range of background color change was from RGB (102, 255, 102) to RGB (153, 255, 153) (Fig. 2). The speed of the color change was determined from the participant's resting heart rate for a time equivalent to four beats, and the system was designed to change the color shade at that speed. This experiment was approved by the Ethical Review Committee of Kogakuin University in Japan.

4   Evaluation Method

4.1   Physiological Index

Three physiological indices are measured: nasal skin temperature, electrocardiogram, and electroencephalogram. Nasal skin temperature is an indicator of sympathetic nerve activity. It is known that arteriovenous and venous anastomoses, called arteriovenous anastomoses, which regulate capillary blood flow, are concentrated in the nasal periphery and are more numerous than in other areas. Because skin temperature depends on changes in blood flow, the psychological state caused by emotional stress is reflected in nasal skin temperature. For example, when a participant is concentrating, sympathetic nerve activity becomes active. This decreases blood flow, which in turn lowers nasal skin temperature. This study focuses on concentration and immersion. Therefore, nasal skin temperature is utilized as an evaluation index of sympathetic nerve activity. A high-function thermometer (Gram LT-200S) is used to measure skin temperature in the nasal region. The sampling frequency is set at 2 Hz. Electrocardiogram is an indicator regarding autonomic nervous system activity. The frequency analysis of the frequency of heart rate (hereinafter referred to as RRI) provides information on sympathetic and parasympathetic nervous system changes. In the frequency domain, there are characteristic frequency bands of LW (Low Frequency) and HF (High Frequency) in the 0.15–0.40 Hz frequency range. The LF reflects the activity of both the sympathetic and parasympathetic nervous systems, and the HF is used as an indicator of the parasympathetic nervous system function. In this study, the degree of immersion of the participant is evaluated from the change in HF content. A biometric sensor (Polymate Pocket MP208) is attached to the participant's left and right earlobes and to the ribs below the heart. The sampling frequency is set at 500 Hz. Electroencephalogram is related to arousal level, relaxation, and sleep, depending on the frequency. The stimuli given in this study are visual stimuli. The occipital area is known as the visual cortex, which receives information about the visual angle. It is known that the visual cortex is particularly responsive to visual stimuli. Therefore, in this experiment, we attached a sensor to the back of the head. Since this experiment focuses on immersion and concentration, the rate of beta wave content, which represents arousal level, is used as an evaluation index. A biometric sensor

(Polymate Pocket MP208) is attached to measure the back of the participant's head. The sampling frequency is set at 500 Hz.

4.2 Psychological Index

Some questionnaires are used to evaluate the effects on users from a psychological aspect. First, the Virtual Reality Sickness Questionnaire (VRSQ) [7] is used to check whether participants are experiencing discomfort such as sickness. In addition, we measure the subjective feelings of concentration and immersion using the Multidimensional Affective Scale [8] and Kim et al.'s questionnaire scale [9]. In addition, an original questionnaire is add to examine immersive feelings in more detail.

4.3 Hypothesis

Based on the findings of a previous study [1,2], our hypothesis for this study was set as "the immersive experience is enhanced by gradually increasing the pulsating tempo of the color environment stimuli with reference to the user's heart rate."

5 Result

The following sections show the results of each evaluation index. Figures 3, 4, and 5 show the results of the analysis of the physiological index, and Figs. 6, 7, 8, and 9 show the results of the four questions that showed significant trends in the psychological index. In each graph, the symbol† indicates a significant trend ($p<0.1$) and * a significance level ($p<0.05$). In addition, "change color" indicates using heart rate condition, "no change color" indicates the nothing their condition, and "N" indicates the number of participants.

5.1 Awareness of Potential Color Stimuli

We asked participants after the experiment whether they noticed the color-environment stimuli presented to them. The results showed that the majority (79.4%) of the participants did not notice any color change. From this, we concluded that the visual information was potentially presented to the users.

5.2 Physiological Index

Figure 3 shows the amount of change in nasal skin temperature. A one-way analysis of variance was conducted using the nasal skin temperature at rest as the reference, with the amount of change per 30 s interval after the start of the task as the dependent variable and the presence of color environmental stimuli as the independent variable. As a result, significant trends were observed at 90 s ($p = 0.0871$), 120 s ($p = 0.0569$), 150 s ($p = 0.0593$), 180 s ($p = 0.0523$), 210 s (p = 0.0637) and 240 s (p = 0.0741) after the start of the game, indicating that the temperature with color change was greater than that without color change. The temperature drop after the start of the experiment task was larger for those with color change than for those without color change.

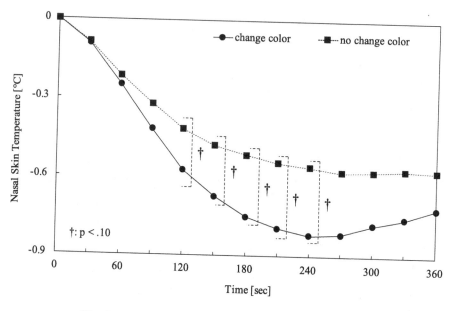

Fig. 3. Time-series variation of nasal skin temperature

Figure 4 shows the percent change in HF values when data from all participants were used. For the heart rate potentials, the RRI (heart rate interval) was calculated from the participants' heart rate potential data. The data were multiplied by spline interpolation to perform frequency analysis, and the HF value, which is a frequency-domain index, was further calculated. A one-way ANOVA was performed using the rate of change in HF values separated by 1 min after the start of the task as the dependent variable and the presence or absence of color environmental stimuli as the independent variable. As a result, when data from all participants were used, significant trends were observed at 180 (p = 0.0720), 210 (p = 0.0786), and 240 (p = 0.0633) s after the start of the game, and a significant difference at 270 s (p = 0.0177). When using data from only the participants who noticed the color change (Sect. 5.1), significant differences were found at 240 s (p = 0.0062) and 300 s (p = 0.0055).

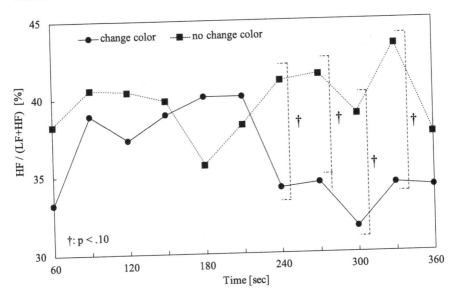

Fig. 4. Time-series variation of heart rate potential (HF content rate)

Figure 5 shows the time-series changes in the EEG. The EEG data was subjected to frequency analysis to obtain the percentage of beta waves. A one-way analysis of variance was conducted using the rate of change of the beta wave as the dependent variable and the presence or absence of color stimuli as the independent variable, separated by one-minute intervals after the start of the task. As a result, a significant trend was observed at 180 s (p = 0.0849) and 360 s (p = 0.0794) after the start of the game when data from all participants were used. When data from only the participants who noticed the color change were used, significant trends were observed at 240 s (p = 0.0809) and 300 s (p = 0.0991), and at 180 s (p = 0.0241) and 360 s (p = 0.0401).

5.3 Psychological Index

For the VRSQ, a one-way ANOVA was conducted with the difference between the post- and pre-test of each subscale as the dependent variable and the presence or absence of color environment stimuli as the independent variable. As a result, significant differences were found in the "feeling of staggering" subscale, and those with pulsation had lower VR sickness than those without pulsation (Fig. 6). For the Multidimensional Affective Scale, Kim et al. questionnaire, and original questionnaire, the Friedman test was conducted using the mean of the questionnaire items belonging to the subscales as the dependent variable (for the original questionnaire, the results of each questionnaire item) and the presence of color environment stimuli as the independent variable. The results showed that there were no significant differences in most of the subscales. On the other hand, a significant trend was found in the inactive pleasantness (p = 0.0588)

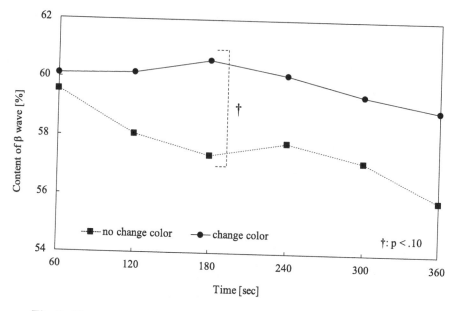

Fig. 5. Time-series variation of electroencephalogram (beta wave content)

subscale of the Multidimensional Affective Scale (Fig. 7). In the original questionnaire surveyed after each experiment, the main effect of the color change condition was significant (p = 0.0947) for the item "Did you forget about the things around you?" (Fig. 8). There was also a significant trend (p = 0.0606) for the item "Did you feel fed up with it?" (Fig. 9).

6 Consideration

6.1 Physiological Index

All physiological indices showed significant differences or significant trends, mainly around 180 s after the start of the game. Compared to the absence of color-environmental stimuli, there was a predominance of sympathetic nerves (nasal skin temperature), lower HF values (heart rate potential), and higher arousal (electroencephalogram). These results generally supported the hypothesis presented in Sect. 4.3 in terms of physiological indices. These results suggest that latent color environment stimuli can enhance the user's sense of immersion. Next, detailed analysis of the graphs shows that there is a difference in heart rate potential (HF content) and nasal skin temperature after 240 and 120 s, respectively, indicating that there is a slight temporal discrepancy between the two, even though they are both indicators of autonomic nervous activity. The possible reason for this is the presence or absence of parasympathetic antagonism. The heart rate is not only a function of the sympathetic nervous system, but also

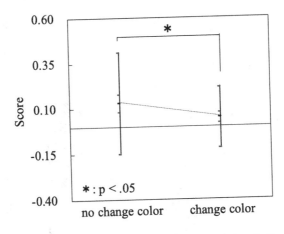

Fig. 6. VRSQ questionnaire (Feeling lightheaded)

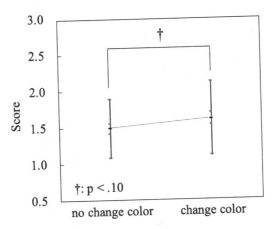

Fig. 7. Multidimensional affective scale questionnaire (Inactive pleasantness)

of the parasympathetic nervous system. The sympathetic and parasympathetic nerves work in such a way that they balance each other. On the other hand, nasal skin temperature change is an index influenced only by sympathetic nerve activity, so there is no antagonism by the parasympathetic nerves. Therefore, we were able to confirm a significant trend in nasal skin temperature from an earlier stage than in heart rate, whereas no significant trend was observed in heart rate until later in the study. Next, the skin temperature of the nasal area did not increase in the no change color condition, while it did increase in the change color condition in the latter half. One possible reason for this may be fatigue caused by the acceleration of sympathetic nerve activity. The temperature in the change color condition was about 0.3°C lower than that in the without change color condition. This difference in temperature is thought to be due to the fact that sympathetic nerve activity was stimulated more strongly in the change color

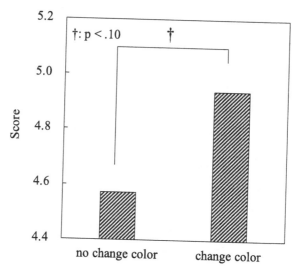

Fig. 8. Original Questionnaire (Have you forgotten about your surroundings?)

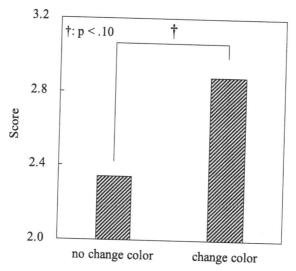

Fig. 9. Original Questionnaire (Have you felt fed up?)

condition than in the no change color condition. As a result, the sympathetic activity may have weakened as the body shifted to a resting state earlier than in the no change color condition.

6.2 Psychological Index

Unlike the physiological measures, many of the psychological measures did not show significant differences or trends, so the hypotheses were not supported by aspects of the psychological measures. However, some items showed some differences among conditions. A significant trend was found in the original questionnaire item "Did you forget about your surroundings?", suggesting that participants in the "with change color condition" may have been more immersed in the experience. In addition, the VRSQ questionnaire on "feeling lightheadedness" showed that participants in the "with change color" condition felt less lightheaded than those in the "without change color" condition. The two results, "I forgot about my surroundings" and "I felt lightheaded," suggest that the participants may have been able to concentrate on the game as a result of suppressing the feeling of lightheadedness by providing potential color environmental stimuli.

7   Summary

In this study, we investigated the effects of latent color stimuli on the user's immersion in a VR game based on the user's heart rate in a VR environment from the physiological and psychological aspects. The results of the experiment using 34 participants showed that, for the physiological index, potential color stimuli had an effect of increasing the user's sense of immersion around 180 s. On the other hand, the psychological index showed no effect of color stimuli on immersion. These results indicate that physiological and psychological factors do not necessarily coincide in terms of their effects on the user's immersive experience during VR games. On the other hand, it was suggested that there is an upper limit to the speed of change to provide a sense of immersion. The color environment stimuli used in this study differed from the stimuli given every beat used in previous studies, in that the stimuli were given based on a time period of four beats. Although the results of this study showed that the participants' sense of immersion was affected, this method of stimulus delivery was not always correct. In previous studies [3], participants' heart rates were obtained in real time, and false heartbeat sounds generated based on the heart beats were used to enhance the subjective experience. What happens when the above changes are made has not yet been verified, and will be a subject for future work. In addition, the results of this study suggest that it is possible that the color stimuli do not need to be changed every beat, since the stimuli were not given every beat as in the case of the false heartbeat sounds. However, the number of beats used as the criterion for change also needs to be considered, since the criterion of four beats used in this study is not necessarily correct.

References

1. Valins, S.: Cognitive effects of false heart-rate feedback. J. Pers. Soc. Psychol. 4(4), 400 (1966)
2. Nishimura, N., Ishi, A., Sato, M., Fukushima, S., Kajimoto, H.: Facilitation of affection by tactile feedback of false heratbeat. In: Extended Abstracts on Human Factors in Computing Systems (CHI 2012), pp. 2321–2326. ACM, New York (2012)

3. Samory, H., Olivier, C., Geoffrey, G., Simon, R.: Effects of voluntary heart rate control on user engagement and agency in a virtual reality game. Virtual Reality **24**, 665–681 (2020)
4. Yasutaka, K., et al.: Driver's drowsiness inhibition by subcutaneous stimulation based on SNS activity. Artif. Life Robot. **20**(4), 341–346 (2015)
5. Ville, N., Aleksi, L., Ville, H., Toni, L., Mikko, J., Perttu, H.: Using heart rate to control an interactive game. In: Proceedings of the SIGCHI Conference on Human Factors in Computing Systems, pp. 853–856. ACM, California (2007)
6. Misha, S., Xuhai, X., Pattie, M.: BreathVR: leveraging breathing as a directly controlled interface for virtual reality games. In: Proceedings of the SIGCHI Conference on Human Factors in Computing Systems, pp. 1–12. ACM, New York (2018)
7. Hyun, K.K., Jaehyun, P., Yeongcheol, C., Mungyeong, C.: Virtual reality sickness questionnaire (VRSQ): motion sickness measurement index in a virtual reality environment. Appl. Ergon. **69**, 66–73 (2018)
8. Masaharu, T., Yoichi, K., Aito, K.: Construction of a multiple mood scale. Jpn. J. Psychol. **62**(6), 350–356 (1992)
9. Taeyong, K., Frank, B.: Telepresence via television: two dimensions of telepresence may have different connections to memory and persuasion. J. Comput. Mediat. Commun. **3**(2), JCMC325 (1997)

Gamification Through the Lens of Safety Engineering

Bryce Bowles[✉] and Vincent G. Duffy

Purdue University, West Lafayette, IN 47907, USA
bdbowles@purdue.edu

Abstract. The purpose of this study was to examine the applications of gamification and game-based learning in the field of safety engineering. This systematic literature review used an extensive set of databases and data analysis tools to defend the rising importance of gamification in safety engineering. Databases such as Scopus, Web of Science, and Google Scholar using Harzing's Publish or Perish were used to analyze existing works, and their metadata was extracted and imported into data analysis tools such as VOSviwer, Citespace, BibExcel, and MAXQDA. Results show that gamification has been used in safety training for industrial jobs to promote learning in the workplace and reduce the risk of accidents. A variety of studies also focus on improving road safety when driving by keeping the driver engaged, reducing boredom, improving hazard recognition, and providing driving recommendations to discourage risky driving habits. Mendeley software was used to generate a bibliography out of all references. This paper utilizes several bibliometric analysis methods for a systematic literature review and explains the potential that gamification has for the future of safety engineering.

Keywords: Gamification · Safety Training · Serious Games · Road Safety

1 Introduction

Since the turn of the 21st century, there has been a rather significant increase in digital game content for entertainment and education. Although games have been a part of human culture and used as entertainment since the dawn of time, it hasn't been until relatively recently that digital games have been sought to improve educational practices. As a result, the term gamification, which refers to the selective incorporation of game elements into an interactive system without a fully-fledged game as the end product, was coined as a sort of game-based learning technique to better introduce subjects for learning and understanding [1]. Gamification today is important to focus on today because it helps motivate people and retain their attention to learn. For example, this is applicable to help educate k-12 students. In safety engineering, gamification can be used as an effective tool to train and encourage employees to uphold safety protocols to prevent accidents and even dissuade drivers from engaging in risky driving behavior.

Currently, employers are finding it hard to keep safety training engaging which raises the risk of injury on the job if workers are bored. With driving, transportation

© The Author(s), under exclusive license to Springer Nature Switzerland AG 2023
J. Y. C. Chen et al. (Eds.): HCII 2023, LNCS 14058, pp. 259–277, 2023.
https://doi.org/10.1007/978-3-031-48050-8_19

accidents claim more than a million lives a year and public awareness campaigns are not engaging enough to constitute a change in driving behaviors to reduce the number of accidents [2]. Autonomous vehicles are being researched and developed to completely remove the human element of driving, but the ability to completely phase out human-operated vehicles is still a distant aspiration. Recently, OSHA has published guidance on the hazards, risks, work to be done, and requirements for photovoltaic systems in industrial settings which has paved the way for gamification to be implemented [3]. Also, the European Commission, as part of Horizon 2020, has helped fund the design and innovation of projects including but not limited to critically reviewing monitoring technologies that provide post-trip interventions, such as retrospective visual feedback, gamification, rewards or penalties, to inform an appropriate driver mentoring strategy delivered after each trip for drivers [4]. Although much progress is being made by such safety organizations, society needs to include more funding for gamification research in driver and safety training applications because most of it now is being focused on fields such as computer science and education.

Figure 1 shows an analysis of the dominant interest in gamification and safety by country using Scopus's "analyze results" feature. Results illustrate that the top countries with the most publications on gamification related to safety are the United States, United Kingdom, Italy, Australia, and Germany. This may be due to their interest in improving their safety measures to improve productivity and quality of life in the workplace.

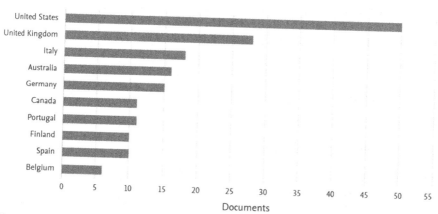

Fig. 1. Number of publications related to keywords "gamification" and "safety" based on country [5]

2 Purpose of Study

The purpose of this study is to conduct a systematic literature review of gamification applied to different facets of safety engineering and determine the feasibility of future developments in the field. Systematic reviews collect data from several different research studies to produce a new integrated result or conclusion, or they may bring together different types of evidence to explore or explain meaning [6]. This unique study will explore how ubiquitous computing technologies have the potential to improve road safety through gamification techniques rather than provide distractions to the driver [7]. This paper will also look at the impact of gamification in safety training situations since effective training requires the stimulation of multiple senses and keeps the employees both challenged and interested [8]. Tools such as VOSviewer, MAXQDA, BibExcel, and Citespace have all been used to evaluate and help compose a summary of the literature.

3 Research Methodology

3.1 Databases

The keywords "gamification" and "safety" were used as a basis for sifting through relevant publications and the metadata from various sources was extracted to be further analyzed. These keywords were chosen as they fit the topic of the paper best. Beginning a methodology with online database searches followed by conducting both trend and co-citation analysis has shown promise in safety engineering for discussing all sorts of topics in the field including injury prevention of electric transportation [9].

Table 1. Databases searched, keywords used for search, and results returned

Databases	Keywords	Number of Results
Scopus	"Safety" AND "Gamification"	261
Web of Science	"Safety" AND "Gamification"	186
Harzing's Publish or Perish (Google Scholar)	"Safety" AND "Gamification"	999

An organized description of each search in three different databases is elucidated in Table 1. As shown, each of the databases used the same keywords but returned a different number of results in which Harzing's Publish or Perish software yielded significantly more publications in Google Scholar. Harzing's software is a useful tool that allows the input of keywords to search databases such as Google Scholar for any articles that contain these words. Parameters can be set to filter results and all articles returned can be sorted by rank, number of citations, year, and more. Considering gamification is a relatively new topic, nearly all of the results were published after 2007. The information in each of these databases was then extracted to pull information such as title, authors, cited references, source, and abstract. Scopus data was extracted into a "CSV" file, Web of Science data was extracted into a ".txt" file, and Harzing's data was extracted into a "WoS" file.

3.2 Trend Analysis

Scopus Analysis. By using the metadata attributed to Scopus, a trend analysis was done to identify the scientific community's interest in gamification applications in safety engineering. Figure 2 reflects this interest as a trendline.

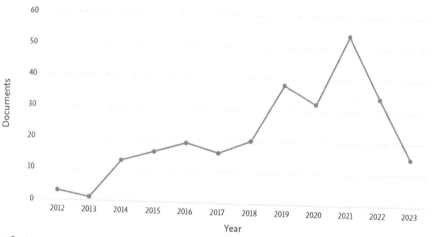

Fig. 2. Number of publications related to the keywords "gamification" and "safety" based on year [5]

Figure 2 depicts the number of papers that have been published globally each year on the topics of applying gamification techniques to safety engineering disciplines. It can be observed that there is a general increase in documents published each year which is indicative of interest in the subject. Although there has been a drop off in publications in 2022 compared to 2021, it should be noted that the number of publications in 2022 is still double the number of publications in 2017. It should also be understood that at the time of writing, the year 2023 is far from over, justifying the significantly fewer articles published.

To demonstrate the same information more succinctly in Fig. 2, Table 2 depicts the exact number of articles published each year since 2012. The number of articles returned each year in Scopus was recorded in an Excel spreadsheet to make the table.

Table 2. Number of documents published each year using Scopus.

Year	Scopus Documents on "gamification" and "safety"
2012	3
2013	1
2014	13

(continued)

Table 2. (*continued*)

Year	Scopus Documents on "gamification" and "safety"
2015	16
2016	19
2017	16
2018	20
2019	38
2020	32
2021	54
2022	34

Google Ngram Analysis. Google Ngram is also a very resourceful tool to graph the popularity of words and phrases throughout history. Figure 3 illustrates the trendline of the phrase "gamification" in comparison to "VR" and "serious game" where VR stands for "virtual reality" and serious games are by definition the kind of computer programs that apply gaming tools to safely simulate different real-life scenarios where the main purpose is not to entertain but to train its users on how to apply certain rules in these scenarios [10]. It is evident that although not as popular as VR, gamification and serious games continued to rise in popularity over the past 20 years.

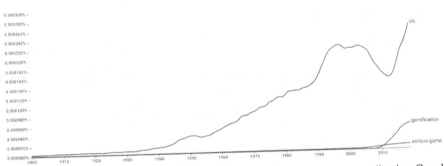

Fig. 3. The popularity of the terms "VR", "gamification", and "serious game" using Google Ngram [11]

Vicinitas Analysis. One last helpful tool in trend analysis is Vicinitas. Vicinitas is a digital tool that analyzes engagement in a topic based on Twitter activity. To better understand the engagement of gamification, a search was conducted based on hashtags and keywords consisting of "gamification" and "safety". Figure 4 displays the resulting word cloud and engagement of the search.

Word Cloud

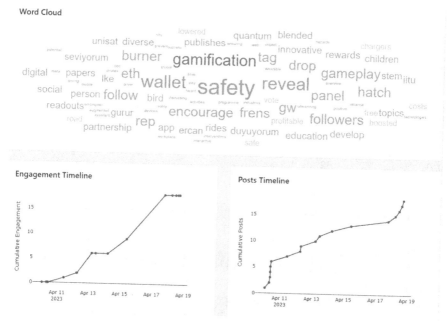

Fig. 4. Twitter activity including "gamification" and "safety" using Vicinitas [12]

4 Results

4.1 Co-citation Analysis

Co-citation analysis is a method of determining sources that have been cited together in other published papers to better understand which sources have made a significant impact in the field. It also is used to define the connectivity between such sources. The metadata was extracted as a "CSV" file from 2000 search results using Scopus based on the keyword "gamification". The file was then imported into VOSviewer and only the articles that were cited at least 22 times were included. This resulted in 9 different articles. Figure 5 shows the cluster produced from the co-citation analysis.

It should be noted that only 8 of the 9 articles that met the criteria were included in the cluster. The results emphasize the importance of these articles which are discussed further in the discussion section of this paper. Table 3 lists these articles of interest.

Each article from Table 2 has been cited with at least another article in the table 22 times. This is indicative of a very historically impactful article in the field of gamification. It is evident that authors such as Juho Hamari and Jonna Koivisto are leading authors in the study of gamification due to the recurrence in their names. Although all of these references are of importance, only a few will be further discussed due to the fact that all of these articles primarily discuss the history of gamification, rather than its impact on safety engineering.

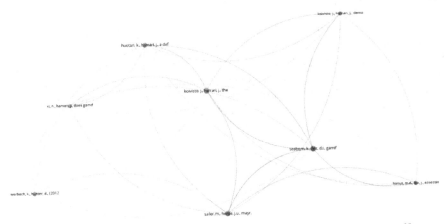

Fig. 5. Co-citation analysis derived from Scopus search using VOSviewer [13]

Table 3. Key articles from co-citation analysis using VOSviewer

Title	Year	Authors
For the Win: How Game Thinking can Revolutionize your Business.	2012	Kevin Werbach & Dan Hunter
Demographic differences in perceived benefits from gamification	2014	Jonna Koivisto & Juho Hamari
Gamification in theory and action: A survey	2015	Katie Seaborn & Deborah I. Fels
Assessing the effects of gamification in the classroom: A longitudinal study on intrinsic motivation, social comparison, satisfaction, effort, and academic performance	2015	Michael D. Hanus & Jesse Fox
How gamification motivates: An experimental study of the effects of specific game design elements on psychological need satisfaction	2017	Michael Sailer & Jan Ulrich Hense & Sarah Katharina Mayr & Heinz Mandl
A definition for gamification: anchoring gamification in the service marketing literature	2017	Kai Huotari & Juho Hamari
The rise of motivational information systems: A review of gamification research	2019	Jonna Koivisto & Juho Hamari
Does gamification satisfy needs? A study on the relationship between gamification features and intrinsic need satisfaction	2019	Nannan Xia & Juho Hamari

4.2 Content Analysis

VOSviewer Content Analysis. VOSviewer is also capable of performing a content analysis using metadata extracted from database searches. Metadata on 2000 articles about gamification were exported as a "CSV" file and used by VOSviewer to investigate common terms. The minimum number of occurrences of each term was 50 of which 270 met the threshold. 162 of the most relevant words (60%) were configured. A depiction of these words and their presence in the articles is shown in Fig. 6.

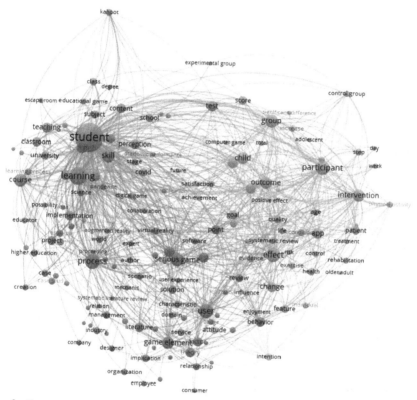

Fig. 6. Content analysis for common terms present in Scopus articles using VOSviewer [13]

Evidently, terms such as employee, company, course, control group, and more may be considered nodes within the clusters. Although there are 162 relevant terms in this content analysis cluster, most words and phrases are referenced about as much as other words, meaning no one term really sticks out. Figure 7 coincides with the analysis by listing the most relevant words in the cluster. These can be considered a reference point for future literature searches.

MAXQDA Content Analysis. MAXQDA is a very useful tool for content analysis after a set of references have been selected and are of interest. The 15 reference sources required in this paper were uploaded to MAXQDA to generate a word cloud, presenting

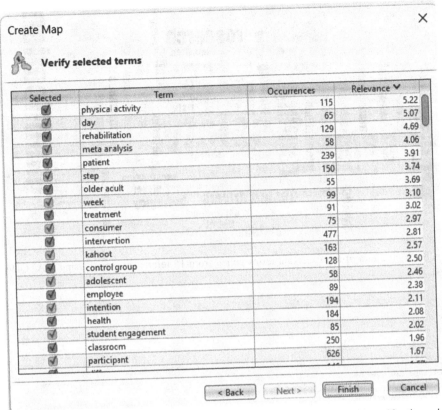

Selected	Term	Occurrences	Relevance ⌄
☑	physical activity	115	5.22
☑	day	65	5.07
☑	rehabilitation	129	4.69
☑	meta analysis	58	4.06
☑	patient	239	3.91
☑	step	150	3.74
☑	older adult	55	3.69
☑	week	99	3.10
☑	treatment	91	3.02
☑	consumer	75	2.97
☑	intervention	477	2.81
☑	kahoot	163	2.57
☑	control group	128	2.50
☑	adolescent	58	2.46
☑	employee	89	2.38
☑	intention	194	2.11
☑	health	184	2.08
☑	student engagement	85	2.02
☑	classroom	250	1.96
☑	participant	626	1.67

< Back   Next >   Finish   Cancel

Fig. 7. List of most relevant terms used throughout Scopus literature regarding gamification using VOSviewer [13]

the most common words in all the articles. Common irrelevant words such as "the", "and", and "an" were removed from the word cloud so that only the important words are included. This helped determine the keywords for the systematic literature review. Figure 8 depicts the resulting word cloud.

As illustrated by Fig. 8, the five most popular words in the literature were "driving", "game", "training", "safety", and "gamification". MAXQDA also has a feature that performed a lexical search such that all mentions of these keywords to find where exactly in each text the keywords are found. Figure 9 shows an example of a lexical search using the keyword "gamification" which returned 875 mentions across the 15 articles.

BibExcel Content Analysis. BibExcel is a program that accepts metadata and returns pivot tables of the most prominent leading authors and leading journals on a given subject. By extracting the metadata from Harzing's Publish or Perish and importing it into BibExcel, the authors that published the most documents on gamification related to safety engineering were found. This data was then copied into a Microsoft Excel sheet to produce a leading authors table. Results are shown in Table 4.

Fig. 8. Word cloud of most relevant terms pulled from 15 reference sources using MAXQDA [14]

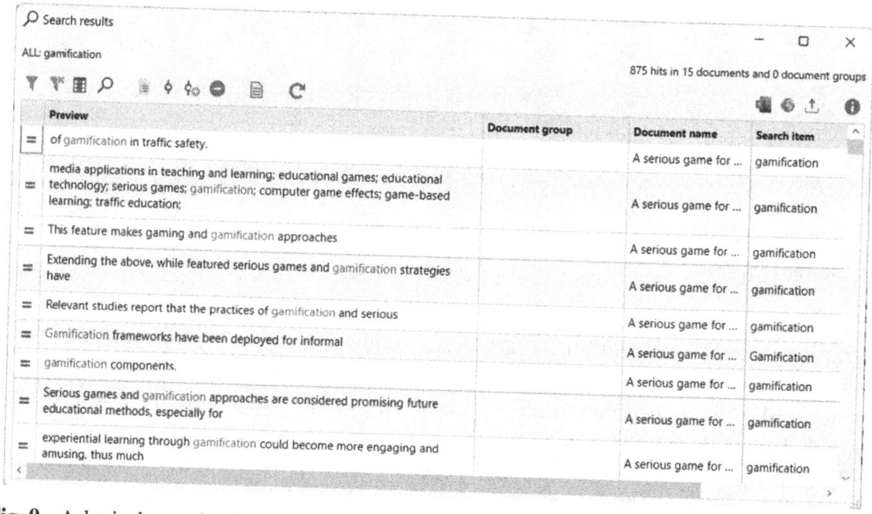

Fig. 9. A lexical search of the phrase "gamification" mentioned in 15 reference sources using MAXQDA [14]

This table demonstrates that 66 of the 999 articles produced by Harzing's software were produced by the 13 leading authors each producing anywhere between 4 and 9 articles. Better visualization for this data is illustrated in Fig. 10 which was formed by graphing the table of leading authors.

A similar method was used to produce a leading table for the top journals that possess an interest in gamification applications for safety engineering. Table 5 depicts this.

Table 4. Leading Authors with most published works in Google Scholar using BibExcel [15].

Author	Article Count
Kim S	9
Hamari J	7
Steinberger F	7
Small DS	5
Rakotonirainy A	5
Yannis G	5
Warmelink H	4
Amaxilatis D	4
Vlahogianni El	4
Katrakazas C	4
Kapp KM	4
Kim TW	4
Patel MS	4
Grand Total	**66**

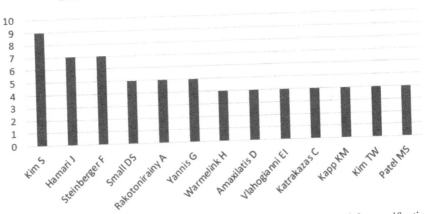

Fig. 10. Graph of leading authors based on BibExcel content analysis tool for gamification in safety engineering.

Table 5. Leading journals with most published works in Google Scholar using BibExcel [15].

Journal Title	Article Count
Safety Science	9
Sensors	7
Cureus	6
Safety	4
Applied Sciences	4
Education Sciences	4
Food Control	4
Grand Total	**38**

Similarly, the top 7 journals interested specifically in applying gamification towards safety engineering have anywhere between 4 and 9 articles published. A better visualization for this data is illustrated in Fig. 11 which was formed by graphing the table of leading journals.

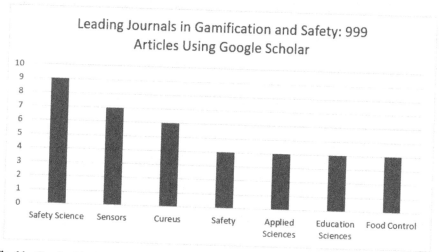

Fig. 11. Graph of leading journals based on BibExcel content analysis tool for gamification in safety engineering.

4.3 Cluster Analysis

Citespace is a software tool that is excellent at producing visual clusters as part of a co-citation analysis and has one distinct advantage over using VOSviewer. Citespace is capable of providing labels for each cluster. To analyze in Citespace, a search for "gamification" and "safety" was performed in Web of Science, yielding 186 results. The data on these articles was extracted into a "txt" file and imported into Citespace. The results of the co-citation analysis were then used to produce a cluster diagram with labels for each cluster. These labels helped produce subheadings to better organize this paper. Figure 12 exemplifies the cluster diagram produced by Citespace. It should be noted that some articles are scattered far from the illustrated clusters. They may be ignored since they are unrelated to the subjects of interest. The cluster diagram broke up all articles in Web of Science into 7 main categories. However, several categories may be intertwined and combined such as "education" and "face-to-face learning". For the purposes of this systematic review, driving recommendations and hazard recognition are combined with some reference to boredom while anything education and learning related is applied to safety training regarding boredom.

Fig. 12. Citespace cluster analysis with labels based on a keyword search using Web of Science [16]

Citespace is also capable of performing a burst analysis. This analysis technique produces a burst diagram that highlights the period of time that an article is the most popular and cited the most. Figure 13 depicts the results of the Citespace burst analysis. Because only two references are articulated in the burst analysis, it can be implied that applying gamification to safety engineering is a fairly new topic.

After all of this analysis, sources of each reference were pulled primarily from Harzing's Publish or Perish (Google Scholar) software. A mix of references were selected

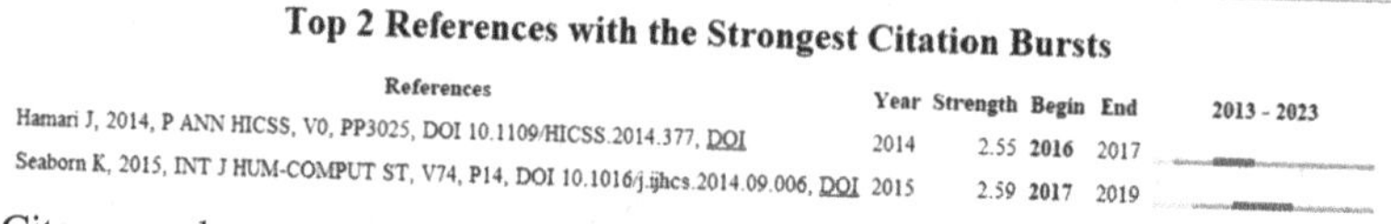

Top 2 References with the Strongest Citation Bursts

References	Year	Strength	Begin	End	2013 - 2023
Hamari J, 2014, P ANN HICSS, V0, PP3025, DOI 10.1109/HICSS.2014.377, DOI	2014	2.55	2016	2017	
Seaborn K, 2015, INT J HUM-COMPUT ST, V74, P14, DOI 10.1016/j.ijhcs.2014.09.006, DOI	2015	2.59	2017	2019	

Fig. 13. Citespace cluster analysis with labels based on keyword search using Web of Science [16]

based on rank and number of citations. Some of these articles were cross-referenced with popular articles that have been cited several times in Scopus and Web of Science as evidenced by the burst analysis and VOSviewer analysis to make sure that they carried pertinent information to gamification applications in safety engineering. It should be understood that papers including the two burst analysis citations stuck out in each of the other types of analysis and were discussed for the systematic review.

5   Discussion

5.1   Gamification in Driving

One effective application for gamification in safety engineering is by complementing road safety with game-based learning techniques. Currently, driving behavior is a leading contributing factor to road safety. One common attribute to driving behavior is the speed at which someone is driving which not only increases the severity of a crash but increases the risk of being in one [4]. Another factor includes the driver's familiarity with the area they are driving in. For example, international drivers have been in a considerably high number of serious vehicle accidents on the road. This has led to road safety training programs using simulations that provide feedback as a gamification element. Results showed that using gamification reduced the likelihood of both driving opposite traffic flow and failing to use proper signaling when driving [10]. Serious games, which are a sub-category of digital games with the purpose to educate rather than entertain, have also been used for traffic education purposes and are proven to benefit the user's behavior after engaging in the game. Current game-based simulations have resulted in not only improving their traffic behavior but their alertness for driving as well. Although these games have demonstrated their efficacy in the driving role, it is also important to consider teaching traffic safety from the perspective of a pedestrian as well to young kids to further promote road safety [17].

Another reason that crashes may be so common is due to boredom. In other words, drivers are not highly engaged in driving which may be due to long-distance drives, low-traffic areas, or familiar routes. This increase in boredom may raise the individual desire to perform risky driving behavior such as speeding and car features that take away driver responsibilities, such as cruise control, do not help keep the driver engaged. Using in-car displays that provide immediate feedback with simple games on them such as being tasked with avoiding speeding while touching the pedal as little as possible, has proven to leave the drivers more stimulated, reduce overall speeds, and increase anticipatory driving behaviors [18]. These in-car ambient displays have shown a rise in popularity to promote safety too while driving. For example, many cars today have a fuel consumption display to engage the driver, reducing the risk of an accident as it encourages them to lower their fuel consumption. Another example comes from a smartphone app called "Driving Miss Daisy" which provides feedback on driving behavior for a smoother and safer driving experience [19]. These gamification techniques over the years have continued to show promise in promoting road safety but still must be cautious to not take too much attention from the driver that they are distracted.

5.2 Gamification in Safety Training and the Workplace

Not only are gamification practices able to be used in promoting road safety they can also be used to encourage safety in the workplace and improve safety training. According to Chapter 12 of Goetsch's book, "Occupational Safety and Health", two common methods of good safety training involve simulation of activity to keep workers engaged and programmed instruction to challenge the participant while providing immediate feedback [20]. This opens the door for innovative gamification techniques.

From a psychological perspective, the self-determination theory presents the argument that humans have psychological and intrinsic needs. Among these are the need for competence, the need for autonomy, and the need for social relatedness. Gamification can help humans meet these needs in unique ways. The need for competence, meaning the need for success and efficiency, can be achieved by delegating points, badges, and providing feedback. The need for autonomy, meaning the need for freedom of choice and making meaningful decisions, can be achieved through the implementation of stories and avatars. The need for social relatedness, meaning the need to feel belonging in a group, can be achieved also through stories and cooperative elements as a group [21]. Using these elements in safety around the workplace and during training has shown exciting results.

Job demands often have a negative effect on the psychological health and safety of an individual. However, as previously noted, gamification takes a psychological approach to meet the needs of the individual. Introducing gamification techniques into the psychosocial safety climate can be a policy formed by an organization through practices and procedures to improve the health and safety of workers which in turn motivates them. This can result in more work engagement among employees since they feel more comfortable with a sense of belonging [22]. An added benefit to this may even be enhanced company performance. In ammonia production sectors where safety is paramount, serious games with elements of gamification have been used to engage workers in safety and promote resilience towards potential accidents [23]. Patriarca et al. also observed that important safety protocols that involve participation in surveys or polls which tend to be low have experienced much more engagement when doing away with traditional check marks in boxes for forms.

In safety training, numerous studies have shown a positive impact on the adoption of gamification principles as well. In the construction industry, more than 20% of work-related fatal incidents occur in the United States. However, introducing safety interventions do not always prove to be useful, requiring organizations to know what characteristics of safety training work well. Using gamification and serious games to train employees in safety may involve using virtual training environments to put on personal protective equipment and other equipment to improve training outcomes [24]. Unintentional injuries in industrial and productive working settings continue to occur today as well, representing an issue of safety culture in the workplace. In response, organizations have focused on safety training to promote workers' perception of work stress, raise their safety commitment, and prevent injury. Although dozens of organizations have used serious games and gamification techniques to effectively engage their employees during safety training, it should be communicated that different levels of immersion come with different levels of cost, and not all organizations are able to support expensive simulations. Still, providing safety training through a game setting has been seen as more enjoyable as it keeps users' attention, and adding player options with realistic outcomes has been appreciated as well. [25]. Since agriculture has similar risks of injury, adopting strategies to train workers using serious games and gamification techniques may be an effective way to promote safety in that sector too.

5.3 Concerns with Gamification

Despite effective elements to improve road safety and safety culture in the workplace, gamification has been extensively studied to gauge the effects of gamification and determine if all people experience the same benefits from it. In one of Juho Hamari and Jonna Koivisto's papers, the educational and psychological aspects of gamification were studied. Results showed that all learning outcomes as a result of gamification were mostly positive. However, some behaviors such as increased competition and task evaluation difficulties surfaced [26]. As evidenced by this paper, not all products of gamification are desirable in a workplace setting and competitive behavior on the road may lead to even less safety. The issue with studying these behaviors out on the road becomes more difficult as experiments are not safe to conduct out in a real environment that may put other drivers on the road in danger.

Demographically, females make up 40% of those playing digital games worldwide which is much higher than ever before. Although this number has continued to increase, males and females tend to be drawn to different types of digital games. When being asked about implementing gamification methods to safety training, male participants preferred more 3D visuals and females preferred simplified 2D visuals with more game variety and levels [26]. Despite these different preferences though, there is no discernable difference in their interest in playing a game related to safety and health. When it comes to reaping the benefits of gamification, females tend to gain more social benefits and the ease of use of gamification tends to decline with age [27]. The reason behind this imbalance of benefits is due to the greater exposure of games in males which reduces the novelty of participating in a gamifying exercise. This novelty in playing a game is linked to learning more from it.

6 Conclusion

This review demonstrates various ways in which gamification elements and techniques can be applied to numerous safety engineering disciplines. Gamification in education and training exercises promotes engagement, learning, and knowledge retention. This can be applied to safety training and interventions at work but also may be applied to help new drivers learn about traffic safety to reduce the likelihood of an accident. Using elements such as points, and badges, leaderboards, avatars, and stories allows organizations to further improve their safety culture and instill a sense of care and belonging in their employees. In regards to road safety, gamification can be used to limit boredom that drivers have, further reducing risky behavior including speeding which may lead to crashes. However, gamification does not come in one form that works for every organization. Depending on the work done, the funding the organization has, and the demographics of the employees, different games and simulations may be needed to optimize the full benefits of safety training and education.

7 Future Work

Gamification is currently being studied for implementation in all sorts of STEM-related fields, but primarily in learning situations. State-of-the-art progress is being made to better understand if k-12 students can learn better through gamification and what elements of game-based learning promote that best. This could even be used to help them pick a career faster with less uncertainty. From a safety engineering perspective, one award focusing on gamification to promote optimal behavior is being funded to study the behavioral effects of gamification which can further prevent people from making poor decisions on the job [28]. Figure 14 displays the currently active award discovered on the National Science Foundation's website. Rather than solely employing these resources to better understand education for students, it is still important to disperse these resources to funding that will improve safety in the workplace and reduce driving accidents that claim so many lives each year.

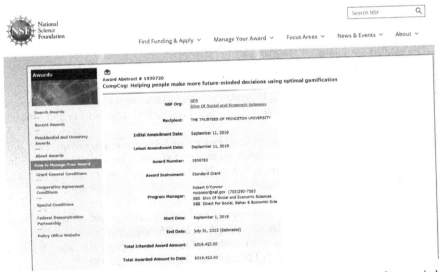

Fig. 14. NSF active award studying gamification's influence to make more future-minded decisions

References

1. Seaborn, K., Fels, D.I.: Gamification in theory and action: a survey. Int. J. Hum. Comput. Stud. **74**, 14–31 (2015). https://doi.org/10.1016/j.ijhcs.2014.09.006
2. Wallius, E., Klock, A.C.T., Hamari, J.: Playing it safe: a literature review and research agenda on motivational technologies in transportation safety. Reliabil. Eng. Syst. Safety **223** (2022).https://doi.org/10.1016/j.ress.2022.108514
3. Erten, B., Oral, B., Yakut, M.Z.: The role of virtual and augmented reality in occupational health and safety training of employees in PV power systems and evaluation with a sustainability perspective. J. Cleaner Prod. **379** (2022).https://doi.org/10.1016/j.jclepro.2022. 134499
4. Michelaraki, E., et al.: Post-trip safety interventions: state-of-the-art, challenges, and practical implications. J. Safety Res. **77**, 67–85 (2021). https://doi.org/10.1016/j.jsr.2021.02.005
5. "Scopus". n.d. https://www.scopus.com/search/form.uri?display=basic&zone=header&ori gin=#basic
6. Pollock, A., Berge, E.: How to do a systematic review. Int. J. Stroke (Vol. 13, Issue 2, pp. 138–156) (2018). SAGE Publications Inc. https://doi.org/10.1177/1747493017743796
7. Schroeter, R., Oxtoby, J., & Johnson, D. (2014, September 17). AR and gamification concepts to reduce driver boredom and risk taking behaviours. In: AutomotiveUI 2014 - 6th International Conference on Automotive User Interfaces and Interactive Vehicular Applications, in Cooperation with ACM SIGCHI - Proceedings. https://doi.org/10.1145/2667317.2667415
8. Brauer, R.: Safety and Health for Engineers, 3rd edn. Wiley & Sons. Chapter 32: Procedures, Rules, and Training (2016)
9. Jung, W.: Promoting safety and injury prevention of electric transportation. Human-Automation Interaction (2023). https://doi.org/10.1007/978-3-031-10784-9_24
10. Alyamani, H., Alharbi, N., Roboey, A., Kavakli, M.: The impact of gamifications and serious games on driving under unfamiliar traffic regulations. Appl. Sci. (Switzerland) **13**(5) (2023). https://doi.org/10.3390/app13053262
11. "Google Ngram," n.d. https://books.google.com/ngrams/
12. "Vicinitas," n.d. https://vicinitas.io/
13. "VOSviewer." n.d. https://www.vosviewer.com/
14. "MAXQDA." n.d. https://www.maxqda.com/
15. "BibExcel." n.d. https://homepage.univie.ac.at/juan.gorraiz/bibexcel/
16. "CiteSpace." n.d. http://cluster.cis.drexel.edu/~cchen/citespace/
17. Gounaridou, A., Siamtanidou, E., Dimoulas, C.: A serious game for mediated education on traffic behavior and safety awareness. Educ. Sci. **11**(3) (2021). https://doi.org/10.3390/edu csci11030127
18. Steinberger, F., Schroeter, R., Watling, C.N.: From road distraction to safe driving: evaluating the effects of boredom and gamification on driving behaviour, physiological arousal, and subjective experience. Comput. Hum. Behav. **75**, 714–726 (2017). https://doi.org/10.1016/j. chb.2017.06.019
19. Rodríguez, M.D., Roa, R.R., Ibarra, J.E., Curlango, C.M.: In-car ambient displays for safety driving gamification. In: ACM International Conference Proceeding Series, 03–05-November-2014, 26–29 (2014). https://doi.org/10.1145/2676690.2676701
20. Goetsch, D.: Occupational Safety and Health for Technologists, Engineers, and Managers, 9th edn. Pearson Education. Chapter 12: Safety & Health Training (2018)
21. Sailer, M., Hense, J.U., Mayr, S.K., Mandl, H.: How gamification motivates: an experimental study of the effects of specific game design elements on psychological need satisfaction. Comput. Hum. Behav. **69**, 371–380 (2017). https://doi.org/10.1016/j.chb.2016.12.033

22. Nurkhori, A., Rahmatia, A., Handari Wahyuningsih, S., Surwanti, A.: Strengthening work engagement through digital engagement, gamification and psychosocial safety climate in digital transformation. J. Innov. Bus. Econ. **5**(01), 35–48 (2021). https://doi.org/10.22219/jibe.v5i01.17477
23. Patriarca, R., Falegnami, A., De Nicola, A., Villani, M.L., Paltrinieri, N.: Serious games for industrial safety: an approach for developing resilience early warning indicators. Saf. Sci. **118**, 316–331 (2019). https://doi.org/10.1016/j.ssci.2019.05.031
24. Albert, L., Routh, C.: Designing impactful construction safety training interventions. Safety **7**(2) (2021). MDPI AG. https://doi.org/10.3390/safety7020042
25. Vigoroso, L., Caffaro, F., Cremasco, M. M., Cavallo, E.: Innovating occupational safety training: a scoping review on digital games and possible applications in agriculture. Int. J. Environ. Res. Public Health **18**(4), 1–23 (2021). MDPI AG. https://doi.org/10.3390/ijerph18041868
26. Hamari, J., Koivisto, J., Sarsa, H.: Does gamification work? - A literature review of empirical studies on gamification. In: Proceedings of the Annual Hawaii International Conference on System Sciences, pp. 3025–3034 (2014). https://doi.org/10.1109/HICSS.2014.377
27. Vigoroso, L., Caffaro, F., Micheletti Cremasco, M., Cavallo, E.: Developing a more engaging safety training in agriculture: Gender differences in digital game preferences. Safety Sci. **158** (2023). https://doi.org/10.1016/j.ssci.2022.105974
28. Koivisto, J., Hamari, J.: Demographic differences in perceived benefits from gamification. Comput. Hum. Behav. **35**, 179–188 (2014). https://doi.org/10.1016/j.chb.2014.03.007
29. Lieder, F., Griffiths, T.L.: Helping people make better decisions using optimal gamification. In: Expected Value of Cognitive Control View project Developing Tools and Theories for Helping People Make Better Decisions View project (2016). https://doi.org/10.13140/RG.2.2.18694.09289

Fitness Bow: An Intelligent Supervised Motion System

Lirong Che[1] , Suzhen Zhang[2] , Yanran Chen[2] , Yan Dong[2] ,
and Qiong Wu[2(✉)]

[1] Beijing University of Posts and Telecommunications, Beijing, China
[2] Tsinghua University, Beijing, China
qiong-wu@tsinghua.edu.cn

Abstract. The development of digital technology and the proliferation of electronic devices have greatly increased people's interaction with the digital world. Work and study increasingly rely on electronic devices, and the popularity of social media and online games reduces our motivation to go out and move, leading to increased sedentary behaviors, which have a negative impact on personal health. The prevalence of COVID-19 has led people to pay more attention to physical health, and the advancement of smart technology has brought new opportunities to fitness. However, traditional fitness methods are monotonous and relatively boring, making it difficult for young people to stick with them. And popular sports like skiing, archery, and rowing have high requirements for venues and professionalism. We have proposed an intelligent supervised sports system that integrates existing software and hardware technologies, aiming to reduce the venue restrictions of popular sports and help individuals use fragmented time for proactive health and fitness improvement.

Keywords: Artificial Intelligence and IoT · Game Design and Game Mapping · Gamification · Proactive Health and Active Design

1 Introduction

The advancement of digitalization and automation has increased screen-based work time, and the lack of physical activity combined with long-term sedentary habits greatly lead to various health risks [1]. Especially with the outbreak of diseases like COVID-19, people are increasingly focusing on physical health [2]. The lack of time for exercise, short-lived enthusiasm, and space restrictions remain significant barriers to people's fitness activities. Traditional fitness methods are monotonous and uninteresting, making it hard for young people to persist. According to a survey by iResearch, an increasing number of young Chinese people are engaging in more niche sports. Among them, skiing, rowing, camping, boxing and golf have attracted more young people's attention [3]. These popular sports are mainly outdoors, requiring specific spaces and equipment, which limits people's ability to exercise anywhere, anytime. To improve the accessibility of popular sports, the restrictions on space and equipment must be reduced.

J. Y. C. Chen et al. (Eds.): HCII 2023, LNCS 14058, pp. 278–297, 2023.
https://doi.org/10.1007/978-3-031-48050-8_20

Advancements in intelligent technology have brought new possibilities for fitness. There are mainly two solutions currently: the first is to recreate outdoor environments indoors, such as building indoor skiing and climbing venues, and introducing virtual reality, mixed reality, and wearable technology to enhance the experience of popular sports indoors. This approach, due to its reproduction of physical scenarios, maintains the user's actual athletic performance but lacks monitoring measures, making it hard to ensure the correctness of exercise movements. Moreover, the issue of space limitation is merely transferred from outdoors to indoors, and it cannot be transformed into an exercise mode that can be carried out anywhere, anytime. The second solution is to create a completely virtual environment, further breaking space constraints, and allowing outdoor sports to be carried out at home anytime. However, this type of research focuses on simulating and reproducing sensory experiences and, because the technology is still in the development stage, it involves cumbersome and expensive equipment to wear. The focus on real sports performance is less, and there's minimal supervision of the correctness of exercise postures.

We propose an intelligent sports supervision system aimed at alleviating the space limitations of popular outdoor sports and providing a more intelligent and accessible way for individuals to proactively improve their health and enhance exercise effects. Through questionnaires, user research, and other methods, we chose archery, a sport loved by young people, as the prototype for initial exercise. Many sports have physical fitness requirements, such as rugby, which is suitable for people with large muscle mass, whereas archery is suitable for people of all body types [4]. It has comprehensive physical and mental benefits, including improving balance, overall body coordination, and alleviating stress and anxiety (World Archery, 2017). Through repeated archery movements, the main upper body muscle groups, such as hands, arms, shoulders, and back, can be exercised [5].

2   Related Works

2.1   HCI and Sedentary Behavior

The advancement of digital technology has transformed people's work and lifestyle, leading to an increase in screen-based time and more time spent on sedentary behavior. Sedentary behavior is any waking behavior characterized by an energy expenditure of less than or equal 1.5 METs while in a sitting, reclining, or lying posture [6]. Prolonged sedentary behavior may have a negative impact on health.

Physical Activity is defined as any bodily movement produced by skeletal muscle contractions that result in energy expenditure above the resting metabolic rate, characterized by its form, frequency, intensity, duration, and exercise context [7]. Incorporating physical activity into daily life is important to mitigate the negative health impacts of sedentary behavior.

Researchers in the field of Human-Computer Interaction have proposed various interventions and corresponding studies for sedentary behavior. This includes adopting active lifestyles to change sedentary behaviors, encouraging them to stay physically active and maintain a healthy lifestyle by tracking personal physical conditions and understanding their health goals [8]. For example, Lithoxoidou et al. [9] developed a health monitoring framework, collecting multimodal data related to activity, location classification, keystroke typing, general phone usage statistics, self-reported questionnaires, and data from wearable devices and popular third-party applications (such as Google Fit and Samsung Health), to infer user daily behaviors and provide persuasive health advice through the persuasive avatar of a virtual coach.

Mobile phones easily integrate into users' daily lives, can be used at any time and place, and inherently possess Bluetooth, Wi-Fi, sensors, GPS, camera, accelerometer, and gyroscope, and can also integrate with games, computers, social networks, etc. This portability and integration make mobile phones an important tool to promote user physical activity [8]. Consolvo et al. [10] proposed Houston, a mobile phone-based fitness APP, which encourages sports by providing personal awareness of activity levels and moderating social interactions related to sports activities among friends. Baretta et al. [11] proposed a smartphone application and wearable device system named Muoviti to promote physical activity in adults. Using gamification to stimulate specific behaviors is also a common approach in such applications. The central idea of gamification is to use the "building block" of games and implement these blocks in the real world. Alizadeh Elizei [12] designed a health and running application that offers a series of diverse exercises of different levels for users, equipped with game components such as scoreboards, competitions among friends, rewards, and achievements to motivate users to achieve personal goals.

Another major research direction is interactive digital games Exergames, which require users to interact through physical exertion, where energy expenditure is a key factor in achieving game objectives [13]. The development of technology has brought many new possibilities for Exergames, from early simple interactions with game hardware devices, like Namco's ski simulation game Alpine Racer, where users can stand on a balance platform and move as if on a ski slope, using vertical rods to support body balance, to the wide application of six-axis gyroscopes and accelerometers, the development of depth-sensing cameras, and series of sports games towards the public, such as Just Dance and Ring Fit Adventure. Now you can use mobile devices such as smartphones to exercise anytime, anywhere, and the development of virtual reality technology further enriches this experience. For example, Pokémon GO uses game mechanics to encourage players to exercise - players need to walk a certain distance to achieve the game goal of hatching pet eggs [14,15].

Many current studies focus on encouraging users to engage in as much physical activity as possible, while we note that for people who sit for long periods, there are issues with musculoskeletal, back diseases, so some specific solutions are needed. A small amount of research focuses on specific body parts like us, such as Ren et al. [16] who proposed an interactive fitness system specifically supporting lower back stretching exercises during work breaks.

2.2 Archery

The mechanics of archery can be divided into four distinct phases: raising, drawing, stabilizing, and releae. Each of these phases engages different muscle groups and contributes to an overall body workout.

The phase of raising the bow engages the deltoid muscles along with static contraction of the muscles in the trunk and legs. Drawing the bow, on the other hand, involves the static contraction of muscles in the legs, buttocks, and trunk, in conjunction with the dynamic contraction of the posterior deltoid, latissimus dorsi, and trapezius muscles. During the stabilizing phase, all muscles previously engaged in the drawing process transition from dynamic to static contraction to achieve the necessary stability for accurate targeting. The final phase, the release of the arrow, primarily involves the coordination of the flexor digitorum superficialis and extensor digitorum muscles [5]. Repeated execution of these archery actions effectively exercises the upper body's main muscle groups, including those in the hands, arms, shoulders, and back. This provides a comprehensive workout for strengthening these muscles (see Fig. 1).

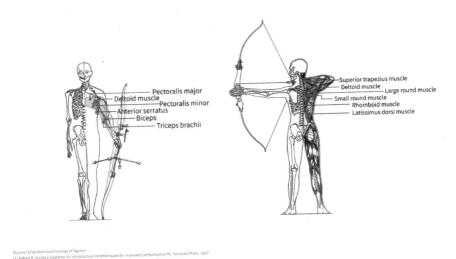

Sources of anatomical drawings of figures.
[1] Axford R. Archery Anatomy: An introduction to techniques for improved performance[M]. Souvenir Press, 2017.

Fig. 1. The effect of archery

The study of interaction design based on the sport of archery focuses on the simulation and reproduction of the archery experience. Commercial solutions like Wii and PlayStation have made attempts in this area. Instead of employing controllers shaped like bows, these platforms use simple interaction metaphors and user gesture mapping to simulate the archery experience, working by tracking user movements [17]. Purnomo et al. [18], on the other hand, designed a virtual reality simulator of traditional archery based on the Oculus Rift S, allowing users to learn and practice traditional archery action sequences in a virtual environment, but still using a joystick as the controller.

The mismatch in the form factor of these controllers to real bows and the lack of tactile feedback limit the fidelity of these simulations. As a result, numerous studies have focused on creating archery simulations based on the original design of the bow. Techno Hunt, for instance, developed an archery simulator maintaining the use of a physical bow and real arrow shooting actions, thereby creating a flat video game experience. This approach provides a high degree of interaction fidelity but necessitates a large physical space to ensure safety due to the use of rubber blunt arrows [19–21].

Incorporating digital technology and remodeling real bows can surmount physical space limitations while retaining the original archery experience. For example, Yasumoto et al. [22] developed "The Electric Bow Interface," a controller designed based on Japanese bow structures and materials, delivering tactile feedback, sensations, and impact almost identical to an original Japanese bow. Thiele et al. [23] proposed a VR archery simulator using a 62-inch bow and a large screen, hoping to provide users with a credible archery experience. The simulator was equipped with a dedicated damping system, negating the need to physically release the arrows and thus reducing spatial requirements. [24] studied the possibilities of creating different archery experiences. The proposed an immersive VR simulator based on a custom haptic interface that could replicate the force characteristics of any type of bow.

In this study, we also use archery as a prototype to recreate the archery experience and ensure physical efficacy. However, unlike the aforementioned studies, we propose the use of mechanical structures and the elimination of actual arrows, further reducing spatial limitations.

3   Design

3.1   System Configuration

FitnessBow integrates intelligent hardware and supervision software into an innovative smart supervision exercise system. Drawing from the action of archery as its physical prototype, FitnessBow retains the exercise efficacy and experience of archery, providing users with targeted muscle training guidance while engaging in entertaining activity. Based on the specifications of compound bows, the axle-to-axle and static draw lengths are set. Combined with arm span and conversion formulas, the draw length range is determined, and through intelligent poundage adjustment, it accommodates users of various physical abilities and exercise habits. This product is highly accessible and has low hardware requirements. It can be used in conjunction with various display devices like mobile phones, computers, and large screens. Using only a mobile phone and an external camera, users can capture motion and scenery (see Fig. 2).

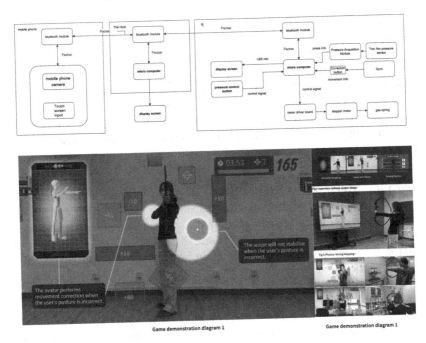

Fig. 2. game demonstration

The primary strategy of FitnessBow is to integrate principles and knowledge of archery, such as the duration of the sport and the rhythm of exertion, into the mechanics of the game. This serves to alleviate the monotony of regular fitness routines while improving professionalism, achieving a balance between professional guidance and entertainment. The system guides users to form standard and consistent postures through character mapping, visual and voice prompts, exercise mechanisms, and scoring mechanisms. Within a stipulated time and arrow count, users earn points by shooting falling boxes. The size of the boxes and the degree of precision correspond to different scores. The screen sight is positioned on the extension line of the bow grip and the bowstring, forming a natural bodily-aiming mapping. The steadiness of sight reflects the user's standard posture.

Using a standard posture dataset, FitnessBow compares the posture landmark data captured by the camera. It employs a virtual character to map users' actions, using visual and voice prompts to correct user posture. Finally, it utilizes an intelligent scoring system that comprehensively scores users based on their posture, finger exertion, and box hitting accuracy.

3.2 Hardware Design

Drawing upon the structural aesthetics of compound and recurve bows, the design of FitnessBow retains the exercise benefits and experience of archery.

The lightweight design eliminates the use of arrows, reduces location restrictions, and enhances safety during exercise. In conventional archery, sometimes occurs whenthe arrow falls off the stringbecause of an illfitting or broken nock. In this case the bow mustdispose of all the energy unaided; almost invariably the bow breaks. If it does not, excessivestrength and hence excessive virtual mass areindicated [1]. Our study replaces the bowstring with a fully rigid mechanical structure and utilizes a hydraulic cylinder to provide recoil force to absorb the kinetic energy of drawing the bow, thereby preventing injuries caused by empty draws.

Appearance Mechanical Structure. The entire bow and arrow structure is rigid, consisting of rigid bow limbs, a rigid bowstring, a central connector and core control panel. The fully rigid mechanical structure prevents damage to the user from empty draws, is easily foldable and disassembled, and facilitates better modular movement system design. The main body of the bow and arrow is made of aluminum alloy and carbon fiber, using a symmetrical structure design that allows the user to alternate training with both hands, achieving better upper limb training objectives.

The core control panel uses an LED screen to display the draw weight of the bow and arrow, and buttons to adjust the draw weight. Below the control panel is the front grip, wrapped in silicone material. Its form is ergonomically designed for a more comfortable grip when holding the bow and arrow. The control panel and front grip form the first grip unit, with two bow limb connectors attached to both ends, each housing a gas spring. The expansion end of the gas spring connects to the rigid bow limb, providing rebound force for the bow and arrow and achieving stable recoil through its resistance. The connector extends outwards, latching onto the rigid bow limb to support the bow and arrow in the draw expansion movement. The rigid bowstring forms the second grip unit, latching onto both ends of the rigid bow limbs, with the center of the bowstring attaching to the draw grip module. This module is also wrapped in silicone material for easier force application during the draw.

When not in use, the bow and arrow are horizontally placed on a bow rack. The bow rack is divided into a base support and a charging pile. The base support features a U-shaped groove design with a built-in wireless charger for the core control panel. The charging pile powers the Bluetooth module inside the bowstring of the bow and arrow. A concealed camera is designed at the top, which can capture the spatial scene where the user is located when placed in front of the user (see Fig. 3).

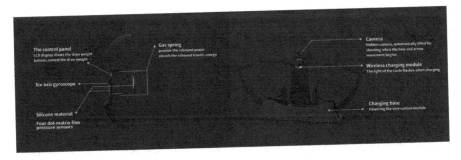

The control panel
LCD display shows the draw weight
buttons control the draw weight

Gas spring
provide the rebound power
absorb the rebound kinetic energy

Camera
Hidden camera, automatically lifted for
shooting when the bow and arrow
movement begins

Wireless charging module
The light of the circle flashes when charging

Six-axis gyroscope

Silicone material

Four dot-matrix film
pressure sensors

Charging base
Powering the core control module

Fig. 3. System framework

Ergonomics Design. For comparison, common compound bows have an axle-to-axle length between 30–35 in. The natural draw length is 14 in., with the maximum draw length extending to 32 in. The bow's poundage can be adjusted through a hydraulic cylinder, with the adjustable poundage range approximately between 20–80 pounds. It can be universally used by individuals with heights from 150–200 cm and arm spans of 60–80 cm. The axle-to-axle length of the Fitness Bow is approximately 44 in. which are set according to the specifications of compound bows, combined with arm span and conversion formulas to determine the draw length. The draw weight is adjusted based on rebound data, using an intelligent poundage system to customize adjustments, accommodating different users' physical abilities and exercise habits.

Internal Circuit Design. Within the archery grip, a microcontroller is installed within the control panel and is connected to two stepper motor driver boards, which in turn are connected to the stepper motors and the hydraulic gas springs. The microcontroller is connected to the pound control button (LBS button) and the display on the control panel, forming an intelligent pound control system used to control the draw weight of the bow (the intelligent pound system will be described in detail below).

Within the bow grip, the microcontroller is connected to a gyroscope and a calibration button, forming the archery aiming system. The gyroscope can measure the acceleration, angular velocity, and magnetic field of the bow's movement and calculate the triaxial angle. The microcontroller transforms the received triaxial angle into cursor movement information recognized by the computer. Once the bow is connected to a display device, it can control the cursor movement on the display device, realizing motion-sensing aiming. The calibration process for the initial position of the motion-sensing aiming is as follows: The user guides the bow to aim at the center of the display device, then presses the calibration button, completing the calibration of the initial position.

Within the bow arm grip, the microcontroller is connected to the pressure acquisition module and a thin-film pressure sensor. The thin-film pressure sensor is placed on the bow grip, wrapped in a silicone shell. The thin-film pressure sensor and the pressure acquisition module collect finger pressure data during use. The cursor movement information and pressure data are packaged and sent to the host via a Bluetooth module. In the bowstring grip, a battery, pressure collection module, Bluetooth module, and thin-film pressure sensor are installed. The pressure collection module is connected to the thin-film pressure sensor and the Bluetooth module. The setting of the thin-film pressure sensor and the principle of collecting the finger pressure data during use is the same as above. The pressure collection module sends the data to the host for processing via the Bluetooth module.

In the bow rack, a microcomputer is installed, which is responsible for controlling the wireless charging module to activate the charging pile. It also receives data sent from the mobile phone and the bow and arrow, processes the data centrally, runs the pre-written program, and transmits the game screen to the display device via a wired connection (see Fig. 4).

3.3 Software Design

The software design consists of three parts as illustrated in the figure (see Fig. 5). The intelligent draw weight system can autonomously adjust the draw force to suit different users' physical fitness and exercise habits. The posture and grip detection system can monitor the standardization of the user's shooting action and compare it with the standard data. Additionally, based on the character mapping, the system offers reminders and a scoring system to help users improve their posture and exercise effect, thus replicating the effectiveness of the sport.

Intelligent Poundage System. The poundage of a bow is generally defined as the amount of force required when the bow is fully drawn, and the unit is pounds (LBS). The force required by the bow at different draw lengths is not entirely the same. However, in actual applications, due to the differences in the height and arm span of different users, the draw length when the bow is fully drawn is different from the full draw length set during production. This discrepancy leads to the bow's poundage not truly reflecting the force used to draw the bow.

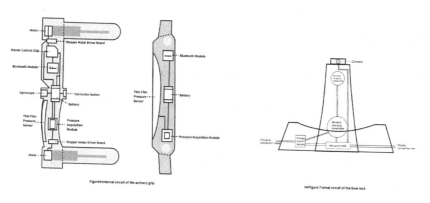

Fig. 4. System framework

This process requires some professional knowledge and skills. Meanwhile, the real poundage size is related to the user's arm span, and the specific adjusted poundage is not accurate. In this paper, we propose an intelligent poundage system where users input their height, the system automatically calculates the user's corresponding arm span and appropriate draw length. The bow poundage output of the current gas spring at the appropriate draw length is displayed on the LED screen. Users can adjust the bow poundage independently through control buttons. After receiving the control button signal, the micro controller controls the motor to rotate the gas spring and adjust the output poundage. To realize the above functions, a mathematical formula is needed to express the relationship between the draw length and the poundage. The user's height, arm span, and optimal draw length are related in the following way:

$$H = S_{arm} = l_{draw} \cdot 2.5 \tag{1}$$

where H is the user's height, S_{arm} is the arm span, and l_{draw} is the optimal draw length.

However, during the process of archery, the gas spring and the grip move horizontally, the bow arm rotates around a fixed point, and the bowstring and the hydraulic spring arm experience both rotation and translation, making the force analysis rather complex. Moreover, the output pressure of the gas spring at different draw lengths does not exhibit a simple linear relationship. The combination of these two factors makes theoretical calculation challenging. Therefore, through actual measurement and data fitting, the following mathematical formula was deduced:

$$F_{out}(s, F_{in}) = (a \cdot s^2 + b \cdot s + c) \cdot F_{in} \tag{2}$$

where a, b, c are the parameters of the fitted quadratic curve, s is the draw length, F_{out} is the poundage, and F_{in} is the output force of the gas spring. The force outputted by the gas spring is only related to the gear position of the gas spring, and the force inputted into the gas spring system is also associated with the draw length. The force outputted by the gas spring can be linearly manipulated by a stepper motor. Therefore, under the same draw length, the variation of the force outputted by the gas spring is linearly related to the draw weight. The Fin parameter is introduced to describe this linear relationship.

We measured n groups of data, each group containing m data points. Within the same data group, Fin is a fixed value, and each data point includes two parameters (F_{out}, s). Error calculation was conducted through different fitting methods, and a binary regression equation was eventually selected for fitting. The parameters a, b, and c are determined by the mechanical structure of the bow. Therefore, according to the mathematical formula derived in reverse, if the current output force Fin of the gas spring is known, and the draw length s is inputted, the corresponding bow poundage F_{out} can be calculated.

The relationship between the three is shown in the figure (see Fig. 6).

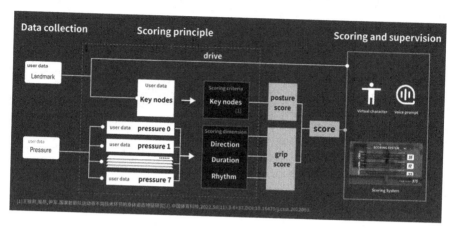

Fig. 5. System framework

Posture and Grip Strength Detection and Monitoring System. The system collects motion and scene data through the front bow stand camera as the background for the game interface. It captures real-time video from the side camera of the user's phone and extracts user skeletal point landmarks based on Mediapipe Pose landmark detection. This technology, characterized by low cost and high frame rate, enables motion capture without the need for more expensive depth cameras. The landmark information will be used to track the user's current actions, which will be processed to serve the scoring and supervision systems.

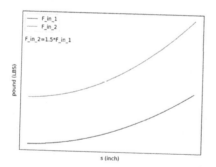

Fig. 6. force analysis

Mediapipe pose landmark detection provides 33 pose landmarks [25]. For subsequent processing, two pose landmarks have been added to the original basis, totaling 35 pose landmarks (see Fig. 8). Each landmark includes the following information:

x, y, z: The three-dimensional coordinates of the landmark, normalized according to the width and height of the image, ranging between [0.0, 1.0]. The video face is the XOY plane, and z represents the depth of the coordinate. The smaller the value, the closer the landmark is to the camera visibility: A value between [0.0, 1.0] that indicates the visibility of the coordinate in the image (Fig. 7).

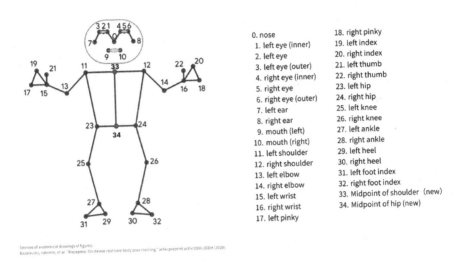

0. nose	18. right pinky
1. left eye (inner)	19. left index
2. left eye	20. right index
3. left eye (outer)	21. left thumb
4. right eye (inner)	22. right thumb
5. right eye	23. left hip
6. right eye (outer)	24. right hip
7. left ear	25. left knee
8. right ear	26. right knee
9. mouth (left)	27. left ankle
10. mouth (right)	28. right ankle
11. left shoulder	29. left heel
12. right shoulder	30. right heel
13. left elbow	31. left foot index
14. right elbow	32. right foot index
15. left wrist	33. Midpoint of shoulder (new)
16. right wrist	34. Midpoint of hip (new)
17. left pinky	

Sources of anatomical drawings of figures:
Bazarevsky, Valentin, et al. "Blazepose: On-device real-time body pose tracking." arXiv preprint arXiv:2006.10304 (2020).

Fig. 7. force analysis

Note: In the following text, the landmark is simply represented as P_n, where the subscript represents the corresponding landmark number. For example, the Midpoint of the shoulder is P_{33}.

The two newly added pose landmarks only contain three-dimensional coordinate information, x, y, z, which are used for numerical calculation and are not displayed on the screen.

Grip strength data is collected through thin film pressure sensors installed on the front and rear grips. Each grip is equipped with a four-channel thin-film pressure sensor, which corresponds to the pressure data of four fingers excluding the thumb. The channel numbers for the bow-holding grip from top to bottom are sequentially A0, A1, A2, A3; and those for the bow-pulling grip from top to bottom are sequentially A4, A5, A6, A7.

The collected data will be used for subsequent grip evaluation, supervision system, and release recognition. When it is detected that the pressure data of channels A4-A7 suddenly drops to around 0, it is considered that the user has completed a release action, and the system will recognize it as shooting an arrow.

Scoring System. The grading system can be divided into posture scoring and grip scoring. The posture scoring system scores based on key posture scoring nodes, and the data of the key scoring nodes is obtained by processing the landmark data captured from the user's movement. The process of motion capture and data processing is collectively referred to as feature extraction. However, during the posture scoring process, pressure data also needs to be incorporated for judgment.

Suppose the direction of the bow aiming is the positive direction of the x-axis, the y-axis is perpendicular to the x-axis and the ground, and the front of the human torso is facing the negative direction of the z-axis. It is defined that the angle of view along the positive direction of the z-axis is the front view angle, and the negative direction of the y-axis is the bird's-eye view angle. At the same time, regardless of whether the user is holding the bow with the left hand or the right hand, they should always face the phone camera. Therefore, in the coordinate system, the "left hand" is always the bow-holding hand.

The definitions and calculation methods of the key nodes for scoring are as follows [26] (Table 1):

When calculating the front-view angle, three adjacent pose landmarks are mapped onto the xoy plane, retaining only the x, y coordinate information for angle calculation (Table 2).

When calculating the trunk angle, the trunk line is defined as the line connecting P_{34} and P_{33}. Let Z-axis be the unit vector along the Z direction, and Y-axis be the unit vector along the Y direction. The shoulder line is defined as the line connecting P_{11} and P_{12}, while the hip line is defined as the line connecting P_{23} and P_{24} (Tables 3 and 4).

Table 1. Front-view angle

Hand type	Joint angle name	Joint angle definition
bow hand	Elbow joint angle	The projection of the angle formed by the line connecting the left wrist, elbow, and shoulder on the XOY plane
bow hand	shoulder joint angle	The projection of the angle formed by the line connecting the left elbow, left shoulder, and right shoulder on the XOY plane
draw hand	Elbow joint angle	The projection of the angle formed by the line connecting the right wrist, elbow, and shoulder on the XOY plane
draw hand	shoulder joint angle	The projection of the angle formed by the line connecting the left elbow, left shoulder, and right shoulder on the XOY plane.

Table 2. trunk angle

Joint angle name	Joint angle definition
Trunk forward flexion angle	The angle between the projection of the line connecting the midpoint of the hip and the midpoint of the shoulder on the YOZ plane and the Z-axis
trunk lateral flexion angle	The angle between the projection of the line connecting the midpoint of the hip and the midpoint of the shoulder on the XOY plane and the Y-axis
trunk torsion angle	The angle between the projection of the shoulder line and the hip line on the ZOX plane

Table 3. Posture angle

Joint angle name	Joint angle definition
Shoulder posture angle	The angle between the projection of the shoulder line on the ZOX plane and the X-axis
hip posture angle	The angle between the projection of the hip line on the ZOX plane and the X-axis

Table 4. Spacing ratio

Distance name	distance definition
Foot distance	Foot distance=ankle distance/shoulder distance

X-axis is the unit vector along the X direction.

The posture rating includes four important stages: raising the bow, drawing the bow, fixing the stance, and releasing. The scoring criteria for the four stages are different.

Raising: The deltoid and trunk, as well as the leg muscles, contract isometrically to provide support.

Drawing: The leg, hip, and trunk muscles isome-trically contract, while the posterior fibers of the deltoid, latissimus dorsi, and serratus anterior muscles contract dynamically.

Stabilizing: The muscle system during the stage of drawing the bow transitions from dynamic contraction to static contraction to complete the aiming action.

Release: The flexor muscles of the forearm and the extensor muscles of the fingers coordinate, while the back muscle group maintains a stable force.

The scoring criteria were generated by studying the professional archery sports literature [27] as well as professional archery videos.

As this system lacks the data source of overhead grip angle in the literature and there are certain errors due to different techniques of collecting stance data, the scoring criteria were generated by combining professional archery videos based on the literature.

By extracting features from the professional archery video, data on the key nodes of the professional archer's scoring during the archery process are extracted and weighted averages are applied in stages according to the four phases of the bow draw to correct as well as supplement the scoring criteria (Tables 5 and 6).

Table 5. Spacing ratio

Distance name	distance definition
Foot distance	Foot distance=ankle distance/shoulder distance

Table 6. Method of stage judgement

Stage	Actual Representative	stage feature
Raising	End point of the bow-raising phase/Start point of the bow-drawing phase	In the vertical direction, the landmarks of both wrists reach the highest point. The pressure exerted by the drawing hand starts to increase from a relatively low value
Drawing	End point of the bow-drawing phase/Start point of the bow-holding phase	The angle of the shoulder joint of the drawing hand increases from less than 90° to around 140°. The pressure exerted by the drawing hand increases from small to large and finally stabilizes
Stabilizing	End point of the stance-fixing phase/Start point of the release phase	The angle of the shoulder joint of the drawing hand essentially reaches its maximum value; the pressure exerted by the drawing hand remains stable over a certain period
Release	End point of the release phase/Start point of the bow-raising phase	The pressure exerted by the drawing hand rapidly decreases to zero.

The mentioned stage is actually an important moment to judge the beginning of the stage, and the stopping point of the previous stage is the starting point of the beginning of the next stage, for example, the stopping point of the bow raising stage is the starting point of the bow opening stage. By detecting the characteristics of different stages, we can determine what stage of bow drawing the current one belongs to.

The scoring criteria include two important concepts: the central value and the scoring gap, the central value is abbreviated as V and the scoring gap is abbreviated as G. The score and the corresponding scoring gap are as follows (Table 7):

Table 7. scoring criteria

score	score range
100	$(V - S, V + S)$
80	$(V - 1.5S, V - S), (V + S, V + 1.5S)$
60	$(V - 2S, V - 1.5S), (V + 1.5S, V + 2S)$
30	$(V - 2.5S, V - 2S), (V + 2S, V + 2.5S)$
0	else

Table 8. Angle of upper limb posture

Stage	Hand type	Joint angle name	Central value	Score gap
Raising	Bow hand	Elbow joint angle	170	15
		Shoulder joint angle	150	30
	Draw hand	Elbow joint angle	155	25
		Shoulder joint angle	20	20
Drawing	Bow hand	Elbow joint angle	175	5
		Shoulder joint angle	170	10
	Draw hand	Elbow joint angle	30	15
		Shoulder joint angle	140	15
Stabilizing	Bow hand	Elbow joint angle	175	5
		Shoulder joint angle	170	5
	Draw hand	Elbow joint angle	30	10
		Shoulder joint angle	140	10
Release	Bow hand	Elbow joint angle	175	5
		Shoulder joint angle	170	10
	Draw hand	Elbow joint angle	20	15
		Shoulder joint angle	170	10

The specific scoring criteria are as follows (Tables 8 and 9):

Table 9. Torso stance

Stage	Name	Center Value	Score gap	Name	Center Value	Score gap
Raising	Trunk forward flexion angle	80	7	Shoulder posture angle	15	5
	Trunk lateral flexion angle	−85	5	Hip posture angle	5	5
	Trunk torsion angle	10	5	Foot distance	1	0.15
Drawing	Trunk forward flexion angle	85	5	Shoulder posture angle	6	5
	Trunk lateral flexion angle	−83	5	Hip posture angle	5	5
	Trunk torsion angle	5	5	Foot distance	1	0.15
Stabilizing	Trunk forward flexion angle	85	5	Shoulder posture angle	7	5
	Trunk lateral flexion angle	−85	5	Hip posture angle	6	5
	Trunk torsion angle	8	5	Foot distance	1	0.15
Release	Trunk forward flexion angle	85	5	Shoulder posture angle	6	5
	Trunk lateral flexion angle	−85	5	Hip posture angle	6	5
	Trunk torsion angle	8	5	Foot distance	1	0.15

The grip score evaluates the user's movement from three levels: force direction, force time, and force rhythm, where the main difference is that the posture detection cannot accurately detect the user's hand movement and the whole body force relationship.

The direction of force: The user's finger pressure data collected by the multi-channel thin-film pressure sensor is compared by channel, and the difference between the channels is compared to restore the user's hand-held posture and analyze the user's direction of force.

Force time: The user needs to go through several different steps when performing a complete archery action, and the pressure sensors' multiple channel characteristic values vary in different steps, so that the user's force condition and time of each process can be judged and the technical problems within a complete action can be analyzed.

Force rhythm: analyze the user's force status and time between multiple complete archery actions, summarize as the user's force rhythm, and analyze the technical problems in the complete process.

A scoreboard is displayed to the user after the user completes a archery session, and the final score is obtained by weighting the stance score and the grip score (see Fig. 8).

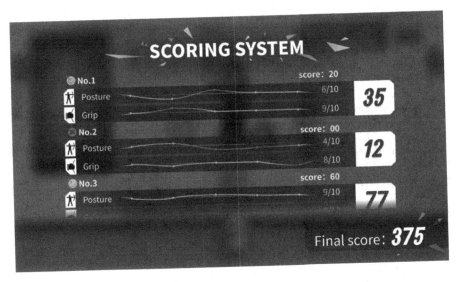

Fig. 8. Force analysis

4   Conclusion and Future Work

The development of human-computer interaction technology has lowered the barriers to many sports, allowing popular activities to transcend physical and equipment limitations. The integration and transformation of traditional fitness equipment provide more systematic services beyond physical activity, such as targeted guidance and personalized training, promoting healthier lifestyles.

In this study, we integrated and designed an intelligent supervised motion system, transforming archery into a more portable and sustainable indoor fitness method while preserving its basic performance and sports experience. It resolves safety and location limitations associated with traditional archery. Simultaneously, it uses more convenient equipment to capture users' body posture data and provides professional guidance.

Surveys show that outdoor sports and aerobic exercises such as skiing, rowing, tennis, and boxing are popular among young people. Nevertheless, they are constrained by geographical space and can't take advantage of fragmented time in daily life for entertaining sports activities. Future research will continue to focus on the integrated application of new technologies to guide individuals in proactive health management. The core control module of the existing design (the core sensor control unit on the bow arm) will be subjected to lightweight, modular expansion design. The existing structure, experience model and user data of the product will be extended to other popular sports fields. The upper limb movement key points in these sports will be extracted and designed into simple, easy-to-learn fitness sports games that can be played anytime in daily life scenarios. Eventually, it will be integrated and designed as an intelligent supervised motion system for sedentary people.

Acknowledgement. This work was supported by the National Social Science Foundation Art Project (19BG127).

References

1. Eurofound. Sixth European Working Conditions Survey - Overview Report: Update, p. 2017. Publications Office of the European Union, Luxembourg (2017)
2. Chiu, W., Oh, G.E., Cho, H.: Impact of COVID-19 on consumers' impulse buying behavior of fitness products: a moderated mediation model. J. Consum. Behav. **21**(2), 245–258 (2022)
3. iResearch. https://mp.weixin.qq.com/s/QYnUjuJiR26nflo2MkW0aQ. Accessed 23 June 2023
4. Axford, R.: Archery Anatomy: An Introduction to Techniques for Improved Performance. Souvenir Press (2017)
5. KaiBin, F., WeiXing, W., ZongHao, L.: Theoretical study on strength training design for archery program. J. Beijing Sport Univ. **1**, 109–110 (2010). https://doi.org/10.19582/j.cnki.11-3785/g8.2010.01.030
6. Tremblay, M.S., et al.: Sedentary behavior research network (SBRN)-terminology consensus project process and outcome. Int. J. Behav. Nutri. Phys. Activ. **14**, 1–17 (2017)
7. Caspersen, C.J., Powell, K.E., Christenson, G.M.: Physical activity, exercise, and physical fitness: definitions and distinctions for health-related research. Publ. Health Rep. **100**(2), 126 (1985)
8. Aldenaini, N., et al.: Mobile phone-based persuasive technology for physical activity and sedentary behavior: a systematic review. Front. Comput. Sci. **2**, 19 (2020)
9. Lithoxoidou, E.-E., et al.: A virtual coach and a worker dashboard to promote well-being and workability: an acceptance study. In: Universal Access in Human-Computer Interaction. Novel Design Approaches and Technologies: 16th International Conference (UAHCI 2022), Held as Part of the 24th HCI International Conference (HCII 2022), Virtual Event, 26 June–1 July 2022, Proceedings, Part I. Springer, Cham (2022). https://doi.org/10.1007/978-3-031-05028-2_19
10. Consolvo, S., et al.: Design requirements for technologies that encourage physical activity. In: Proceedings of the SIGCHI Conference on Human Factors in Computing Systems (2006)
11. Sailer, M., et al.: How gamification motivates: an experimental study of the effects of specific game design elements on psychological need satisfaction. Comput. Hum. Behav. **69**, 371–380 (2017)
12. Alizadeh Elizei, Z.: A user-centered mobile interface design, promoting physical activity in the Covid 19 pandemic's sedentary lifestyle. In: Stephanidis, C., Antona, M., Ntoa, S. (eds.) HCII 2021. CCIS, vol. 1421, pp. 539–550. Springer, Cham (2021). https://doi.org/10.1007/978-3-030-78645-8_68
13. Finco, M.D., Maass, R.W.: The history of exergames: promotion of exercise and active living through body interaction. In: 2014 IEEE 3nd International Conference on Serious Games and Applications for Health (SeGAH). IEEE (2014)
14. Nigg, C.R., Mateo, D.J., An, J.: Pokémon GO may increase physical activity and decrease sedentary behaviors. Am. J. Publ. Health **107**(1), 37 (2017)
15. Hashim, H.L., Kamaruddin, A., Jantan, A.H.: The mobile exergames design model to encourage physical activity for sedentary generation Z. In: Proceedings of the 5th International ACM In-cooperation HCI and UX Conference (2019)

16. Ren, X., et al.: HealthSit: designing posture-based interaction to promote exercise during fitness breaks. Int. J. Hum. Comput. Interact. **35**(10), 870–885 (2019)
17. Geiger, C., Thiele, S., Meyer, L., Meyer, S., Hören, L., Drochtert, D.: Goin' goblins - iterative design of an entertaining archery experience. In: Reidsma, D., Katayose, H., Nijholt, A. (eds.) ACE 2013. LNCS, vol. 8253, pp. 284–295. Springer, Cham (2013). https://doi.org/10.1007/978-3-319-03161-3_20
18. Purnomo, F.A., et al.: Archery training simulation based on virtual reality. In: 2022 1st International Conference on Smart Technology, Applied Informatics, and Engineering (APICS). IEEE (2022)
19. TechnoHunt. https://www.technohuntbyai.com/systems. Accessed 23 June 2023
20. Butnariu, S., et al.: An interactive haptic system for experiencing traditional archery. Acta Polytech. Hungar. **15**(5), 185–208 (2018)
21. Thiele, S., et al.: Virtual archery with tangible interaction. In2013 IEEE Symposium on 3D User Interfaces (3DUI). IEEE (2013)
22. Yasumoto, M., Ohta, T.: The electric bow interface. In: Shumaker, R. (ed.) VAMR 2013. LNCS, vol. 8022, pp. 436–442. Springer, Heidelberg (2013). https://doi.org/10.1007/978-3-642-39420-1_46
23. Thiele, S., et al.: Virtual archery with tangible interaction. In: 2013 IEEE Symposium on 3D User Interfaces (3DUI). IEEE (2013)
24. Butnariu, S., et al.: An interactive haptic system for experiencing traditional archery. Acta Polytech. Hungar. **15**(5), 185–208 (2018)
25. Bazarevsky, V., Grishchenko, I., Raveendran, K., Zhu, T.L., Zhang, F., Grundmann, M.: BlazePose: on-device Real-time body pose tracking. arXiv preprint arXiv:2006.10204 (2020)
26. Zhang, X.: Research on the Archery Action Comprehensive Test and Technique Evaluation Index. Dissertation. Beijing Sport University, Beijing (2008)
27. Wang, J., Wu, G., Yin, J.: Research on body posture characteristics of national archery athletes in different technical links. Chin. Sport Sci. Technol. **58**(11), 3–6+37 (2022). https://doi.org/10.16470/j.csst.2022069

The Incorporation of Gamification into Safety: A Systematic Review

Sara Herrera, Stephen Petters, and Vincent G. Duffy(✉)

School of Interdisciplinary Engineering, Purdue University, West Lafayette, IN 47906, USA
{herre110,spetter,duffy}@purdue.edu

Abstract. The primary goal of this report is to review literature regarding gamification in the context of safety. Utilizing tools such as Scopus Analysis, Google Scholar, Dimensions AI, Springer link, Scite.AI, VOSviewer, and CiteSpace, a bibliometric analysis was conducted to explore the connections in published literature between "Gamification" and "Safety". The paper explores potential trends in publication on these topics and focuses specifically on three major fields where gamification has been used to enhance safety, namely, Patient Health, Transportation, and Workplace Safety.

Keywords: Gamification · Safety · Patient Safety · Workplace Safety · Transportation Safety

1 Introduction and Background

1.1 Problem Statement

The benefits of Gamification have been well documented and include aiding cognitive development, increased engagement from learners, and makes learning more accessible to students [24]. However there is substantially less research available that correlates how the benefits of gamification have been applied to industries to increase safety outcomes. There are studies that have already utilized gamification to enhance the ergonomic experience of the user such as using mobile apps to encourage users to relax [22]. Gamification can be used in a wide variety of applications to give a much more thoughtful and flexible approach to increasing safety in the workplace and several examples will be shown in this paper.

Games have always played an important part in society. Gamification has been linked to positive impacts on motivation, behavior, cognitive performance, and learning outcomes [12]. This area of research is especially important where the psychology of what motivates us is concerned- gamification has been shown to have sustained and lasting effects on those that participate [16]. If the success of traditional game methods can be applied to increase safety in varying industries the aforementioned benefits could be realized to a new sector and therefore deserves attention for research purposes. The authors of this paper respectively submit the following as evidence that gamification should be expounded to increase safety learning and application wherever possible.

© The Author(s), under exclusive license to Springer Nature Switzerland AG 2023
J. Y. C. Chen et al. (Eds.): HCII 2023, LNCS 14058, pp. 298–316, 2023.
https://doi.org/10.1007/978-3-031-48050-8_21

1.2 Purpose of This Study

The main purpose of this report is to review published literature whose topics connect "Gamification" and "Safety" and explore instances where gamification has been successfully implemented to increase safety in various applications.

Before continuing it is helpful to first define gamification and outline its principles. Gamification can be defined as "the application of game design principles to education" [2]. Another author described it aptly as "the intentional use of game elements for a gameful experience of non-game tasks and contexts [23]. Principles of gamification can be applied to what would normally be classified as menial or even boring tasks to increase engagement and learning potential. The core principles of gamification are: (1) clear and relevant goals, (2) immediate feedback, (3) positive reinforcement, (4) comparisons to peers, (5) Common goals, (6) Content that adapts to the learner and situation, (7) "nudges" or guided paths which guide learners to determined outcomes, (8) multiple choices in problem solving, and (9) simplify the user experience [16]. Gamification also has two main components: "it is used for non-entertainment purposes, and it draws inspiration from games, particularly the elements that make up games, without engendering a fully-fledged game" [23].

Table 1 shows other common elements that exist in games along with their definitions Table 2 shows common game dynamics and motives. Both can be a helpful reference when reading the remainder of this paper.

Table 1. Common Game Elements [4]

Game element	Definition
Feedback	Immediate notification that keep users constantly aware of progress or failures
Goals	Activity goals that are adapted as challenges for the user
Badges	Optional rewards and goals outside the scope of a service's core activities
Point system	Reward for completing actions (that is, a numeric value that's added to the total points)
Leaderboard	Tracking and displaying desired actions to drive desired behavior through competition
User levels	Indication of the user's proficiency in the overall gaming experience over time

Table 2. Game Design Elements, Dynamic, and Motives [23]

Game design elements, dynamics, and motives from Blohm and Leimeister (2013).

Game element: mechanics	Game element: dynamics	Motives
Documentation of behavior	Exploration	Intellectual curiosity
Scoring systems, badges, trophies	Collection	Achievement
Rankings	Competition	Social recognition
Ranks, levels, reputation points	Acquisition of status	Social recognition
Group tasks	Collaboration	Social exchange
Time pressure, tasks, quests	Challenge	Cognitive stimulation
Avatars, virtual worlds, virtual trade	Development/ organization	Self-determination

1.3 Literature Review

Data Collection

Multiple databases were utilized to gather a variety of results and sources in this review. Analysis from all databases was conducted using the same search terms, "Safety" and "Gamification". Table 3 shows the databases and results of each search.

Table 3. Database search table.

Database	Search Term	Results
Scopus	"Safety", "Gamification"	260 documents
Google Scholar	"Safety", "Gamification"	3,080 articles
Springer Link	"Safety", "Gamification"	4,207 results
Web of Science	"Safety", "Gamification"	185 results
Dimensions	"Safety", "Gamification"	26,122 publications

Trend Analysis

Scopus and Dimensions AI were the primary databases used for trend analysis. Parameters for both databases were set to search between 2012 and 2022. Figures 1 and 2 show increasing trend lines of articles published since 2012 that discuss gamification and safety. Before 2012, interest in gamification was not evident in published articles, but both figures show steady increases in trendlines after 2014, showing increasing interest.

Documents by year

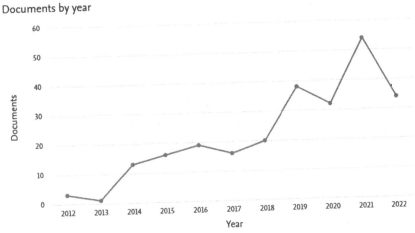

Fig. 1. Trend Analysis of articles per year on "Safety" and "Gamification" (Scopus)

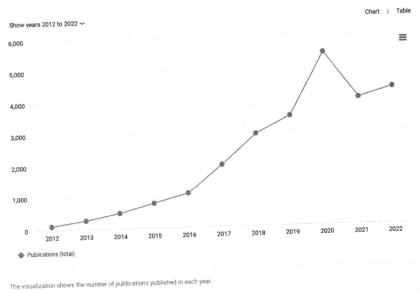

Fig. 2. Trend Analysis of articles per year on "Safety" and "Gamification" (Dimensions)

Proof of Interest

Vicinitas was used to search for proof of relevance from the last 10 days of Twitter posts, as of 16 April 2023. The search for both "Gamification" and "Safety" returned 35 twitter posts, while solely searching "Gamification" returned 1342 posts with an influence of 4.1 million. As shown in Fig. 3, 'Benefit' 'Rewards' and 'Gamification' were prominent buzzwords for tweets about "Gamification". As shown in Fig. 4, 'Encourage' 'Gameplay' and 'Safety' were prominent buzzwords for tweets about both "Safety" and "Gamification".

Fig. 3. Twitter relevance of "Gamification" (Vicinitas)

Fig. 4. Twitter relevance of "Gamification" and "Safety" (Vicinitas)

2 Co-citation Analysis/Co-author Analysis

The concept of gamification is by no means a new idea, although the use of the term gamification has gained popularity in recent years [13]. When performing a systematic literature review, it is important to consider multiple resources that can be used to collect information on all relevant work [15]. To help parse through all the ideas from multiple authors and studies that have been completed on the subject, a co-citation analysis is necessary. Figure 5 illustrates the amount of articles that were written on the subjects of "Gamification" and "Safety" per author.

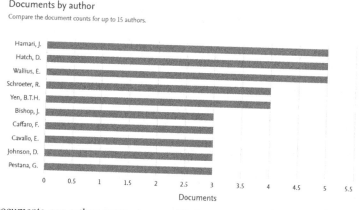

Fig. 5. Documents per author comparison on "Safety" and "Gamification" Years 2012–2023 (Scopus)

A co-citation analysis is unique in its ability to perform an examination of articles researching a similar topic and drawing comparisons between them. This analysis is particularly useful when the findings can be summarized using visual charts with clusters of images based on information density concerning common themes or citations [26]. The following tools were used for the co-citation analysis of this paper.

2.1 VOS Viewer

Figure 6 was created using the VOSviewer basic tool. A database was first collected by searching "Gamification" and "Safety" using the Scopus search website. A total of 261 results were generated from this search. All options were selected and extracted into a csv file. Once in a csv file the database was ready to be analyzed using VOSviewer. A map was created based on bibliographic data and then prompts were followed to read data from bibliographic database files [30]. Once the csv database was selected, VOSviewer constructed the map shown in Fig. 6 based on the following criteria: Co-authorship analysis, full counting method, authors as the unit of analysis, and the maximum number of authors per document set at 20. Finally, the minimum number of documents of an author was set to 1. This result prompts VOSviewer to reduce the set of connected items to a list of 21. Figure 6 is the result. It shows three main clusters of co-citations and the three most cited authors within this database are Yannis G., Brijs K., and Katrakazas C.

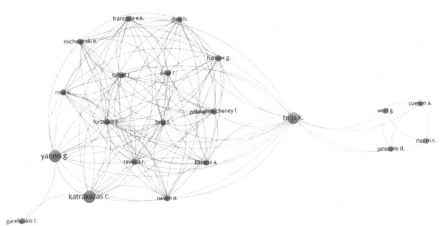

Fig. 6. Co-citation Network Visualization (VOSviewer)

The same database was analyzed for text content using VOSviewer. The database was uploaded using the create a map based on text data option. Title and abstract fields were extracted and a binary counting method was utilized. The minimum number of occurrences for the term to be selected was set to 10 and the number of terms to be selected was set to 88% as a relevance score. Figure 7 is the result. The most common terms under these parameters were, in no particular order: user, analysis, process, topic, behavior, and level.

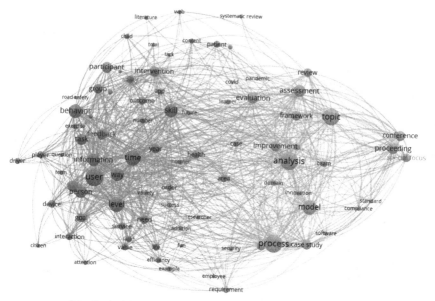

Fig. 7. Article Text Data Network Visualization (VOSviewer)

2.2 Cite Space

Cite space has some added functionality that VOSviewer does not allow, one among them being the option to automatically extract names to the clusters for better visual organization. The database used for the cite space analysis was extracted from Web of Science using the keywords "Gamification" and "Safety". A total of 185 results were generated from this search. These were extracted into a plain text file using full record and cited references. These were then opened within Citespace and cluster names were extracted using keywords of similar articles. Results are shown in Fig. 8 below. The top three most common themes based on keywords are: Infection Prevention, Driving recommendations, and safe driving. The themes of patient, workplace safety education, and transportation safety as they pertain to gamification are discussed at length later on in this document and this analysis validates why those discussion topics were chosen. Figure 9 shows the citation "burst" with two articles shown to have the strongest citations.

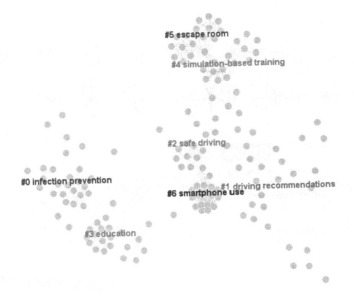

Fig. 8. Article Cluster Map (Cite Space)

Top 2 References with the Strongest Citation Bursts

References	Year	Strength	Begin	End	2013 - 2023
Hamari J, 2014, P ANN HICSS, V0, PP3025, DOI 10.1109/HICSS.2014.377, DOI	2014	2.55	**2016**	2017	
Seaborn K, 2015, INT J HUM-COMPUT ST, V74, P14, DOI 10.1016/j.ijhcs.2014.09.006, DOI	2015	2.59	**2017**	2019	

Fig. 9. Strongest Citation Bursts (Cite Space)

3 Discussion

3.1 Research Fields

Dimensions AI, Scopus, and Springer Link were used as the primary databases for separating discovered articles, resulting from the search "Safety" and "Gamification", into specific research fields. The search parameters were set between 2012 and 2022 for all to keep the results comparable between the three databases. Despite having three distinct result sizes, 260 for Scopus, 4,207 for Springer Link, and 46,122 for Dimensions AI, the results of all three searches, Fig. 10, Fig. 11, and Fig. 12 support the same findings, that the primary research field that the search results of "Safety" and "Gamification" fall into is Computer Science.

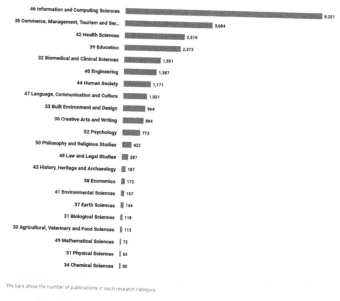

Fig. 10. Dimensions AI Fields of Research Classification

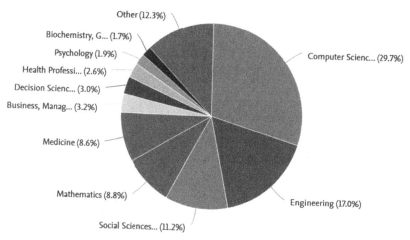

Fig. 11. Scopus Documents by Subject Area

Three subtopics, "Patient Safety", "Transportation Safety", and "Workplace Safety", were identified in the earlier Cite Space Cluster Map, and Fig. 13 shows their comparison to the main topic of "Gamification" according to Google nGram from the year 2002 to 2019.

Discipline	see all
Computer Science	1,213
Engineering	855
Business and Management	722
Education	348
Medicine & Public Health	268

Subdiscipline	see all
Artificial Intelligence	853
User Interfaces and Human Computer Interaction	708
Computational Intelligence	494
Information Systems Applications (incl. Internet)	430
Computer Communication Networks	346

Fig. 12. Springer Link Documents by Discipline

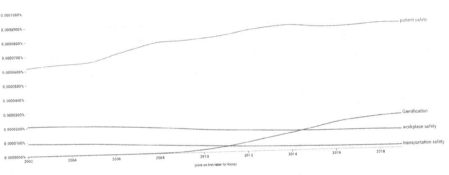

Fig. 13. Google nGram of Chosen Subtopics

3.2 Patient Safety

CiteSpace cluster analysis discussed previously revealed "Escape Room" as a common text theme in articles related to gamification and safety. Figure 14 shows a word cloud of the patient safety articles referenced in this paper and it is clear "escape", "room", and "simulation" were common themes. An Escape room is a popular activity in which an individual or group of individuals are "locked" in a room and must solve a series of puzzles and perform certain activities in order to leave or progress. These activities are typically coupled with the added requirement of completion within a certain time limit. Escape rooms as instructional methods have become incredibly popular to train a wide-range of health care professionals including nurses, physicians, pharmacists and medical technicians [3]. We will explore a few examples of how this gamification technique has been applied in the field of patient safety.

Teaching patient safety to medical students is a difficult task. Some of the challenges involve constraints associated with traditional classroom teaching, difficulty of teaching the soft skills of patient safety, and the lack of opportunity to develop communication

Fig. 14. MaxQDA word cloud of patient gamification safety articles

and teamwork skills, among others [2]. Simulation through escape rooms overcomes several of these challenges by allowing dynamic interaction in a team-based setting to discover answers and apply learning. In one particular application, medical students were given a portable "suitcase-based" escape room that required them to complete diagnoses and prescribe medication all within a 30 min window. The setup allowed them to fail within safe boundaries and provided rapid feedback to assess their performance after the simulation [2].

The COVID-19 pandemic caused a large-scale disruption to several nurse education and training programs [29]. Not only were staff needing to care for an influx of high risk patients, gathering in person for training was no longer an acceptable setup for fear of "super spread" events that could expose a large number of workers to the SARS-CoV-2 virus. It became a necessity to conduct online virtual training in lieu of in person alternatives. Escape rooms that had been used successfully to train nursing students now needed to be tested in a virtual space to verify if this method of gamification learning could still be effective remotely. Dubbed "Online Escape room" or "OER", students in a course obtaining their Bachelor of Science in Nursing (BSN) degrees trialed the methodology. Google forums were designed with prompts and quizzes intended to simulate the same decision making and creative thinking from in-person escape rooms. The end result was a success and student nurses reported similar benefits seen from in-person escape room experiences [29].

The medical field is rich with other non-escape room examples of gamification in practice. These include: the use of exercise equipment to encourage physical activity in older adults [17], the use of a mobile app to motivate and reward children diagnosed with type 1 diabetes to accurately track glucose levels [23], and the use of game-like elements to improve chest radiography skills [5]. In all cases gamification is used to promote patient safety using the core concepts of game design and reward discussed earlier in this paper.

3.3 Workplace Safety

Being involved in a workplace accident can have severe physical and psychological effects for workers. This knowledge resulted in the Operational Safety and Health (OSH) Act of 1970, to "assure so far as possible every working man and woman in the nation safe and healthful working conditions." OSHA was created to enforce the standards set forth by the OSH Act, and requires every employer to be responsible for the safety of the workplace they require their workers to be in [9]. Part of these requirements are the need to educate their workers and create safety and health programs, but despite the existence of these programs, workplace accidents still cost the United States over $155 billion every year [14].

Unfortunately, safety training can be boring and the knowledge required to learn is very technical and specific to each individual worksite. Occupational safety mainly focuses on prevention, with the goal to have each worker proficient in identifying health and safety risks, reviewing their specific work practices when faced with these risks, and to identify and take preventative actions. Gamification involvement in health and safety organizations adds 'fun elements', with the outcome of reducing risks and having financial savings due to decreased accidents [20]. Gamification elements that are be utilized in the workplace, like points, positive feedback, timers, badges, upgrades, and monetary rewards are linked to increased productivity, collaboration, employee engagement, communication, and innovation [28].

A simple gamification method that is used to motivate workers to learn about workplace safety is quizzing in Jeopardy or Family Feud formats, with the quizzing games serving as a way to "...capture the interest of those workers putting themselves in harm's way" and to present them with the knowledge to work in a safer manner [6]. A more involved gamification technique was implemented at EnTrans International, the company-wide program Safety Matters, where different facilities competed against each other to accumulate safety points gained in eight categories like safety improvements and audits. Along with the typical gamification reward of points, the Safety Matters system was also linked to a financial reward system, a monthly bonus. Facilities improved from typically earning 26 points a month to 30–34 out of a possible 36 after implementation. EnTran recorded a reduction of more than 50% in recordable injuries and a Total Recordable Incident Rate (TRIR) from 6 to 2.1, with the industry standard TRIR at 7.32 [10]. An automotive company in Poland also utilized a gamification system based on points to increase the safety of their workplaces. While they did not make participation in the safety program game required, it was discovered that the majority of their employees were interested in the competition [7].

3.4 Transportation Safety

CiteSpace cluster analysis discussed previously revealed "safe driving", "driving recommendations", "situation-based simulations" and "education" as common themes for research, which were all combined to examine safety in the transportation field. Transportation accidents persist as the major cause of death globally. A variety of strategies have been attempted to try to mitigate transportation safety risks, like awareness campaigns, regulation, and mandated training, but these approaches fail to effectively reduce accidents [31]. The need for positive motivation in regards to transportation safety can be addressed with gamification.

There are three phases of accidents when dealing with transportation systems: pre-event (injuries can be prevented), during-event (injuries can be managed), and post-event (injuries can be treated). The majority of roadway studies, for cars and cyclists, focused on pre-event by promoting safe behaviors to avoid accidents. Air travel studies focused on during-event safety, using gamification to better educate passengers on what to do in emergencies in order to minimize injuries. Waterway studies, ferries, commercial boats, and military vessels, focused on pre-event safety, as accidents in this sector tend to be catastrophic and expensive [31].

One roadway study looked into effective motivation to increase commute by cycling with a gamification system as a smartphone app. Increased cycling is desired as it increases health status as a physical activity and it decreases roadway accidents as cities become more 'liveable' with reduced car use. This study compared the effectiveness of gamification when paired with financial rewards, and found both smart gamification motivation techniques and small financial rewards resulted in increased cycling, with a combination of the two being most effective [18].

The majority of roadway studies look into the motivation effects of gamification on drivers of motor vehicles. Simple examples of gamification applications with cars are the ECO score function in the Prius and the growing Efficiency Leaves and Vines in Fords [6, 21]. Both continuously rate a user's driving and give visual feedback, which encourages the drivers to drive smarter and fix their driving shortcomings while keeping the user engaged. Driving is characterized by tasks that are predictable, monotonous, and repetitive, which results in frustration, 'mind wandering', and boredom. Common coping methods to alleviate boredom reported among drivers are speeding, 'semi-automated driving', and cell phone use, all of which are dangerous and not desired [25]. Gamification strategies to decrease boredom and increase active engagement offer safety benefits, but do pose the risk of decreasing hazard reactions due to increased off-road glances to the gamification system. Accidents are twice as likely when drivers' eyes are away from the road for more than two seconds [32].

Studies on specific driving gamification techniques tended to employ the use of simulators, as shown in Fig. 15 below. One technique was the CoastMaster, a mobile application that functioned as a speedometer and "encouraged anticipatory driving by gamifying transitions to new speed limits." This study determined that using CoastMaster as a boredom intervention resulted in significantly reduced speeding incidents and increased lateral control of the vehicle during straight slow sections [25]. Another gamification technique was The Road Hero, a mobile application that provided during-event and post-event feedback on driving performance. The Road Hero engaged the driver with a mission narrative, where if the driver mastered three safety driving skills, keeping eyes on the road, distance to prior vehicle, and lane keeping, the mission was successfully completed and the driver was rewarded virtually. Results from this study showed drivers experienced enhanced motivation towards safe driving [32]. A third study utilized Smooth Driver, a mobile application that encourages ecologically friendly driving to increase driving safety, and looked at the effects of both visual and auditory feedback. Smooth Driver monitors good acceleration and braking behavior, which reduces the risk of traffic accidents, specifically nose-to-tail accidents. The results of this study suggested that real-time gamification applications improve eco-driving behaviors and decreased safety risk, with drivers enjoying a visual only experience over a gamification system that utilized visual and auditory feedback [11].

Fig. 15. A sample driving simulator from two perspectives (Driver and Researcher) [25]

Not only is it important for drivers to practice good driving behavior, but drivers must also establish adequate levels of driving and vehicle specific knowledge. Gamification has been shown to increase learning motivation and performance, and gamification techniques could be utilized to enhance driver knowledge compared to current user manuals. A study was performed looking specifically on how to increase drivers' knowledge of the ever increasing levels of Advanced Driver Assistance Systems (ADAS) in vehicles. Results suggested that gamification techniques increased driver knowledge and trust of the ADAS, promoting safer driver-vehicle interactions compared to traditional classroom style teaching or information booklets like user-manuals. As shown in Fig. 16, Users who received gamification style education felt they understood the ADAS better and received more correct answers about the ADAS when tested. Figure 17 reveals that drivers who were administered ADAS education through gamification had better driving when tested on use of ADAS-equipped vehicles [12].

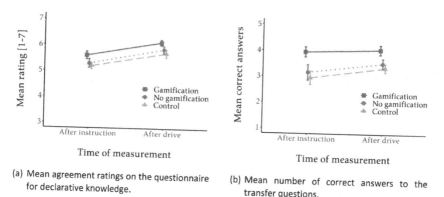

(a) Mean agreement ratings on the questionnaire for declarative knowledge.

(b) Mean number of correct answers to the transfer questions.

Fig. 16. ADAS knowledge after Gamification style education [12]

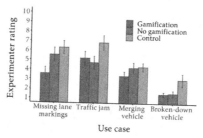

Fig. 17. Driving event failures in ADAS-equipped vehicles after Education [12].

4   Conclusions

A systematic literature of published articles in the field of safety with the application of gamification is crucial to set a baseline for research into gamification and to discover what needs further study. Gamification is a relatively novel concept and its abilities and applications are not fully defined or understood. The majority of the literature reviewed framed gamification in a positive light, with initial results showing the promise of the application of gamification to increase safety. Unfortunately, there are still a lack of studies that show grand qualitative evidence to prove without a doubt the usefulness of gamification, and many studies that do exist test different aspects of the applicability and cannot be fully compared.

4.1   Future Sponsored Research

Completing a search on the National Science Foundation website utilizing the search terms, "Gamification" and "Safety" only results in nine awards. A broader search of just

"Gamification" reveals 106 award results. Funding into gamification covers a variety of fields, like increasing student motivation in STEM [8], developing technologies to improve adolescent executive function [19], applications to help children deal with daily tasks of medical conditions [1], and cyberlearning environments [27]. Research into already published gamification studies for safety funded by sponsors on scopus, shown in Fig. 18, reveal that funding is coming from large organizations, like the Department of Transport, the Australian Research Council, the European Regional Development Fund, and a National Institute for Occupational Safety.

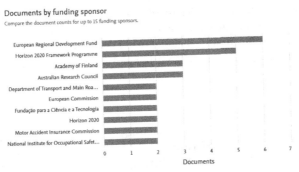

Fig. 18. Research Sponsors in "Gamification" and "Safety"

4.2 Further Applications of Gamification in Safety

In this report, applications of Gamification in the field of safety were explored more intimately in the Workplace Safety, Transportation Safety, and Patient Safety subtopics, but gamification has the potential to be applied in many more fields. Gamification itself has not yet been fully defined, and certain elements and applications have not been fully tested. Future studies of gamification should look into the motivational effects of different gamification elements for different applications [23]. Research into gamification elements should look into how those elements motivate, and how to more effectively utilize those elements [16]. Research should also look into the short-term and long-term motivational effects of gamification elements [31]. Feedback methods for gamification elements and how effective different sensory stimuli affects the user's receipt of the element could be studied. Feedback could use both auditory and visual stimulation, or one or both methods could be preferred by users, depending on the situation. Driving is a visual task, but users tend to find auditory feedback methods as distractions. In a fitness environment, users may be too busy to look at visual feedback and auditory feedback would be more useful [11]. As research into gamification continues, it can be expected to see that even small design changes in gamification systems will have major impacts on the motivation of users, and optimizing gamification systems will be more important than ever.

4.3 Challenges

There are a few major challenges with the application of gamification techniques that designers and developers of programs need to consider. Motivation from gamification tends to decrease when the novelty of the new program wears off, so continuous improvements to the gamification elements used will need to be tailored to the program to maintain the positive effects. Some users may determine a way to cheat the system to get extra rewards, causing other users to feel disadvantaged. Program Managers need to also consider privacy and data collection of gamification methods, ensuring only to use 'public' data and not breach data and privacy regulations. Gamification elements can distract from the user's main responsibilities, and their quality of their tasks and productivity may suffer if the gamification system is not tailored correctly [4]. The distraction caused by certain gamification elements must also be considered, as distractions can easily increase risk during activities like driving [31].

References

1. Ahn, H.: Award Abstract # 1738560 STTR Phase II: User-Friendly Spirometer and Mobile App for Self-Management and Home Monitoring of Asthma Patients. National Science Foundation. KNOX MEDICAL DIAGNOSTICS INC (n.d.). https://www.nsf.gov/awardsearch/showAward?AWD_ID=1738560&HistoricalAwards=false
2. Backhouse, A., Malik, M.: Escape into patient safety: bringing human factors to life for medical students. BMJ Open Qual. 8(1), e000548 (2019). https://doi.org/10.1136/bmjoq-2018-000548.PMID:31206043;PMCID:PMC6542456
3. Barker, N., Kaulback, M., Yocom, D.: Fluid and electrolyte escape room. J. Nurs. Educ.Nurs. Educ. 59(5), 298 (2020). https://doi.org/10.3928/01484834-20200422-14. PMID:32352549
4. Basten, D.: Gamification. IEEE J. Mag. (2017). https://ieeexplore.ieee.org/document/8048643
5. Chen, P., Roth, H., Galperin-Aizenberg, M., Ruutiainen, A., Gefter, W., Cook, T.: Improving abnormality detection on chest radiography using game-like reinforcement mechanics. Acad. Radiol.Radiol. 24(11), 1428–1435 (2017)
6. Christ, G.: Treading gingerly: the gamification of safety. EHS Today, 29 April 2016. https://www.ehstoday.com/environment/article/21917568/treading-gingerly-the-gamification-of-safety
7. Cierniak-Emerych, A., Pietron, A.: Gamification as a tool to improve the level of occupational safety and health in the company. In: Scientific Papers of Silesian University of Technology 2019 Organization and Management Series No. 136 (2019). https://www.researchgate.net/publication/338875710
8. Claville, M.: Award Abstract # 1623236 Targeted Infusion Project: Increasing Student Motivation and Engagement in STEM Courses through Gamification. National Science Foundation. Winston-Salem State University. https://www.nsf.gov/awardsearch/showAward?AWD_ID=1623236&HistoricalAwards=false
9. Congress: OSH Act of 1970 | Occupational Safety and Health Administration. OSHA.gov. United States Department of Labor, 1 January 2004. https://www.osha.gov/laws-regs/oshact/completeoshact
10. Czor, K.: Using gamification to enhance safety. Trailer/Body Builders; Nashville vol. 60, no. 4. EnTrans, February 2019

11. Degirmenci, K., Breitner, M.: Gamification and sensory stimuli in eco-driving research: a field experiment to reduce energy consumption in electric vehicles. Transport. Res. Part F Psychol. Behav. **92**, 266–282 (2023). Pergamon, 12 December 2022. https://www.sciencedirect.com/science/article/pii/S1369847822002492

12. Feinauer, S., Schuller, L., Groh, I., Huestegge, L., Petzoldt, T.: The potential of gamification for user education in partial and conditional driving automation: a driving simulator study. Transport. Res. Part F Psychol. Behav. **90**, 252–268 (2022). Pergamon, 11 September 2022. https://www.sciencedirect.com/science/article/pii/S1369847822001760

13. Fitz-Walter, D.Z.: What is gamification? education, Business & Marketing (2021 examples). What is Gamification? Education, Business & Marketing (2021 Examples) (n.d.). https://www.gamify.com/what-is-gamification#:~:text=There%20are%20many%20different%20definitions,is%20not%20a%20new%20concept. Retrieved 18 Apr 2023

14. Goetsch, D.L., Ozon, G.: Occupational Health and Safety for Technologists, Engineers, and Managers, 9th edn. Pearson Canada Inc., North York, Ontario (2019). Chapter 6

15. Khan, K.S., Kunz, R., Kleijnen, J., Antes, G.: Five steps to conducting a systematic review. J. R. Soc. Med. **96**(3), 118–121 (2003). https://doi.org/10.1177/014107680309600304.PMID:12612111;PMCID:PMC539417

16. Krath, J., Schürmann, L., von Korflesch, H.F.O.: Revealing the theoretical basis of gamification: a systematic review and analysis of theory in research on gamification, serious games and game-based learning. In: Computers in Human Behavior. Pergamon, 2 August 2021. https://www.sciencedirect.com/science/article/pii/S0747563221002867

17. Lee, E.L., et al. The effect of convergence gamification training in community-dwelling older people: a multicenter, randomized controlled trial. J. Am. Med. Dir. Assoc. **23**(3), 373–378 (2022). e3. https://doi.org/10.1016/j.jamda.2021.05.041. Epub 30 June 2021. PMID: 34216552

18. Máca, V., Ščasný, M., Zvěřinová, I., Jakob, M., Hrnčíř, J.: Incentivizing commuter cycling by financial and non-financial rewards. Int. J. Environ. Res. Publ. Health (2020). Multidisciplinary Digital Publishing Institute. https://www.mdpi.com/1660-4601/17/17/6033

19. Mehta, R.: Award Abstract # 1747260 STTR Phase I: Developing a Technological Intervention to Improve Adolescent Executive Functioning. National Science Foundation. STUDENTIVITY INC. (n.d.). https://www.nsf.gov/awardsearch/showAward?AWD_ID=1747260&HistoricalAwards=false

20. Pingle, S.: Gamification and benchmarking to achieve occupational health at workplace - tools and good practices to improve OSH at the workplace, examples from India. Saf. Health Work. Elsevier (2022). https://doaj.org/article/a21c5de67dcd42c9a2b80d81b3f275cf

21. Roy, R.: Ford's green goddess grows leaves. Autoblog (2009). https://www.autoblog.com/2009/10/29/ford-smart-gauge-engineer/

22. Salvendy, G., Karwowski, W.: Handbook of Human Factors and Ergonomics, 5th edn. Wiley, Hoboken (2021). Chapter 41

23. Seaborn, K., Fels, D.I.: Gamification in theory and action: a survey. Int. J. Hum.-Comput. Stud. Academic Press (2014). https://www.sciencedirect.com/science/article/pii/S1071581914001256

24. Smithsonian: 5 benefits of Gamification. 5 Benefits of Gamification. Smithsonian, 8 January 2014. https://ssec.si.edu/stemvisions-blog/5-benefits-gamification

25. Steinberger, F., Schroeter, R., Watling, C.: From road distraction to safe driving: evaluating the effects of boredom and gamification on driving behaviour, physiological arousal, and subjective experience. Comput. Hum. Behav. **75**, 714e726 (2017). Pergamon, 13 June 2017. https://www.sciencedirect.com/science/article/pii/S0747563217303904

26. Surwase, G., Sagar, A., Kademani, B.S., Bhanumurthy, K.: Co-citation analysis: an overview. In: Beyond Librarianship: Creativity, Innovation and Discovery, Mumbai (India), 16–17 September 2011 (2011)

27. Tymann, P.: Award Abstract # 1525414 Collaborative Research: Engaged Student Learning - Design and Development Level II: Using a Cyberlearning Environment to Improve Student Learning and Engagement in Software Courses. National Science Foundation. NORTH DAKOTA STATE UNIVERSITY (n.d.). https://www.nsf.gov/awardsearch/showAward?AWD_ID=1525414&HistoricalAwards=false

28. Uppalike, M.: Gamification impact on human aspects of the organization. J. Games Game Art Gamification **07** (2022). https://www.researchgate.net/publication/365650326_Gamification_Impact_on_Human_Aspects_of_the_Organization/fulltext/637d90e937878b3e87d3a84a/Gamification-Impact-on-Human-Aspects-of-the-Organization.pdf

29. Vestal, M.E., Matthias, A.D., Thompson, C.E.: Engaging students with patient safety in an online escape room. J. Nurs. Educ. **60**(8), 466–469 (2021). https://doi.org/10.3928/01484834-20210722-10. Epub 1 Aug 2021. PMID: 34346812

30. https://www.vosviewer.com/

31. Wallius, E., Carolina, T.K.A., Hamari, J.: Playing it safe: a literature review and research agenda on motivational technologies in transportation safety. Reliabil. Eng. Syst. Saf. **223**, 108514 (2022). Elsevier. https://www.sciencedirect.com/science/article/pii/S095183202201727. Accessed 5 April 2022

32. Xie, J., Chen, H.-Y.W., Donmez, B.: Gaming to safety: exploring feedback gamification for mitigating driver distraction. In: Proceedings of the Human Factors and Ergonomics Society 2016 Annual Meeting (2016). https://www.researchgate.net/publication/307944248_Gaming_to_Safety_Exploring_Feedback_Gamification_for_Mitigating_Driver_Distraction

Comparing Photorealistic and Animated Embodied Conversational Agents in Serious Games: An Empirical Study on User Experience

Danai Korre[✉]

The University of Edinburgh, Edinburgh, UK
d.korre@ed.ac.uk

Abstract. Embodied conversational agents (ECAs) are paradigms of conversational user interfaces in the form of embodied characters. While ECAs offer various manipulable features, this paper focuses on a study conducted to explore two distinct levels of presentation realism. The two agent versions are photorealistic and animated. The study aims to provide insights and design suggestions for speech-enabled ECAs within serious game environments. A within-subjects 2 × 2 factorial design was employed for this research with a cohort of 36 participants balanced for gender. The results showed that both the photorealistic and the animated versions were perceived as highly usable with overall mean scores of 5.76 and 5.71 respectively. However, 69.4% of participants stated they preferred the photorealistic version; 25% of participants stated they preferred the animated version; and 5.6% of participants had no stated preference. The photorealistic agents were perceived as more realistic and human-like while the animated characters made the task feel more like a game. Even though the agents' realism had no significant effect on usability, it positively influenced participants' perceptions of the agent. This research aims to lay the groundwork for future studies on the impact of ECA realism in serious games across diverse contexts.

Keywords: conversational user interfaces · speech interaction · multimodal interaction · embodied conversational agents · serious games · user experience · realism · human-centered AI

1 Introduction

There are two information processors in human-computer interaction (HCI): a computer and a human. These two entities communicate with each other through a constrained interface. Understanding and studying the design of this interface is crucial for overcoming its inherent limitations [1].

Conversational user interfaces (CUIs) are one of the modes of interaction that can be employed in HCI. Recent technological developments in artificial intelligence (AI) and the increasing popularity of voice assistants such as Google Home and Amazon Echo, have sparked a growing interest in conversational user interfaces (CUIs) [2]. Embodied conversational agents (ECAs) are CUI paradigms in the form of virtual characters

© The Author(s), under exclusive license to Springer Nature Switzerland AG 2023
J. Y. C. Chen et al. (Eds.): HCII 2023, LNCS 14058, pp. 317–335, 2023.
https://doi.org/10.1007/978-3-031-48050-8_22

designed to emulate human-to-human interaction using a combination of verbal and non-verbal communication [3]. In this paper's study, the focus lies on the utilization of speech-enabled ECAs.

Previous work has shown that the interaction with spoken dialogue systems, either in the form of an embodied agent or not, is still inferior to other approaches that allow direct manipulation, despite the theoretical advances of ECAs and dialogue systems [4]. The reasons for the reluctance of using ECAs in multimodal HCI are multi-fold. On the human side of the interaction, when communicating audio-visually via speech people convey extra-linguistic information instinctively. In HCI this information that works complementary to speech is not reliably communicated since machines are usually not able to interpret and extract this type of information. On the machine side of the interaction, current technology is still somewhat limited to generating extra-linguistic information the way humans do. Furthermore, such attempts are not always interpreted correctly by users [3, 4].

Considering the factors mentioned earlier, the evaluation of these ECAs still poses several challenges, especially within the encompassing design process that entails prototyping and testing. Designing ECAs is a time-consuming task that involves multidisciplinary fields such as human-computer interaction (HCI), computer science, behavioral science, psychology, and linguistics [3]. This paper aims to shed light on these interaction paradigms by evaluating the design of speech-enabled ECAs in the context of a serious game application and providing insights based on both quantitative and qualitative data and observations.

1.1 Embodied Conversational Agents, Their Roles, and Characteristics

Embodied conversational agents, as they exist today, are the outcome of various interdisciplinary fields. The specific disciplines involved in the development of each ECA vary depending on its functionalities and modes of interaction. For instance, an ECA utilizing speech input requires speech recognition and speech-to-text technology, whereas ECAs with text input do not. Overall, ECAs inherently embody a multidisciplinary nature, as depicted in Fig. 1

There are many theoretical advantages regarding ECAs and spoken dialogue systems since they provide a more "natural interaction" [3, 8]. Their visual design has been deemed important beyond the aesthetic aspect of it [4].

Previous research has identified the possibilities of using ECAs for mission rehearsal training [5], for military leadership and cultural training [6, 7], as museum guides and in installations [8], as sales agents [9–11], as medical advisers [12, 13], as companions [14], e-commerce and finance [15–17], as TV-style presenters [18], for psychological support [19] and in various other roles [3].

Embodied conversational agents serve as animated pedagogical agents in a variety of roles [20–23] when used in an educational context. According to Kim and Baylor, [24], pedagogical agents have been found in four major roles: 1) an expert who provides information, 2) a mentor who advises, 3) a motivator who encourages, and 4) a companion who collaborates.

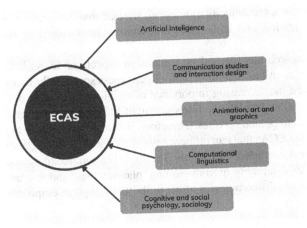

Fig. 1. Contributing disciplines to the field of ECAs

According to De Vos, [25], ECAs share the following five features: anthropomorphic appearance, virtual body that is used for communication purposes, natural communication protocols, multimodality, and a social role.

1.2 Embodied Conversational Agent Appearance

According to Nass [26], appearance influences people's cognitive assessments. According to Churchill et al. [27, 28], the character's appearance plays a significant role in naming which design aspects should be examined for situated conversational characters. Gulz and Haake [29] proposed five dimensions of agent look to be explored:

1. the degree or level of human likeness,
2. the degree of stability versus changeability in terms of appearance,
3. animation or movement versus static or immobility,
4. 2D or 3D visual rendering and
5. the degree of realism ranging from photorealism to stylized.

The presented study focuses on the fifth dimension of the degree of realism.

Although conducting a comprehensive review of the literature on ECA realism is beyond the scope of this paper, indicative previous research examining the level of ECA realism has provided mixed findings. In a study comparing two levels of pedagogical agent realism, specifically a cartoon-like animal and an anthropomorphic agent with a voice-only tutor as a control, no definitive advantage was found for the agents in terms of the learning effect. However, the results did show that the appearance of the agent does have an impact [30]. In another study looking at the design implications of a virtual learning companion robot, the participants preferred the robot-like appearance over the human-like agent [31]. Another study with three degrees of agent representation, computer vs. virtual vs. human agent, showed that participants' decision to trust the agent by adopting task-specific advice was not affected [32]. Finally, a research study on the effect of embodiment for a group facilitation agent, showed that the agent embodiment, non-verbal communication, and human-like face had an effect improving user perceptions [33].

Previous research has focused on the design aspects of ECAs but there are limited empirical evaluations regarding their effectiveness specifically focusing on serious games [3]. Given the increasing importance of usability in modern development processes, it is crucial to evaluate the introduction of ECAs in such environments. Failing to do so can lead to potential issues. Therefore, it is highly necessary to investigate the specific aspects of ECAs that can influence usability within serious game environments, surpassing current interaction paradigms. The study is a comparative evaluation between two design styles commonly used in gaming, photorealism, and animated design, and investigates how the different styles affect usability through an empirical study.

2 Research Question/hypothesis

The primary objective of this study is to examine how ECA design decisions affect the usability of a serious game application. Specifically, this experiment investigates user reactions to two versions of multimodal interaction with ECAs. One version contains photorealistic ECAs and the second contains animated ECAs. This experiment aims to present an examination of how and if ECAs' aesthetics affect the usability of the application.

3 Methodology

A user study was conducted to compare two ECA designs. The study aimed to compare the two ECA designs in terms of user preference and usability.

3.1 Participants

A cohort of 36 participants (18 females and 18 males; aged 18 to 40) was recruited to take part in the experiments. The participants were balanced for gender, version order, and shopping list order. Participants were selected from a list of bank customers who signed up for user studies. All participants were comfortable using a desktop computer. There were no prerequisites for taking part in the study. The only limitation was that participants had to be between 18 and 40 years of age. The age limit was calculated based on the context of the game (on pre-decimalized currency) that was used up until the 70s therefore, it is highly unlikely for someone under 40 years old to have used the old money system.

3.2 Apparatus

The experiment was conducted on a desktop computer. The interface was presented on a Dell Precision T3600 with NVIDIA Quadro K2000 3D vision Pro graphics card, a standard 24" PC monitor with a resolution of 2220×1080 pixels, and an Intel® Xeon® Processor E5–1603, 10M Cache, 2.80 GHz, 0.0 GT/s Intel® QPI processor.

The software was developed using Unity. The overall application was not specifically designed for the evaluations reported in this paper, but the different ECA designs were designed specifically for the study.

The game that was used is called Moneyworld. Moneyworld is a computer-based game where the player is asked to travel back in time and use the pre-decimal money system to purchase a list of items in a corner store back in the 60 s. All the transactions need to be made by using the following pre-decimal coins: penny, threepence, sixpence, shilling, and florin. The scene is composed of the corner store, the shopkeeper with whom the player interacts to buy the items that Alex dictates, Alex on the top right corner, and on the left side is the inventory of the items purchased and the rewards system. When asked to pay for the items, the screen fades to dark and the user is presented with the coins (Figs. 2 and 3).

Fig. 2. Store scene with photorealistic Alex

Fig. 3. Photorealistic shopkeeper with the inventory and coins

3.3 Procedure

The experiment was conducted in a dedicated laboratory setting within the university.

Participants were welcomed and informed of the purpose of the study. The experiment session lasted approximately 45 min. After experiencing each version, participants completed a set of 7-point Likert scale usability questions as well as an exit interview to explore issues raised in the experiment. The usability questionnaire used in this evaluation is the CCIR MINERVA usability questionnaire, a standardized and validated metric for assessing usability with 18 usability statements [34].

The first scene of the game introduces the participant to Moneyworld and a tutorial introducing the old money system used throughout the game. The tutorial is introduced by a disembodied voice and the agent is not present, as the tutorial is the same for both versions and experienced once at the beginning of the session to avoid overexposure to one style over the other. After the tutorial, the game starts with a small introduction to the gameplay delivered by Alex the instructor. The gameplay is straightforward, the player is asked by Alex to buy a list of items one at a time from the shopkeeper. For each item, the player is rewarded with points and stars. The reward system is based on the evaluation of correct payment, no help required (ex. Ask twice for the money), and using as fewer coins as possible in the transaction.

3.4 Experimental Design

We used a 2 × 2 within-subjects factorial design with the following independent variables and levels:

- ECA design: Photorealistic, Animated
- Shopping list: Shopping list 1, Shopping list 2 (different shopping lists were used to avoid overexposure but no hypothesis was attached to them)

The dependent variables were the usability questionnaire and the explicit preferences. Each participant experienced both versions and was counterbalanced using a Latin square method (Table 1). In this study, a mixed methods approach was used with a combination of qualitative and quantitative research methods.

Table 1. Latin square for 2 × 2 factorial design

2 × 2 Design		ECA Design	
		Photorealistic	Animated
Shopping list	1	P1	A1
	2	P2	A2

The participants were allocated randomly into equal and balanced groups with all group subjects experiencing both design options.

In the photorealistic version (Figs. 4 and 5), the user experienced and interacted with photorealistic ECAs. The photorealistic style is used to simulate reality in a way that is believable to the user. This kind of style is mainly used for real-life simulations and immersive entertainment games [35].

Fig. 4. Photorealistic shopkeeper

Fig. 5. Photorealistic Alex

In the animated version (Figs. 6 and 7), the user experienced and interacted with animated ECAs. The animated style is based on our ability as humans to interpret abstraction quickly and effectively [36]. The animated style has been used in numerous games and gives the notion that we are not in the real world; therefore, we are not bound by its rules. The animated version was designed using the masking effect. The concept of the masking effect entails depicting characters in a stylized manner while maintaining a realistic background. Disney has successfully employed this technique for many years, achieving remarkable results in terms of character engagement [29].

Fig. 6. Animated shopkeeper

Fig. 7. Animated Alex

4   Results/Findings

4.1   Quantitative Results

Usability Results. An overall mean usability score was calculated from the 18 usability attribute scores for each of the two treatment groups. Overall mean scores for the questionnaire taken did not differ between the two versions. After detecting and treating the data for outliers, the overall mean for the Photorealistic version was 5.76, indicating a positive attitude toward the application. The mean score for the Animated version was similar at 5.71.

A repeated-measures ANOVA with *version* as the within-subjects factor, and *gender*, version order (*v-order*), and shopping list order (*list-order*) as between-subjects factors showed that the difference in mean attitude score was not significant. Figure 8 shows the scores for each of the 18 usability attributes for each version (PH = photorealistic, AN = animated).

To examine any differences between the two versions for each of the individual attributes on the questionnaire, a repeated measures ANOVA was run on the mean

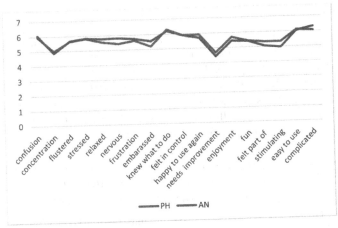

Fig. 8. Usability attributes for both versions

scores; the version was the within-participants factor and the order of participation was the between-participants factor. None were found to yield significant results. There were, however, significant interactions between the versions and the order that the versions were experienced for usability statement No 2 "I had to concentrate hard to use Money-world." ($p = 0.007$). This result signifies that the participant concentration levels were dependent on the order they experienced it. More specifically, this result indicates that men felt they had to concentrate significantly more when using the animated version compared to the photorealistic one while women rated the two versions similarly on this issue (Fig. 9).

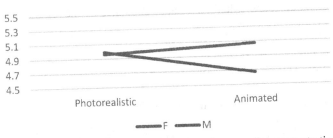

Fig. 9. Interaction between version and gender regarding concentration

4.2 Qualitative Results

After experiencing each version, participants were asked to comment on their experience with the application and then specifically on each version they experienced. The exit interview consisted of both open and closed questions.

The overall perception of the tutorial was positive with 91.7% finding it helpful. It was mentioned in the comments that the tutorial was clearly explained and informative as they learned a lot about old money. Following the tutorial, 97.2% felt they understood the old money. When asked about the voice introducing the tutorial, all comments were positive. Even though this was an open question, the answers were organized and analyzed for recurring themes. In terms of what participants liked in the voice used in the tutorial, 16 responded that the voice was well-paced and clear; 10 mentioned it was friendly, welcoming, and pleasant, and the rest that the voice was good and fine.

Shopkeeper. During the exit interview, participants were asked "What did you think of the shopkeeper". An initial sentiment analysis was performed that was then followed by manual annotation and qualitative analysis to validate and refine the results obtained from sentiment analysis. Regarding the photorealistic shopkeeper, 19 participants had a positive impression based on their comments on the human characteristics of the ECA, saying that he was realistic, funny, polite, friendly, and kind which prompted them to be polite when talking to him. Some of their comments were:

- "Very realistic, smartly dressed. Makes you feel engaged as part of the shop."
- "Good character, naturally warm, he made me want to be polite as I would be to an elderly person."

Nine participants had neutral opinions about the shopkeeper saying he was fine or ok with comments like:

- "Eyebrows were funny, but it was OK in general."

Lastly, 8 participants made negative comments about the ECA, saying that he was creepy, strange looking, and stilted; this can be explained by the uncanny valley theory. Some of their comments were:

- "He was ok but a bit creepy looking."
- "Pretty creepy. More realistic but unappealing."

Participants were also asked their opinion about the animated shopkeeper. Based on the positive comments (7), the animated shopkeeper was funnier and more stylized which made the participants have less expectations of him with comments like:

- "Much more stylized, you know it is not real because of the exaggerated features. More successful because you know it is not real. Better facial expressions."

The neutral comments (12) were mostly about the basic and avatar-like graphics. Some of the comments were:

- "Short of standard computer graphic"
- "Basic graphic, clearly non-human"

Finally, negative comments (17) were mostly about the ECAs' proportions, cartoon-like appearance, and unpleasant disposition. A few of the comments were:

- "He looks like a puppet with a big head."
- "Quite scary, cartoony, and weird looking."

Figure 10 demonstrates the different sentiments between the two shopkeeper versions.

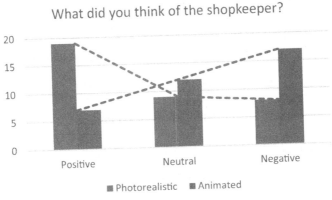

Fig. 10. Comparison of participant comments between the two shopkeeper versions

Instructor. Participants were asked about the two instructor versions as well. Regarding the photorealistic instructor, most comments were positive with 17 participants reporting that they felt she was friendlier and more realistic. Some of the positive comments were:

- "Much more human looking and friendlier."
- "Very real looking, I took information from her more seriously than the other one."

The neutral comments (13) had to do with the fact that they did not interact with her directly and did not pay too much attention to her. An example comment follows:

- "Neutral, not involved in the learning process she was the instructor."
- "Didn't mind her in either version."

The negative comments (6) had to do with the lip-synching that was off and that she looked a bit robotic. A few of these comments were:

- "Felt a bit robotic, not as realistic as the shopkeeper."

- "Fine but the mouth didn't move as it was meant to."

When asked about the animated instructor, the positive comments (8) had to do with her pleasant cartoon-like appearance and the exaggerated features that made it easier to follow what she was saying. Some of the comments were:

- "Easier to watch than the first cause facial features were more eccentric."
- "It was a non-human computer-generated face but pleasant nonetheless."

The neutral comments (5) were mostly about how they did not pay as much attention to her as her role was not as interactive as the shopkeeper. One comment was:

- "I didn't notice much difference between the first and the second."

The negative comments (4) had to do with her exaggerated features that made her robotic, her face did not add to the experience or was off-putting. Some negative comments were:

- "Distracting. Doesn't look like a person."
- "Very cartoon-looking and unnatural. Maybe good for kids"

Figure 11 demonstrates the different sentiments between the two instructor versions.

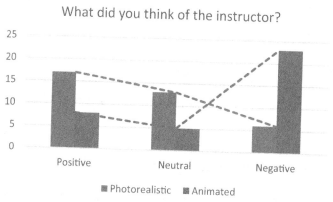

Fig. 11. Comparison of participant comments between the two instructor versions

4.3 Explicit Preference

Finally, participants were asked which version of Moneyworld they preferred. Participants were asked to give their answers in terms of their first or second version experienced, and the answers were re-ordered for each version. Twenty-five out of thirty-six participants (69.4%) preferred the photorealistic version while 9 (25%) preferred the animated one and 2 (5.6%) had no preference (Fig. 12).

Participants were asked to elaborate on their answers. The reasons for those who preferred the Photorealistic version were realism (10), better graphics (8), more engaging (4), more approachable and friendly (3), human-like (3), and clearer (2). Some sample comments made by participants are:

- "Felt more engaging cause the characters looked more realistic, I found it less distracting."
- "The human face makes it more approachable."
- "Felt more engaging cause the characters looked more realistic, I found it less distracting."

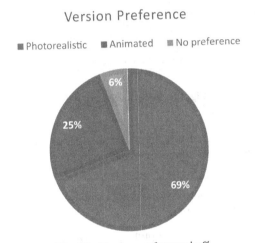

Fig. 12. Version preference in %

The participants who preferred the animated version justified their preference by saying that the photorealistic characters were too real and creepy (5), or they preferred the animated characters better (4). Some sample comments made by participants are:

- "Didn't feel like a test because the characters were cartoon-like."
- "Less creepy and wasn't as frustrating."
- "I preferred the look of the animated character. The first ones (photorealistic) were old, too realistic, and disconcerting. The second one fitted better with the game."

The participants were also asked which set of agents they preferred. Twenty-eight (77.8%) chose the Photorealistic agents, 7 (19.4%) the Animated agents and 1 (2.8%) had no preference (Fig. 13). The Photorealistic agents were preferred due to their realism (7), better graphics (5), human-likeness (3), expressiveness (3), natural interaction, especially when using speech interaction (3), engagement (2), friendliness, personality, trust and interactivity (1). Some sample comments made by participants are:

- "More engaging, didn't feel as silly talking to realistic people."

- "Liked talking to a person rather than a cartoon."
- "See people's emotions is better and fitted better with the game."

Agent Preference

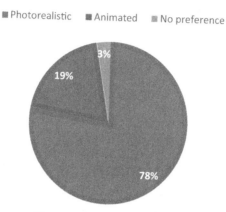

Fig. 13. Agent preference in %

Three people who preferred the Animated version stated that they preferred the Photorealistic characters. Their comments were:

- "You trust the realistic one more."
- "The cartoon was funnier, but I felt like I got it right with the human."
- "Bit more human. Not as creepy."

Participants justified their choice of preferring to interact with the Animated agents by stating that it was more like a game (3), more fun, and more relaxing. Some of their comments were:

- "They are characters that don't look like real people. That's the point of playing a game."
- "Polite and didn't like the photo real one in comparison. Meant to be on a computer so you expect to see computerized people more."

Only one person who preferred the Photorealistic version liked the Animated characters better and their comment was:

- "Look more fun and playful."

Regarding the agents' voices, participants were asked if they believed that the voice matched the appearance of the agent. Even though both Photorealistic and Animated agents had the same animations and voices (real actor recordings), participants stated that the voice matched the Photorealistic agents more than the Animated ones as shown in Fig. 14.

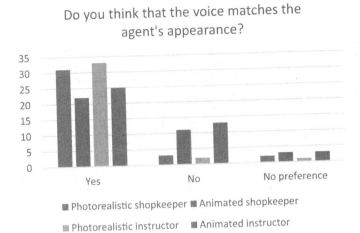

Fig. 14. Voice-visual perception

5 Discussion and Limitations

The selection of agents for the photorealistic version was based on their realism. However, it is important to acknowledge the limitations of this academic project in terms of funding, technology, and expertise, which prevented the creation of hyper-realistic industrial game characters. Despite these limitations, participants still perceived the photorealistic agents as human-like and realistic, as evident from their comments. Furthermore, the limitations mentioned above also imposed a constraint on the animations, specifically the synchronization of lip movements. This aspect influenced the participants' perception of the agents and led to various effects, which will be explored and discussed in detail later in the section.

The quantitative data did not reveal a significant usability difference between the two versions with scores that suggested a relatively positive evaluation of usability for both. Regardless, there was an interesting effect between gender and version when it came to concentration levels which can be explored further in the future.

The analysis of qualitative data provided valuable insights into participants' preferences. While some participants found both the animated and photorealistic shopkeepers to be "creepy", there was a higher level of anticipation and expectations associated with the shopkeeper that had a realistic appearance. This phenomenon can be explained by the uncanny valley theory [37] which is a common risk when developing human-like interfaces. Many comments associated the animation of facial features, eyebrows, and lip-synching, with this feeling of uneasiness. According to Gratch [37], gesturing without any facial expression can look peculiar and vice versa. The same is true for the movement of hands without any involvement of the torso. Moreover, facial expressions should accomplish any attempts of emotions because, otherwise, the lack of facial involvement could detract from the expected result even if the character's speech and gestures are synched [37]. Saygin et al. [38] derived the conclusion that the effect can be based on perceptual mismatch where ultra-realistic human-like robots are expected to behave in an equally realistic human-like way. Therefore, the strength of the effect relies on how high the expectation is [4].

Overall, the photorealistic agents were perceived as friendlier, realistic, and engaging highlighting that the human-like characteristics of the ECA made that version appealing to the participants. An interesting observation is that even though both versions had the same animations and voices, most participants stated that the voices matched the photorealistic agents better. This could be because the voices were actor recordings and not computer generated thus finding the more realistic-looking ECAs as a better fit.

Another noteworthy aspect was the effect of speech interaction with the ECAs. Several comments indicated that participants felt a greater sense of naturalness when engaging in conversation with a realistic, human-like character. This preference can be attributed to the familiarity with speech interaction in human-to-human communication. Consequently, participants tended to gravitate more towards realistic agents when replicating this form of communication as it enhances the sense of authenticity and relatability in human-computer interactions. This could be explained by the media equation theory [39, 40] and the illusion of humanness effect [3]. The media equation theory implies that people tend to interact with computers and media in an inherently social way [39]. Reeves and Nass [40] demonstrated that interactions between humans and agents exhibit comparable fundamental patterns to those observed in human-to-human interactions [29]. An extension of the media equation is the illusion of humanness. The illusion of humanness is defined as the user's involuntary reaction to a humanoid and anthropomorphic interface which gives them the perception that the system possesses human attributes and/or cognitive functions [3]. Essentially, as the agent's realism increases, so do the social and cognitive expectations placed upon it, an effect that was observed in this study as well.

6　Summary and Conclusions

In conclusion, this study provides empirical data on the effect of design styles of ECAs within serious games. It contributes to the ECA literature by providing insights into the role of aesthetics in user interaction with serious games. It also offers design suggestions for ECAs within serious games by shedding light on the preferences and experiences of users when interacting with photorealistic and animated ECAs. A 2 × 2 within-subjects factorial design was utilized with participants experiencing both conditions. While the quantitative results indicated that there were no significant differences in the overall usability scores, qualitative findings offered valuable insights into the way participants perceived the ECAs. Comments on the photorealistic shopkeepers were mostly positive due to their realism, human likeness, and engagement despite the uncanny feelings evoked due to the animation. On the other hand, the animated shopkeeper was praised for its funny and stylized appearance but also received negative comments on its disproportionate features and cartoon-like appearance. Regarding the instructors, the photorealistic version was perceived as more friendly and realistic, while the animated version received mixed comments on its cartoon-like appearance and exaggerated features.

Overall, the results of the comparative evaluation of animated versus photorealistic ECAs in a serious game generate insights into best practices for designing ECAs in serious game applications. These results indicate that the visual appearance of ECAs can impact user preferences, with photorealistic agents generating more favorable reactions among participants. However, these preferences may not lead to significant variations in the overall usability of the agents. Nonetheless, while the results indicated a preference for photorealistic ECAs in serious games, ECAs should be evaluated in various contexts to establish this effect. This research aims to lay the groundwork for future investigations into the impacts of ECA realism in serious games across diverse contexts.

Acknowledgments. I would like to thank Dr. Nancy Gunson, Dr. Hazel Morton, Professor Mervyn Jack, and Dr. Simon Doolin for their invaluable input and assistance. This research was funded by Lloyds TSB.

References

1. Perez-Marin, D., Pascual-Nieto, I. (eds.): Conversational Agents and Natural Language Interaction: Techniques and Effective Practices. IGI Global (2011). https://doi.org/10.4018/978-1-60960-617-6
2. Li, Z., Xu, Y.: Designing a realistic peer-like embodied conversational agent for supporting children's storytelling. In: Proceedings of the CHI Workshop on Child-centered AI Design: Definition, Operation and Considerations, Apr. 23, Hamburg, Germany, pp. 1–10. ACM, New York, NY, USA (2023)
3. Korre, D.: Usability evaluation of spoken humanoid embodied conversational agents in mobile serious games, Ph. D thesis (2019)
4. Weiss, B., Wechsung, I., Kühnel, C., Möller, S.: Evaluating embodied conversational agents in multimodal interfaces. Comput. Cogn. Sci. 1(6), 1–21 (2015)
5. Hill, R., et al.: Virtual humans in the mission rehearsal exercise system. Künstliche Intelligenz (KI Journal), Special issue on Embodied Conversational Agents 17(4), 5–10 (2003)
6. McCollum, C., et al.: Developing an immersive, cultural training system. In: Proceedings of the Interservice/Industry Training, Simulation, and Education, pp. 1–2. National Training Systems Association (2004)
7. Raybourn, E., et al.: "Adaptive thinking & leadership simulation game training for special forces officers." ("[pdf] adaptive thinking & leadership simulation game training for ...") In: Proceedings of the Interservice/Industry Training, Simulation, and Education Conference, pp. 1–10. Orlando, FL (2005)
8. Kopp, S., Gesellensetter, L., Krämer, N.C., Wachsmuth, I.: A conversational agent as museum guide – design and evaluation of a real-world application. In: Panayiotopoulos, T., Gratch, J., Aylett, R., Ballin, D., Olivier, P., Rist, T. (eds.) IVA 2005. LNCS (LNAI), vol. 3661, pp. 329–343. Springer, Heidelberg (2005). https://doi.org/10.1007/11550617_28
9. Andre, E., et al.: "The automated design of believable dialogues for animated presentation teams." ("the automated design of believable dialogues for animated ... - CORE") In: Cassell, J. (ed.) Embodied Conversational Agents, pp. 220–255. MIT Press (2000)
10. Cassell, J., Stone, M.: Living hand to mouth: psychological theories about speech and gesture in interactive dialogue systems. In: Proceedings of the AAAI Fall symposium 1999, pp. 34–42 (1999)
11. Hayes-Roth, B.: Jennifer James, celebrity auto spokesperson. In: SIGGRAPH 1998 ACM SIGGRAPH 98 Conference abstracts and applications, pp. 1–6. Orlando, Florida, USA (1998)

12. Pelachaud, C., De Carolis, B., de Rosis, F., Poggi, I.: Embodied contextual agent in information delivering application. In: Proceedings of the First International Joint Conference on Autonomous Agents and Multi-agent Systems, pp. 758–765. ACM Press (2002)
13. Poggi, I., Pelachaud, C., de Rosis, F., Carofiglio, V., De Carolis, B.: Greta. a believable embodied conversational agent. In: Stock, O., Zancanaro, M. (eds.) Multimodal Intelligent Information Presentation, pp. 3–25. Springer Netherlands, Dordrecht (2005). https://doi.org/10.1007/1-4020-3051-7_1
14. Cavazza, M., et al.: 'How was your day?': an affective companion ECA prototype. In: Proceedings of the 11th Annual Meeting of the Special Interest Group. Collin, S., Jack, M. & Anderson, J., 2004. "A comparison of the effectiveness of single and multiple 3D embodied synthetic agents in eBanking." ("S. Collin | Semantic Scholar") In: Proceedings of Third International Conference on Intelligent Agents, Web Technology, and Internet Commerce (IAWTIC 2004), s.l.: s.n., pp. 564–575 (2010)
15. Matthews, A., Anderson, N., Anderson, J., Jack, M.: Individualised product portrayals in the usability of a 3D embodied conversational agent in an eBanking scenario. In: Prendinger, H., Lester, J., Ishizuka, M. (eds.) Intelligent Virtual Agents, pp. 516–517. Springer Berlin Heidelberg, Berlin, Heidelberg (2008). https://doi.org/10.1007/978-3-540-85483-8_67
16. Foo, N., Douglas, G., Jack, M.: Incentive schemes in the financial services sector: moderating effects of relationship norms on customer-brand relationship. Int. J. Bank Mark. 26(2), 99–118 (2008)
17. Noma, T., Zhao, L., Badler, N.I.: Design of a virtual human presenter. IEEE Comput. Graphics Appl. 20(4), 79–85 (2000)
18. Hayes-Roth, B., Amano, K., Saker, R., Sephton, T.: Training brief intervention with a virtual coach and virtual patients. In W. BK & R. G. (Eds.), Annual Review of CyberTherapy and Telemedicine, pp. 85–96. Interactive Media Institute (2004)
19. Andre, E., et al.: The automated design of believable dialogues for animated presentation teams. In: Cassell, J. (ed.) Embodied Conversational Agents, pp. 220–255. MIT Press (2000)
20. Lester, J., et al.: The persona effect: affective impact of animated pedagogical agents. In: Proceedings of the Human Factors in Computing Systems Conference, pp. 359–366. ACM Press (1997)
21. Moreno, R., Mayer, R., Spires, H.: The case for social agency in computer-based teaching: do students learn more deeply when they interact with animated pedagogical agents? Cogn. Instr. 19, 177–213 (2001)
22. Moundridou, M., Virvou, M.: Evaluating the persona effect of an interface agent in an intelligent tutoring system. J. Comput. Assist. Learn. 18(3), 253–261 (2002)
23. Kim, C., Baylor, A.: A virtual change agent: motivating pre-service teachers to integrate technology in their future classrooms. Educ. Technol. Soc. 11(2), 309–321 (2008)
24. De Vos, E.: Look at that doggy in my windows, Ph. D. thesis, Utrecht University (2002)
25. Nass, C., Moon, Y.: Machines and Mindlessness: Social Responses to Computers. Soc. Psychol. Study Soc. Issues 56(1), 81–103 (2000)
26. Churchill, E., et al.: Design issues for situated conversational characters. In: Proceedings of the 1st Workshop on Embodied Conversational Characters (WECC 1998), pp. 149–158. AAAI and ACM (1998)
27. Churchill, E., et al.: "May I help you?": Designing Embodied Conversational Agent Allies, MIT Press, (2000)
28. Gulz, A., Haake, M.: Design of animated pedagogical agents–a look at their look. Int. J. Hum. Comput. Stud. 64(4), 322–339 (2006)
29. Sträfling, N., et al.: Teaching learning strategies with a pedagogical agent: the effects of a virtual tutor and its appearance on learning and motivation. J. Media Psychol. Theor. Methods Appl. 22(2), 73–83 (2010)

30. Ahmed, E., Ahtinen, A.: Design implications for a virtual language learning companion robot: considering the appearance, interaction, and rewarding behavior. In: Proceedings of the 9th International Conference on Human-Agent Interaction (HAI 2021), pp. 56–65. Association for Computing Machinery (2021)

31. Kulms, P., Kopp, S.: More human-likeness, more trust? the effect of anthropomorphism on self-reported and behavioral trust in continued and interdependent human-agent cooperation. In: Proceedings of Mensch und Computer 2019 (MuC'19), pp. 31–42. Association for Computing Machinery (2019)

32. Shamekhi, A., et al.: Face value? exploring the effects of embodiment for a group facilitation agent. In: Proceedings of the 2018 CHI Conference on Human Factors in Computing Systems (CHI 2018) (Paper 391), pp. 1–13. Association for Computing Machinery (2018)

33. Jack, M.A., Foster, J.C., Stentiford, F.W.M.: Usability analysis of intelligent dialogues for automated telephone services. Applications of Speech Technology (1993)

34. IEEE Research: How Photorealistic Should a Virtual Human Be? (2016). https://innovate.ieee.org/innovation-spotlight/humanizing-vr-part-3-how-photorealistic-should-a-3d-virtual-human-be/

35. Lakoff, G., Johnson, M.: Metaphors we live by. University of Chicago Press (2003)

36. Mori, M.: The uncanny valley. Energy 7(4), 33–35 (1970). (In Japanese)

37. Gratch, J., Hartholt, A., Dehghani, M., Marsella, S.: Virtual humans: a new toolkit for cognitive science research. In: Proceedings of the Annual Meeting of the Cognitive Science Society, p. 35 (2013)

38. Saygin, A.P., et al.: The thing that should not be predictive coding and the uncanny valley in perceiving human and humanoid robot actions. Soc. Cogn. Affect. Neurosci. 7(4), 413–422 (2011)

39. Nass, C., Moon, Y.: Machines and mindlessness: social responses to computers. J. Soc. Issues 56, 81–103 (2000)

40. Reeves, B., Nass, C.: The Media Equation: How People Treat Computers, Television, and New Media Like Real People and Places. Bibliovault OAI Repository, The University of Chicago Press (1996)

From Teams to Games: Connecting Game Development to Game Characteristics

Emil Lundedal Hammar[1]([⊠]), Alessandro Canossa[1], Michael S. Debus[2],
Johannes Pfau[3], Magy Seif El-Nasr[3], Jesper Juul[1], and Ahmad Azadvar[4]

[1] Royal Danish Academy of Fine Arts, Copenhagen, Denmark
eham@kglakademi.dk
[2] Copenhagen, Denmark
[3] University of California at Santa Cruz, Santa Cruz, CA 95064, USA
[4] Massive Entertainment, Malmö, Sweden

Abstract. The objective of this paper is to explore potential associations between development teams and the characteristics of the games they produce. Through a production study of Danish game companies and a design analysis of their games, we propose that there are statistically significant associations between features of the game and the team that produced them. The game features that we selected for this analysis refer to the game structure, the relations between players, the tone, and controls, whereas the team composition consists of the demographics of game professionals and approaches to concept generation.

Keywords: Computer games · Design tools/technologies · Development methodology · Digital games/Online games · Game improvement · Games and Society · Gender and games · Interaction design of games · Video games · game production studies

1 Significance

The paper is motivated by studies into how the characteristics of game companies result in (un)successful game products [1–3]. Using a bottom-up approach to our collected data on game development teams, we defined 6 categorical features describing the games and 8 categorical features characterizing the developers. The categories were selected for statistical significance from a long list of features collected through interviews from 42 game development teams in 2021–22 (see "Methods" section). Subsequently we estimated the measure of how strongly these 2 groups of features are associated.

Because games as played processes are in large part predisposed by the game structure [4] and the game structure is encoded through production [5], then production contexts are important to the kinds of games being made and how they influence player experiences [6, 7]. Our research bridges the recent advancements of game production studies [8, 9], game design [10], and ontological approaches to games [11–13] through an analysis of the effect size of associations between variables describing game companies and their products to explore the dynamics between creator, artifact, and user.

M. S. Debus—Independent Researcher.

© The Author(s), under exclusive license to Springer Nature Switzerland AG 2023
J. Y. C. Chen et al. (Eds.): HCII 2023, LNCS 14058, pp. 336–340, 2023.
https://doi.org/10.1007/978-3-031-48050-8_23

2 Methods

In 2021–22, we interviewed and analyzed 42 Danish game companies on how they operated internally, and we conducted game analysis of their released games (N = 142) [3]. The qualitative and quantitative data was analyzed and inserted into 201 different frames through a grounded theory approach [14, 15]. These 201 frames were more broadly divided into company information, business metrics, success assessment, production evaluation & creative processes, while the analysis of each company's released game products was divided into design analysis and product analysis. Out of these broader categories, we selected the features that directly related to player experience in the game (game structure, fiction/tone, play setting, player relation, controls) – leaving out meta-information, for example distribution platform, or release year – and the most heavily populated business metrics that involved team composition (age, gender, nationality, parenthood, survival index) and production methods (concept generation). The frames that showed a correlation were the following:

2.1 Game Features

- **Play setting**: The type of settings in which players were able to play alone or with each other. The subcategories were solo, social / local multiplayer, online multiplayer, or MMO.
- **Player relation**: How players are positioned to each other with the options of being either single- (solo play by oneself) or multiplayer (FFA, 1vs1, team vs team, cooperative play). While using popular terminology, "Player Relation" refers to an "Operator Positions" (Debus, 2019). This means that a racing game with bots will be tagged "FFA" as long as the positions could theoretically be filled by humans
- **Fiction / tone**: The game's 'valence' that refers to "whether an emotion inclines you to approach something or to avoid it" [13].
- **Emergence vs progression**: This refers to the types of game structure where progression has players "[…] perform a predefined set of actions in order to complete the game", whereas emergence "[…] is the primordial game structure where a game is specified as a small number of rules that combine and yield large numbers of game variations." [13]. It is possible for games to contain both forms, which we also accounted for in our data categorization with a mixed label.

2.2 Production Method and Team Composition

- **Concept generation**: How game producers develop their design concepts that players play either through horizontal or vertical incorporation of the company's professionals. Horizontal is when design ideas and game concepts by all professionals within the studio are considered and analyzed for a potential next game product. Vertical is when the design ideas and concepts for the next game product is hierarchical and entirely decided on by those in the upper echelons of the company.
- **Age of the game professionals**: Here we inquired into the age demographics of the companies in question with a segmentation of 20–29/30–39/40–49/ + 50 of age groupings in percent of the company at the time of the interview.

- **Nationality of game professionals**: The percentage of game professionals who are of native nationality and how many are non-native within the company at the time of interview.
- **Male composition of game professionals**: The overall male gender percentage within the company at the time of interview.
- **Parenthood of game professionals**: The percentage of game professionals who had children within the company time of interview.

The variables were all quantified as either ordinal categorical data, that is non-numerical pieces of information with implied order (i.e. survival index) or nominal categorical data for the total amount of cases (N = 142), that is non-numerical pieces of information without any inherent order (game structure). Since all our variables are categorical, we adopted Cramér's V [16] as an effect size measure of the strength of association between two variables.

We conducted 53 tests in total. In order to rule out type 1 errors and false positives when conducting multiple comparisons, we applied the "False Discovery Rate" [17]. This method is better suited for the task than the Bonferroni correction as it does not simply multiply the threshold for every p-value, but instead it is based on the expected rate of false positives and it ranks results, so only the weakest results are discarded in the end. This procedure returns 17 significant results.

Cramér's V can only tell us the association, not the direction. So the data in Table 1 does not allow to draw conclusions like "lower parenthood is associated with lower user scores", because it could also be that "lower parenthood is associated with higher user scores". Typically, the effect size of Cramer's V is considered weak if lower than 0.2, moderate between 0.2 and 0.6 and strong if above 0.6, which we then filtered into Table 1 below.

Table 1. Strength of association with Cramer V value = > 0.2 and significance = < 0.05

Production	Game artifact	Cramer's V	Valid Data Points
Parenthood	User Score	0,718	51
Nationality %	Play Setting	0,634	54
Age 30–39%	Player Relation	0,572	91
Age 30–39%	Game Structure	0,554	92
Age 40–49%	Player Relation	0,538	91
Age 30–39%	Play Setting	0,529	97
Age 20–29%	Play Setting	0,527	97
Age 20–29%	Player Relation	0,514	91
Age 30–39%	Controls	0,509	89
Age 20–29%	Game Structure	0,508	92

(continued)

Table 1. (*continued*)

Production	Game artifact	Cramer's V	Valid Data Points
Age 40–49%	Play Setting	0,483	97
Age 40–49%	Game Structure	0,473	92
Age 40–49%	Controls	0,45	89
Parenthood	Play Setting	0,385	94
Concept Generation	Game Structure	0,339	79
Concept Generation	Player Relation	0,326	78
Parenthood	Controls	0,305	86

3 Discussion

Through these values we test the first hypothesis that specific types of concept generation are associated with specific game designs. Our analysis shows that if a game company's approach to concept generation is horizontal, then it has a larger association with solo game experiences. If the approach is vertical, then there is an equal association with both solo and free-for-all experiences. Regarding a game's structure, horizontal approaches to concept generation are associated with games of progression, while a vertical approach has an equal chance for both. This means that vertical teams are more commonly associated with games of emergence than horizontal teams. Furthermore, the association between horizontal concept generation and solo experiences and games of progression is unsurprising to the authors. Games of emergence are the older of the two structures, while games of progression are the newer structure that gained popularity especially with the invention of digital – and especially adventure – games [13]. Games of emergence are, historically, especially linked with card games, board games and sports – all of them often multiplayer. Our data indicates a connection between games of progression and solo experiences through their similarity in association.

Our second hypothesis that teams with a high percentage of national developers may be tied to more social settings due to both being comfortable with intra-group interactions and being less sensitive to different kinds of players proved true. Our data analysis showed that game companies with higher percentages of nationals are associated with producing free-for-all types of games that are more socially oriented, whereas companies with a higher number of foreign professionals are associated with solo experiences.

Our third hypothesis claimed that having children may make developers more interested in creating games for audiences other than themselves, and specifically games of progression. Our analysis showed that the teams with a high number of parents are associated with positive reception, touch controls as typically seen on smartphones and haptic controllers like the Playstation Move, and games of progression. Those with zero or low amounts of parenthood were associated with lower user scores and use of virtual reality headset. We did not test for non-violent content aimed at children.

These are some of the examples of the results from our data analysis and testing of hypotheses. It should be noted that our study is limited by grounding our hypotheses from our methods, as there is a limit to how much we are able to infer from our methods. Future work could potentially fix this limitation by conducting more research on precisely the relation between game development teams and the games themselves. Nevertheless, our work identifies some of the associations across production and game artifacts and we tested possible interpretations of the reasons behind these associations. Future work, such as the use of support vector machines, could help unpack the nature of these relations between production and game.

References

1. Paul, T.: The intelligence engine: game outcomes project methodology. The intelligence engine (blog) (2014). https://intelligenceengine.blogspot.com/2014/11/game-outcomes-project-methodology-in.html. Accessed 16 Apr 2023
2. Aleem, S., Capretz, L.F., Ahmed, F.: Critical success factors to improve the game development process from a developer's perspective. J. Comput. Sci. Technol. **31**(5), 925–950 (2016). https://doi.org/10.1007/s11390-016-1673-z
3. Pfau, J., Debus, M., Juul, J., Hammar, E.L., Canossa, A., El-Nasr, M.S.: Predicting success factors of video game titles and companies. In: Göbl, B., van der Spek, E., Hauge, J.B., McCall, R. (eds.) Entertainment Computing – ICEC 2022: 21st IFIP TC 14 International Conference, ICEC 2022, Bremen, Germany, November 1–3, 2022, Proceedings, pp. 269–282. Springer, Cham (2022). https://doi.org/10.1007/978-3-031-20212-4_22
4. Debus, Michael S., Grabarczyk, P.: What's important to a game?: adding a hierarchy to the cybermedia model (2017)
5. Hammar, E.L.: Producing & playing hegemonic pasts: historical digital games as memory-making media, Doctoral thesis, UiT Arctic University of Tromsø (2020). https://munin.uit.no/handle/10037/17717
6. Hammar, E.L., Pötzsch, H.: Bringing the Economy into the Cybermedia Model: Steps towards a Critical-Materialist Game Analysis'. IT University of Copenhagen (2022)
7. Srauy, S.: Professional norms and race in the North American video game industry. Games Culture **14**(5), 478–497 (2019). https://doi.org/10.1177/1555412017708936
8. Sotamaa, O., Švelch, J.: Introduction: why game production matters? In: Sotamaa, O., Švelch, J. (eds.) Game Production Studies, pp. 7–26. Amsterdam University Press (2021). https://doi.org/10.2307/j.ctv1hp5hqw.3
9. Sotamaa, O.: Studying game development cultures. Games Culture **16**(7), 835–854 (2021). https://doi.org/10.1177/15554120211005242
10. Kultima, A.: Game Design Praxiology (2018)
11. Debus, M.S.: Unifying game ontology: a faceted classification of game elements. IT-Universitetet i København (2019)
12. Aarseth, E., Calleja, G.: The Word Game: The Ontology of an Undefinable Object. Foundations of Digital Games, Pacific Grove, CA, USA (2015). http://www.fdg2015.org/papers/fdg2015_paper_51.pdf
13. Juul, J.: Half-Real: Video Games between Real Rules and Fictional Worlds. MIT Press, Cambridge, Mass, London (2005)
14. Charmaz, K.: Constructing Grounded Theory: A Practical Guide through Qualitative Analysis. Sage, London (2006)
15. Birks, M., Mills, J.: Grounded Theory: A Practical Guide. Sage, London (2015)
16. Cramér, H.: Mathematical Methods of Statistics. Princeton: Princeton University Press, page 282 (Chapter 21. The two-dimensional case) (1946). ISBN 0-691-08004-6
17. Benjamini, Y., Hochberg, Y.: Controlling the false discovery rate: a practical and powerful approach to multiple testing. J. Roy. Stat. Soc. B **57**(1), 289–300 (1995). MR 1325392

Let the Players Go!

Substituting Excessive Handholding with Autonomous Experiences

Milas Ray Manley Norman[✉] and Alessandro Canossa[iD]

Royal Danish Academy, Philip De Langes Allé 10, 1435 Copenhagen, Denmark
milas-norman@live.dk, acan@kglakademi.dk

Abstract. This paper explores how games can facilitate greater autonomous experiences. The project describes possibilities of how a certain kind of simulation can be a viable substitute for the often overwhelming and explicit communications of information that characterize many instances of handholding in video games. We hypothesize that consistently supporting the players' expectations regarding their interactions with the world can result in decisions informed by players' knowledge and experiences from the real world and consequently can lead to feelings of autonomy over their own actions. To test these hypotheses a vertical slice of a video game was developed with mechanics that were chosen to support the players' natural intuition and what they want to do, rather than restrict them to what they can do. An experiment was conducted where 12 participants tested the first version of the game, then answered questions and filled a survey based on the Player Experience Inventory (PXI). Based on the feedback, an improved second version of the game was made. The results of the two versions were then compared. Overall findings show how leveraging implicitly communicated information, consistent simulation and logical mechanics enhance the players perceived autonomy and can teach players complex systems without resorting to handholding strategies. The methods used can be turned into practical steps that game developers can take into consideration if developers want to facilitate more autonomous experience for their players.

Keywords: games · Self Determination Theory · autonomy · simulation · handholding · user interface · information transfer · experimental validation · satisfaction · agency · volitional engagement · choice · opportunity · gameflow · affordance · diegetic puzzles

1 Introduction

As time progresses, game systems are getting increasingly more complex. From the first arcade games to the modern AAA blockbusters shooters, developers are always finding new and exciting ways to give players satisfying experiences. Technology evolves and thus developers can easier implement more functionalities into their games, often to the satisfaction of the players. However, with more functionalities follows a risk of overwhelming the players to the point of less satisfaction. If games fail to train players

© The Author(s), under exclusive license to Springer Nature Switzerland AG 2023
J. Y. C. Chen et al. (Eds.): HCII 2023, LNCS 14058, pp. 341–369, 2023.
https://doi.org/10.1007/978-3-031-48050-8_24

on the available functionalities, players will end up frustrated and might quit playing entirely. Out of this need for informing players emerged a tendency to overexplain. How, why, and what players must or can do are often explicitly communicated to the point where they don't have to think for themselves. This experience of a game overexplaining something which the player could have figured out themselves, had the game supported it, is often referred to as the game holding the players' hands, or simply: handholding. In this paper the term means exactly that. It is a well-known term but has not been precisely defined before.

Handholding consequently reduces the players' feeling of ownership over their actions and being self-governing. This feeling is known as autonomy and is considered a basic human need as well as a highly satisfying feeling [7].

2 Background: Previous Research

2.1 Autonomy in Games

Games are artefacts which evolve when dedicated developers find new ways to create satisfying experiences for their players. One of these can be supporting their perceived autonomy. Psychological studies found that the feeling of having control and agency over one's own choices is a basic human need. Not only is it rewarding in and of itself, but it also increases one's overall life satisfaction [8]. This need for autonomy together with need for relatedness and competence was included in the Self-Determination meta theory (SDT) [1].

Rigby and Ryan have expanded upon the term in relation to games: they define which criteria are required for autonomous experiences to happen in a game:

"At its heart, autonomy means that one's actions are aligned with one's inner self and values. [...] Even if you have only a single pathway open to you, you still feel autonomous if it is the one you want to travel down." [7], [p 40].

In practice, increased autonomous feelings in players happens when two criteria are present: meaningful choices and volitional engagement [7], [p 49]. Providing these consists of presenting opportunities that match the personal desires, intentions, and values of players. Each choice needs to be something players internally want to do and aligns with their values for it to be truly volitional. Having more volitional choices motivates them to come back. It can have positive implications to have more meaningful choices. However, even if a game only presents the player with a single path, that path can make the player feel autonomous if their engagement with it is volitional [7].

At Ubisoft, an instrument (Ubisoft Perceived Experience Questionnaire) was developed to assess both players' motivations as well as games' affordances based on the basic psychological needs described by SDT [1]. In order to provide an overview of how autonomy is operationalized in games, here are the items contained in the UPEQ survey [12]:

- I was free to decide how I wanted to play.
- I could approach the game in my own way.
- The game allowed me to play the way I wanted to.
- I had important decisions to make when playing.

- The choices I made while playing influenced what happened.
- My actions had an impact on the game.

2.2 Informed Choices and Handholding

Before players will engage with meaningful choices presented by a game, they need to be informed about them. How this is achieved is also important for the autonomous experience. How handholding negatively affects volitional choices is explained in the next section. This section accounts for the positives of handholding: how it can lead to less frustrations because the player is well-informed. It accounts for some goals game developers might have when developing their games, and how handholding can help achieve these. It is important to note both positive and negative effects of handholding so that the alternative suggested in Sect. 2.5 is to achieve the positives and avoid the negatives of it.

It is difficult to find good definitions of handholding on paper, however it is discussed many places on the web. One example is a reddit thread where players discuss what handholding in games mean to them. This discussion shows the importance and significance it has to players, but also the unsureness of what the definition should be [15].

Handholding and GameFlow. GameFlow is a model that can be used to evaluate the player's satisfaction in a game [9, p 65]. It can be a tool for developers to design their game around, or just account for what affects the satisfaction of a game. Here we use it to see how handholding affects it positively, so we know what the hypothesis must achieve. According to GameFlow a satisfying game incorporates the following steps [10]:

1. A task that can be completed.
2. The ability to concentrate on the task.
3. Concentration is possible because the task has clear goals.
4. Concentration is possible because the task provides immediate feedback.
5. The ability to exercise a sense of control over actions.
6. A deep but effortless involvement that removes awareness of worries and frustrations of everyday life.
7. Concern for self disappears but sense of self emerges stronger afterward.
8. Sense of duration of time is altered.

Primarily, steps 3, 4, 5 and 6 can be achieved by overexplaining information. Steps 3 and 4 requires information that is given to the player about what they must do and how their actions affect it. An example of communicating these could be a quest-log which consists of a list of tasks that needs to be completed to get a reward. Another is waypoints, which are UI elements that point to the players' next goal in the game space.

Step 5 implies the need for players to know the game's button-mapping[1].

The effortless involvement mentioned in step 6, could encourage developers to accommodate less experienced players. Effortless involvement can simply be attained if the game does not allow the player to think for themselves but does it for them. The players need not put in effort if the game constantly hold their hands.

---

[1] A scheme which overviews which buttons to press to act out the specific functionalities. For example, press space to jump.

Handholding in Casual Games. The free-to-play market has grown to staggering proportions [11]. Many free-to-play games have a business model that focus on in-game transactions which usually give advantages to the player. To increase the chances of purchases, playtime and retention have become the focus. Games need to be more user friendly and easy to learn to avoid players getting frustrated and stop playing. Additionally, casual games, have a broad audience. Therefore, their user experiences must also accommodate less experienced players. From these emerged new ways to cater to players which bled into other types of games other than casual ones.

2.3 The Negative Effects of Handholding

In Glued to games Ryan and Deci maintain that bad games overexplain what players must do, and how it limits volitional engagement:

> "[Bad games] have characters that literally command the player to "Keep moving!" But a well-designed video game never <u>drags</u> or <u>prods</u> the player along in these ways. Instead, they use well-crafted <u>stories</u> and compelling <u>rationales</u> to awaken in the player an <u>internal desire</u> to walk the path ahead. We call this experience in games volitional engagement." [1]

Drags, prods and command are all verbs that could describe handholding. A game with less volitionally engaging choices is one that overexplain how, why, and what the player must do. Handholding consequently happens at the expense of meaningful choices and volitional engagement, and thus it reduces the player's sense of autonomy. Instead, games can tap into rational thinking and support the player's internal desires which in turn will increase their perceived autonomy.

2.4 Benefits of Agency

Image of the city [5] is a book that explores how people identify objects and structures in cities by taking in their visual information and turning it into cognitive maps. It explains that the visual qualities of the city images can help people navigate, but also that easy to identify structures that inspire little imagination can make navigation easier but be boring as a result. The images a person might observe has a significant impact on the satisfaction linked to the city. Cities that are maze-like and hard to navigate can be very satisfying to experience, because the cognitive act of mapping and deducting new information from the visuals is satisfying:

> "We stare into the jungle and see only the sunlight on the green leaves, but warning noise tells us that an animal is hidden there. The observer then learns to single out clues and reweighting previous signals. [...] Finally, by repeated experience the entire pattern of perception is changed, and the observer need no longer consciously search for giveaways [...] Quite suddenly the animal appears among the leaves, clear as day." [5].

In games this same deduction happens when players must look at different cues, contrasting visuals, compositions, and landmarks to figure out how to navigate, what to do and how to do it.

Informing via Visuals. Image of The City explain that an environmental image can be analyzed into three components:

" [...] identity, structure and meaning" [5].

Identity is the visual aspects of the object. How does it stand out? What are the qualities that an observer identifies? Simply put: what are its distinctive visual qualities?

Structure is how it relates to the surroundings. Where is it usually seen; how does it affect being grouped together with something else?

Meaning is something the observer gives the object. Objects can be familiar which means the meaning has been defined long time ago. For example: doors. We do not have to spend much time identifying a door and its meaning because we know it, but also because it has a very distinctive visual identity. If an object is unfamiliar the quality and distinctiveness of its identity will affect how long it takes for an observer to apply meaning. Similarly, if it has meaning already but the visual identity of the object instance is far from the familiar identity of it, it can also take a long time to identify it. The meaning of an interactable object in a game can be leveraged to inform the players of its functionality. This is called affordance and is defined as what opportunities an observer perceives when looking at the visual qualities of an object.

Or we might even exercise clearer identities of objects the player can interact with, to let the player explore its meaning and function by themselves:

" If it is our purpose to build cities for the enjoyment [...] we may even concentrate on physical clarity of the image and allow meaning to develop without our direct guidance." [5].

Thusly, players can be informed of the games functionalities through visuals which identities are easy to identify, as well as either ensuring meaning through a predefined familiarity with the said identity or let the player develop meaning themselves.

2.5   How Simulation Can Hypothetically Achieve Autonomous Experiences and Substitute Handholding

Based on the insights derived from literature on autonomy and handholding, this section will describe the kind of consistent simulation that can hypothetically be used to avoid handholding while still informing the player enough to avoid frustration.

Our hypothesis is this:

Simulations that can consistently support players' expected outcomes during their interactions with a game will result in players being informed by their inherent knowledge and experiences from the real world. Information gained by players in this manner can lead to an increased sense of autonomy over their own actions.

Instead of communicating every aspect of the games system with explicit information, which restricts autonomy, utilizing consistent simulations will leverage players own ability to think and act on their own accord. Players already possess some of the required information, the game must only support and incentivize them to use it.

For example, players know that a rock should follow a parabolic trajectory if thrown. If the game does not support this, either the parabolic trajectory is wrong or the rock just falls flat, then players will not feel supported and will be less incentivized to think for themselves from that point on. This upholding of illusion is referred to as suspension-of-disbelief, and players perception of it can be an indicator of how well the game scaffolds this illusion.

Some information is harder to communicate implicitly. Meta information like which buttons to press to act out functionalities, player health, and score each should be explicitly communicated without restricting autonomy. This is because this information exists in the context of playing a game. They belong to long established game conventions and do not necessarily come from within the in-game universe. In other words, they are not diegetic[2] but they do not interfere with the players' suspension-of-disbelief. Without explicit communication, players might feel frustrated because they do not know how to use controls to play the game. Additionally, the feedback from their interactions which affect the health or score for example might not be present, thus removing the meaning behind their choices. Informing the player enough to avoid frustration while still avoiding overexplaining therefore becomes a matter of balance. A balance that is hard to perfect.

3   Background: Games that Foster Autonomous Experiences

In these following subsections we will analyze three critically acclaimed games. The first two serve as examples of what implication the absence or presence of handholding have on autonomous experiences. The last one is a newer example that successfully achieves the consistent simulation defined so far, hence it possesses many elements that support player autonomy and comparing it to our hypothesis serves as an example of how applying it can be successful.

3.1   Elden Ring

Elden ring is a game developed by FromSoftware. It received great critical acclaim. In short, the game is an open-world 3rd-person action-roleplaying game where you explore and make your way towards a massive golden-tree. The playable space is very big and dense with branching paths and choices.

It separates itself from other open-world games with how little it holds the hands of the players. From Software games are held as some of the most difficult games, but also very rewarding, which can be tied to that players must figure out how, why, and what they should do. It supports and helps the player mainly with implicit communication. For example, it uses perspective, composition, landmarks, shapes, color, and the like

---

[2] Diegetic. Something which exists in the in-game universe.

Fig. 1. Elden Ring. Possible paths implicitly communicated in the environment.

to help the player navigate. The big glowing tree is used as a landmark to orient them as well as an indication of where the player must go to complete the game. The castle creates a composition which implies what stands between you and your goal. The layout uses levels of rock formations and verticality to further point the player in the right or optional directions (see Fig. 1).

One aspect which was chosen to be not communicated is the progression of optional quests in the game. Many open-world games like Elden Ring utilize a quest-log system. In Elden Ring the players must find out what to do with no indication of their progression. Because there is no way to view the players' progression many sites and YouTube videos have been made to explain step by step how each quest should be completed. This creates an incentive for investing time away from the game, minimizing immersion. This information is also explicit and non-diegetic which breaks suspension-of-disbelief.

If the game had given players the tools to obtain an overview of their progression without explicitly explaining the next goal, it would have reduced the incentive to get information outside of the game while still encouraging volitional engagement.

3.2 Deathloop

Deathloop is a game designed by Arkane Studios. It was published in September 2021.

The game takes place on an island where the player progress by finding clues on how to kill certain NPC's. These clues are collected and can be viewed in the UI menu. Here the player can get an overview of how the clues connect to each other, however, players do not have to connect them themselves. The game presents the answer and tells players where to go next instead of letting them figure it out themselves (Fig. 2).

The clue overview has many similarities to a conventional quest-log, which is a list of tasks to complete to advance the game [4].

Ultimately because the game gives the player the answers, they are not incentivized to think for themselves thus restricting their volitional engagement.

Deathloop received good reviews [6] however, has also been noted as a lost potential by some players. One reviewer reports:

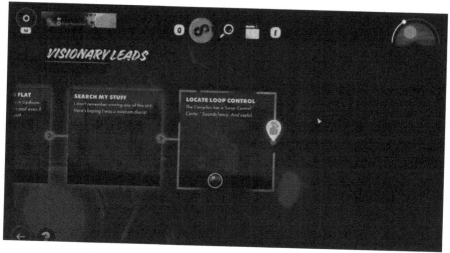

Fig. 2. Deathloop UI clue-overview resembles a quest-log.

" *Instead of giving players the satisfaction of figuring it out for themselves, and crafting their own ending, Deathloop simply supplies players a screen (UI) with all the answers, where you are given specific tasks to figure out the next step of the puzzle.*" [3].

Deathloop has many great mechanics which leans into its detective narrative; however it fails to capitalize on these to let the player deduct new information from the clues themselves. The player's experience of their own autonomy could have been more realized.

If the game would let players figure out the answers, one clue obtained might for example show the image of the next objective without a specific location. It might describe a building with a visual metaphor resembling a mirror, and the average player would be able to find it given that the building does indeed reminds of a mirror. Here prior knowledge of the physical world has an impact on players successfully finding the correct building. In the unlikely event of a player not knowing what a mirror is, they would be lost. This is why it can be beneficial to present several different opportunities to gain information and advance. More meaningful choices mean higher chances of volitional engagement.

3.3 Design Guidelines

This section concludes the analysis and lists the guidelines that inspired our game's design, which will be accounted for in the next section.

Elden Ring primarily inspired the navigation and pathfinding. It demonstrates how minimizing handholding and instead guiding the players with visual landmarks, cues and inherent knowledge, the players are incentivized to think for themselves and progress through logical thinking. Also, the idea of letting the player figure things out themselves and not being afraid of letting players fail to experience a bigger sense of accomplishment when completed was inspired by this game.

Deathloop inspired the game to make use of a detective narrative and a set of mechanics that support this narrative. The idea was that the narrative presentation serves as a guide for the players motive and actions.

A second hypothesis formed:

If players know they play the role of detective, this information will incentivize them to perform detective related actions they know from the physical world or other media. They will have the required information to start roleplaying by searching for clues, deducting answers from them, and solving puzzles. Because they know what a detective is they already have a set of information they can actively or passively apply to how, why, and what they can or want to do.

4 The Game

The game was developed in Unreal Engine 5. This engine has photorealistic qualities as well as thorough physics simulation, which serves as a bonus for supporting players' suspension-of-disbelief. A video of a playthrough is linked in Appendix 3.

In the game the players enter a little village on a small Faroe island. They play as a detective who has received a job about a missing woman named Alma. They then must explore it while collecting clues, deducting new information from them, interacting with the environment, and solving small puzzles and navigating the level to receive one of three possible endings. The only explicit meta information they get is the control-scheme and the context of being a detective, which is presented in a locked-off section at the start of the map. The players must learn the controls by selecting a key, opening a door with it, and pushing a box to gain access to the small open world that is the island.

The control scheme can be seen any time the game is paused. There is a HUD element which indicates when the players can interact with something they are looking at. The objects that can be interacted with have distinct identities and affordances that communicate to the player that they can be interacted with. Some objects have meaning, and some only rely on identity to allow meaning to develop without direct guidance [5]. Keys and tools can be picked up and placed in an inventory which is displayed in the in-game characters hands. Keys are picked up in the left hand and tools in the right hand (see Fig. 3).

The axe can be used on weak-looking objects like fragile doors, boards, and windows. Smaller to medium sized objects can also be held in front of the players and then be thrown

Fig. 3. In-game overview of the items the player has picked up.

(see Fig. 4), and players movement actions involve walking, jumping, and climbing up on objects.

The interactions with objects are physics simulated to act as we expect from the real world.

Fig. 4. Screenshot from the game. The player is holding a rock.

The Detective Presentation. The players are also introduced to a diegetic tablet which the player character will place in front of the screen view when the keyboard button TAB is pressed (see Fig. 5). This acts as a classic detective board but as an in-universe app where the detective can overview all the collected clues. It supports players while directing them implicitly with the information contained in the clue. The clues do not tell players exactly what to do, but highlights important points that can be coupled together with other clues. For example, one clue informs players that Alma might be located at lighthouse, a second one that she is unnaturally dangerous and strong while a third one informs of a book that has information about dealing with evil demons. Players might then deduce that the book is important to deal with Alma at the lighthouse.

The detective narrative also helps guide players while also giving meaning behind their choices. Each choice and functionality are not isolated but are supported with dynamics that mean progression can be advanced in several ways: one player might find a key to a door and enters a house this way. Another player might find a rock, throws it

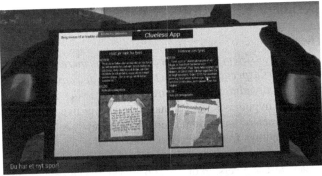

Fig. 5. The in-game tablet that overviews the collected clues, which give indirect information.

at a window and climbs inside the house this way. The clues are not necessary to finish the game, however a single key is needed to open a door to finish the game. The clues give information needed to acquire certain items that can change the ending. In the end, players are met with these choices and it is up to them to decide how they want to deal with Alma in the lighthouse. There are clues that each gives the player the necessary information to have an idea of what each option might result in. If players are unhappy with the choice they made, they can simply play it again and try out a different one.

Environment and Level Design. The environment and level consist of five distinctive houses: a dock house at the start area, two residential houses, one shed and one old prayer house. There is also a lighthouse on a cliff which must be accessed via a locked door, a beach, a main road, and off-road and the dock where players start.

The lighthouse and the cliff are landmarks that acts as navigational guides. It is also at the lighthouse where players finish the game.

The water and the cliffs act as a natural barrier to enclose the playable space (Fig. 6).

Fig. 6. The lighthouse on the cliff.

5 The Experiment

We stipulated two hypotheses:

H1: Thorough and consistent simulations can lead to an increased sense of autonomy.
H2: Framing players expectations within the role of a detective and supporting these with detective-like functionalities will encourage players to act autonomously.

In order to test the hypotheses, we conducted tests over five iterations of the game, after which a questionnaire was administered. Each new version of the game was improved using the findings from the previous test, until a version had been achieved that was to our satisfaction and gave good insight into how the autonomous experiences had improved. Each test of a version involved between two and 8 participants, roughly split evenly between genders and with age ranging from 21 to 29. The first and last test had the most participants of 6 and 8. In total 12 different participants tested the game.

The protocol of each test included probes designed to evaluate the autonomous experiences of the participants.

Firstly, participants were introduced to the game. The only information they were given was that they were detectives solving a mystery.

When they finished it, they were asked questions relating to their experience of the video game about their actions and thoughts. The questionnaire can be found in the appendix.

In the first and last version, they were given a questionnaire based on the Player Experience Inventory, PXI, which is a model used to evaluate the players emotional responses to games. The questionnaire focused on PXI questions relating to autonomy, immersion ease of control, goals and rules, progress feedback audiovisual appeal, meaning, curiosity, and narrative [13, 14]. These can be seen in Appendix 1 and 2.

6 Results

The most relevant findings are:

Overall better autonomous responses from the participants in the improved version (see Figs. 7 and 8). Participants felt freer to think for themselves in the final version. Some of the participants that had experienced high feelings of autonomy, said it was because they felt free to figure things out themselves in their own pace. It was when the players expectations were fully supported with functionality, that they reported very high levels of satisfaction.

Misinterpretations of object affordances and not knowing which buttons to press resulted in worse autonomous experiences because participants tried to interact with non-functional objects. This was also backed when the later versions had tutorials that explained how to control the game on the keyboard, which increased autonomy. Functionalities that did not act as expected or the lack of functionality where players expected it significantly reduced the players incentive to find new clues.

Interpretations of implicit information in clues had to be supported. In some instances, the participants interpreted them differently than we had imagined, resulting in incidents of feeling restricted or frustrated. If their interpretations of clues aligned with their actual meaning, they reported intense feelings of reward. This was improved by making important information in clues clearer. A balance between implicit and explicit.

Their sense of progression was improved in later versions. We figure it is due to clearer goals deducted from clearer clues.

Some reported being satisfied with how they had to explore and connect the clues to gain new information, which backs up the importance of letting players develop meaning themselves from object identity.

The participants of the first versions were not informed that they played as a detective, where the participants in the later versions did. We observed that players that had this information played differently. They more often interacted with actual interactable objects because they knew what to look for. They also commented that this was indeed the case.

All responses from the questionnaire can be found in the appendix.

3. Goals and Rules

6 Responses

ID ↑	Name	Responses		
		I grasped the overall goal of the game	The goals of the game were clear to me	I understood the objectives of the game
1	anonymous	4 Agree	5 Strongly agree	5 Strongly agree
2	anonymous	3 Neither agree nor disagree	2 Disagree	3 Neither agree nor disagree
3	anonymous	5 Strongly agree	4 Agree	4 Agree
4	anonymous	5 Strongly agree	4 Agree	3 Neither agree nor disagree
5	anonymous	5 Strongly agree	4 Agree	5 Strongly agree
6	anonymous	5 Strongly agree	4 Agree	4 Agree

Fig. 7. Autonomy responses on first version

10. Autonomy

8 Responses

ID ↑	Name	I felt free to play the game in my own way	I felt like I had choices regarding how I wanted to play this game	I felt a sense of freedom about how I wanted to play this game
1	anonymous	5 Strongly agree	5 Strongly agree	4 Agree
2	anonymous	5 Strongly agree	5 Strongly agree	4 Agree
3	anonymous	5 Strongly agree	5 Strongly agree	5 Strongly agree
4	anonymous	5 Strongly agree	5 Strongly agree	5 Strongly agree
5	anonymous	5 Strongly agree	5 Strongly agree	5 Strongly agree
6	anonymous	4 Agree	3 Neither agree nor disagree	4 Agree
7	anonymous	5 Strongly agree	4 Agree	4 Agree
8	anonymous	5 Strongly agree	5 Strongly agree	5 Strongly agree

Fig. 8. Autonomy responses on final version

6.1 Discussion

This section serves first and foremost as a discussion of the findings, and a list of ways these findings constitutes to which developers can utilize when developing a game that focus on the players' autonomy.

Logical Functionalities. It is not technologically feasible to simulate the real world one to one easily. We can however filter the functionalities we implement into games, with the criteria that they must satisfy to the players expectations when it comes to their interactions. If their suspension-of-disbelief is negatively affected, it might be a sign these expectations have not been accommodated. Affordances tell the player what they can do with an object, and misinterpretations of them, such as not being able to pick up a knife in a game where you must defend yourself, can have significant negative long-lasting effects on the players' motivation to think for themselves.

Consistency incentivizes creative thinking. The player will look for opportunities based on their experience from interacting with the game's system. For example, if they can throw a rock to destroy a window, they might think about throwing a rock at another object that has a visual identity that resembles a weak structure. In the opposite way, if they cannot destroy the window, they might be less incentivized to explore other tactics and interactions, this ending up being lost and frustrated.

However, there is also a satisfaction to be had in letting players apply meaning themselves to their interactions and explore the functionalities and new information this way.

Implicit Information and the Advantages of More Choices. Primarily informing the player implicitly is usually a sure way to make the player not feel handheld. However, it requires a setup where the player will obtain this information one way or another. Because implicit information can be overlooked or simply misinterpreted, it can be an advantage to have several ways to find one point of information, so one way or another the player will very likely find it.

Tools Instead of Explicit Guides. Because humans have deductive abilities, supporting their deduction with tools is a great way to incentivize them to think for themselves. Instead of giving explicit guiding on why, how, and what to do, games can supply players, for example, with a diegetic map where they can pin important points of interests themselves, instead of the game automatically doing it. Diegetic elements instead of UI can be a great way to inform the player of explicit information while it still upholding the players' suspension-of-disbelief. For example, a physical map instead of a UI map.

Navigation. It is evident from the experiments and the analysis of Elden Ring, that navigation can be thoroughly enjoyable without a mini-map, quest-log, or waypoints: Contrast, color, shape language, affordance, visual identity, landmarks, and structures can all help with the cognitive mapping of the environment to the players' navigation satisfaction.

7 Conclusion

On the notion that autonomous experiences are crucial for players to feel in control and satisfied with their choices in games, this paper has accounted for the broad criteria for them to be facilitated in games. It has also notably explored the concept of handholding in games and its impact on players' autonomous experiences. Handholding refers to the tendency of games to overexplain and guide players excessively, reducing their sense of ownership and self-governance. The term handholding is not well defined in the domain of games and this paper hopes to validate its importance. We have discussed the positive effects of handholding, such as reducing frustration and providing clear guidance to players. It can be beneficial for certain goals. However, excessive handholding can limit players' volitional engagement and meaningful choices, ultimately diminishing their autonomy.

Analyzing critically acclaimed games, we observed the implications of handholding on players' autonomous experiences. Games like Elden Ring by FromSoftware demonstrated the success of implicit communication and minimal handholding. These games rely on environmental cues, landmarks, and visual elements to guide players, allowing them to figure out how to progress and make meaningful choices independently.

To substitute handholding and its negative effects while still providing enough information to avoid frustration, we offered a hypothetical approach of simulation. This proposed that by simulating players' expected outcomes based on their inherent knowledge and real-world experiences, games can inform players implicitly and support their autonomy simultaneously.

A game was developed to test the hypotheses laid out at the end of Sects. 2 and 3. The game was tested and iterated upon, resulting in a version which satisfied the autonomous experiences of the participants. They were each conversed with and answered a questionnaire. Findings from these tests included that the players' autonomous and immersive experiences were heavily affected by the simulation qualities of aspects like affordances, visual cues, contrasting elements, logical interactions and functionalities, and environmental navigation. If the players' expectations of alle these systems were met, the autonomous experience were better. The importance of balancing explicit communication of meta information, such as button-mapping and feedback, with implicit communication of in-game functionalities became essential to strike the right balance.

In conclusion, while handholding can provide benefits in terms of less frustration, it heavily hinders the autonomous experience of the players. By leveraging implicit information in the form of composition, visual identities, meaning, form language, color, affordance, and simulating expected outcomes, games can empower players to think for themselves and take ownership of their actions, in turn resulting in more satisfying experiences and motivations to play the game again. Future research and game development should continue to explore ways to enhance autonomy in games and create less trivialized and more satisfying player experiences.

Appendix 1. PXI Based Questionnaire Results from Testing First Version of the Game

1. I regularly play games on PC or console (Playstation, Nintendo, Xbox and so on...)

6 Responses

ID ↑	Name	Responses
1	anonymous	1 Strongly disagree
2	anonymous	1 Strongly disagree
3	anonymous	5 Strongly agree
4	anonymous	2 Disagree
5	anonymous	2 Disagree
6	anonymous	2 Disagree

2. Ease of control

6 Responses

ID ↑	Name	Responses		
		It was easy to know how to perform actions in the game	The actions to control the game were clear to me	I thought the game was easy to control
1	anonymous	2 Disagree	4 Agree	4 Agree
2	anonymous	5 Strongly agree	4 Agree	4 Agree
3	anonymous	4 Agree	4 Agree	5 Strongly agree
4	anonymous	4 Agree	3 Neither agree nor disagree	4 Agree
5	anonymous	4 Agree	3 Neither agree nor disagree	3 Neither agree nor disagree
6	anonymous	4 Agree	5 Strongly agree	5 Strongly agree

6 Responses

ID ↑	Name	Responses		
		I grasped the overall goal of the game	The goals of the game were clear to me	I understood the objectives of the game
1	anonymous	4 Agree	5 Strongly agree	5 Strongly agree
2	anonymous	3 Neither agree nor disagree	2 Disagree	3 Neither agree nor disagree
3	anonymous	5 Strongly agree	4 Agree	4 Agree
4	anonymous	5 Strongly agree	4 Agree	3 Neither agree nor disagree
5	anonymous	5 Strongly agree	4 Agree	5 Strongly agree
6	anonymous	5 Strongly agree	4 Agree	4 Agree

4. Progress Feedback

6 Responses

ID ↑	Name	Responses		
		The game informed me of my progress in the game	I could easily assess how I was performing in the game	The game gave clear feedback on my progress towards the goals
1	anonymous	3 Neither agree nor disagree	5 Strongly agree	4 Agree
2	anonymous	3 Neither agree nor disagree	5 Strongly agree	4 Agree
3	anonymous	3 Neither agree nor disagree	3 Neither agree nor disagree	3 Neither agree nor disagree
4	anonymous	3 Neither agree nor disagree	3 Neither agree nor disagree	2 Disagree
5	anonymous	4 Agree	4 Agree	4 Agree
6	anonymous	3 Neither agree nor disagree	4 Agree	3 Neither agree nor disagree

5. Audiovisual Appeal

2 Responses

ID ↑	Name	Responses		
		I enjoyed the way the game was styled	I liked the look and feel of the game	I appreciated the aesthetics of the game
1	anonymous	5 Strongly agree	4 Agree	5 Strongly agree
2	anonymous	5 Strongly agree	5 Strongly agree	5 Strongly agree

6. Meaning

6 Responses

ID ↑	Name	Responses		
		Playing the game was meaningful to me	The game felt relevant to me	Playing this game was valuable to me
1	anonymous	5 Strongly agree	4 Agree	5 Strongly agree
2	anonymous	4 Agree	5 Strongly agree	5 Strongly agree
3	anonymous	3 Neither agree nor disagree	4 Agree	4 Agree
4	anonymous	4 Agree	5 Strongly agree	4 Agree
5	anonymous	3 Neither agree nor disagree	4 Agree	3 Neither agree nor disagree
6	anonymous	5 Strongly agree	4 Agree	5 Strongly agree

7. Curiosity

6 Responses

ID ↑	Name	I wanted to explore how the game evolved	I wanted to find out how the game progressed	I felt eager to discover how the game continued
1	anonymous	5 Strongly agree	5 Strongly agree	5 Strongly agree
2	anonymous	5 Strongly agree	5 Strongly agree	5 Strongly agree
3	anonymous	4 Agree	5 Strongly agree	4 Agree
4	anonymous	5 Strongly agree	5 Strongly agree	5 Strongly agree
5	anonymous	5 Strongly agree	5 Strongly agree	5 Strongly agree
6	anonymous	5 Strongly agree	5 Strongly agree	5 Strongly agree

8. Immersion

6 Responses

ID ↑	Name	I was no longer aware of my surroundings while I was playing	I was immersed(fordybet) in the game	I was fully focused on the game
1	anonymous	3 Neither agree nor disagree	4 Agree	3 Neither agree nor disagree
2	anonymous	4 Agree	4 Agree	4 Agree
3	anonymous	4 Agree	4 Agree	4 Agree
4	anonymous	4 Agree	5 Strongly agree	4 Agree
5	anonymous	4 Agree	4 Agree	4 Agree
6	anonymous	4 Agree	4 Agree	4 Agree

9. If there was something that retracked from your immersion, can you explain what it is?

1 Responses

ID ↑	Name	Responses
1	anonymous	other sound and noises

10. Autonomy

6 Responses

ID ↑	Name	I felt free to play the game in my own way	I felt like I had choices regarding how I wanted to play this game	I felt a sense of freedom about how I wanted to play this game
1	anonymous	4 Agree	3 Neither agree nor disagree	4 Agree
2	anonymous	5 Strongly agree	5 Strongly agree	5 Strongly agree
3	anonymous	5 Strongly agree	4 Agree	4 Agree
4	anonymous	4 Agree	4 Agree	4 Agree
5	anonymous	5 Strongly agree	4 Agree	4 Agree
6	anonymous	3 Neither agree nor disagree	3 Neither agree nor disagree	3 Neither agree nor disagree

11. Autonomy ekstra

2 Responses

ID ↑	Name	I felt constrained by the mechanics in the game	I felt the game did not let me do things I would have liked to, to solve problems my own way
1	anonymous	2 Disagree	3 Neither agree nor disagree
2	anonymous	2 Disagree	3 Neither agree nor disagree

12. Narrative

2 Responses

ID ↑	Name	I would be able to retell the story to someone	I felt immersed in the story	I wanted to see how the story progressed	I felt the story was believable
1	anonymous	5 Strongly agree	4 Agree	4 Agree	4 Agree
2	anonymous	4 Agree	5 Strongly agree	5 Strongly agree	5 Strongly agree

Appendix 2. PXI Questionnaire Results from Testing Final Version of the Game

1. I regularly play games on PC or console (Playstation, Nintendo, Xbox and so on...)

8 Responses

ID ↑	Name	Responses
1	anonymous	3 Neither disagree nor agree
2	anonymous	1 Strongly disagree
3	anonymous	2 Disagree
4	anonymous	5 Strongly agree
5	anonymous	1 Strongly disagree
6	anonymous	1 Strongly disagree
7	anonymous	5 Strongly agree
8	anonymous	1 Strongly disagree

2. Ease of control

8 Responses

ID ↑	Name	It was easy to know how to perform actions in the game	The actions to control the game were clear to me	I thought the game was easy to control
1	anonymous	5 Strongly agree	5 Strongly agree	5 Strongly agree
2	anonymous	4 Agree	5 Strongly agree	5 Strongly agree
3	anonymous	4 Agree	5 Strongly agree	4 Agree
4	anonymous	4 Agree	4 Agree	4 Agree
5	anonymous	4 Agree	3 Neither agree nor disagree	3 Neither agree nor disagree
6	anonymous	4 Agree	4 Agree	4 Agree
7	anonymous	4 Agree	5 Strongly agree	5 Strongly agree
8	anonymous	5 Strongly agree	5 Strongly agree	5 Strongly agree

3. Goals and Rules

8 Responses

ID ↑	Name	Responses		
		I grasped the overall goal of the game	The goals of the game were clear to me	I understood the objectives of the game
1	anonymous	4 Agree	4 Agree	4 Agree
2	anonymous	4 Agree	4 Agree	4 Agree
3	anonymous	5 Strongly agree	5 Strongly agree	5 Strongly agree
4	anonymous	5 Strongly agree	5 Strongly agree	5 Strongly agree
5	anonymous	4 Agree	2 Disagree	3 Neither agree nor disagree
6	anonymous	4 Agree	4 Agree	4 Agree
7	anonymous	4 Agree	5 Strongly agree	4 Agree
8	anonymous	5 Strongly agree	5 Strongly agree	5 Strongly agree

4. Progress Feedback

8 Responses

ID ↑	Name	The game informed me of my progress in the game	I could easily assess how I was performing in the game	The game gave clear feedback on my progress towards the goals
1	anonymous	4 Agree	4 Agree	4 Agree
2	anonymous	3 Neither agree nor disagree	4 Agree	3 Neither agree nor disagree
3	anonymous	4 Agree	3 Neither agree nor disagree	4 Agree
4	anonymous	5 Strongly agree	5 Strongly agree	5 Strongly agree
5	anonymous	2 Disagree	2 Disagree	3 Neither agree nor disagree
6	anonymous	2 Disagree	3 Neither agree nor disagree	3 Neither agree nor disagree
7	anonymous	4 Agree	3 Neither agree nor disagree	3 Neither agree nor disagree
8	anonymous	4 Agree	5 Strongly agree	4 Agree

5. Audiovisual Appeal

8 Responses

ID ↑	Name	I enjoyed the way the game was styled	I liked the look and feel of the game	I appreciated the aesthetics of the game
1	anonymous	5 Strongly agree	5 Strongly agree	5 Strongly agree
2	anonymous	5 Strongly agree	5 Strongly agree	5 Strongly agree
3	anonymous	5 Strongly agree	5 Strongly agree	5 Strongly agree
4	anonymous	5 Strongly agree	5 Strongly agree	5 Strongly agree
5	anonymous	5 Strongly agree	5 Strongly agree	5 Strongly agree
6	anonymous	5 Strongly agree	4 Agree	5 Strongly agree
7	anonymous	4 Agree	4 Agree	4 Agree
8	anonymous	5 Strongly agree	5 Strongly agree	5 Strongly agree

6. Meaning

8 Responses

ID ↑	Name	Responses		
		Playing the game was meaningful to me	The game felt relevant to me	Playing this game was valuable to me
1	anonymous	5 Strongly agree	5 Strongly agree	5 Strongly agree
2	anonymous	5 Strongly agree	4 Agree	5 Strongly agree
3	anonymous	4 Agree	3 Neither agree nor disagree	4 Agree
4	anonymous	5 Strongly agree	5 Strongly agree	5 Strongly agree
5	anonymous	4 Agree	3 Neither agree nor disagree	4 Agree
6	anonymous	4 Agree	4 Agree	4 Agree
7	anonymous	5 Strongly agree	4 Agree	4 Agree
8	anonymous	5 Strongly agree	5 Strongly agree	5 Strongly agree

7. Curiosity

8 Responses

ID ↑	Name	Responses		
		I wanted to explore how the game evolved	I wanted to find out how the game progressed	I felt eager to discover how the game continued
1	anonymous	5 Strongly agree	5 Strongly agree	5 Strongly agree
2	anonymous	4 Agree	5 Strongly agree	5 Strongly agree
3	anonymous	5 Strongly agree	4 Agree	5 Strongly agree
4	anonymous	5 Strongly agree	5 Strongly agree	5 Strongly agree
5	anonymous	5 Strongly agree	4 Agree	5 Strongly agree
6	anonymous	5 Strongly agree	4 Agree	5 Strongly agree
7	anonymous	4 Agree	4 Agree	4 Agree
8	anonymous	5 Strongly agree	5 Strongly agree	5 Strongly agree

8. Immersion

8 Responses

ID ↑	Name	Responses		
		I was no longer aware of my surroundings while I was playing	I was immersed(fordybet) in the game	I was fully focused on the game
1	anonymous	5 Strongly agree	5 Strongly agree	5 Strongly agree
2	anonymous	3 Neither agree nor disagree	4 Agree	4 Agree
3	anonymous	4 Agree	5 Strongly agree	5 Strongly agree
4	anonymous	4 Agree	4 Agree	4 Agree
5	anonymous	4 Agree	5 Strongly agree	5 Strongly agree
6	anonymous	4 Agree	5 Strongly agree	4 Agree
7	anonymous	3 Neither agree nor disagree	4 Agree	4 Agree
8	anonymous	4 Agree	4 Agree	4 Agree

9. If there was something that retracked from your immersion, can you explain what it is?

4 Responses

ID ↑	Name	Responses
1	anonymous	sound
2	anonymous	I was surrounded by friends, and we had great fun talking
3	anonymous	If I was unable to accomplish something I wanted to do (like hit something with the axe, walk into the water etc) it could effect my focus on the game.
4	anonymous	lav FPS

10. Autonomy

8 Responses

ID ↑	Name	I felt free to play the game in my own way	I felt like I had choices regarding how I wanted to play this game	I felt a sense of freedom about how I wanted to play this game
1	anonymous	5 Strongly agree	5 Strongly agree	4 Agree
2	anonymous	5 Strongly agree	5 Strongly agree	4 Agree
3	anonymous	5 Strongly agree	5 Strongly agree	5 Strongly agree
4	anonymous	5 Strongly agree	5 Strongly agree	5 Strongly agree
5	anonymous	5 Strongly agree	5 Strongly agree	5 Strongly agree
6	anonymous	4 Agree	3 Neither agree nor disagree	4 Agree
7	anonymous	5 Strongly agree	4 Agree	4 Agree
8	anonymous	5 Strongly agree	5 Strongly agree	5 Strongly agree

11. Autonomy ekstra

8 Responses

ID	Name	the game	solve problems my own way	interacted with them	... much	... ending	... looking at them
1	anonymous	2 Disagree	3 Neither agree nor disagree	5 Strongly agree	5 Strongly agree	4 Agree	5 Strongly agree
2	anonymous	2 Disagree	2 Disagree	5 Strongly agree	4 Agree	4 Agree	4 Agree
3	anonymous	1 Strongly disagree	1 Strongly disagree	5 Strongly agree	5 Strongly agree	4 Agree	4 Agree
4	anonymous	1 Strongly disagree	1 Strongly disagree	5 Strongly agree	5 Strongly agree	4 Agree	5 Strongly agree
5	anonymous	3 Neither agree nor disagree	1 Strongly disagree	5 Strongly agree	5 Strongly agree	2 Disagree	3 Neither agree nor disagree
6	anonymous	4 Agree	4 Agree	3 Neither agree nor disagree	4 Agree	4 Agree	4 Agree
7	anonymous	2 Disagree	2 Disagree	4 Agree	5 Strongly agree	3 Neither agree nor disagree	5 Strongly agree
8	anonymous	2 Disagree	2 Disagree	5 Strongly agree	5 Strongly agree	4 Agree	4 Agree

12. Anything you would like to add to your answers about autonomy?

3 Responses

ID ↑	Name	Responses
1	anonymous	limitation of physical movement
2	anonymous	Had some difficulties differentiating between my bag, my clues, and what i had in my left and right hand. Sometimes you should left click sometimes you should press E. While it was easy to figure out, it wasn't intuitive
3	anonymous	Det var fedt, at man kunne tage tingene i sin egen rækkefølge og selv gå rundt og udforske

13. Narrative

8 Responses

ID ↑	Name	I would be able to retell the story to someone	I felt immersed in the story	I wanted to see how the story progressed	I felt the story was believable
1	anonymous	4 Agree	5 Strongly agree	5 Strongly agree	5 Strongly agree
2	anonymous	4 Agree	5 Strongly agree	5 Strongly agree	5 Strongly agree
3	anonymous	5 Strongly agree	5 Strongly agree	4 Agree	5 Strongly agree
4	anonymous	5 Strongly agree	4 Agree	5 Strongly agree	5 Strongly agree
5	anonymous	4 Agree	4 Agree	4 Agree	4 Agree
6	anonymous	4 Agree	4 Agree	4 Agree	4 Agree
7	anonymous	3 Neither agree nor disagree	3 Neither agree nor disagree	3 Neither agree nor disagree	4 Agree
8	anonymous	5 Strongly agree	5 Strongly agree	5 Strongly agree	5 Strongly agree

14. Want to add something else?

2 Responses

ID ↑	Name	Responses
1	anonymous	I loved that I could jump and sprint <3
2	anonymous	Great to play around in the game while collecting the clues. If you are a bit unfocused you can always just go and explore the game. Even if you just want to throw a rock at someones window. :-)

YouTube Video of a Playthrough of the Game Experiment

https://www.youtube.com/watch?v=o_eBtfHb90Q.

References

1. Deci, E.L., Ryan, R.M.: Intrinsic Motivation and Self-Determination in Human Behavior. Springer (2013). https://doi.org/10.1007/978-1-4899-2271-7
2. Calleja, G.: In-Game: From Immersion to Incorporation. MIT Press (2011)
3. Deathloop Should Be Amazing - But Isn't [YouTube Video]. YouTube (2022). https://www.youtube.com/watch?v=uOs5QPUuvKQ&t=267s
4. GamersPrey: Deathloop - Full Gameplay Walkthrough [HD 1080P] [Video]. YouTube (2021). https://www.youtube.com/watch?v=HaEqzsYzTwI
5. Kevin, L.: The Image of the City. MIT Press (1960)
6. Metacritic: Deathloop. Metacritics (2023). https://www.metacritic.com/game/pc/deathloop
7. Rigby, S., Ryan, R.M.: Glued to Games: How Video Games Draw Us In and Hold Us Spellbound. AbC-CLIo (2011)
8. Shodhan, S.: Intrinsic vs Extrinsic Motivation in Games. Medium (2017). https://medium.com/@SharanShodhan/intrinsic-and-extrinsic-motivation-in-games-a8bbc06aac4
9. Sweetser, P.: Emergence in Games. Game Connect Asia Pacific (2008)
10. Sweetser, P., Wyeth, P.: GameFlow: a model for evaluating player enjoyment in games. Comput. Entertainment 3(3), 3–3 (2005). https://doi.org/10.1145/1077246.1077253
11. Thomas, I.: How free-to-play and in-game purchases took over the video game industry. CNBC (2022). https://www.cnbc.com/2022/10/06/how-free-to-play-and-in-game-purchases-took-over-video-games.html
12. Azadvar, A.; Canossa, A.: UPEQ: ubisoft perceived experience questionnaire: a self-determination evaluation tool for video games. In Proceedings of the 13th International Conference on the Foundations of Digital Games, pp. 1–7. ACM, Malmö, Sweden (2018)
13. Abeele, V.V., Spiel, K., Nacke, L., Johnson, D., Gerling, K.: Development and validation of the player experience inventory: a scale to measure player experiences at the level of functional and psychosocial consequences. Int. J. Hum. Comput. Stud. 1(135), 102370 (2020)
14. Vanden Abeele ,V., Nacke, L.E., Mekler, E.D., Johnson, D.: Design and preliminary validation of the player experience inventory. In: Proceedings of the 2016 Annual Symposium on Computer-Human Interaction in Play Companion Extended Abstracts, pp. 335–341 (2016)
15. xwatchmanx: How would you define hand-holding in games? reddit r/truegaming (2014). https://www.reddit.com/r/truegaming/comments/1ufccn/how_would_you_define_handholding_in_games/

Design and Research of an Interactive Game Based on Motion-Sensing Technology for Huizhou Brick Carvings

Jie Wang and Rongrong Fu(✉)

College of Art Design and Media, East China University of Science and Technology, Shanghai, China

ieiewang@163.com

Abstract. As an important part of Huizhou culture and art, Huizhou brick carving integrates social customs, folk beliefs and carving art, and has high cultural and artistic values. At present, the ageing of Huizhou brick carving craftsmen, the loss of illustrated plates and the lack of attention to it by younger groups have led to a crisis of survival for the inheritance of this folk cultural heritage [1]. In order to solve the problem of the lack of protection and inheritance of Huizhou brick carvings, this paper adopts a somatosensory interactive game design applied to the study of the inheritance of Huizhou brick carvings, by recognizing and analyzing the user's body movements to trigger the interaction between the game character and the scene, so as to give the user a sense of immersion and thus stimulate the interest and attention of the young group to Huizhou brick carvings. EEG, eye-movement and focus group interviews were used to obtain the user's preferences on the factors of the craft physical interactive game experience from both rational and emotional perspectives. In order to assist the subsequent design practice of the emblematic brick carving somatic interactive game. Finally, the design effect of the game was evaluated to verify that the approach can effectively enhance users' attention and awareness of Huizhou brick carving art, providing a method for the application of somatosensory technology in the study of the living Intangible Cultural Heritage (ICH).

Keywords: Huizhou brick carving · physical interactive games · intangible cultural heritage

1 Introduction

Huizhou brick carving is one of the most important decorative tools in ancient and modern architecture, fused by exquisite craftsmanship, profound historical and cultural heritage and unique artistic techniques, and is a wonder in the field of ancient Chinese architecture. In recent years, with social changes and cultural transformations, as well as architectural changes, Huizhou brick carving is gradually moving away from its original application space and heritage, and is one of the first national intangible cultural heritages in China to be rescued and supported. It has been found that the heritage of

J. Y. C. Chen et al. (Eds.): HCII 2023, LNCS 14058, pp. 370–393, 2023.
https://doi.org/10.1007/978-3-031-48050-8_25

traditional Huizhou carving art is mostly passed on to a few inheritors, through word and example rather than a popular cultural heritage system, which severely limits the efficiency of handicraft transmission [2]. Secondly, the manual knowledge system and the popularization of science is relatively single, lacking in interactivity and experience, making it difficult to attract the interest of young groups to Huizhou brick carving leading to less attention to it, and the protection of Huizhou brick carving craft is imminent. Nowadays, physical interactive games cater to the preferences and lifestyles of a new generation of young audiences, which is an important opportunity for digital innovation of intangible cultural heritage [3].

In this study, the user participates in the production process of Huizhou brick carvings through an interactive physical game, which emphasises the use of visuals, stories and movements to stimulate participants' interest in brick carvings, enabling the heritage to be better inherited and protected in everyday life. Therefore, transforming the intangible heritage craft into a tangible physical game is conducive to developing ways to showcase the NRM. In order to design a physical interactive game that meets the cultural needs of contemporary people. The author applied EEG experiment, eye movement experiment, focus group and questionnaire research based on user experience hierarchy theory to complete the design practice of physical interactive game for Huizhou brick carving.

2 Related Research

2.1 Analysis of the Application of Somatic Games in Intangible Cultural Heritage

Craft knowledge is complex, and the traditional form of popular science introduction is monotonous and boring, lacking interactive experience of the craft process, movement and body, etc., which is not ideal. Through the use of visual content and somatosensory interactive technology, abstract and incomprehensible craft knowledge can be presented through a richer sensory experience and interaction. It is highly feasible.

By combing through the relevant literature, we found that scholars have already made attempts, such as Lu Wen, who, from the perspective of revitalising the inheritance of folk non-heritage skills, combined somatosensory technology with the Phoenix blue-printed fabric printing and dyeing skills to design an interactive game with the process as the main line, promoting the inheritance and protection of the blue-printed fabric craft [4] From the perspective of traditional folk craft heritage, Yu Yali combines the conservation of Tujia brocade techniques with somatosensory technology to design and implement an interactive Tujia brocade virtual weaving science system, deepening people's basic knowledge of Tujia brocade culture [5]. Lu Yi combined virtual reality and somatosensory interaction with digital technologies to design a popular weaving game, taking cloud brocade weaving techniques as an example, to develop a more flexible and efficient way to pass on the weaving skills [6].

2.2 Research on the Importance of User Experience in Physical Games

Games are a form of experience with fun and entertainment at its core, and the immersive experience of users helps them to gain more fun and relevant knowledge during the gaming experience. Some scholars have demonstrated that immersion plays a significant role in the behavioural intention to use a game experience. Chin-Lung Hsu demonstrated that there is indeed a very strong link between immersion and gaming, and that immersion substantially enhances the experience and intention to use a game [7]. Shin verified that immersion plays a significant role in the satisfaction and intention to use an online game learning platform [8]. Bai Yu constructed a model of the influence of individual persistent behavioural intention to use regarding online games and the results showed that immersion experience is not only an important factor in constituting student players' satisfaction but also the most significant and direct influence factor on their persistent behavioural intention [9]. Ju Yu argues that the sense of experience can significantly influence the behavioural intention to learn games [10]. Wei Ting constructs a model of the factors influencing participants' behavioural intention to play, and verifies that the sense of experience has a significant effect on behavioural intention to play, which in turn influences users' usage behaviour [11].

2.3 Summary

Therefore, this study determines that the starting point is to enhance the user's sense of experience and to investigate which factors in intangible cultural heritage craft-based physical games affect the sense of experience and thus the behavioral intention to play, so as to make traditional crafts more appealing to the public and to achieve the effective inheritance of Intangible Cultural Heritage crafts.

3 Research on Factors Influencing User Experience of Emblematic Brick Carving Physical Interactive Game

3.1 Extraction of User Experience Layers of Emblematic Brick Carving Physical Interactive Game

Donald.A.Norman put forward the theory of universal experience layering in Emotional Design, which divides the cognitive processing of users into three levels: instinctive layer, behavioral layer and reflective layer [12]. Emotion is a human psychological response to external things when they act on themselves, determined by needs and expectations [13]. This is a method of analysing users based on their psychological perspective. There have been attempts by scholars to apply the theory of experience hierarchy to design. Chen Weiwen analyses the application of the three-level theory to the interaction design of information products such as the Florence game to enhance the user experience and the fun of the game [14]. Zhang Lude and Li Zhichun propose a method of using design elements to express culture. Through the cultural symbols of the product, the user will be able to associate and resonate with the relevant experience or emotion, thus perceiving the cultural imagery in the product [15]. Therefore, based on the experience layering theory proposed by Norman, combined with the characteristics of the brick carving process and the audience's game experience preference, the author further refined the experience layers of the physical interactive game of Huizhou brick carving. The instinctive layer corresponds to the aesthetics of the game scene design, the behavioral layer corresponds to the rationality of the interactive action and the clarity of the narrative structure, and the reflective layer corresponds to the intangible cultural heritage connotation and audience expectations conveyed by the physical interactive game.

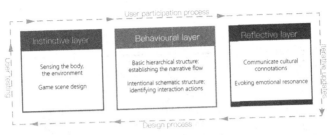

Fig. 1. Diagram of the three-level theoretical model of experience

3.2 Establishing the Target Users of the Huizhou Brick Carving Interactive Game

The original purpose of the handicraft game is to stimulate people's interest in traditional handicrafts through digital games, so that users can have a better experience of traditional handicrafts and thus achieve the popularisation and inheritance of handicrafts. As youth is a critical period of cultural plasticity, it is important to integrate the heritage of traditional crafts into the process of cultivating cultural confidence in youth. The digital nature of interactive games makes it easier for young people who are used to using media to learn about handicrafts. Therefore, this paper takes young people such as primary and secondary school students and university students (14–28) as the main target users.

3.3 EEG Experiment to Obtain a Sample of User Preferences

Experimental Design. The EEG and focus group interviews were selected to obtain user preferences on the factors of cultural physical interactive game experience from both rational and emotional perspectives.

In order to obtain the games with higher user preference among the existing games on the market for further research, three groups of cultural communication games were selected as samples, and the Muse rationality test was used as the basis to obtain the user's preference for different interactive games through EEG data. The top three games in terms of overall preference were selected for the subsequent focus group perceptual analysis.

Experimental Sample. The author selected national cultural public welfare institutions - Guangzhou Cultural Museum, Zhenjiang Folk Culture and Art Museum; well-known museums - Cleveland Museum of Art, Xinqi Technology Company - Little Gyro Technology, and the somatosensory game company - Guangzhou Feitai Digital, etc. Six somatosensory interactive games with the role of cultural science popularization were selected as samples for comparative study, namely: "Chen's Needle Technique", "Muscle and Bone with Treatment", "Dragon Boat Noon Tea", "The Legend of the White Snake Wall is Coming", "Herzhe Fishing and Hunting Culture", and "Shadow Somatosensory Interactive Game" (Tables 2, 3 and 4).

Table 1. Somatic interactive game sample numbers

No.	1	2	3	4	5	6
Games						
Culture	Acupuncture	Herb Picking	Muscle and bone treatment	Tale of the White Snake	Fishing and hunting	Leather Shadow

Experimental Subjects. Fifteen target users aged 20–30 years were invited to participate in the experiment, so that the subjects volunteered to participate in the experiment, were in good physical and mental health, had normal vision or corrected vision before the experiment, and had no a priori knowledge of the content of the experiment. In order to exclude confounding factors, the subjects were asked to wash their hair and keep their face plain before conducting the experiment.

Experimental Equipment. Muse2, iPad, Muse: the app for Meditation& Sleep.

Experimental Indicators. A higher value of Active means that the sample is more stimulated, more aroused and more interested in the subject; conversely, a higher value of Neutral and Calm means that the sample is less stimulated, less aroused and less interested in the subject, On the contrary, the higher the value of Neutral and Calm, the weaker the stimulus and the lower the arousal level of the sample, and the less interested the subject.

Experimental Procedure. The subjects were guided to perceive the overall picture and text of the physical game to be shown, and were guided to look at the cross in the centre of the iPad screen for 10s, followed by the presentation of the first stimulus material, informing the subjects that they had 1 min 30 s to understand the game action style, the game interface display and the game narrative background through the picture and text independently, and to save the EEG data through the app; then a white screen of 1000 ms was presented, followed by the presentation of the second stimulus material for 1 min 30 s, and so on, until all 6 models were understood at the end.

Table 2. Summary of Muse data statistics for the somatic interactive game sample

Active/Neutral	Sample 1		Sample 2		Sample 3		Sample 4		Sample 5		Sample 6	
	A	N	A	N	A	N	A	N	A	N	A	N
Subject 1	5	21	0	8	0	35	2	16	0	17	0	27
Subject 2	6	12	0	25	1	7	0	18	0	20	0	22
Subject 3	0	30	0	30	0	13	0	30	0	38	4	28
Subject 4	4	67	2	70	0	35	0	35	2	40	9	29
Subject 5	1	78	2	76	1	79	0	81	0	72	0	71
Subject 6	0	76	0	30	0	57	1	64	0	39	6	49
Subject 7	0	71	3	30	0	9	0	64	0	76	3	67
Subject 8	0	4	3	28	3	39	0	76	0	57	0	64
Subject 9	0	7	0	29	0	77	0	16	0	85	0	6
Subject 10	0	27	4	63	43	21	0	32	0	75	0	12
Subject 11	0	21	0	21	0	32	0	87	0	87	0	60
Subject 12	6	2	3	103	61	23	0	19	0	74	5	24
Subject 13	6	26	0	68	0	47	2	69	0	70	0	33
Subject 14	0	33	0	78	0	79	0	57	0	73	0	24
Subject 15	0	39	0	30	3	72	0	21	0	24	0	72
Total	28	514	17	689	112	625	5	675	2	847	27	588

Analysis of Experimental Results. The Active values of the six game samples are shown in Table 1, where the three with the highest Active values are divided into Sample 3, Sample, Sample 1 and Sample 6, corresponding to "Dragon Boat Noon Tea", "Chen's Needlework" and "Shadow Physical Interactive Game". The three physical interactive games have a high level of brain arousal for the subjects and can be used for further research.

3.4 Eye-Movement Experiments to Obtain User Preferences

Experimental Design. The subjects were eight design professionals, six females and two males, with no eye disease occurring within 1 month prior to the experiment. The subjects had a clear understanding of the cultural connotations and meanings associated with the text and were not involved in the EEG experiment for the physical game described above.

Experimental task: In order to obtain the focus of the user's attention on the overall information of the game scene images, the subjects were asked to randomly view 6 images of scenes from sample 5, the game "Herdzhe Fishing and Hunting Culture", with a 3D complete story scene, to find the area that best matches the cultural allegory and to keep viewing it. The number of times each subject looked at each area and the

Table 3. Outline of the interviews

Interview dimensions		Content of the interview
Instinctive layer	Game interface design	What are your impressions of the painting style and composition of the three sensory games? Do you think there are any visual and aural aspects of these sensory games that need to be improved?
Behavioural layer	Interaction rationality	1. Does the whole operation move properly? Are there any parts that are good or bad? 2. Is the physical motion of entering or switching scenes appropriate?
	Narrative content architecture design	1. Which of the three sensory games do you like better? What are the reasons for this? 2. Was the cultural knowledge told by these games clear to you through understanding them? 3. Which point of the story structure of the three interactive physical games appealed to you the most and which point did you dislike?
Reflective layer	Audience expectations	1. Please describe your first impressions of these three interactive games 2. What kind of craft games do you have in mind? Do the current games meet your expectations?

time spent in each area were obtained using the SMI EMG eye-tracking device to record the subjects' research attention process to find the best points of interest. Typical parts were classified using distance clustering methods and the typicality of each part was ranked quantitatively using the average attention duration as the basis for calculation.

Presenting each image for 20 s allows subjects to fully understand and perform the task without losing interest in the area of interest due to increased eye fatigue from looking at it for too long.

Analysis of Experimental Data. Figure 4 shows the eye-tracking attention span hotspots for the main scenes of the somatosensory game sample, with the areas of highest relative attention represented in red on each hotspot and the remaining areas differentiated using a colour gradient (Fig. 5).

From the figure, we can see that the eye-movement attention areas of the interactive games are mainly focused on the characters, costumes and other props. Combining the

Table 4. User interview data

Subjects	Highlights of interview responses	Elements of experience to consider
Student Yu	• The interface is not aesthetically pleasing and is too simple • Lack of immersion in the game's interactive actions • Expect craft-based physical games to have a real sense of experience and showcase homemade achievements	1. Beautiful graphics 2. Action design ensures ease of use and a sense of control 3. Fun gameplay mechanics
Student Wang	• The game's rewards and the loss of a sense of achievement in playing the game • Availability of audio feedback such as "good job", "go for it", etc	1. Game mechanics, such as leveling 2. Multi-sensory feedback methods e.g. auditory feedback
Student Li	• Consider balance, some will find it easy others find it difficult • Some operations are not known and the lack of help makes the experience impossible	1. User skill levels are balanced 2. guidance for novice users
Student Wang	• Interactive action is slightly one-dimensional • The game is set in a setting that has substance and conveys cultural values	1. The difficulty of the target content is reasonable 2. The game graphics should be in keeping with the craft culture
Student Sun	• No innovation in the form of interaction, a single imitation of intangible cultural heritage crafts • Game content that generates empathy can increase player interest	1. Smooth system and feedback on the progress of the action content 2. The game is connected to life and close to the public
Student Cui	• What is the relationship between the action and the real craft, and the rationale for such a setup • Can cultural physicality be edgy and bold, with visual diversity	1. Realistic fit of target content and action 2. Content and variety, freedom of choice 3. Simple information and balanced interaction settings
Student Jin	• The action is displayed immediately after it is done and the device is stable without lagging • Is the game scene closely integrated with the craft culture	1. Smooth system and fast action triggers 2. Targeted content with authentic cultural
Student Chu	• The game's graphics lack authenticity • The game needs to give the user a rewarding point	1. Beautifully designed and authentic graphics and experience content 2. Multi-dimensional feedback and cultural atmosphere

(continued)

Table 4. (*continued*)

Subjects	Highlights of interview responses	Elements of experience to consider
Student Pan	• Interface design elements that are culturally relevant, such as screen shapes • Visually recreate the cultural atmosphere of intangible cultural heritage crafts • Simple action but requires its own space to operate, with a sense of immersion	1. Backgrounds, images and text are in harmony with each other 2. The storyline presents cultural knowledge 3. Interaction design is easy to use and allows for the dissemination of cultural knowledge
Student Qi	• Narrative explanation about the science and technology vehicle, don't just come up and do operations that you can't understand • I don't know how far I've gone in the case of long-stage learning tasks	1. Narrative explanation 2. Fast scene switching and loading with progress display

(a) Muse equipment

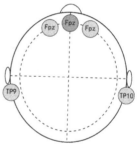
(b) Muse device sensor click position

Fig. 2. Schematic diagram of the EEG equipment (source: author's own)

eye-movement attention areas and the relative duration of attention, we can calculate the typical preference elements of users for physical interactive games.

3.5 Selection of Factors for Experiencing the Effect of Physical Play on Huizhou Brick Carvings

Test Materials. Considering that some of the interviewees did not know enough about the sense of action experience of the somatic game, which might affect the real validity of the interview data. Therefore, the author selected the "Dreamland" somatic game and invited the subjects to fully understand and experience the somatic game after the EEG experiment. As shown in Figs. 1, 2, 3 and 4 Dreamland is a highly artistic VR interactive somatic game with cute and rich characters, poetic scenes, and emotionally delicate music, forming a warm and healing rescue story that captures the movement of

Fig. 3. Diagram of the EEG experiment process (source: photographed)

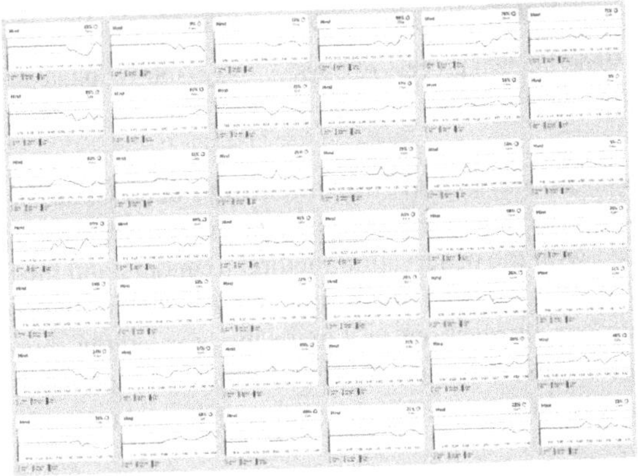

Fig. 4. Schematic of Mind Meditation app data (source: author's own)

Fig. 5. "Herdzhe Fishing and Hunting Culture" physical game scene screen eye movement hotspot map

the body and hands, enabling interactive somatic exploration in this "amazing journey". It also allows the subjects to experience the physical action from a multi-dimensional perspective (Fig. 6).

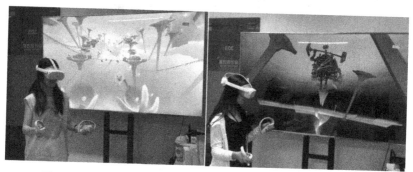

Fig. 6. Experimental process of physical play (source: photographed)

Designing Interview Questions and Implementing Focus Groups. In the use of the interview method, more detailed research and interviews are conducted with the test population, combined with the observation method to understand the obvious problems in the experience process, to understand in depth the reasons for the problems, to understand the game operations or reactions will make the user tedious, bored, intimidated or frustrated, which operations or reactions will make the user motivated, pleasure, immersion, etc. This summarises the impact of the craft science and technology physical game experience Factors.

The aim of the focus group was to make a perceptual analysis of the reasons why the first three games have a higher level of arousal in the user's brain, and at the same time to propose secondary influencing factors that affect the experience of the emblematic brick carving somatic game, taking into account the characteristics of the emblematic brick carving intangible cultural heritage craft. The specific interview outline is as follows:

After the interviews, the author summarised the results of the interviews and combined them with the sub-projects obtained from the aforementioned experimental eaves picking and literature research to further distil the seven design indicators that affect the experience of physical interactive games, as shown in Table 5. They are divided into four aspects: scene and screen design, interactive action design, narrative structure design and audience targeting.

Extraction of Influencing Factors of Emblematic Brick Carving Somatic Interactive Game. According to the influencing factors of the user experience of the physical interactive game summarized above, combined with the craft characteristics of the intangible cultural heritage Huizhou brick carving, the influencing factors affecting the game experience of Huizhou brick carving are proposed, as shown in Table 6.

Table 5. Factors influencing user experience of physical interactive games

Dimensions		Extraction of key elements	Explanations
Instinctive layer	Scene design	Overall style Realism of content scenes Diversification of sensory interactions Rationalisation of the interface layout	Coordinated scenery, music and character style in line with the non-fiction cultural atmosphere Realistic experience content and authentic experience atmosphere scenes Close connection between scenes and sound effects, enhancing the sense of participation through multi-sensory presentation Clear core messages and functional distinctions
Instinctive layer	Interaction Motion Design	Easy to operate	Crafting corresponds to an easy action interaction and is not particularly difficult
		Action available	The presentation is process specific and the logic of the process interaction is clear
		Movement guidelines	The corresponding action is introduced before the interaction and can be studied for reference
		Smooth system	Stable interaction system, fast and sensitive scene switching and motion recognition, no lag
		Freedom of movement	Freedom of choice of interaction, free from guidance control

(continued)

Table 5. (*continued*)

Dimensions		Extraction of key elements	Explanations
	Narrative Architecture Design	Contextual narrative	Presenting cultural knowledge in a way that is engaging and interesting through storytelling, etc
		Process Levels	Experience a wide range of craft content by gradually unlocking pipe cards
		Playfulness Effect presentation	By setting up interactive social interaction, achievement incentive system, competition and other modes of fighting to make users have continuous learning fun There could be some sort of reward mechanism at the end of the game, or a spin-off of my participation in the design
Reflective layer	Market audience expectations	Emotional objectives	Ability to connect with users emotionally and drive the full user experience
		Cultural Objectives	Enables the dissemination of cultural knowledge of non-traditional crafts

3.6 Conclusion

Through the analysis of experience preferences in the above experiments, it was found that the subjects' concerns and interests in somatic interactive games fell on the immersion of scene graphics, the sense of interactive action experience, narrative design and emotional-cultural expectations. Therefore, this study takes scene graphics, interactive action, narrative structure and cultural-emotional content as the key elements to guide somatic design and provide solutions for the heritage of Huizhou brick carvings.

Table 6. Factors influencing the user experience of the emblematic brick carving physical interactive game

Dimensions	Tier 1 Influencing Factors	Secondary influences
Scene design	Overall style Content scene immersion Diversification of sensory interactions Rationalisation of interface layout	Ancient Chinese Style Three-dimensional brick workshop scene construction Soft and gentle music Highly saturated or low saturation style
Interaction design	Usable and easy to use actions	A single line of story advances through the brickwork process User-adapted process exploration Somatosensory devices as motion capture
	Movement guidance mechanism	Text or voice prompts
	Movement presentation	3D animated scenes with text Animated with audio explanation
Narrative Architecture Design	Story Narrative Situation Selection	The Story of a Non-Generic Inheritor The History of Huizhou Brick Carving
	Process Levels	Brick making process as a barrier
	Effect presentation	Presenting a homemade brick sculpture Redeem the reward value and finish straight away
Market audience expectations	Emotional objectives	A sense of immersion and experience A sense of achievement in the game
	Cultural Objectives	Easy-to-learn knowledge of brickwork culture﹑Interesting

4 Design Practice

4.1 Game Objectives and Strategies

This study uses Leap Motion combined with the Unity3D game development platform to design a physical game that promotes the inheritance and promotion of the Huizhou brick carving craft to achieve an immersive experience display effect to enhance the experience of the brick carving craft. In response to the current relatively homogeneous inheritance and boring exhibition methods of Huizhou brick carving, the steps, techniques, tools and technologies required for the production of Huizhou brick carving are presented in a virtual, dynamic form, allowing the audience to understand the process of brick carving more intuitively while deepening the degree of impact of Huizhou brick carving's intangible cultural heritage culture.

The design uses Leap Motion to obtain hand motion information (Fig. 7), which enhances human-computer interaction, and proposes a game to simulate the production process of Huizhou brick carving, allowing the user to experience the whole process through hand motion. --scene graphics, interactive movements, narrative structure, cultural and emotional content, providing users with a sense of immersive experience. The interactive game will motivate the participants and promote their interest in Huizhou brick carving (Fig. 8).

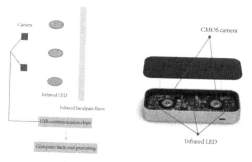

Fig. 7. Schematic diagram of how Leap Motion works

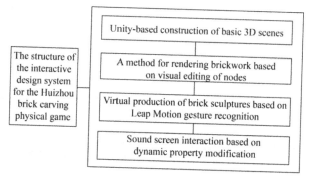

Fig. 8. Interaction design system architecture diagram (source: author's own)

This dynamic display of physical interaction can vividly realise the digital conservation and inheritance of the Huizhou brick carving process, providing a new solution to promote the intangible cultural heritage culture of brick carving. It enables the audience to understand the process of brick carving more intuitively and can attract more people to pay attention to the Huizhou brick carving culture.

4.2 Design Options

3D Scene Design. The game is based on Unity to build a 3D scene depicting the process of Huizhou brick carving, which includes the design of scenes, characters, actions, production tools and other screen content (Fig. 9). The scene design style matches the unique square foot green and grey brick colour of Huizhou brick carving, combined with the characteristics of Huizhou architectural doorways and lintels, to meet the user's need to experience Huizhou brick carving culture in a more realistic scene [16] (Fig. 9).

Fig. 9. D3D scene diagram for physical game - scene, characters, production tools (source: author's own production)

Interaction Gesture Design. The Leap Motion device sets 10 gestures, captures and collects the player's joints in real time to determine the player's movement, and matches the collected gesture information with the gestures in the pre-set gesture model library to obtain the final The game flow is shown in Fig. 10, with the corresponding Huizhou brick carving steps being shown on the screen, where the system sets out the actions of bowing to the master, smoothing the bricks, drawing the pattern, hammering the bricks (as shown), and assembling the bricks (Fig. 11).

Narrative Architecture Design. Narrative design is the telling of a story to an audience in a specific way, while narrative design is the use of design methods to cleverly combine

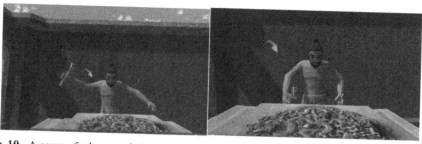

Fig. 10. A scene of a hammer being swung and chiselled during the bashing of a Huizhou brick carving

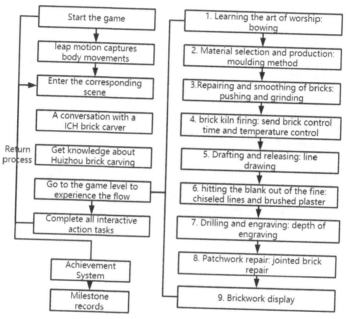

Fig. 11. Flow chart of the game experience (source: author's own)

elements such as story subjects, targets, props and scenes to ultimately achieve immersive communication between people and design works [17]. This is the most critical aspect of the whole session, and also the difficult part of the design. The use of narrative design in physical games can effectively attract players to participate, guide them to actively switch their identity roles to participate in the game, promote the development of the storyline, and better enhance the players' experience. This study uses narrative thinking to convey information about the scenes, making it easier for players to understand the content of the game. Players take on the role of "apprentice" to naturally integrate into the game process (as shown in the figure), which can produce a change from "entertainment" to "story", and then from "story The transformation from "entertainment" to "story" and then from "story" to "Huizhou brick carving craft" enriches the emotional journey of the player [18] (Fig. 12).

Fig. 12. The start of the game "learning from a master" scene

The game is called "Craftsmanship" and takes the workflow of Huizhou brick carving as the main narrative line, so that the player is brought in as an "apprentice" to build a half-virtual, half-realistic world. According to the Huizhou brick carving process, the narrative structure of the game can be broken down into nine key processes, and the narrative screen design is shown in Table 7. The 'master' will lead the player into the brick carving workshop and teach the player the craft of brick carving through the scenario elements set in the game (Fig. 13) (Tables 8 and 9).

4.3 Application Scenarios

The main application scenario of the game is in museums related to Huizhou brick carvings. The introduction of brick carving culture in Chinese museums is mostly based on static display collections and textual introduction boards and voice explanations. The application of physical interactive games can change the original written and one-way introduction in museums, with the characteristics of intuitiveness, vividness and experience in terms of storytelling, visual presentation and interactive design [19], and broaden the way of inheritance of intangible cultural heritage Huizhou brick carvings. Users can learn about the relevant cultural knowledge while participating in the somatic interactive game, and also connect the process with the offline collection [20], enhancing the effect of preserving and passing on the Huizhou brick carving process, and providing a demonstration value for the digital innovative display of other craft museums. Secondly, somatic interaction is gradually being used in many fields due to its unique advantages, such as civic and entertainment venues, educational organisations, shop windows and exhibition halls.

Table 7. Game narrative architecture diagram

Designing a narrative structure for a physical game of Huizhou brick carving				
Process plot		Movement	Scene screen content	Scenery
Join the shop and learn from a teacher		The protagonist pays homage to his master Bend over and bow	Huizhou Brick Carving Craft Workshop	Panorama
Pre-kiln process	1. Selection of material for making the blank	Moulded brick moulding Stepping clay	The brick carver uses a wooden mould on the ground to form the bricks	Panorama
	2. Brick kiln firing	Brick delivery for firing	The embryo of the brick sculpture is sent to a brick kiln to be fired into water-ground green fine bricks	Panorama
Post kiln process	3. Brick repair and smoothing	Pushing the mill	Manual or instrumental polishing of the side to be engraved	Medium view
	4. Drawings	Sketches In-depth contouring	Depicting floral motifs, figures, etc	Special Features
	5. Blanking out fine	Tool chisel line Painting grey	A burin or tapping hand is used by hand to make a shallow groove along the handwriting Remove dust with a brush	Medium view Special Features

(continued)

Table 7. (*continued*)

Designing a narrative structure for a physical game of Huizhou brick carving			
Process plot	Movement	Scene screen content	Scenery
6. Nail the hole 7. Carving open face	Drill pattern outer profile The knocker and burin carve out the shades	The master picks up a burin and other tools to do detailed carving of brickwork, such as figures with open faces Hollowed out layered effect	Medium view Special Features
8. Patchwork repair	Two brick sculptures combined Repairing damage	Gluing the carved brickwork together The bonding compound is applied to the bricks for repair	Special Features
Artwork presentation	Display	The work is shown enlarged in the scene	Panorama

5 Design Validity Assessment

5.1 Experimental Design

In order to verify whether "Crafting Emblem Carving" can form effective communication among youth groups, the EEG data of different types of users in feeling the game scenes were recorded using the Muse experiment, and at the same time, the subjects were allowed to experience the game after increasing the questionnaire to make subjective assessment. The secondary influencing factors affecting the experience of the emblematic brick carving physical interactive game obtained in the previous section were combined with the experimental sample to create a questionnaire according to the Likert scale method.

Table 8. Summary of Muse data statistics

	Active
Subject 1	8
Subject 2	3
Subject 3	14
Subject 4	5
Subject 5	1
Subject 6	16
Subject 7	0
Subject 8	30
Subject 9	17
Subject 10	6
Subject 11	4
Subject 12	21
Subject 13	11
Subject 14	3
Subject 15	5
Total	144

Table 9. Post-test questionnaire data statistics

	Scene visualisation	Interactive actions	Introductory mechanism	Narrative	Interesting	accomplishment
Average	3.66	4.33	3.89	4.56	4.22	3.67

5.2 Experimental Subjects

A total of 15 subjects were invited and divided into two groups: 8 in group A were experienced players who experienced physical games at a high frequency, but did not know about Huizhou brick carving; 7 in group B were brick carving enthusiasts, but had almost no contact with physical games.

5.3 Experimental Procedure

Subjects were informed of the overall perception of the emblematic brick carving physical game that was about to be presented. Nine game scene images and text of the game "Craftsmanship Huizhou Carving" were presented, and the user experienced the game independently for 1min30s, and the experiment ended. The subjects are then asked to experience the "Craftsmanship Brick Carving" physical game and a questionnaire is distributed after the experience (Fig. 14).

01拜师学艺	02选料制坯	03砖窑烧制
04修砖磨平	05画稿放样	06打坯出细
07钻孔雕刻	08拼接修补	09作品呈现

Fig. 13. Example of a game with multiple craft scenes

Fig. 14. Game experience site (source: photo)

The data from the Muse EEG experiment showed that the Active value of Crafted Emblem was higher than the six experimental samples in the previous section, indicating that users' preference for the game was higher than that of several existing cultural and physical interactive games on the market. At the same time, questions were asked in the form of a questionnaire on important experience factors such as scene graphics, interactive actions and narrative design, which were highly preferred by users in the preliminary research of the game, and the results of the questionnaire showed that users rated Crafted Emblem Carving relatively high overall.

6 Conclusion

This study takes Huizhou brick carvings as the research object, based on EEG experiments, focus groups and questionnaire analysis, and the specific research results are as follows: firstly, a research model of cultural science and popularization of physical interactive games was constructed from the perspective of combining physiology and psychology; secondly, by exploring the preference of different influencing factors on the experience of Huizhou brick carvings, a research method was proposed to increase the viscosity of young people to cultural science and popularization of physical interactive games through quantitative analysis; thirdly, using physical interactive games as a carrier for the heritage of intangible cultural heritage crafts, it provides a method for the contemporary heritage of Huizhou brick carvings and other Chinese crafts. Thirdly, using interactive games as a vehicle to inherit the intangible cultural heritage crafts, it provides a new solution for the contemporary inheritance of Huizhou brick carving and other intangible cultural heritage crafts in China.

References

1. Zhu, M., Kai, H.: The heritage and innovation of Huizhou brick carving. J. Tongling College **8**(04), 89–90 (2009)
2. Jun, C.: Study on the "resurrection" of traditional "extinct" handicrafts: an example of Huizhou brick carving "nine-layer hollowing" technique .J. Decoration (05), 99–101 (2017)
3. Tang, J, Zhu, X.: Exploring the development and application of serious game projects in digital non-genetic heritage .J. Library Intell. Work **64**(10), 35–45 (2020)
4. Lu, W., Ouda, Y.: Interactive game design of Phoenix blue print based on somatosensory technology .J. Packaging Eng. **43**(04),182–188 (2022)
5. Yu, Y.: Design and implementation of an interactive virtual weaving system for Tujia brocade weaving. D. Huazhong Normal University (2017)
6. Lu, Y.: Virtual technology as a wing - Exploring the digital practical heritage of Nanjing cloud brocade weaving techniques. J. Nanjing Art College J. (Art and Design) (06), 157–160 (2020)
7. Choi, D., Kim, J.: Why people continue to play online games: in search of critical design factors to increase customer loyalty to online contents. J. Cyberpsychology Behav. (2004)
8. Shin, N.: Online learner's flow experience: an empirical study. J. British J. Educational Technol. **37**(5), 705–720 (2006)
9. Bai, Y.: A theoretical model and empirical study of the factors influencing individuals' intention to continue using online games. Shaanxi Normal University (2014)
10. Yu, J.: Study on the factors influencing behavioral intention of game-based learning and strategies to enhance it. Nanjing University of Posts and Telecommunications (2021)
11. Wei, T.: Modeling and empirical research on the factors influencing the behavioral intention of educational game participants. Nanjing Normal University (2011)
12. Norman, D.A., Fu, Q., Zheng, J.: Emotional Design. Electronic Publishing House, Beijing (2005)
13. He, C., Zhang, W.: Emotional design of tableware for preschool children. J. Design **34**(17), 139–141 (2021)
14. Weiwen, C.: Research on emotional interaction design in mobile phone games: the example of the game Florence. J. Design **32**(11), 31–33 (2019)

15. Tan, A., Li, H.: A literature review of product emotional design research. J. Design (01), 74–75 (2016)
16. Shuo, H.: Report on the study of brick carving in Huizhou. J. Brick and tile **05**, 55–59 (2009)
17. Hai-ya, W.: Narrative design of cultural and creative products based on experience level. J. Packaging Eng. **41**(16), 30–335 (2020)
18. Zhang, K., Gao, Z.: Study on the design of child medical products based on the narrative design. J. Zhuangshi (1), 11 (2018)
19. Garzotto, F., Rizzo, F.: Interaction paradigms in technology-enhanced social spaces: a case study in Museums. ACM Press, New York (2007)
20. Zhao, X.T., Wu, H.S., Su, Q.Y., et al.: A case study in museums. J. Compar. Study cultural Innovation **5**(35), 157–160 (2021)

Research on Design Strategy of Puppetry Based on Octalysis Framework

Lu Xu[⊠] and Tianhong Fang

College of Art Design and Media, East China University of Science and Technology, Shanghai,
China
1625223757@qq.com

Abstract. Puppetry is one of the representative important cultural heritages in China. However, in the digital age, the survival environment of puppetry has been strongly impacted by digital media, and its inheritance and development face enormous challenges. Meanwhile, the use of serious games (SG) in education and culture and their teaching effectiveness are widely recognized. Therefore, this paper aims to help such intangible cultural heritage to achieve effective digital inheritance and cultural dissemination among young people by combining puppetry with serious games. This study first conducted a literature review to summarize the commonly used Octalysis framework in serious game design. Based on this analysis framework, the subsequent research focused on the design strategies for puppetry serious games. Firstly, extensive user interviews and surveys were conducted to obtain young people's design expectations for puppetry serious games, and KJ method was used to preliminarily summarize the user needs. Secondly, using the eight-aspect model analysis framework as the research dimension, the preliminary design requirements were further classified into design demand indicators, and the Analytic Hierarchy Process (AHP) was used to analyze the weight of the requirements and rank them. Finally, the design strategies for puppetry serious games were deduced based on the weight of the requirements, providing valuable design ideas for the inheritance and development of puppetry and a reference for the digital dissemination of traditional culture.

Keywords: Puppetry · Serious Games · Octalysis Framework · Analytic Hierarchy Process

1 Background and Purpose of the Research

Puppetry is one of the representatives of Chinese traditional culture, and it is a performing art that uses puppets as a medium to spread Chinese traditional folk customs. This traditional art contains Chinese traditional aesthetic thought and is a common treasure of the world. However, with the process of modernization and urbanization, the traditional venues for puppet shows are gradually decreasing, the number of actors is also gradually decreasing, and the audience's interest is weakening. At the same time, the development of digital media enables people to access more cultural and entertainment resources through the Internet, which also leads to the loss and forgetting of traditional culture.

© The Author(s), under exclusive license to Springer Nature Switzerland AG 2023
J. Y. C. Chen et al. (Eds.): HCII 2023, LNCS 14058, pp. 394–407, 2023.
https://doi.org/10.1007/978-3-031-48050-8_26

The rise of digital media has had a huge impact on traditional culture, and the value and charm of traditional culture are gradually being ignored by people.

The emergence of digital cultural heritage provides new ways and means for the protection and inheritance of traditional culture. The preservation and dissemination of digital cultural heritage can make traditional culture more widely disseminated and recognized, and can also protect traditional culture from being forgotten and disappearing to a certain extent. Serious games are a form of games for education and training purposes, which can combine games and education to improve the learning effect and interest of learners. Serious games have been widely used in the protection of cultural heritage. Through the form of serious games, learners can have a deeper understanding of the connotation and value of traditional culture, and at the same time, they can improve their interest and attention to traditional culture, thereby promoting the protection and inheritance of traditional culture.

The combination of puppetry and serious games can make traditional culture more widely disseminated and recognized, and at the same time can improve learners' interest and attention to traditional culture, thereby promoting the protection and inheritance of traditional culture. Digital technology provides the possibility for the combination of puppetry and serious games, and digital protection strategy is an important way to promote the inheritance and development of puppetry. This study uses the octagonal model analysis and AHP method to quantitatively analyze the design needs of serious games of puppetry and explore the design potential of serious games of puppetry, which is of great significance to the protection and dissemination of puppetry culture.

2 Theoretical Background and Research Method

2.1 Theoretical Background

Serious games, also known as functional games, were first proposed by American scholar Abt in 1970. The ultimate purpose of these games is to educate rather than entertain. According to their application field, serious games can be divided into cultural, commercial, educational, and other functional categories [1]. Among them, cultural functional games focus on attracting users to play various interesting games in order to display culture and spread knowledge. Currently, the number of theoretical studies on serious games is increasing, and comprehensive studies have verified that serious games play a positive educational role for players to a certain extent. In 2010, Thompson et al. proposed a conceptual model for serious video game design [2]. Arnab et al. integrated game research and learning theory systems and proposed the Learning-Play (LM-GM) mechanism model for serious games, which makes up for the lack of integration of educational and playful elements in serious games [3]. M. J. Callaghan et al. presented a scenario case of game development and design based on the learner-game mechanism model [4]. Silva proposed a framework for digital game design, which separates the learning and entertainment elements of games and analyzes their respective characteristics [5].

Octalysis framework was first proposed by game designer Marc LeBlanc in 2001. He believed that the success of a game is not only related to the game mechanics and plot, but also to whether the game meets the needs and spiritual expectations of the players, and whether it provides players with spiritual pleasure. The octagonal gamification framework consists of eight core drivers that motivate players to engage in the game. These drivers are: Epic meaning and sense of mission, Progress and achievement, Ownership and sense of control, Scarcity and desire,Loss and avoidance, Unknown and curiosity, Social influence and relevance, Creative empowerment and feedback. These eight core drivers can be divided into four categories: external, internal, positive (white hat gamification), and negative (black hat gamification), as shown in the figure. The octagonal model analysis is a common gamification design analysis method used in serious game design to explore the driving factors that affect user participation in the game. In our discussion, we used the octagonal model to analyze the user needs and preferences for the design of a serious game that combines traditional culture and digital media. By categorizing and prioritizing the user needs using the octagonal model, we were able to derive the design strategies for the serious game based on the traditional Chinese puppet show. Daphne Economou et al. propose an SG platform based on an octagonal model analysis framework that provides educators with tools for dynamically creating three-dimensional (3D) scenes and verbal and non-verbal interactions with fully embodied dialogue agents (ECAs) that can be used to simulate numerous educational scenarios [6]. DeCusatis et al. developed a virtual network security escape room game development platform based on 3D Unity based on the octagonal model analysis framework to improve network security awareness [7]. Based on the analysis framework of octagonal model and theories related to serious games, Sunar et al. provide a lasting, scaffolding and satisfactory online learning experience platform for undergraduates [8]. Ewais et al. introduces gamification and the octagonal model analysis framework to explore the use of gamification in mobile health applications, identifying design principles that are more suitable for enhancing the intrinsic motivation of people seeking self-stress management [9]. KANG, LI YONG conducted gamification design of mobile fitness application based on octagon game analysis framework and discussed the design elements [10] (Fig. 1).

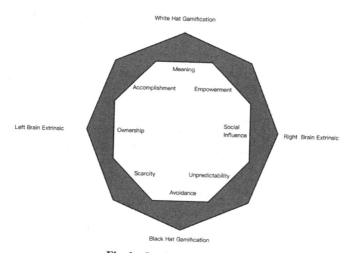

Fig. 1. Octalysis framework

2.2 Research Method

KJ method, also known as the affinity diagram method, involves collecting related facts, opinions, or ideas about unknown problems and unfamiliar fields through language and text. Through brainstorming, the internal relationships are identified, categorized, and merged to uncover the essence of the problem from complex information. This method can help find solutions to the problem.

AHP method refers to the decomposition of elements related to the final decision into goals, criteria, and programs, and other levels. Evaluate and score the elements at each level. Scoring and evaluation indicators are developed using a 1–9 scoring table, with experts assigning values based on the level of importance: very important, relatively important, general, relatively unimportant, and very unimportant. Finally, the weight of each element is calculated, and the importance of each element is sorted. This method is useful for decision-making.

3 User Research and Demand Analysis

3.1 Research Object and Sample Selection

The purpose of this study is to promote traditional puppet show culture to young people through serious games. Therefore, the research object is young people. According to the World Health Organization, youth is defined as individuals aged 15 to 44 years old. However, this age range is too broad to select core research samples. Hence, this study will further select and determine the age group of the study samples. According to the game industry research report, people aged 18–26 account for the largest proportion of young game users in the global game market, which is expected to reach $180.3 billion in 2021. Therefore, the age range of research samples is set to be 18 to 26 years old. Moreover, since the final design strategy of this study aims at the transformation design strategy of puppet shows and functional games, the research population should include a representative group of game users. Additionally, the research is related to traditional cultural puppetry, and in the follow-up user survey, it is necessary to understand users' expectations and demands for serious games of puppetry. Therefore, the research sample population also needs to have a certain level of knowledge and interest in puppetry.

3.2 User Interview and Questionnaire Survey

To understand the expectations and potential needs of the core research population for serious games of puppetry, we released questionnaires in game-related and puppetry forums and invited puppetry enthusiasts and game enthusiasts to participate. We distributed 120 semi-open questionnaires to these two core groups through online channels and received 105 valid questionnaires from the game hobby forum and 101 valid questionnaires from the puppet show hobby forum, respectively. After collecting a large number of questionnaire data, we filtered out meaningless questionnaire data with high repeatability and statistically analyzed the remaining questionnaire results. The summarized content is shown in the table 1 below.

Table 1. Survey results

User sample	As the user's expectation of the puppet show function game	As the designer of the puppet show functional game expectations	Design requirement transformation
Gaming enthusiasts (18–22 years old)	A. The game mechanics are new B. Beautiful visual effects of the game C. The setting of traditional puppetry characters D. Includes multiple selectable levels of puppet-themed games E. Interesting game controls and mechanics F. Adventure, leisure, healing type of game G. Have a certain degree of difficulty and challenge H. You can buy beautiful game accessories	A. Beautifully designed puppet-style game screen B. Puppet show story as the game setting C. Choose different puppet characters as the protagonists of the game D. Can simulate puppet show interaction E. Background Settings of puppet shows with different themes F. The game screen is bright and warm G. There are different levels of difficulty	Interactive way of puppetry performance Cultural connotation of puppet show Interesting visual style Innovative game mechanics Immersive game story experience Multi-gradient game difficulty
Puppeteers (22-28 years old)	A. Learn about interesting puppetry B. Socialize and make game friends C. Type of relaxing and casual games D. Learn the culture and knowledge of puppetry E. Run the puppet show yourself F. Tell the classic puppet show story	A. The game community can communicate together B. Beautiful game characters and scenery C. Points system to redeem game gifts D. Learn puppet-making game levels E. Open treasure chest to redeem mysterious shadow play characters	The free open world Exploratory mission Collaborative play and social A positive reward system Puppetry knowledge popularization

In the survey questionnaire, the results of the preliminary survey were analyzed to guide game users in clarifying their expectations for serious games of puppet show. The analysis showed that the two core user groups had an expectation of more than 80% for serious games of puppet show and believed that the design and research of serious games of puppet show could have a positive effect on the dissemination of puppet show culture. About 70% of the survey users expressed a strong interest in puppet culture and considered it the most attractive part of the game. Additionally, about 80% of the survey users had strong expectations for the gamification design of puppetry, hoping that the puppetry culture could carry out innovative design in the game and produce interesting functional games with rich puppet elements and puppet knowledge. The final research results of puppetry demand were summarized as follows: "Interactive Way of Puppet Show", "Cultural Connotation of Puppet Show", "Interesting Visual Style", "Innovative Game Mechanism", "Immersive Game Story Experience", "Multi-Gradient Game Difficulty", "Free Open World", "Exploratory Task", "Collaborative Play and Social Interaction", "Positive Reward Mechanism", and "Puppetry Knowledge Popularization". These 11 vague demand words indicate that survey users generally hoped that serious games of puppet show could not only bring users a sense of pleasure but also create a good cultural experience of puppet show. The design of puppetry functional games received positive feedback from young groups, proving that puppetry functional games have a certain interest base and potential users among young groups.

To gain a deeper understanding of the needs of core users, the research continued by selecting 40 young people from the questionnaire group for in-depth interviews. Based on the questionnaire theme and users' answers, the research further extended the questions to explore users' more detailed and specific needs for the design of serious puppetry games. For example, questions were raised on the basis of questionnaires, such as "What aspect of puppetry culture do you think you most want to learn about in the game?" By integrating the results of the questionnaire and interview, 16 vague user demand words were preliminarily obtained: "Clear Game Tasks", "Puppetry Knowledge Popularization", "Exploratory Tasks", "Positive Reward Mechanism", "Cultural Connotation of Puppetry", "Interesting Visual Style", "Immersive Game Story Experience", "Puppetry Performance Interaction", "Collaborative Play and Social Interaction", "Multi-Gradient Game Difficulty", "Sense of Achievement", "Free Open World", "Creation of New Game Mechanics", "Punitive Game Mechanics", "Negative Feedback for Failed Operations", and "Puppetry Art Sound Experience".

These 16 demand words are the expectations put forward by users who have not actually experienced the functional games of puppet show. Therefore, to make the research more convincing, the subsequent research will combine the game framework of the octagonal model, KJ method, and AHP to further qualitatively and quantitatively summarize and screen user needs and make a sort and comparison.

3.3 The Establishment of User Demand Index System

In the initial user survey, a total of 16 vague demand words were obtained. To systematically study user needs, the KJ method was adopted to identify internal correlations among user needs by brainstorming and drawing inspiration. As a result, more complex user needs were extracted and refined into concise design demand words.

Through brainstorming, related design needs were refined. For example, the connection between "interesting visual style" and "puppetry art sound experience" is puppetry and sensory experience. Therefore, these two needs were summarized as "multi-sensory experience of puppetry." "Popularization of puppetry knowledge" and "cultural connotation of puppetry" were combined and summarized as "perception of cultural connotation of puppetry." "Exploratory quests" and "innovative game mechanics" are both requirements for game mechanics and gameplay, and can therefore be distilled into "unknown and innovative game mechanics." After brainstorming, the final design requirement vocabulary was summarized and presented in Table 2. The 10 design requirement vocabulary words are: "clear design task," "positive reward mechanism," "perception of puppet cultural connotation," "interesting interactive feedback," "immersive story experience," "multi-level game challenge," "collaborative play and social interaction," "multi-sensory experience of puppetry show," "unknown and innovative game mechanics," and "negative feedback and punishment mechanism.

Table 2. User requirements summary

Core user	Design requirement
Gaming enthusiasts puppeteers	Clear game tasks positive reward mechanism
	Puppetry cultural connotation perception interesting interactive feedback
	Immersive story experience multi-layered game challenges
	Collaborative play and social Puppetry multi-sensory experience
	Unknown and innovative game mechanics Negative feedback and punishment opportunities

After obtaining the preliminarily refined user needs, the research needs to take an advanced step to summarize and sort out the needs and establish the demand evaluation index system. To adopt the AHP method to quantitatively study the weight of demand, the user demand summarized by KJ method is subjective and needs to be improved for accuracy and professionalism. Therefore, the four main design driving factors of the octagonal model analysis framework are adopted as the main dimensions of the demand further summarized. These four dimensions are: external driving force, internal driving force, positive driving force, and negative driving force. External driving forces are associated with externally set goals, and extrinsic factors are needed to drive intrinsic motivation. Internal driving force does not need to be guided by external goals and focuses on the user's internal experience. Positive drivers are positive drivers, such as progress and achievement, positive feedback. Negative drivers are negative drivers, such as loss, avoidance, etc. The octagonal model analysis is a common game design method for serious games, which can effectively summarize the motivation factors for users to actively participate in games. Therefore, it is feasible and effective to extract the main dimension of octagonal model analysis framework as the main dimension of demand induction. Since the user needs obtained from the preliminary research may not completely summarize the design elements of the serious game of puppetry, some design principles and design elements commonly used in game design are used to supplement and revise the acquired needs and enhance the professionalism of the research. Common design elements include clearly setting goals for the game and motivating the user to achieve them, clear rules and feedback mechanisms to help users understand the rules of the game and get feedback, a sense of achievement and reward mechanism to enhance user's game participation and loyalty, social interaction to increase interaction and cooperation between users, and personalization and customization to meet the game interests and needs of different users.

Combining the four main dimensions of the preliminary user survey and the octagonal model analysis framework, as well as the common design elements as supplements, the final user demand evaluation index system is summarized in Table 3.

Table 3. User needs evaluation index system

External needs	Internal needs	Positive needs	negative needs
Clear game mission Puppetry art style Achievement accumulation and reward mechanism	Collaborative play and social Cultural connotation perception of puppet show Fun interaction Timely feedback	Personalized expression and creation Immersive story experience Multi-level game challenge	Negative feedback and punishment mechanism Exploration and innovation mechanism

Based on the octagonal model analysis framework, four main dimensions of user demand classification have been determined: external demand, internal demand, positive demand, and negative demand. External needs include clear game tasks, puppet art-style experiences, achievement accumulation, and reward mechanisms. Internal needs include collaborative play and social interaction, cultural connotation perception of puppet shows, interesting interaction, and timely feedback. Positive demands include personalized expression and creation, immersive story experiences, and multi-layered game challenges. Negative needs include negative feedback and punishment mechanisms, as well as exploration and innovation mechanisms. The follow-up study establishes a hierarchical analysis model through AHP to conduct a systematic quantitative analysis of user needs based on the demand index evaluation system.

3.4 User Demand Weight Analysis

Establishment of User Hierarchy Model. Through AHP, the core user demand evaluation index system constructed in the early stage is transformed into A hierarchical model: the target layer is set as "Research on the design strategy of the serious game of puppetry", represented by the letter A. According to the four main dimensions of user demand evaluation index system, the criterion layer is set as "external demand", "internal demand", "positive demand" and "negative demand", which are represented by B1, B2, B3 and B4 respectively. The scheme level is set as "clear game tasks", "puppet art style experience", "Achievement accumulation and reward mechanism", "collaborative play and social interaction", "puppet cultural connotation perception", "fun interaction", "timely feedback", "personalized mandatory answer and creation", "immersive story experience", "multi-level game challenge", "negative feedback and punishment mechanism", "exploration" Sex and innovation mechanism ", respectively, b4, b5, b6, b7, b8, b9, b10, b11, b12, b13, b14, b15. See Fig. 2 for the construction of hierarchical model.

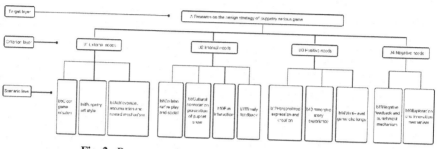

Fig. 2. Puppetry serious game hierarchical analysis model

After constructing the analytic hierarchy model, experts were invited to assign scores to the hierarchical model and construct a judgment matrix. In order to ensure the credibility of the study, 4 game experts with experience in serious game design related to traditional culture and 4 college teachers majoring in game design were selected for pairwise comparison and scoring using a scale of 1–9. Prior to weight calculation, a consistency test was conducted on the judgment matrix. Firstly, the consistency index (CI) was calculated, followed by querying the consistency index random average (RI) according to the table. Finally, the consistency ratio (CR) was calculated. If CR < 0.1, it indicates that the judgment matrix has passed the consistency test, and the weight of scheme elements can be calculated based on the judgment matrix.

CR calculation formula:

$$CR = CI/RI \tag{1}$$

CR calculation formula:

$$CI = (\lambda max - n)/(n-1) \tag{2}$$

Weight calculation formula:

$$\omega i = \frac{\left(\Pi j = 1\ a_{ij}\right)^{\frac{1}{n}}}{\sum_{k=1}^{n}\left(\Pi j = 1\ a_{ij}\right)^{\frac{1}{n}}} \tag{3}$$

where λmax is the largest eigenvalue of the matrix and n is the dimension of the matrix. According to the above calculation steps, the shadow play function game is assigned and scored to construct a judgment matrix and the weight results of each element are calculated. The final calculation results are shown in the Tables 4, 5, 6, 7 and 8.

Table 4. Weight calculation result 1

A	B1	B2	B3	B4	W_i	C.R	λ-max
1	1.0000	0.3333	0.4000	2.0000	0.1646	0.0701	4.1873
2	3.0000	1.0000	0.8000	3.0000	0.3655		
3	2.5000	1.2500	1.0000	1.5000	0.3356		
4	0.5000	0.3333	0.6667	1.0000	0.1343		

Table 5. Weight calculation result 2

B1	b5	b6	B7	Wi	C.R	λ.max
b5	1.0000	1.5000	1.4000	0.4176	0.0311	3.0324
b6	0.6667	1.0000	1.6000	0.3332		
b7	0.7143	0.6250	1.0000	0.2492		

Table 6. Weight calculation result 3

B2	b8	b9	b10	b11	W_i	C.R	λ-max
b8	1.0000	0.6000	1.3333	1.5000	0.2545	0.0234	4.0624
b9	1.6667	1.0000	1.8000	1.2000	0.3384		
b10	0.7500	0.5556	1.0000	1.2500	0.2059		
b11	0.6667	0.8333	0.8000	1.0000	0.2013		

Table 7. Weight calculation result 4

B3	b12	b13	b14	W_i	C.R	λ-max
b12	1.0000	0.5556	1.3333	0.2865	0.0036	3.0037
b13	1.8000	1.0000	2.0000	0.4852		
b14	0.7500	0.5000	1.0000	0.2283		

3.5 Data Analysis

Based on the weight data analysis results obtained through the analytic hierarchy model, it can be concluded that the internal demand of target users is more important than

Table 8. Weight calculation result 5

B4	B15	B16	W_i	C.R	λ-max
b15	1.0000	0.3333	0.2500	0.0000	2.0000
b16	3.0000	1.0000	0.7500		

Table 9. Weight calculation result 6

Target layer	Criterion layer	Criterion layer weight	Scenario level	Scheme level weight
Research on the design strategy of puppetry serious game	B1External needs	0.1646	b5 Clear game mission	0.0687
			b6 Puppetry art style	0.0548
			b7Achievement accumulation and reward mechanism	0.0410
	B2Internal needs	0.3655	b9 Cultural connotation perception of puppet show	0.1237
			b8 Collaborative play and social	0.0930
			b10 Fun interaction	0.0752
			b11 Timely feedback	0.0736
	B3Positive needs	0.3356	b13 Immersive story experience	0.1629
			b12 Personalized expression and creation	0.0961
			b14 Multi-level game challenge	0.0766
	B4negative needs	0.1343	b16 Exploration and innovation mechanism	0.1007
			b15 Negative feedback and punishment mechanism	0.0336

positive demand, external demand, and negative demand. This indicates that internal demand is the primary demand that motivates users to participate in the game. The user's internal needs include puppet show cultural connotation perception, collaborative games and social interaction, fun interaction, and timely feedback. The user's positive demand includes immersive story experience, personalized expression and creation, and multi-level game challenge. The user's external needs include clear game tasks, puppet art style, and achievement accumulation and reward mechanism. The user's negative needs include exploratory and innovative mechanisms, negative feedback, and punishment mechanisms. Therefore, the first nine requirements with weight values are selected for subsequent design strategy derivation, based on the priority of user requirements. This comprehensive analysis of user needs for serious games of puppetry indicates that target users are highly interested in the traditional culture of puppetry contained in the game, and they require a balance between entertainment and education. Utilizing the octagonal model analysis framework, the following design strategies are proposed.

3.6   Strategy Proposal

Intrinsic Needs

Puppetry is an artistic performance that uses puppets as a medium and has a rich cultural connotation. Traditional Chinese aesthetics are reflected in the creation ideas of puppetry, and the folk stories and opera performances depicted through puppetry showcase time-honored cultural customs. By integrating the production and performance techniques of traditional puppets into the design of serious games, young people can learn about traditional culture and aesthetic thoughts while experiencing the fun of handmade production.

In Maslow's hierarchy of needs theory, social needs are essential for human growth and enable individuals to find a sense of belonging in a group. By increasing the level of cooperation and social interaction between users in the serious game of puppetry, users can be motivated to participate in the game and obtain a sense of belonging and pleasure. For example, the game could include leaderboards and the ability to play together, as well as open game forums and reviews to allow users to exchange feelings about the game and receive advice from each other.

Fun interaction refers to the sense of pleasure and enjoyment that users experience during gameplay. In the serious game of puppetry, the game can integrate the performance of the puppet show by including a game section where the user can choose to play music and operate the puppet to complete performance actions. The user can receive feedback on the success of the performance, which adds to the fun of the game.

Prompt feedback is essential in a game to help users confirm whether their actions are correct and to track their progress. In the serious game of puppetry, timely feedback is necessary, including whether the user has completed the performance operation of the puppet show, whether the puppet has been produced, and whether the task has been successful or failed, and if the user needs to try again.

Extrinsic Needs

In the serious game of puppetry, it is important to have a clear game mission and plan the game function information on the home page of the game interface, so that users can quickly understand the functions and objectives of the game and participate with minimal learning costs.

Positive Needs

In a serious game of puppetry, an immersive story experience is crucial, as it allows users to be fully immersed in the traditional cultural atmosphere by using the attractive puppet show story as the background of the game.

By allowing the user to complete the performance and tasks of the puppet show story in the first person, the user can absorb the puppet show knowledge more efficiently during the game.

To enhance the user's participation and pleasure in the game, serious games of puppetry can encourage users to use their imagination to create customized puppets and develop their own puppet stories.

Negative Demand

Exploration and innovation mechanism. Users can in the puppet show serious game in an open world way to let users freely explore, and in the unknown situation to give users a certain surprise and feedback. For example, in unknown situations, users can freely explore a puppet show, and can participate in it, deepening the user's sense of surprise.

4 Prospect and Deficiency

Based on the traditional culture of puppetry, this study explores the design requirements of functional games of puppetry by combining them with serious game design strategies. The design requirements are analyzed using qualitative and quantitative analysis methods. Through research, several design strategies and requirements are identified that should be taken into consideration in the design of functional games of puppetry. The user needs of serious games of puppetry are classified into internal needs, external needs, positive needs, and negative needs, and the corresponding design strategies are elaborated upon to help today's young people better understand the culture of puppetry and experience the fun in it. This study provides a new design approach for the protection and dissemination of traditional culture. The design exploration utilizes qualitative and quantitative analysis methods to deduce the design strategy, which provides a reference for designs similar to traditional culture.

One limitation of the research is the small number of design samples and the fact that the research samples are all Chinese people, which limits the international design vision. Future studies should pay more attention to the selection of research samples to make the research more universal.

References

1. Lee, C.W., Oh, S.H.: A study on design factors of serious game considering senior layer. In: Proceedings of the 10th International Conference on Information and Communication Technology Convergence (ICTC) - Ict Convergence Leading the Autonomous Future, Jeju, South Korea, 16–18 Oct. IEEE (2019)

2. Thompson, D., Baranowski, T., Buday, R.: Conceptual model for the design of a serious video game promoting self-management among youth with Type 1 diabetes. J. Diabetes Sci. Technol. Diabetes Sci. Technol. **4**(3), 744–749 (2010)
3. Arnab, S., Ger, P.M., Lim, T., et al.: A conceptual model towards the scaffolding of learning experience. In: Proceedings of the 3rd International Conference on Games and Learning Alliance (Gala), Bucharest, Romania, 02–04 Jul (2015)
4. Callaghan, M.J., Mcshane, N., Eguiluz, A.G., et al.: Practical application of the learning mechanics game mechanics (Lm-Gm) framework for serious games analysis In engineering education. In: Proceedings of the 13th International Conference on Remote Engineering and Virtual Instrumentation (REV), Madrid, Spain, 24–26 Feb (2016)
5. Silva-Vasquez, P.O., Rosales-Morales, V.Y., Benitez-Guerrero, E.: Automatic code generation of user-centered serious games: a systematic literature review. In: Proceedings of the 8th International Conference In Software Engineering Research And Innovation (CONISOFT), Inst Tecnologico Chetumal, Chetumal, Mexico, 04–06 Nov (2020)
6. Economou, D., Doumanis, I., Pedersen, F., et al.: Evaluation of a dynamic role-playing platform for simulations based on octalysis gamification framework. In: Proceedings of the 11th International Conference on Intelligent Environments (IE), Prague, Czech Republic, Jul 13–14 (2015)
7. Decusatis, C., Gormanly, B., Alvarico, E., et al.: A cybersecurity awareness escape room using gamification design principles. In: Proceedings of the IEEE 12th Annual Computing and Communication Workshop and Conference (CCWC), Electr Network, 26–29 Jan (2022)
8. Kian, T.W., Sunar, M.S., Su, G.E.: The analysis of intrinsic game elements for undergraduates gamified platform based on learner type. IEEE Access **10**, 120659–120679 (2022)
9. Ewais, S., Alluhaidan, A., Assoc Informat, S.: Classification of stress management mhealth apps based on octalysis framework. In: Proceedings of the 21st Americas Conference on Information Systems (AMCIS), Fajardo, Pr, 13–15 Aug (2015)
10. Kang, L.Y.: A study on the application of gamification in fitness apps based on octalysis framework. J. Brand Design Association Korea **20**(4), 59–70 (2022)

Climate Change Literacy Gamified: How Gamification Mechanics Affect User Experience Factors in the User Interfaces

Xinyue Zhang[✉]

University of Leeds, Leeds LS3 1FF, UK
sd22x3z@leeds.ac.uk

Abstract. The disposal of kitchen waste (KW) has become one of the most critical issues for society due to the many contaminants present. Kitchen waste disposal needs to be improved due to the limited understanding of the requirements for source separation of kitchen waste. This limited understanding hinders behavioural change and affects young people's sense of urgency and perception of their actions. With this in mind, this study created a concept prototype for the UK government to teach Chinese students about the UK's disposal and recycling system to promote sustainable living. Second, thirty Chinese students aged 18 to 25 studying in the United Kingdom were recruited to test the prototype. The study uses quantitative research to examine how scores, badges, and leaderboards affect target users' learning results and why this phenomenon occurs. The study also investigates how the gameplay elements of the educational game influence the user experience and how the game teaches users about kitchen waste sorting.

Keywords: Gamification · Climate change literacy · Kitchen waste · Educational technologies · Cognitive learning · Motivation

1 Introduction

How to correctly dispose of kitchen waste (KW) has become one of the most pressing global problems due to kitchen waste's extensive production and challenging treatment [1, 2]. In Europe and North America, the annual per capita production can reach between 95 and 115 kg, which represents nearly a half of the total agricultural production in these regions [3]. KW accounts for 1.6 Tg of domestic residual waste in Australia. As a result of China's enormous population, the increase in the quantity of KW generated places a tremendous strain on the environment [4]. Moreover, KW contributes to 8% of greenhouse gas emissions [7] and uses a substantial quantity of water and land resources during disposal. Weak awareness of KW segregation and improper management of the waste treatment cycle [5, 6] is to blame for such a substantial amount of kitchen waste production. Developing awareness and action on KW disposal in diverse cultural and educational contexts [8] is thus an enormous challenge today.

Nevertheless, KW is worthwhile. If KW is utilised intelligently, it will provide numerous benefits [100]. Life cycle assessments indicate that KW recycling contributes to the energy balance. As KW is abundant in hydrocarbons, sugars, and proteins, it provides favourable conditions for microorganisms and is a valuable resource [11]. In addition, after dehydration, KW can be utilised to reduce atmospheric pollution by extracting biodiesel, methane, hydrogen, and fuel ethanol for fuel production [9].

In this study, a prototype game was created to conceptualise the repurposing and classification of KW. The participants were 18–35 year old Chinese pupils studying in the United Kingdom. Through the development of the game's concept, the study examined how to educate young people on the correct separation and reuse of KW. A gamified user experience was also required to help Chinese students rapidly adapt to the UK's kitchen waste sorting and disposal system. In order to maximise the user experience, this study compared the relationship between user experience and user learning outcomes when using gamified mobile applications with different game reward mechanisms and game elements, such as points, badges, leaderboards, and product redemption.

This study focuses on whether and how various game elements influence users' learning outcomes and experiences. It also provides recommendations for optimising the user experience in the future development of educational games. Despite the study's solid foundation, it still has some limitations. Although the test sample was small, it demonstrated that systematic evaluation of various game elements revealed distinct game characteristics. Moreover, various reward mechanisms can have varying degrees of influence on participants' learning experiences and outcomes. It also suggests that the gamification of applications as a learning instrument can effectively promote user engagement, interaction motivation, and knowledge acquisition.

2 Research Objectives:

1. What is the impact of using various game elements on users' learning outcomes in educational game projects?
2. What factors contribute to this phenomenon?
3. What are the recommendations for future development of educational games regarding user experience?

3 Literature Review

3.1 Kitchen Waste Treatment and Reuse

Kitchen Waste Disposal and Recycling. Currently, the improper disposal of kitchen waste contributes in some measure to climate change [8]. In addition to consuming vast quantities of water and land resources, the deposition and disposal of KW account for 8% of total greenhouse gas emissions [14]. In addition, improper KW disposal results in the emission of toxic gases such as NH3 and H2s, which contribute to atmospheric pollution [13]. In the meantime, kitchen waste is one of the most significant municipal solid residues [13] and a significant source of global economic and environmental contamination (1:15). Wang, Xu, and Sheng [13] noted that KW production is so high that effective kitchen waste disposal has become a global issue.

KW is a mixed waste of oil, water, fruit peelings, vegetables, rice, fish, poultry, bones, polymers, and paper towels, making its treatment more challenging [13]. The complex composition of KW, rich in water, organic matter, oil, and sodium, combined with its perishable nature, makes it susceptible to noxious substances [17]. Moreover, KW is complicated to manage, resulting in a resource efficiency of less than 30% [13].

The Significance of Kitchen Waste Management and Recycling. In the last 18 years, it has been noted that European countries have implemented various systems for the separate collection of KW and its subsequent biological treatment. Many European countries already have efficient solving systems based on source separation of domestic KW in place [19]. However, Bernstad [18] contends that household participation in KW sorting is crucial as a source segregation behaviour in all sorting systems; otherwise, the efficiency of KW disposal at a later stage is drastically reduced.

The effective treatment and utilisation of KW have numerous additional advantages [23–25]. First, KW has a variety of industrial and agricultural applications [13]. Wang, Xu, and Sheng [13] demonstrate that KW can be utilised in industry to produce fuels. In agriculture, it can be used to produce animal feed and organic fertiliser; And in industry, it can be used to reduce carbohydrates, carbon materials, and lactic acid. Also, KW can be converted into humic acid fertiliser and bioethanol, among other products, due to its high nutrient content [23, 36].

Second, KW remediation reduces the environmental impact of landfills and combustion [24]. Most notably, organic residue can be converted into biofuels [26]. Several studies have indicated that organic residue can produce biohydrogen [29, 31–33]. Dark fermented biohydrogen is a non-polluting, highly productive, renewable, sustainable, and efficient use of various organic substrates [28]. Simultaneously, dark fermented biohydrogen can be utilised as a potent alternative to fossil fuels in order to significantly reduce the production of greenhouse gases and thus safeguard the environment [60].

Factors Influencing Kitchen Waste Segregation. There are numerous contributors to the high levels of KW and improper disposal. Thyberg and Tonjes [38] contend that individuals' awareness and comprehension of waste segregation directly influence their behaviour. Ali et al. [39] contend that education and communication can improve awareness and understanding of KW segregation. People's awareness and comprehension of KW sorting can be increased through education and communication, making individuals aware of its positive effects on environmental protection, resource conservation, and sustainable development and encouraging them to participate actively. This will direct the development of the prototype's functionality.

Secondly, the convenience and practicability of disposal options are also significant factors [43], and Bernstad [18] suggests that individuals are more likely to actively participate in waste sorting if facilities and systems are designed to be user-friendly, provide convenient sorting methods, and reduce operational difficulties.

In addition, Li et al. [40] suggest that incentives are one of the factors that encourage people to sort KW actively. People can be motivated and satisfied with their participation in sorting by using a reward system, such as a point system, offering physical rewards or other incentives [41]. Huang and Tseng [42] suggest that individuals are likelier to follow and partake in such organisations.

3.2 Theories of Gamified Education and Learning

Gamification and Game-Based Learning. Currently, there are numerous examples of gamification in education [44]. According to Kapp [45], educational gamification can motivate and engage students by employing game design elements, mechanics of games, aesthetics, and game thinking. Hu [47] argues that applying gamification elements can utilise specific characteristics of games to accomplish non-entertaining goals. In most gamified applications, users need to have clear learning objectives from the outset [48], making adding gamified elements simpler to achieve the desired educational effect. By presenting learning objectives through gamified content and combining gamification objectives with game design elements, the elements' motivational effect, and the user's psychological requirements, better educational objectives can be attained [44].

Huang and Soman [49] contend that there is no substantial distinction between learning and game objectives. The primary goal of gamification is to influence motivational factors associated with learning, such as involvement with training content and achieving educational results. Therefore, gamification aims to "influence the psychological factors that regulate learning outcomes" [53, pp:4]. However, the presentation of educational content also significantly influences learning outcomes. This is because although increased participation and effort may result in improved performance or knowledge and skills, if presented ineffectively, it may result in poorer learning outcomes [49]. Therefore, the gamification-targeted learning environment must be meticulously designed, with specific reference to the mentioned elements of play and clear and explicit instructions supplied [51]. Otherwise, learners may be distracted from concentrating on the learning objectives, negatively influencing the learning outcomes [52, 53].

Advantages of Game-Based Learning. The gamification model of education can increase user motivation to learn by stimulating their interest and motivation through reward mechanisms, competitive elements, and immediate feedback, thereby increasing their engagement in learning activities [57]. According to Sánchez-Mena et al. [54], education is becoming increasingly interested in gamification. Smiderle et al. [56] and Ribeiro et al. [55] also argue that gamification is effective because it keeps students engaged with electronic technologies and devices in an informal setting. According to Kapp [59], gamification can increase student engagement in the learning process.

Moreover, gamification also improves the learning experience [58]. First, it creates active, dynamic, and challenging atmospheres for learning that engage and motivate students [82]. Second, gamification can provide learners with immediate insight and individualised pathways to assist them in understanding their progress and making improvements [61]. Additionally, emotional and affective stimulation can increase learning enthusiasm and involvement [58]. In conclusion, gamified education provides learners with enjoyable, interactive, and individualised learning experiences that stimulate interest and motivation, thereby fostering deeper learning and improved learning outcomes.

Another benefit of modern gamification is the increased emphasis on active learner participation [65]. Saleem et al. [70] argue that this approach engages and motivates students to remain active in their learning because it provides them with multiple forms of stimulation. According to Alsawaier [66], gamification boosts student engagement. Thus, student achievement can be improved. This view is also supported by Chan et al.

[66], Dichev and Dicheva [63], Sepehr and Head [67], and Szegletes et al. [68]. The primary reason for this is that gamification attempts to reward students with elements such as challenges, badges, leaderboards, levels, points, and badges [64, 66, 68].

Game Mechanics and Elements. In gamified education, reward systems and feedback mechanisms are crucial [71]. A reward system initially motivates and engages learners in learning [72]. According to Gibson et al. [73], setting rewards that can be obtained, such as badges, points, leaderboards, and levels, can increase students' motivation to learn.

Based on the literature review, this study identifies the game elements chosen for this thematic study: emblems, leaderboards, and points, as well as their corresponding reward mechanisms.

1. Badges

According to Nah et al. [71], badges are viewed as an indication of appreciation or task completion in achieving an objective, which is one of the primary reasons badges were selected for this study. Badges effectively motivate students to work towards future objectives while also assisting students in maintaining motivation and remaining engaged in later learning tasks [61]. Santos et al. [74] found that most students thought insignia kept them engaged, and inspired them to learn.

2. League Table

Furthermore, Nah et al. [71] suggest that leaderboards can keep students motivated and foster a sense of competition as they strive to improve their name ranking. In their study, gonzález et al. [75] explain that the reason most leaderboards only display the top five or ten scorers is to prevent lower-ranked players from losing motivation while enhancing the sense of competition. According to Odonovon et al. [61], leaderboards are highly effective in motivating students.

3. Points and benefits

Brewer et al. [76] demonstrated the effectiveness of rewards in motivating learners, and Raymer [77] believed reward timing and form affected learner motivation. Additionally, he suggested that multiple minor rewards are more effective than a single large reward [78]. Moreover, the schedule for awarding incentives should be distributed evenly throughout the learning process [77].

4 Research Experiment

4.1 Survey Background

This study examines the relationship between the use of various game elements and learning outcomes in the design of the educational game "Kitchen no waste." The public service environmental brand "Kitchen no waste" was developed for this investigation. The game aims to increase Chinese students' knowledge of the UK's kitchen waste processing system and encourage them to adopt a sustainable lifestyle. Similarly, "Kitchen no Waste!" has partnered with them to provide a promotional and commercial platform and business for various sustainability-focused brands'. Users can redeem items via an in-game reward system. This study generated a user-friendly interface and a prototype for the testing phase.

The prototype is an educational game incorporating previous research outcomes to foster a scientific understanding of KW sorting and wet waste disposal for waste recycling. The application of the research tool includes three functions:

- Educating about the correct sorting of KW (Fig. 1).
- Gratifying KW reuse and wet waste disposal (Fig. 2).
- Promoting recycling and providing a platform to promote the products of environmental brands (Fig. 3).

This research employed a participatory design [20] methodology to evaluate comprehensively. This test used three versions of the application corresponding to points, badges, and leaderboards to test different game elements' impact on the kitchen waste knowledge gained by users [12].

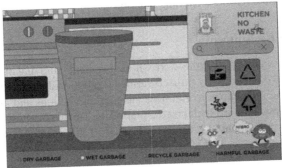

Fig. 1. Function 1: Science on the correct separation of kitchen waste

Fig. 2. Function 2: Gamified format to promote kitchen waste reuse and wet waste disposal

Fig. 3. Function 3: Provide a platform to promote the products of relevant environmental brands

This study included a user assessment of the prototype and observational methods. In addition to observing users while they utilised the prototype, the study utilised a post-test to collect data. Users were required to remark on their learning experience and were assigned a score. Later, these scores were used to analyse the feedback from the three versions regarding the learner's learning outcomes.

4.2 Participant Recruitment

The selection criteria for participants were Chinese students studying in the UK between the ages of 18 and 35. The study utilised various promotional strategies to recruit participants, including on-campus recruitment via email invitations and publishing a link to the research application on social media platforms. Thirty target users were successfully recruited to participate in the survey. Fifteen of these scholars were enrolled in undergraduate programmes, and 15 were postgraduate (master's and doctoral) students. Because the target users were all educated, there was slight variation between the samples, barring minimal variations. The survey data collection process occurred in 2023 and was evaluated to ensure validity.

4.3 Survey Methodology

Thirty participants were required to complete three sets of experiments, with prototype versions corresponding to points, certificates, and leaderboards in each set. The complete testing procedure consisted of three stages. First, a one-week observation period was required. During this week, users were required to utilise the prototype to answer their kitchen waste-related queries. To assess their learning, after the observation, the users completed a questionnaire on kitchen waste classification and wet waste recycling. This data examined how reward mechanisms affect motivation and learning.

4.4 Summary of the Experiment

Each of the badges, points, and leaderboards corresponds to a distinct reward mechanism in this endeavour. In the version that uses badges, the user will receive a badge certification that can be redeemed for prizes in function three after a certain number of earned badges. For the version with points, users will acquire points for the first two functions that can be redeemed for prizes during the third function. Within the ranking version, users will be compared to one another. Also, the best ten's scores are updated daily; scores 11–30 are not displayed. Simultaneously, the version's scores will be accumulated.

Users are required to complete a learning assessment questionnaire at the conclusion of each version's observation period. The questionnaire scored 88 points. It consists of eight questions on general knowledge (with fixed answers) and two open-ended questions (with varying scores for various options depending on the level of choice). The general knowledge questions are selected based on the categories of kitchen waste sorted by the user during use. The results of this questionnaire will be used to provide feedback on the user's current learning outcomes.

4.5 Experimental Results and Analysis

This study selected linear regression to examine the relationship between the impact of display points, badges, leaderboards and scores. In addition, descriptive analysis was employed to illustrate the variable influence of points, insignia, and leaderboards on scores.

This study's objective was to examine, through linear regression analysis, the relationship between distinct game elements (badges, points, and leaderboards) and user test scores after the observation period. As the dependent variable, the participants' total scores on the learning assessment questionnaire served as the prediction objective. In addition, certificates, points, and leaderboards were considered predictor variables. Before conducting the analysis, we examined the variables for chi-square and normality. The Levin test [34] was utilised to test the variance chi-square assumption, while the Shapiro-Wilk test [93] was utilised to examine the normality assumption. We utilised an inverse square root transformation to convert the corresponding variables into proportional variables to satisfy the normality assumption.

The study determined the extent to which each independent variable influenced the user test scores by analysing the coefficients of the regression equations. Positive or negative coefficients imply a correlation between independent and dependent variables. By evaluating the significance of the coefficients, we can determine which independent variables have a statistically significant impact on users' test scores.

Group 1: Points version use. In this test group, the points earned by users in the prototype were compared to the final learning outcomes, as shown in Table 1. More points indicate more use.

The preceding table demonstrates that a linear regression analysis was performed with points serving as the independent variable and scores serving as the dependent variable. The model R-squared value is 0.327, indicating that points account for 32.7% of the variance in scores. The model equation is scored = 52.959 + 0.454*points, and the model R-squared value is 0.327. The model passed the F-test (F = 13.585, p = 0.0010.05), indicating that points must influence the score, and the final specific analysis reveals that the regression coefficient value for points is 0.454 (t = 3.686, p = 0.0010.01), indicating that points will have a significant positive influence relationship with the score.

Table 1. Points version use.

Results of linear regression analysis ($n = 30$)

	Unstandardised coefficients		Standardised coefficients	t	p	covariance diagnostics	
	B	Standard Error	Beta			VIF	Tolerance
Constant	52.959	5.770	–	9.179	0.000**	–	–
Rank	0.454	0.123	0.572	3.686	0.001*	1.000	1.000
R^2	0.327						
AdjustmentR^2	0.303						
F	$F(1,28) = 13.585, p = 0.001$						
D-W value	1.287						

Dependent variable: score
* $p < 0.05$ ** $p < 0.01$

Group 2: Badge version use. In this test group, the user's badge rating in the prototype was compared to the final learning outcome, and the calculated results are displayed in Table 2. Badges were assigned a rating between 1 and 5. Higher levels indicate greater usage frequency.

Table 2. Badge version use.

Results of linear regression analysis ($n = 30$)

	Unstandardised coefficients		Standardised coefficients	t	p	covariance diagnostics	
	B	Standard Error	Beta			VIF	Tolerance
Constant	51.593	3.268	–	15.786	0.000**	–	–
Rank	5.593	0.917	0.755	6.098	0.000*	1.000	1.000
R^2	0.570						
AdjustmentR^2	0.555						
F	$F(1,28) = 37.187, p = 0.000$						
D-W value	0.724						

Dependent variable: score
* $p < 0.05$ ** $p < 0.01$

With grade as the independent variable and score as the dependent variable, a linear regression analysis was conducted; the model formula is score $= 51.593 + 5.593*$grade, and the model R-squared value is 0.570, indicating that grade explains 57.0% of the variance in the score. The model passed the F-test (F = 37.187, p = 0.0000.05), indicating that there must be a correlation between rank and scores. The final specific analysis reveals that the regression coefficient for rank is 5.593 (t = 6.098, p = 0.0000.01), indicating that rank has a significant positive influence on scores.

Group 3: Leaderboard version use. In this test group, users' points were accumulated and ranked, and only the top 10 users and scores were displayed on the visible daily leaderboard. This version allows points to be accumulated based on the number of days. For this ornament analysis, we analysed the complete rankings of 30 users, and the results are shown in Table 3.

Table 3. Leaderboard version use.

Results of linear regression analysis ($n = 30$)							
	Unstandardised coefficients		Standardised coefficients	t	p	covariance diagnostics	
	B	Standard Error	Beta			VIF	Tolerance
Constant	71.000	1.577	–	45.023	0.000**	–	–
Rank	−0.219	0.089	−0.423	−2.470	0.020*	1.000	1.000
R^2	0.179						
AdjustmentR^2	0.150						
F	$F(1,28) = 6.100, p = 0.020$						
D-W value	1.671						

Dependent variable: score
* p < 0.05 ** p < 0.01

The model formula is scored = 71,000 −0.219 * ranking, and the model R-squared value is 0.179, indicating that ranking accounts for 17.9% of the variance in scores. The model passed the F-test (F = 6,100, p = 0.0200.05), indicating that there must be a significant relationship between ranking and scores. The final specific analysis reveals that the regression coefficient for ranking is −0.219 (t = −2.470, p = 0.0200.05), indicating that ranking has a statistically significant negative influence relationship. In addition, the ranking has no influence on the motivation of users' learning outcomes.

The study also descriptively collected the learning outcomes' data to determine their characteristics and distribution to demonstrate variability. The descriptive analysis offered a quantitative description of the learning outcomes scores' concentration, variability, and distribution trends.

According to the descriptive analysis data (Table 4), the sample size for all three sets of experiments was thirty. The points version of the exam had a maximum score of 78 and a minimum score of 63. The leaderboard version had a maximum score of 76 and a minimum score of 50. The badge version had a maximum score of 78 and a minimum score of 60. The points version had the highest mean score, while the leaderboard variant had the lowest mean score. According to the graph contrasting the averages (Fig. 4), there is little difference between the average scores for points and badges. In contrast, the difference between the leaderboard and the other two averages is more pronounced.

Table 4. Descriptive analysis data.

Basic Indicators						
Name	Sample size	Minimum	Maximum	Average	Standard deviation	Median
Points	30	63.000	78.000	74.100	4.105	75.000
Leaderboard	30	50.000	76.000	67.600	4.568	68.000
Badges	30	60.000	78.000	71.167	5.052	70.000

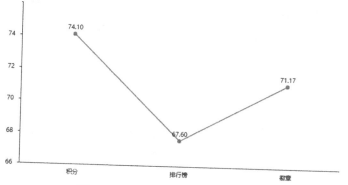

Fig. 4. Average score comparison chart

In conclusion, the correlation between the variables indicates that points and badges affect the learning outcomes of users. In contrast, the leaderboard has no significant effect on the learning outcomes of users. By analysing the differences between the variables, it is possible to conclude that there is little difference between points and badges regarding their impact on users' learning outcomes. Conversely, the leaderboard has a significantly lower positive impact on learning outcomes than the other two variables.

5 Discussion

The widespread use of gamification has enhanced user experience design across multiple media, increasing user engagement [62]. Incorporating gamification elements into education makes it more engaging, and the game's objective is not simply to win [83]. Badges, leaderboards, and points are common elements in educational games [101]. "The characteristic of 'playability' can result in a pleasurable experience, which is the foundation for designing an intrinsically motivating learning environment [12]. However, forcing game-like elements without comprehending their purpose can negatively affect the user experience [35]. Thus, game elements within gamified educational applications have to balance what the learner is learning and having fun while ensuring that it enhances the appeal and efficacy of the learning knowledge [12].

5.1 Learning How to Use the Prototype

Before approaching the app, the user need only be aware of its principles. In the first function, the user can examine the sorting criteria for KW to sort at the source correctly. After use, the user's familiarity with the various kitchen waste categories increased considerably, and the outcomes aligned with expectations. In the second application, guidelines for the reuse of KW and the disposal of wet waste were developed. This function focused on increasing user awareness of reducing KW and reusing them. Typically, in gamification, the user proceeds directly to the prototype. As gamification's unique characteristic is plot progression [46], users only need to understand how to use it after some time. This also demonstrates that gamification somewhat increases user satisfaction and product usability [46].

5.2 Effects of Various Gameplay Elements

The primary aim was to determine the impact of various game elements on learning outcomes, representing various reward mechanisms and user experiences. The study's findings indicate that game-like applications comprising various game elements affect the motivation of learning outcomes.

Experimentally, points and badges significantly positively affect students' learning outcomes, and there is a strong correlation between them. Contrarily, there is no correlation between leaderboards and learning outcomes. In addition, there was no statistically noteworthy distinction between the effects of points and insignia on learning outcomes., but evaluators outperformed the leaderboard. This result is nearly consistent with findings from prior research. The experimental results indicate that users are more engaged with reward mechanisms like points and certificates. Higher positive engagement is more likely to produce a positive response regarding learning outcomes [99].

The experiment results indicate that the leaderboard version is less preferable than points and badges for user learning outcomes. This indicates that the leaderboard version of the game mechanics does not engage players as effectively as the other two versions. Çakıroğlu [94] notes that competition, the most conspicuous negative aspect of leaderboards, may cause some users additional stress and anxiety. They may become preoccupied with ranking and performance and lose interest in the game experience and information acquisition. This anxiety may harm their learning outcomes [95], resulting in a lack of evident connection to the leaderboards. As leaderboards are the more frequently employed gamification element, it is essential to note that using such game design elements in a learning process may negatively impact the learning process of learners, thereby reducing the achievement of desired learning outcomes [12].

Different game elements offer unique user experiences, with varying degrees of positive experiential impact leading to distinct outcomes [96]. Lister [98] demonstrates that leaderboards need to provide all users with a comprehensive view of the game experience. As leaderboards can provide immediate feedback to increase the likelihood of ranking, they can motivate students who are good at winning. However, they can be demotivating for students who could be better, causing them to perform less well. As game usage increases and some players accumulate many points, it becomes increasingly more work for new players to reach the top of the leaderboard, which can significantly impact the user experience and even the frequency of use [97].

5.3 Analysis of the Study

Although this study has a solid foundation, it still has some limitations. With only 30 participants, the sample was modest. This may compromise the reliability of the statistical results and the credibility of the findings [84]. Second, the evaluation duration was brief. Participants played the prototype game for only one week, making its impact on long-term learning outcomes challenging to determine [85]. Finally, a subjective selection of evaluation criteria was present. After one week of use, the questionnaire included highly subjective queries [86]. The evaluation of participants' learning outcomes may rely on their subjective feedback or self-reports. This subjectivity may result in biased or inaccurate evaluation outcomes [87].

5.4 Research Suggestions for the Future

This paper makes suggestions for future research directions on kitchen waste education. First, educational research on KW knowledge could multiply and compare various educational approaches [88] and evaluate the user experience from multiple angles when selecting game elements. Second, comprehending the psychology of human behaviour and motivational research [89] would enable comprehension of the psychological factors and motivations influencing people's behaviour towards KW sorting. This enables a focused examination of the attitudes and perceptions that influence people's participation in KW sorting and provides effective interventions and application mechanisms [90]. Additionally, more alternatives can be provided in terms of format and medium. Technological innovations and digital tools, such as mobile phone applications and virtual reality, can increase the interactivity and engagement of KW education. Lastly, the research could also concentrate on designing and developing more engaging and effective learning tools [91].

6 Summary

Game elements can motivate students and enhance their ability to solve problems [92]. This study used gamification to teach KW separation and reuse. Also, a comparison of badges, points, and leaderboards was used to examine how different game features affect learning outcomes and address the research question.

As a reward for traditional games, leaderboards have a dramatically different effect on student outcomes than points and badges. The competitive nature of leaderboards makes it hard to encourage users and affects learning outcomes.

This study's tests show users' KW sorting knowledge. However, limited sample sizes, brief observation times, and subjective assessment criteria limit it. At the same time, this study also provides some suggestions for future education and popularisation of kitchen waste-related knowledge: 1. Using different educational methods and considering user experience from multiple perspectives when selecting game elements; 2. Understanding the psychological factors and motivations of people's kitchen waste sorting behaviour from a psychological perspective. 3. To improve user experience, technical breakthroughs and digital tools should expand media and format options.

References

1. Li, P., et al.: Bioconversion of welan gum from kitchen waste by a two-step enzymatic hydrolysis pretreatment. Appl. Biochem. Biotechnol. **183**, 820–832 (2017)
2. Thompson, K., Haigh, L.: Representations of food waste in reality food television: an exploratory analysis of Ramsay's kitchen nightmares. Sustainability **9**, 1139 (2017)
3. Masson, M., Delarue, J., Blumenthal, D.: An observational study of refrigerator food storage by consumers in controlled conditions. Food Qual Prefer **56**, 294e300 (2017)
4. Ding, LK., Cheng, J., Qiao, D., Yue, LC., Li, YY., Zhou, JH., et al.: Investigating hydrothermal pretreatment of food waste for two-stage fermentative hydrogen and methane co-production. Bioresour. Technol. **241**, 491e9 (2017)
5. Yu, Q., Li, H.: Moderate separation of household kitchen waste towards global optimization of municipal solid waste management. J. Clean. Prod. **277**, 123330 (2020)
6. Cerda, A., Artola, A., Font, X., Barrena, R., Gea, T., Sánchez, A.: Composting of food wastes: Status and challenges. Biores. Technol. **248**, 57–67 (2018)
7. Scialabba, N.E., et al.: Food wastage footprint: full-cost accounting. Final Report (2014)
8. Wang, H., et al.: Key factors influencing public awareness of household solid waste recycling in urban areas of China: a case study. Resour. Conserv. Recycl. **158**, 104813 (2020)
9. Liu, D., Liu, Q., Zhang, Y.: Research progress on zero discharge and resource utilization of industrial high-salt wastewater. Clean: soil, air, water **49**(5), 2000410–n/a (2021)
10. Wang, H., Xu, J., Sheng, L., Liu, X., Lu, Y., Li, W.: A review on bio-hydrogen production technology. Int. J. Energy Res. **42**(11), 3442–3453 (2018)
11. Kang, X., Liu, Y.: Chemically enhanced primary sludge as an anaerobic co-digestion additive for biogas production from food waste. Processes **7**(10), 709 (2019)
12. Leitão, R., Maguire, M., Turner, S., Arenas, F., Guimarães, L.: Ocean literacy gamified: a systematic evaluation of the effect of game elements on students' learning experience (2022)
13. Wang, H., Xu, J., Sheng, L.: Study on the comprehensive utilization of city kitchen waste as a resource in China. Energy (Oxford). **173**, 263–277 (2019)
14. Yu, Q., Li, H.: Moderate separation of household kitchen waste towards global optimization of municipal solid waste management. J. Clean. Prod. **277**, 123–330 (2020)
15. Thompson, K., Haigh, L.: Representations of food waste in reality food television: an exploratory analysis of ramsay's kitchen nightmares. Sustainability (Basel, Switzerland). **9**(7), 1139 (2017)
16. Masson, M., Delarue, J., Blumenthal, D.: An observational study of refrigerator food storage by consumers in controlled conditions. Food Qual. Prefer. **56**, 294–300 (2017)
17. Lee, Z.-K., et al.: Thermophilic bio-energy process study on hydrogen fermentation with vegetable kitchen waste. Int. J. Hydrogen Energy **35**(24), 13458–13466 (2010)
18. Bernstad, A.: Household food waste separation behavior and the importance of convenience. Waste Manage. **34**(7), 1317–1323 (2014)
19. European Compost Network.: Country Reports for Austria, Germany, Sweden, the Netherlands and Spain. http://www.compostnetwork.info/country-reports-world/. Accessed 2017

20. Spinuzzi, C.: The methodology of participatory design. Tech. Commun. **52**(2), 163–174 (2005)
21. Brockmyer, J.H., Fox, C.M., Curtiss, K.A., McBroom, E., Burkhart, K.M., Pidruzny, J.N.: The development of the game engagement questionnaire: a measure of engagement in video game-playing. J. Exp. Soc. Psychol. **45**(4), 624–634 (2009)
22. Kalogiannakis, M., Papadakis, S., Zourmpakis, A.I.: Gamification in science education. a systematic review of the literature. Educ. Sci. **11**(1), 22 (2021)
23. Hafid, H.S., Shah, U.K.M., Baharuddin, A.S., Ariff, A.B.: Feasibility of using kitchen waste as future substrate for bioethanol production: a review. Renew. Sustain. Energy Rev. **74**, 671–686 (2017)
24. Srivastava, N., Srivastava, M., Abd_Allah, E.F., Singh, R., Hashem, A., Gupta, V. K.: Biohydrogen production using kitchen waste as the potential substrate: a sustainable approach. Chemosphere, **271**, 129537 (2021)
25. Peng, L., Zheng, P., Siswanto, I.: Good earthworm-kitchen waste decomposition device. In: Journal of Physics: Conference Series (2020)
26. Trivedi, J., Bhonsle, A.K., Atray, N.: Processing food waste for the production of platform chemicals. In: Refining Biomass Residues for Sustainable Energy and Bioproducts. Academic Press, 427–448 (2020)
27. Weitemeyer, S., Kleinhans, D., Vogt, T., Agert, C.: Integration of renewable energy sources in future power systems: the role of storage. Renew. Energy **75**, 14–20 (2015)
28. Fatima, A., Basak, B., Ganguly, A., Chatterjee, P.K., Dey, A.: Biohydrogen production through dark fermentation of food wastes by anaerobic digester sludge mixed microbial consortium. In: Recent Developments in Waste Management: Select Proceedings of Recycle, vol. 2018, pp. 57–70 (2020)
29. Dahiya, S., Sarkar, O., Swamy, Y.V., Mohan, S.V.: Acidogenic fermentation of food waste for volatile fatty acid production with co-generation of biohydrogen. Bioresour. Technol. **182**, 103–113 (2015)
30. Kumar, G.R., Chowdhary, N.: Biotechnological and bioinformatics approaches for augmentation of biohydrogen production: a review. Renew. Sustain. Energy Rev. **56**, 1194–1206 (2016)
31. Linder, T.: Making the case for edible microorganisms as an integral part of a more sustainable and resilient food production system. Food Secur. **11**, 1–14 (2019)
32. Show, K.Y., Lee, D.J., Chang, J.S.: Bioreactor and process design for biohydrogen production. Bioresour. Technol. **102**(18), 8524–8533 (2011)
33. Kumar, G., et al.: Recent insights into the cell immobilization technology applied for dark fermentative hydrogen production. Biores. Technol. **219**, 725–737 (2016)
34. Firnhaber, C., et al.: Evaluation of a cervicography-based program to ensure quality of visual inspection of the cervix in HIV-infected women in Johannesburg, South Africa. J. Low. Genit. Tract Dis. **19**(1), 7 (2015)
35. Kornevs, M., Hauge, J.B., Meijer, S.: Gamification of a procurement process for professional training of public servants. Int. J. Serious Games **6**(2), 23–37 (2019)
36. Junzhe, W.A.N.G., Lihua, T.A.N.G., Jianxin, G.U.O.: Alkali catalysis hydrothermal conversion of cabbage leaf in kitchen waste. Chin. J. Environ. Eng. **11**(1), 578–581 (2017)
37. Aschemann-Witzel, J., De Hooge, I., Amani, P., Bech-Larsen, T., Oostindjer, M.: Consumer-related food waste: causes and potential for action. Sustainability **7**(6), 6457–6477 (2015)
38. Thyberg, K.L., Tonjes, D.J.: Drivers of food waste and their implications for sustainable policy development. Resour. Conserv. Recycl. **106**, 110–123 (2016)
39. Ali, Y., Jokhio, D.H., Dojki, A.A., Rehman, O.U., Khan, F., Salman, A.: Adoption of circular economy for food waste management in the context of a developing country. Waste Manage. Res. **40**(6), 676–684 (2022)

40. Li, C.J., Huang, Y.Y., Harder, M.K.: Incentives for food waste diversion: exploration of a long term successful Chinese city residential scheme. J. Clean. Prod. **156**, 491–499 (2017)
41. Limon, M.R., Villarino, C.B.J.: Knowledge, attitudes and practices on household food waste: Bases for formulation of a recycling system. Glob. J. Environ. Sci. Manag. **6**(3), 323–340 (2020)
42. Huang, C.H., Tseng, H.Y.: An exploratory study of consumer food waste attitudes, social norms, behavioral intentions, and restaurant plate waste behaviors in Taiwan. Sustainability **12**(22), 9784 (2020)
43. Matiiuk, Y., Liobikienė, G.: The impact of informational, social, convenience and financial tools on waste sorting behavior: assumptions and reflections of the real situation. J. Environ. Manage. **297**, 113323 (2021)
44. Richter, G., Raban, D.R., Rafaeli, S.: Studying gamification: the effect of rewards and incentives on motivation. In: Gamification in Education and Business; Springer: Cham, Switzerland, pp. 21–46 (2015) https://doi.org/10.1007/978-3-319-10208-5_2
45. Kapp, K.M.: The gamification of learning and instruction: game-based methods and strategies for training and education. Int. J. Gaming Comput. Simul **4**, 81–83 (2012)
46. Klock, A.C.T., Ogawa, A.N., Gasparini, I., Pimenta, M.S.: Does gamification matter: a systematic mapping about the evaluation of gamification in educational environments. In: Proceedings of the ACM Symposium on Applied Computing; Association for Computing Machinery: New York, vol. 7, pp. 2006–2012 (2018)
47. Hu, J.: Gamification in learning and education: enjoy learning like gaming. Br. J. Educ. Stud. **68**, 265–267 (2020)
48. Kalogiannakis, M., Papadakis, S., Zourmpakis, A.-I.: Gamification in science education.: a systematic review of the literature. Educ. Sci. **11**(1), 22 (2021)
49. Huang, H.-Y.W., Soman, D.: A Practitioner's Guide to Gamification of Education. Research Report Series Behavioural Economics in Action (2013)
50. Kam, A.H., Umar, I.N.: Fostering authentic learning motivations through gamification: a self-determination theory (SDT) approach. J. Eng. Sci. Technol. **13**, 1–9 (2018)
51. Strmečki, D., Bernik, A., Radošević, D.: Gamification in E-learning: introducing gamified design elements into e-Learning systems. Comput **11**, 1108–1117 (2015)
52. Huang, H.M., Rauch, U., Liaw, S.S.: Investigating learners' attitudes toward virtual reality learning environments: based on a constructivist approach. Comput. Educ. **55**, 1171–1182 (2010)
53. Ijaz, K., Bogdanovych, A., Trescak, T.: Virtual worlds vs. books and videos in history education. Interact. Learn. Environ. **25**, 904–929 (2017)
54. Sánchez-Mena, A., Martí-Parreño, J., Aldás-Manzano, J.: The role of perceived relevance and attention in teachers' intention to use gamification. In: European Conference on e-Learning. Academic Conferences International Limited, pp. 615 (2016)
55. Ribeiro, L.A., da Silva, T.L., Mussi, A.Q.: Gamification: a methodology to motivate engagement and participation in a higher education environment. Int. J. Educ. Res. **6**(4), 249–264 (2018)
56. Smiderle, R., Rigo, S.J., Marques, L.B., de Miranda Coelho, J.A.P., Jaques, P.A.: The impact of gamification on students' learning, engagement and behaviour based on their personality traits. Smart Learn. Environ. **7**(1), 1–11 (2020)
57. Saleem, A.N., Noori, N.M., Ozdamli, F.: Gamification applications in E-learning: a literature review. Tech Know Learn **27**, 139–159 (2022)
58. Nah, F.F.H., Zeng, Q., Telaprolu, V.R., Ayyappa, A.P., Eschenbrenner, B.: Gamification of education: a review of literature. 22-27, 401-409 (2014)
59. Kapp, K.M.: Games, gamification, and the quest for learner engagement. Training Dev. **66**(6), 64–68 (2012)

60. Balraj, K., Parul, K..: Gamification in education – learn computer programming with fun. Int. J. Comput. Distrib. Syst. **2**(1), 46–53 (2012)
61. O'Donovan, S., Gain, J., Marais, P.: A case study in the gamification of a university level games development course. In: Proceedings of the South African Institute for Computer Scientists and Information Technologists Conference, pp. 242–251 (2013)
62. Dicheva, D., Dichev, C., Agre, G., Angelova, G.: Gamification in education: a systematic mapping study. J. Educ. Technol. Soc. **18**(3), 9 (2015)
63. Hoe, T. W.: Gamifikasi dalam pendidikan: Pembelajaran berasaskan permainan (2015)
64. Tsay, C.H.H., Kofinas, A., Luo, J.: Enhancing student learning experience with technology-mediated gamification: an empirical study. Comput. Educ. **121**, 1–17 (2018)
65. Alsawaier, R.S.: The effect of gamification on motivation and engagement. Int. J. Inf. Learn. Technol. **35**(1), 56–79 (2018)
66. Chan, K.Y.G., Tan, S.L., Hew, K.F.T., Koh, B.G., Lim, L.S., Yong, J.C.: Knowledge for games, games for knowledge: designing a digital roll-and-move board game for a law of torts class. Res. Pract. Technol. Enhanc. Learn. **12**(1), 7 (2017)
67. Sepehr, S., Head, M.: Competition as an element of gamification for learning: an exploratory longitudinal investigation (2013)
68. Szegletes, L., Koles, M., Forstner, B.: Socio-cognitive gamification: general framework for educational games. J. Multimodal User Interfaces **9**(4), 395–401 (2015)
69. Alexiou, A., Schippers, M.C.: Digital game elements, user experience and learning: a conceptual framework. Educ. Inf. Technol. **23**(3), 1–23 (2018)
70. Saleem, A.N., Noori, N.M., Ozdamli, F.: Gamification applications in E-learning: a literature review. Technol. Knowl. Learn. **27**(1), 139–159 (2022)
71. Nah, F.F.H., Zeng, Q., Telaprolu, V.R., Ayyappa, A.P., Eschenbrenner, B.: Gamification of education: a review of literature, pp. 401–409 (2014)
72. Eleftheria, C.A., Charikleia, P., Iason, C.G., Athanasios, T., Dimitrios, T.: An innovative augmented reality educational platform using gamification to enhance lifelong learning and cultural education. In: 4th International Conference on Information, Intelligence, Systems and Applications, pp. 1–5 (2013)
73. Gibson, D., Ostashewski, N., Flintoff, K., Grant, S., Knight, E.: Digital Badges in Education. Education and Information Technology. Springer, New York (2013)
74. Santos, C., Almeida, S., Pedro, L., Aresta, M., Koch-Grunberg, T.: Students' perspectives on badges in educational social media platforms: the case of SAPO campus tutorial badges. In: IEEE 13th International Conference on Advanced Learning Technologies, pp. 351–353 (2013)
75. González, C.S., et al.: Learning healthy lifestyles through active videogames, motor games and the gamification of educational activities. Comput. Hum. Behav. **55**, 529–551 (2016)
76. Brewer, R., Anthony, L., Brown, Q., Irwin, G., Nias, J., Tate, B.: Using gamification to motivate children to complete empirical studies in lab environments. In: 12th International Conference on Interaction Design and Children, pp. 388–391 (2013)
77. Raymer, R.: Gamification - Using Game Mechanics to Enhance eLearning. eLearn Magazine (2011)
78. Denny, P., McDonald, F., Empson, R., Kelly, P., Petersen, A.: Empirical Support for a Causal Relationship between Gamification and Learning Outcomes (2018)
79. Johnson, D., Gardner, M.J., Perry, R.: Validation of two game experience scales: the player experience of need satisfaction (PENS) and game experience questionnaire (GEQ). Int. J. Hum. Comput. Stud. **118**, 38–46 (2018)
80. Denisova, A., Nordin, A. I., Cairns, P.: The convergence of player experience questionnaires. In: Proceedings of the 2016 Annual Symposium on Computer-Human Interaction in Play, pp. 33–37 (2016)

81. Nacke, L., Drachen, A.: Towards a framework of player experience research. In: Proceedings of the Second International Workshop on Evaluating Player Experience in Games at FDG (2011)

82. Kumar, B., Khurana, P.: Gamification in education – learn computer programming with fun. Int. J. Comput. Distrib. Syst. **2**(1), 46–53 (2012)

83. Zichermann, G., and C. Cunningham.: Gamification by Design: Implementing Game Mechanics in Web and Mobile Apps. Sebastopol (2011)

84. Boddy, C.R.: Sample size for qualitative research. J. Cetacean Res. Manag. **19**(4), 426–432 (2016)

85. Hoyle, R.H. (Ed.).: Statistical strategies for small sample research (1999)

86. Kortum, P., Peres, S.C.: The relationship between system effectiveness and subjective usability scores using the system usability scale. Int. J. Hum. Comput. Interact. **30**(7), 575–584 (2014)

87. Zimmermann, P.G.: Beyond usability: Measuring aspects of user experience (2008)

88. Onyesolu, M.O., Eze, F.U.: Understanding virtual reality technology: advances and applications. Adv. Comput. Sci. Eng. 53–70 (2011)

89. Brown, L. V.: Psychology of motivation (2007)

90. Gollwitzer, P.M., Bargh, J.A.: The psychology of action: Linking cognition and motivation to behavior. Guilford Press (1996)

91. Huda, A., Azhar, N., Almasri, A., Hartanto, S., Anshari, K.: Practicality and effectiveness test of graphic design learning media based on android (2020)

92. Chen, H.R., Jian, C.H., Lin, W.S., Yang, P.C., Chang, H.Y.: Design of digital game-based learning in elementary school. In: International Journal of Innovation, Management and Technology, Vol. 7, No. 4, August 2016 135math-ematics. In: Proceedings of 2014 7th International Conference on UbiMedia Computing and Workshops, pp. 322–325 (2014)

93. Razali, N.M., Wah, Y.B.: Power comparisons of shapiro-wilk, kolmogorov-smirnov, lilliefors and anderson-darling tests. J. Stat. Model. Analytics **2**(1), 21–33 (2011)

94. Çakıroğlu, Ü., B. Başıbüyük, M., Güler, M., Atabay, Yılmaz Memiş, B.: Gamifying an ICT course: influences on engagement and academic performance. Comput. Hum. Behav. **69**, 98–107 (2017)

95. Ibáñez, M.B., Di Serio, Á., Villarán, D., Kloos, C.D.: Experimenting with electromagnetism using augmented reality: impact on flow student experience and educational effectiveness. Comput. Educ. **71**, 1–13 (2014)

96. Alsaleh, N., Alnanih, R.: Mapping gamification mechanisms to user experience factors for designing user interfaces. J. Comput. Comput **15**(5), 736–744 (2019)

97. Ashaari, S.A.H.A.R.I.: Quantifying user experience in using learning gamification website. J. Theor. Appl. Inf. Technol. **96**(23), 7783–7793 (2018)

98. Lister, M.: Gamification: the effect on student motivation and performance at the post-secondary level. Issues Trends Educ. Technol. **3**(2), 22 (2015)

99. Chou, Y.K.: Actionable gamification: Beyond points, badges, and leaderboards. Packt Publishing Ltd. (2019)

100. Edwards, J., Othman, M., Crossin, E., Burn, S.: Life cycle assessment to compare the environmental impact of seven contemporary food waste management systems. Biores. Technol. **248**, 156–173 (2018)

101. Warmelink, H., Koivisto, J., Mayer, I., Vesa, M., Hamari, J.: Gamification of production and logistics operations: status quo and future directions. J. Bus. Res. **106**, 331–340 (2020)

Achieving a Balance Between Work and Rest Through Interaction Design

Jiancheng Zhong◉ and Qiong Wu(✉)◉

Academy of Art and Design, Tsinghua University, Beijing 100084, China
qiong-wu@tsinghua.edu.cn

Abstract. With the advancement of technology, we have entered the Information Age. The arrival of the Information Revolution has liberated human productivity, but it has not led to a reduction in working hours. A significant number of white-collar office workers need to spend considerable time sitting in front of computers, and the detrimental work habits, such as prolonged sedentary behavior, seriously jeopardize the physical and mental well-being of employees. This paper examines the concept of work micro-breaks as a theoretical framework and aims to establish a work-rest balance for users through digital means and user-centric interactive applications. Building upon existing productivity applications, we incorporate novel interactive methods to enhance the mandatory nature of reminders and the enjoyable aspects of user habits, ultimately achieving equilibrium between work and rest, fostering positive work-rest routines, maintaining the physical and mental health of workers, and improving overall work efficiency.

Keywords: Interaction design · Application design · Interface design · User experience design · Heuristic design · Era of overwork · Sedentary lifestyle · Work and rest · Active rest · Microbreaks · Work efficiency · Pomodoro Technique · Gamification

1 Introduction

This is an era of "work to death". With the advancement of technology and the accelerated pace of urban life, the pressure of life, study and work is increasing, leading to a growing phenomenon of overwork. According to the "2018 National Time Use Survey Report," the average daily working hours for employed men in 2018 were 7 h and 52 min, while for women, it was 7 h and 24 min. These figures represent an increase of 1 h and 26 min for men and 1 h and 20 min for women compared to 2008. Comparing the data to a decade ago, both male and female workers experienced a 22% increase in their working hours [4]. According to the "China Labor Statistical Yearbook," the average weekly working hours of urban employed individuals in China reached 47.6 h in 2022 [1]. Despite people's income and material wealth far surpassing any previous historical period, the average leisure time has been diminishing, with many individuals frequently experiencing a state of exhaustion and busyness [2].

Prolonged high-pressure work can lead to even more severe consequences. In recent years, there have been frequent reports of sudden deaths caused by long working hours,

J. Y. C. Chen et al. (Eds.): HCII 2023, LNCS 14058, pp. 426–442, 2023.
https://doi.org/10.1007/978-3-031-48050-8_28

highlighting the increasingly serious issue of work-related fatalities. A study released by the World Health Organization and the International Labour Organization on May 17, 2021, revealed that hundreds of thousands of people worldwide die each year from fatal diseases caused by excessive working hours [5]. In just one year, 745,000 people globally died due to long working hours, translating to nearly 1.5 deaths every minute attributed to overwork. Among professions such as programmers, designers, media personnel, doctors, police officers, public relations practitioners, finance professionals, e-commerce workers, couriers, and financial personnel, the occurrence of sudden death due to overwork is most prevalent.

The arrival of the information revolution has liberated human productivity, but it has not resulted in a reduction of working hours. In his book "The Age of Overwork" [3] Takao Morioka points out that new information and communication technologies serve as powerful tools for reducing and eliminating workload. However, they simultaneously accelerate business operations, intensify time competition, diversify the range of goods and services, and foster a trend towards borderless and 24/7 economic activities. Consequently, both at the collective and individual levels, workloads have not decreased but rather increased. Additionally, new information and communication technologies enable faster business processing and shorter working hours. However, due to the interconnectedness of work and personal life through networks, working hours have the potential to expand infinitely. As long as individuals have access to mobile electronic devices and networks, they can work from anywhere, blurring the boundaries between work and personal life.

These various phenomena seem to indicate that, with the combined influence of factors such as globalization, the information and communication revolution, maturation of consumer markets, and relaxation of employment and labor restrictions, we are entering an era of overwork.

In the current information age of high-intensity work, it inevitably provokes reflection on how to find a balance between work and rest for white-collar workers who require long hours facing computer screens and working in office environments. This paper aims to explore the use of digital means and interactive methods, with a user-centric approach, to establish a balance between work and rest for users. The objective is to cultivate users' healthy rest habits, improve rest efficiency, and consequently enhance their work performance, enabling them to complete tasks within working hours and reduce overtime consumption. Our research aims to design an application specifically targeting the young Chinese population who face high-intensity work rhythms, with the goal of fostering users' proactive engagement in work micro-breaks to address the contradiction between work and rest.

2   Theoretical Studies

2.1   The Hazards of Prolonged Computer Work

The development of the information age and the advent of mobile internet have brought us convenience while becoming an inseparable part of our lives. In the era of the internet, whether it is for work, study, or entertainment, individuals inevitably require long hours of computer work. A public opinion survey revealed that the average time office workers spend staring at a computer annually is 1700 h. A study on screen time disclosed that office workers spend an average of 6.5 h per day using a computer, with a prolonged sedentary time of up to 8 h.

Intense and prolonged computer-based work imposes a significant burden on the physical and mental well-being of workers. In 2016, globally, there were 488 million people (8.9% of the global workforce) engaged in long working hours (≥55 h per week). It resulted in 745,000 deaths attributable to ischemic heart disease (347,000) and stroke (398,000), along with 23.3 million disability-adjusted life years attributed to these long working hours. Estimations indicate that in 2016, there were 745,000 deaths attributed to ischemic heart disease and stroke caused by long working hours or overtime, with strokes accounting for 53% (398,000) and ischemic heart disease accounting for 47% (347,000) of the cases. Between 2000 and 2016, there was a 42% increase in deaths from ischemic heart disease due to long working hours, and a 19% increase in stroke-related deaths. Prolonged high-pressure work continuously activates the autonomic nervous system and immune system, leading to associated stress responses and excessive release of stress hormones, triggering cardiovascular reactions and tissue damage. Additionally, many individuals adopt harmful coping mechanisms, such as smoking, alcohol consumption, unhealthy diets, lack of exercise, and insufficient sleep, in response to the pressures of long working hours. These factors are known risk factors for ischemic heart disease and stroke [6].

Previous data released by the World Health Organization (WHO) has shown that prolonged sedentary behavior and an increase in BMI significantly elevate both overall mortality and cardiovascular mortality rates. Ford et al. found in their study that adults aged 18 and above who spend more than 2 h sitting per day have a 5% increase in cardiovascular disease mortality rate [7]. Similarly, research by Grontved et al. revealed that individuals who spend over 2 h watching television daily experience a 13% increase in overall mortality rate [8]. Furthermore, Wilmot et al. reported that compared to individuals with lower sedentary time, adults who spend a substantial amount of time in a sedentary state exhibit a noticeable increase in overall mortality rate and cardiovascular mortality rate attributed to prolonged sitting [9].

Through desktop research, we have identified a range of issues associated with high-intensity computer work, including increased mental stress, prolonged sitting, excessive eye strain, reduced work efficiency, and diminished attention. Simultaneously, within the explosion of information on the Internet, individuals are required to process an excessive amount of complex information, further contributing to a loss of attention focus. This necessitates a significant expenditure of effort to combat attentional distractions and procrastination behaviors, resulting in decreased work efficiency and unnecessary prolongation of work hours.

2.2 Literature Research on Microbreaks During Work Hours

In today's information-driven society, office workers are inevitably exposed to long hours of computer work. To address the negative impact of prolonged work hours, such as increased mental stress, elevated risk of cardiovascular diseases, and decreased attention, it is necessary to find a balance between work and rest and adopt proactive rest strategies. This allows for the restoration of personal resources, such as energy and attention, while promoting both physical and mental well-being and performance [10].

The World Health Organization's guidelines on physical activity and sedentary behavior, published in 2020, recommend that adults should limit their sedentary time and engage in various intensities of physical activities, including light-intensity activities, to reap health benefits [11].

Workplace Micro-break Concept Explained. In the field of management, there has been considerable research on strategies for incorporating rest periods into the workday. The concept of microbreaks, which aims to restore energy and attention through brief periods of rest, has emerged as a topic of study in the field of recovery research. Microbreaks are intended to counteract the physical and mental fatigue resulting from continuous work, and most employees require breaks during the workday to reduce resource depletion and replenish their physical and mental resources.

The term "microbreak" was initially used to describe spontaneous, informal, and brief rest periods taken during work, but it lacked a clear definition [12]. McLean adopted the term "microbreak" and defined it as organizationally planned rest time to prevent employees from experiencing cumulative physical trauma caused by uninterrupted repetitive work. In recent years, with improvements in technology and the increasing knowledge levels of employees, work has become more unstructured, and employees have greater autonomy in determining their work schedules and pace. As a result, employees are often able to independently decide on their work time arrangements and engage in spontaneous short rest activities between work tasks [13].

Impact of Workplace Micro-breaks. According to research findings [14], microbreaks have been found to have an impact on physical health, psychological well-being, work engagement, and job performance among workers.

In terms of physical health, longer and less frequent microbreaks have been shown to better alleviate discomfort in the lower extremities of workers. Stretching activities and guided physical exercises have been found to reduce pain in the neck, lower back, shoulders, upper back, wrists/hands, knees, and ankles after surgical procedures [15].

Regarding psychological well-being, microbreaks contribute to employees' mental health by increasing positive affect, vigor, energy, and recovery experience, while reducing negative affect, emotional exhaustion, and fatigue [14].

In terms of work engagement, Rzeszotarski found that appropriate microbreaks after several hours of task duration can reduce the risk of attentional lapses and enhance employees' work engagement [16].

In terms of job performance, Kim raises objections from a speculative perspective, suggesting that the relationship between the duration of microbreaks and task performance is not strictly monotonic, either increasing or decreasing. They propose that there may be an optimal duration for microbreaks, where employees achieve optimal performance, and exceeding this duration may have a detrimental effect. The reason behind this could be that longer microbreaks do not necessarily reduce the workload, but instead result in a backlog of tasks. As a result, employees may experience pressure to complete the accumulated tasks within a limited time frame after the break, leading to "anxiety" or "pursuit of speed at the expense of quality," ultimately resulting in reduced task performance [17].

In summary, appropriate microbreaks have been shown to have clear positive effects on workers in terms of physical, psychological, and work efficiency aspects. However, these effects are not solely determined by the duration of the breaks. Regarding job performance, excessively long microbreak durations can lead to psychological anxiety due to an inability to complete work tasks. There appears to be an optimal duration for microbreaks, where reaching this optimum yields positive effects, but further increasing the duration may not continue to enhance these effects and could potentially diminish them gradually [17].

2.3 Active Rest Planning Study

The secret to effectively utilizing human energy, which is limited, lies in learning to take proactive rest. Ling Zhou's book "Cognitive Awakening" [18] describes two patterns of energy depletion. Left chart (Fig. 1) represents the energy fluctuation curve of individuals who persistently work hard, race against time, and are reluctant to take breaks. Their overall energy level follows a continuous downward trend. Once energy is depleted to a certain level, such as below 70%, attention starts to involuntarily wander, and thinking speed slows down. If energy continues to be depleted, learning efficiency further decreases, and it becomes easy to become distracted. Although diligent individuals may appear extremely hardworking, their effectiveness diminishes over time, and they experience more pain than pleasure in the process, resulting in severe energy depletion. Right chart (Fig. 2) illustrates the energy fluctuation curve of individuals who have mastered the skill of taking proactive rests. They never excessively deplete themselves and, whenever they feel low on energy, they proactively stop and rest, leading to a rapid replenishment of their energy levels.

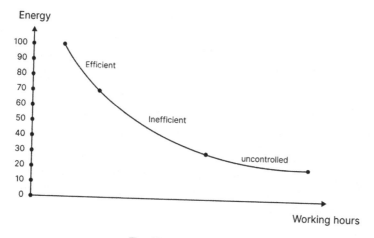

Endless work

Fig. 1. The energy fluctuation curve of individuals who persistently work hard.

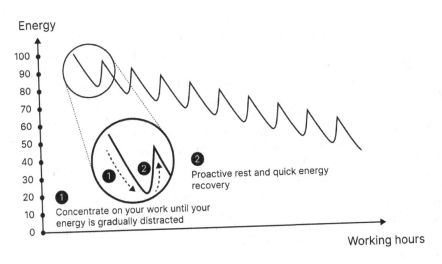

Active rest

Fig. 2. The energy fluctuation curve of individuals who have mastered the skill of taking proactive rests.

If we consider the range above 70% of energy level as the zone for efficient learning, we can observe from Fig. 3 that individuals who are more relaxed have a much larger efficient learning zone compared to those who are diligent. Therefore, it can be seen that

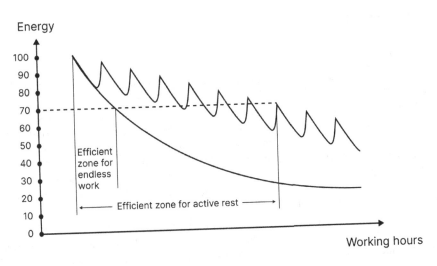

Efficient zone:endless work vs active rest

Fig. 3. Endless work versus active rest in the work efficiency zone (70% + energy)

the more effective and scientific utilization of energy involves a combination of intense focus and proactive rest, repeated in a cycle [18].

In the scientific methodology of integrating rest and work, the Pomodoro Technique is a typical representative. In the late 1990s, Francesco Cirillo invented a time management method called the Pomodoro Technique. The objective of this technique is to perceive time as a value rather than an enemy. It has been proven to enhance the work efficiency of individuals, enabling them to be more focused on their tasks within a given timeframe while alleviating time-related anxiety. The technique divides time into 25-min work intervals known as "pomodoros." During each pomodoro, the individual is required to concentrate on the task at hand without any distractions. After completing one pomodoro, a 5-min break is taken before starting the next one. Through this approach, the Pomodoro Technique assists individuals in maintaining high levels of concentration and efficiency. Additionally, it helps reduce anxiety and stress, promoting a more relaxed and confident work environment. The Pomodoro Technique also aids individuals in better time management, optimizing daily workflow and improving work efficiency. It helps individuals allocate time effectively, ensuring each task receives appropriate attention and handling while avoiding time wastage during work [20].

The research on the aforementioned theories provides substantial evidence that learning to take proactive breaks is crucial for balancing and mitigating the negative impacts of intense computer work prevalent in today's society. Therefore, identifying opportunities to effectively manage and integrate microbreaks becomes a focal point. It is desirable to explore the intersection of human-computer interaction field with the aim of enhancing user productivity and maintaining their physical and mental well-being through scientific work and rest methodologies.

3 Methodology

3.1 Related Product Research

There are numerous cases utilizing digital means to assist users in managing their work and rest time. Jasmijn Franke et al. discovered that office workers often lead sedentary lifestyles, which contribute to increased risks of cardiovascular diseases, stroke, diabetes, and premature death. To address this issue, they employed a virtual agent to deliver daily summaries and encourage users to engage in more physical activity at designated reminder times. The virtual agent was embedded within the HealthMe smartphone application, which connected to an activity tracker to monitor and visualize users' physical activity, sleep patterns, heart rate, and other indicators. The virtual agent utilized the Recurring Sedentary Period Detection (RSPD) algorithm to accurately identify recurring sedentary periods, generate appropriate daily summaries, and determine precise reminder times. Jasmijn Franke et al. [19] aimed to provide more personalized reminders based on algorithmic monitoring and guide users to engage in physical movements during prolonged periods of sitting through virtual human conversations.

In the existing application market, there are also numerous applications based on the theory of the Pomodoro Technique that aim to balance work and rest. This study selected six commonly found applications for phased experiences and analyzed their commonalities and experiential issues to derive design insights.

The six applications are "Focus List," "Focus City," "iFocus," "Session," "Focus Keeper," and "Flow." The experiential testing in the study focused on the core task of time management for maintaining focus. The task was divided into three stages: work-in-progress, work completion, and rest periods, with each stage representing one Pomodoro time cycle. The objective was to achieve a state of focused work and efficient rest. While some of the applications also offered features such as time planning and task management, these were not the core focus of the testing and thus not discussed in detail in the study.

Stage 1: At Work. As shown in Fig. 4, all six applications run in the background while the user is in a working state, and they display a countdown of the remaining work time in the status bar. The difference lies in the presentation style, with some apps using a dial format and others using a digital countdown format. However, in practical experience, the countdown of work time in the status bar can induce a sense of time pressure and anxiety in users, creating an invisible pressure during work. Additionally, as the countdown approaches its end, users may experience a relaxation in their level of focus. These two factors have an impact on the user's state of concentration during work, and we believe this is not the optimal user experience.

Fig. 4. 6 apps working on the status bar

Stage 2: End of Work. As shown in Fig. 5, among the six applications, some of them display a pop-up reminder for users to take a break after the work countdown, while others do not provide any reminders for rest time. When users are engaged in high-intensity focused work, these reminders often fail to have an effective prompting effect, and users frequently dismiss them and continue working. As a result, users often overlook the designated rest time and maintain a prolonged working state. This inadequate reminder experience fails to cultivate a rhythmic work pattern in users. Prolonged high-intensity work not only reduces efficiency but also increases the risk of health issues associated with sedentary behavior and excessive eye strain.

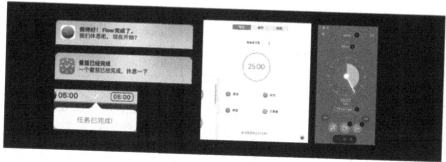

Fig. 5. 6 end-of-work reminders for apps

Stage 3: During the Break. As shown in Fig. 6, the six applications also provide users with feedback during the rest phase in the form of countdown timers. However, as we have learned earlier, prolonged sitting is a significant contributing factor to cardiovascular diseases among office workers. Therefore, during the rest phase of the application, it is beneficial to provide users with prompts to leave their seats and engage in physical activities.

Fig. 6. 6 apps resting in state

From the analysis of the aforementioned three phases of user experience, the following insights can be derived:

- During the work phase, minimize user distractions;
- Strong reminders are needed when the work phase ends to encourage users to take a break;

- During the rest phase, users should be given appropriate guidance and encouragement to engage in physical activities.

Due to time constraints, the sample size for the experience testing was limited, and the feedback received was subjective. Future testing will involve a larger number of participants to obtain more accurate experience reports.

3.2 Framework and Process

Office workers who engage in prolonged periods of work are unable to avoid extended computer screen usage. Our design objective is to utilize digital means to balance work and rest time. We aim to use computer applications as a medium to cultivate users' mental models and establish new, positive work habits through enjoyable and obligatory methods.

Based on our design objective of using digital means to balance work and rest time, we have formulated the following design strategies:

- Utilize the Pomodoro Technique to cultivate users' habit of taking active breaks;
- Employ mandatory reminder modes to help users establish a mental model of taking proactive breaks;
- Use interactive and engaging elements to guide users in leaving their sedentary positions and engaging in restorative activities during break time.

As depicted in Fig. 7, we have constructed a framework based on the traditional Pomodoro clock productivity software, where the core mode is the cycle of work and rest. The innovation lies in the implementation of mandatory reminder modes to end users' work and prompt them to engage in short rest periods. Additionally, we aim to use a fun interaction to guide users to leave their seats. We consider implementing a surprise element and achievement system to cultivate users' habits effectively.

Within the framework, we can observe the Image Gallery page, which functions to collect and unlock achievements as a means to develop users' mental models. Through the Statistics page, users can view their past completion of Pomodoro cycles. For each completed cycle, users can record the work task associated with that cycle and track the time spent on each task.

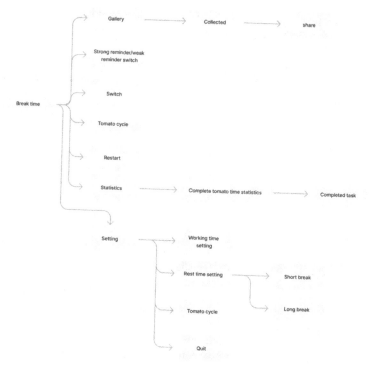

Fig. 7. Framework diagram for Break time

The core task flow diagram generated during the initial conceptualization phase, as shown in Fig. 8, illustrates a complete usage process from work to work-ending reminder to rest. Considering scenarios where rest cannot be enforced, such as group meetings, users can autonomously choose between strong and weak reminder modes before initiating their work time. Once in the work state, Break time operates in the background, and the work timer countdown is not visible on the user's desktop to minimize distractions during work. When the work time ends, the weak reminder mode displays a pop-up dialog box to remind the user to take a break, while the strong reminder mode overlays the user's work desktop with a full-screen pop-up window, urging them to engage in a break. During the break period, Break time utilizes the computer's camera to determine whether the user is still seated in front of the computer. If the user is still seated, Break time displays a bubble pop-up to remind them to leave the desk and engage in physical activity. When the user returns to the computer after taking a break and prepares to resume work, they will receive a new island (surprise point) as an enjoyable reward mechanism to foster a sense of achievement and cultivate habit formation.

3.3 Low-Fidelity Prototyping

Based on the aforementioned application framework and user flow, a low-fidelity prototype design was completed using Figma, as shown in Fig. 9. The skeletal framework

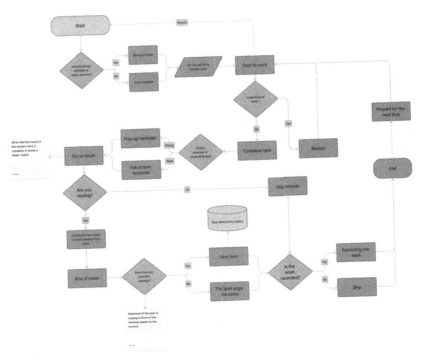

Fig. 8. Flow chart of Break time core tasks

of Break time was established, serving as the foundation for subsequent high-fidelity prototype design. Basic interactive transitions were implemented in Figma, and a simple usability test was conducted to ensure the completeness of the user flow.

3.4 High-Fidelity Prototyping

The high-fidelity prototype in Fig. 10 is an improved version based on the low-fidelity prototype. The visual design of the entire software revolves around islands, with floating islands creating a sense of tranquility and peace. The islands serve as core surprise elements within the application, employing a low-poly style that aligns with the aesthetic preferences of younger user demographics and introduces a gamified feel, resulting in an overall more relaxed and lively experience. Imagine that every time you take a break, leave your desk, grab a cup of coffee, and come back to work, you encounter a new island. This sense of achievement encourages you to continuously collect new islands, gradually cultivating a habit of avoiding prolonged sitting. In terms of interface design, a flat design style that is widely embraced by younger users has been incorporated.

Fig. 9. Low-fidelity prototype for Break time

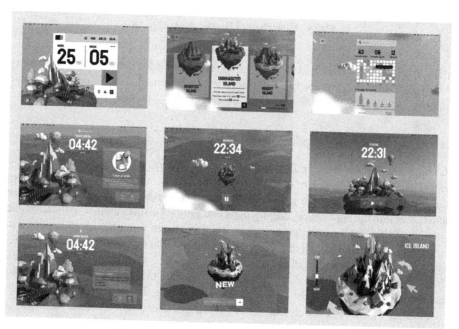

Fig. 10. High-fidelity prototype for Break time

4 Result

4.1 The Design Explanation

Break Time is guided by the theory of tomato work method, and every 25 min of work time is a cycle, and 4 cycles are a group. Users can also set longer or shorter working time according to their own working habits. After working, users are reminded to take a 5-min break to relax their body and mind to ensure that they can maintain good concentration in the next working time. In order to avoid users skipping the break, which leads to fatigue of long working hours, we set a switch for forced interaction in the application. Before users start working, they can turn on the switch of strong reminder to ensure that by the rest time, the computer is forced to enter the rest mode, and the mandatory interaction cultivates users to develop the habit of reasonable rest. During the break, the program will dispatch the computer's camera to determine whether the user is still sitting in front of the computer, and if the user is still sitting in front of the computer, Break Time will remind the user to leave the desktop to move his body and carry out relaxation activities that do not consume cognition instead of sitting on the seat and playing with the phone, so that the break can really let us quickly rejuvenate. Another creative point of Break Time Break Time is a fun habit-forming system that revolves around "islands". After the user completes a cycle, if the user leaves his seat and moves his body, he will be surprised to find that he unlocks new "islands" when he returns to the studio. The user can explore the "island", browse its details, and the "island" will accompany you to the next round of

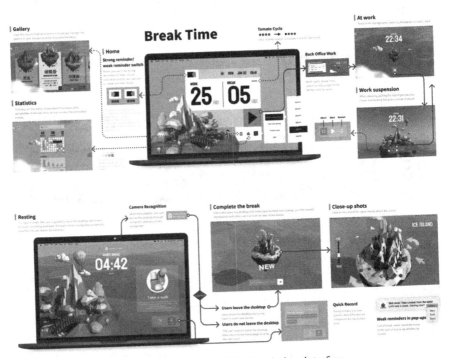

Fig. 11. Description of the Break time interface

work cycle. With this exploratory gamification mechanism, users can develop the habit of using it and learn to take active micro-breaks between jobs. Currently, Break Time has completed its conceptual design. We will conduct usability testing with users in the next phase to determine the feasibility of the program (Fig. 11).

4.2 Steps to Use

The steps for using the application, as illustrated in Fig. 12., are explained below, considering a user's first-time usage scenario. The initial island is a deserted island. The following parameters are set for this cycle: work time of 25 min, rest time of 5 min, 4 cycles, and strong reminders. Rest determination: user leaves the desktop for a break.

1. Before starting work, the user needs to set the work time, rest time, and the number of tomato cycles based on their work and rest habits. It is crucial to choose between strong or weak reminders for breaks, depending on the work environment.
2. Click on the "Start Work" button.
3. The Break time application runs in the background as the user begins to focus on their work.
4. When the work time is completed, Break time overlays the user's work interface in the form of a strong reminder, indicating the start of the rest period.
5. A dialog box pops up, reminding the user to leave the desktop and engage in physical activities.
6. Break time activates the computer's camera to determine whether the user has left the desktop.

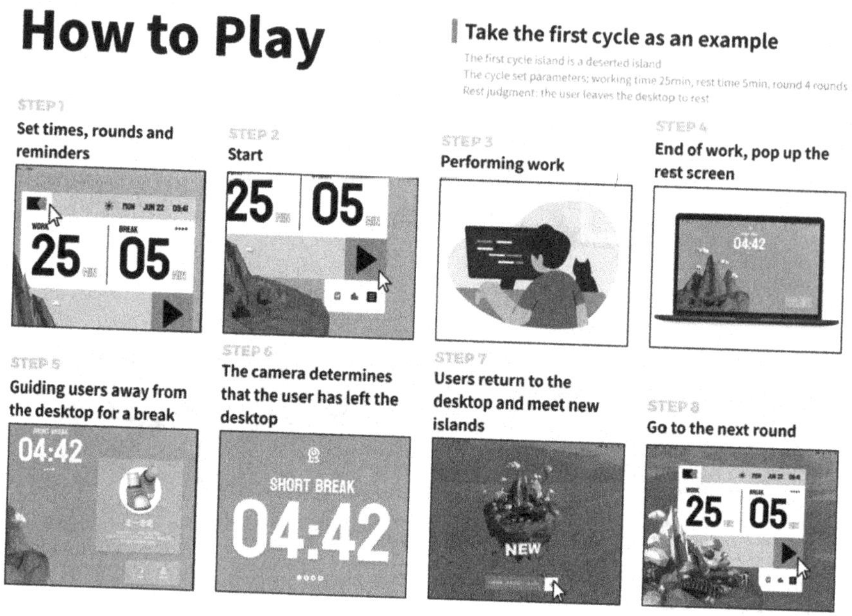

Fig. 12. Flow of Break time usage

7. Once the user finishes their rest and returns to the desktop, they will encounter a new island.
8. The user prepares to enter the next work cycle.

5 Conclusion

With the advent of the information age, computers have become an indispensable tool for people. In urban office environments, there are a significant number of office workers who need to spend long hours facing computers daily, resulting in significant physical and psychological burdens. In this study, we attempt to address the work-rest balance of office workers through digital means. Through desktop research, we recognize the importance of taking short breaks during work hours, and many teams have made efforts to assist workers in proactively taking breaks through computer applications. Building upon the traditional concept of the Pomodoro Technique, we propose innovations that enhance the mandatory nature of reminders and introduce gamification elements to foster user habits.

Currently, the concept design of Break Time has been completed. However, user experience design still needs to revolve around user-centered approaches. In the next phase, we will conduct usability testing with users to evaluate the practical effectiveness of the design solution based on their experiential feedback. This assessment will determine whether the solution effectively cultivates a habit of proactive work breaks and will help assess the feasibility of the proposed design.

Acknowledgement. This research was supported by "Dual High" Project of Tsinghua Humanity Development (No. 2021TSG08203).

References

1. I. General. 1–52 Average weekly working hours in urban employment survey. Page 93. In: China labour statistical yearbook. China Statistical Publishing House, Beijing (2022)
2. Wei, L.: "The Age of Overwork" and "Transparent Society". China Book Review. 27–36 (2023)
3. Morioka & Mi.: The Age of Overwork. New Star Press, Beijing (2019)
4. National Statistical Office: National Time Use Survey Bulletin 2018 http://www.stats.gov.cn/sj/zxfb/202302/t20230203_1900224.html
5. Teixeira, L., Dzhambov, A.M., Gagliardi, D.: Response to letter to the editor regarding "the effect of occupational exposure to noise on Ischaemic heart disease, stroke and hypertension: a systematic review and meta-analysis from the who/ilo joint estimates of the work-related burden of disease and injury." Environ. Int. **161**, 107105 (2022). https://doi.org/10.1016/j.envint.2022.107105
6. Pega, F., et al.: Global, regional, and national burdens of ischemic heart disease and stroke attributable to exposure to long working hours for 194 countries, 2000–2016: a systematic analysis from the WHO/ILO joint estimates of the work-related burden of disease and injury. Environ. Int. **154**, 106595 (2021). https://doi.org/10.1016/j.envint.2021.106595

7. Ford, E.S., Caspersen, C.J.: Sedentary behaviour and cardiovascular disease: a review of prospective studies. Int. J. Epidemiol. **41**, 1338–1353 (2012). https://doi.org/10.1093/ije/dys078

8. Grøntved, A., Hu, F.B.: Television viewing and risk of type 2 diabetes, cardiovascular disease, and all-cause mortality: a meta-analysis. JAMA **305**, 2448–2455 (2011). https://doi.org/10.1001/jama.2011.812

9. Wilmot, E.G., et al.: Sedentary time in adults and the association with diabetes, cardiovascular disease and death: systematic review and meta-analysis. Diabetologia **55**, 2895–2905 (2012). https://doi.org/10.1007/s00125-012-2677-z

10. Trougakos, J.P., Beal, D.J., Green, S.G., Weiss, H.M.: Making the break count: an episodic examination of recovery activities, emotional experiences, and positive affective displays. AMJ. **51**, 131–146 (2008). https://doi.org/10.5465/amj.2008.30764063

11. Okely, A.D., Kontsevaya, A., Ng, J., Abdeta, C.: 2020 WHO guidelines on physical activity and sedentary behavior. Sports Med. Health Sci. **3**, 115–118 (2021). https://doi.org/10.1016/j.smhs.2021.05.001

12. Hennfng, R.A., Sauter, S.L., Salvendy, G., Krieg, E.F.: Microbreak length, performance, and stress in a data entry task. Ergonomics **32**, 855–864 (1989). https://doi.org/10.1080/001401 38908966848

13. McLean, L., Tingley, M., Scott, R.N., Rickards, J.: Computer terminal work and the benefit of microbreaks. Appl. Ergon. **32**, 225–237 (2001). https://doi.org/10.1016/S0003-6870(00)000 71-5

14. Qi, N., Jie, Z., Jian, P., Yanzhao, B.: Recuperate and build up energy: a literature review and prospects of micro-break in the workplace. Foreign Econ. Manag. **42**, 69–85 (2020). https://doi.org/10.16538/j.cnki.fem.20200410.301

15. Park, A.E., et al.: Intraoperative "micro breaks" with targeted stretching enhance surgeon physical function and mental focus. Ann. Surg. **265**, 340–346 (2017). https://doi.org/10.1097/SLA.0000000000001665

16. Rzeszotarski, J., Chi, E., Paritosh, P., Dai, P.: Inserting micro-breaks into crowdsourcing workflows. Proc. AAAI Conf. Hum. Comput. Crowdsourcing. **1**, 62–63 (2013). https://doi.org/10.1609/hcomp.v1i1.13127

17. Kim, S., Park, Y., Headrick, L.: Daily micro-breaks and job performance: general work engagement as a cross-level moderator. J. Appl. Psychol. **103**, 772–786 (2018). https://doi.org/10.1037/apl0000308

18. Lin, Z.: Cognitive Awakening: Unlocking the Dynamics of Self-Change. The People's Posts and Telecommunications Press, Beijing (2020)

19. Franke, J., Grünloh, C., Hofs, D., Schooten, B.V., Bondrea, A., Cabrita, M.: Breaking up long sedentary periods of office workers through a virtual coach using activity data. In: 2nd International Workshop on Smart, Personalized and Age-Friendly Working Environments (2023)

20. Notteberg, S. Big Fat.: The tomato work method illustrated: a simple and easy way to manage time. Posts & Telecom Press, Beijing (2011)

Author Index

J. Y. C. Chen et al. (Eds.): HCII 2023, LNCS 14058, pp. 443–444, 2023.
https://doi.org/10.1007/978-3-031-48050-8

Printed in the United States
by Baker & Taylor Publisher Services